MORGAN STATE SERIES IN AFRO-AMERICAN STUDIES

Walter Fisher, General Editor
Benjamin Quarles, Consulting Editor

The Series has been assisted by a grant from the Ford Foundation. Technical editorial support was provided by the Metropolitan Applied Research Center.

ALSO BY PHILIP BUTCHER

The William Stanley Braithwaite Reader
George W. Cable
George W. Cable: The Northampton Years

THE MINORITY PRESENCE IN AMERICAN LITERATURE, 1600–1900

A Reader and Course Guide

Edited by PHILIP BUTCHER

Volume II

 HOWARD UNIVERSITY PRESS, WASHINGTON D.C. 1977

Printed in the United States of America

Library of Congress Cataloging in Publication Data
Main entry under title:

The Minority presence in American literature, 1600-1900.

   Includes bibliographical references and index.
   1. American literature.   2. Minorities—United
States—Literary collections.   I. Butcher, Charles
Philip.
PS509.M5M53   810'.9'353   77-5687
ISBN 0-88258-102-3 (v. II)
ISBN 0-88258-100-7 (v. II) pbk.

Edith, Nellie, Jennie, and James: For Them and Theirs

Preface

The Minority Presence in American Literature is designed both for the general reader pursuing an interest in American life and literature or in the role and status of minorities in the development of the nation and for the college student engaged in formal study of these subjects. While black Americans and American Indians are emphasized, the readings and study materials deal also with other minority groups, with some references to writing after 1900, and they provide a basis for examining the literary representation of any minority in any period.

This book will be most useful to persons who have had some exposure to the formal study of literature, who are capable of objective appraisals of various kinds of writing, and who are acquainted with the broad outlines of the writing and history of the United States. The reader must take care to deal with the selections in the context of the time of publication, to understand the writers and their works rather than to judge them, and to appreciate the authors' accomplishments rather than to disparage their work for flaws more easily detected from our perspective than from theirs. I have not meant to exalt poor writers unduly merely because they had social vision or humanitarian motives or to condemn fine writers whose genius did not include a generous understanding of some particular minority; but I consider that an author's response to the minority presence of his time and place is part of his record as a person and an artist and should not be disregarded. Yet I have wished to avoid chauvinism in preparing this book, and I would not want readers to use what they find here for chauvinistic purposes.

Incorporating the introductory essay in both volumes of this work assures that all readers are provided with two essentials for an intelligent response to the selections: a synthesis of the experience of "the other American" over three hundred years of our history and a guide to the principles that operate in the representation of minorities in literature. The readings are presented in chronological order, generally, the determining factor being the date of publication of the first selection by each writer. Each author's work is followed by a study guide that consists, in most instances, of a list of additional treatments of minorities, some recommended references, and questions and projects. The work from which a selection is taken is not listed among "Suggested Readings," and the selection, often given a title of my own, may not exhaust the relevance of that work. The projects differ greatly in scope and difficulty; students and teachers must adjust them to suit their needs, taking into account the library and other resources that are at hand. Students should be careful about inferring answers to the questions they do not pursue and should not undertake any project without checking the index and employing appropriate references from the bibliography at the end of the book. Some of the books I cite have been issued in several editions, including paperback, but I refer to one edition only. I make no comment about study tools such as the *Dictionary of American Biography*, the bibliographies in *American Literature*, *PMLA*, and other scholarly journals, or the standard references students are expected to use in advanced work in American literature, since it is assumed, as a matter of course, that these will be consulted as needed.

In my graduate classes in the minority presence I have found it helpful to insist that required reports treat more than one period and literary form and deal with more than one minority group. A particular student might discuss in one presentation the Indian woman in selected poetry of the romantic period, in a second the Quaker abolitionist as a character in certain fugitive slave narratives, and in a third Thoreau and the Irish. The range of the reports should allow the student to develop a topic related to his or her interests and should involve the study of unfamiliar material examined from an objective point of view. The stress should be on literary rather than other considerations. Reports may concentrate on a single minority as represented in several works or by several authors, a problem affecting several minorities (e.g., segregated housing or mixed marriage), a period (the age of local color), or a setting (the urban ghetto).

If readers of this book are to avoid the very sins they condemn when their indignation is aroused by bigotry and racism, they must keep in mind the human inclination toward xenophobia—the fear and hatred of strangers and foreigners—and the dismaying fact that man's reluctance to accept his fellows as equals is not limited to any single time or place or race or culture. Walther von der Vogelweide, a thirteenth century Minnesinger, observed in "My Brother Man" that "Mankind arises from one origin; / We are alike both outward and within." Yet many Christians, Jews, and heathens who worship God lack the true love that should be their salvation:

> *"For many call Thee Father, who*
> *Will not own me as brother too."*

PHILIP BUTCHER

CONTENTS

---

*Some titles, like this one, have been supplied by the editor. Sources from which selections are taken are identified in the headnotes.

THE MINORITY
PRESENCE IN
AMERICAN LITERATURE, 1600–1900

INTRODUCTION

I. The Minority Presence: Principles, Practices, and Prospects (1600–1800)

> Do we call this the land of the free? What is it
> to be free from King George and continue the
> slaves of King Prejudice?
>
> THOREAU.

In "Waiting at the Station," from *Sketches and Travels in London*, written more than a hundred years ago about class distinctions in England, William Makepeace Thackeray dramatized the conscience-salving rationalizations that the dominant group in a society uses in dismissing its subordinates as essentially alien and beyond the pale:

> We are amongst a number of people waiting for the Blackwell train at the Fenchurch Street Station. Some of us are going a little farther than Blackwell—as far as Gravesend: some of us are going even farther than Gravesend—to Port Phillip in Australia, leaving behind the *patriae fines* and the pleasant fields of Old England. . . .
>
> Some eight-and-thirty women are sitting in the large Hall of the station, with bundles, baskets, and light baggage, waiting for the steamer, and the orders to embark. . . .
>
> You and I, let us suppose again, are civilised persons. We have been decently educated: and live decently every day, and wear tolerable clothes, and practise cleanliness: and love the arts and graces of life. As we walk down this rank of eight-and-thirty female emigrants, let us fancy that we are at Melbourne, and not in London, and that we have come down from our sheep-walks, or clearings, having heard of the arrival of forty honest, well-recommended

3

young women, and having a natural longing to take a wife home to
the bush—which of these would you like? If you were an Australian
Sultan, to which of these would you throw the hankerchief? I am
afraid not one of them. I fear, in our present mood of mind, we
should mount horse and return to the country, preferring a solitude,
and to be a bachelor, than to put up with one of these for a companion. There is no girl here to tempt you by her looks: (and, world-
wiseacre as you are, it is by these you are principally moved)—there
is no pretty, modest, red-cheeked rustic,—no neat, trim little
grisette, such as what we call a gentleman might cast his eyes upon
without too much derogating, and might find favour in the eyes of a
man about town. No; it is a homely bevy of women with scarcely
any beauty amongst them—their clothes were decent but not the
least picturesque—their faces are pale and care-worn for the most
part—how, indeed, should it be otherwise, seeing that they have
known care and want all their days?—there they sit, upon bare
benches, with dingy bundles, and great cotton umbrellas—and the
truth is, you are not a hardy colonist, a feeder of sheep, feller of
trees, a hunter of kangaroos—but a London man, and my lord the
Sultan's cambric handkerchief is scented with Bond Street perfumery—you put it in your pocket, and couldn't give it to any one of
these women.

They are not like you, indeed. They have not your tastes and feeling: your education and refinements. They would not understand a
hundred things which seem perfectly simple to you. They would
shock you a hundred times a day by as many deficiencies of polite-
ness, or by outrages upon the Queen's English—by practices entirely ·
harmless, and yet in your eyes actually worse than crimes—they
have large hard hands and clumsy feet. The woman you love must
have pretty soft fingers that you may hold in yours: must speak your
language properly, and at least when you offer her your heart, must
return hers with its *h* in the right place, as she whispers that it is
yours, or you will have none of it. If she says, "Hedward, I ham so
unappy to think I shall never behold you again,"—though her emotion on leaving you might be perfectly tender and genuine, you
would be obliged to laugh. If she said, "Hedward, my art is yours for
hever and hever" (and anybody heard her), she might as well stab
you,—you couldn't accept the most faithful affection offered in such
terms—you are a town-bred man, I say, and your handkerchief
smells of Bond Street musk and millefleur. A sun–burnt settler out
of the Bush won't feel any of these exquisite tortures: or understand
this kind of laughter: or object to Molly because her hands· are

coarse and her ankles thick: but he will take her back to his farm, where she will nurse his children, bake his dough, milk his cows, and cook his kangaroo for him.

But between you, an educated Londoner, and that woman, is not the union absurd and impossible? Would it not be unbearable for either? Solitude would be incomparably pleasanter than such a companion. . . . Well! out with it at once: you don't think Molly is your equal—nor indeed is she in possession of many artificial acquirements. She can't make Latin verses, for example, as you used to do at school; she can't speak French and Italian, as your wife very likely can, etc.—and in so far she is your inferior, and your amiable lady's.

What Thackeray perceived as estranging England's lower classes from their betters—"They are not like you, indeed"—may be seen as basic to the predicament of subordinate groups in a society concerned about religion, nationality, and race as well as class. Americans subscribe to assorted religious faiths, trace their ancestry to nations on scattered continents, and bear skins that are black, brown, red, white, yellow, and all possible mixtures thereof. But only white Anglo-Saxon Protestant males, the dominant group in our culture, entirely escape the stigma of minority[1] designation. All other Americans have been regarded historically as inferior to them on the convenient notions that, on the one hand, minorities are "all alike" (that is, are all like one another in their group) and, on the other, are fundamentally "different" (that is, are lamentably unlike the established norm for human beings as determined and supposedly exemplified by the male WASP). To the extent that these concepts have been in force in our culture at a given time, they have found expression in our literature.

Yet it has been the very presence on these shores of various ethnic groups, classes, and cultures that has characterized the American experience and has made American literature something more than writings in English composed on the North American continent.

[1]The term is used in this book in accordance with the statement adopted by the Modern Language Association's Commission on Minority Groups: "A minority group is not construed here simply in terms of relative numbers in the population—a voting booth minority. Rather it is construed as a group of significant size in the society whose culture not only differs from the conventional culture but is systematically underrepresented in the preferred activity of the society and undervalued in its eyes." *MLA Newsletter,* 5, No. 3 (May, 1973), 3.

American literature deals with the encounter of Europeans and the native inhabitants of the New World, with the frontier, advancing ever westward, providing a unique setting. It deals also, since Africans arrived here before the Pilgrims and Puritans, with a massive black-white confrontation and accommodation, once concentrated on, but not limited to, the plantation, and now taking place in almost all aspects of our highly complex society. And it includes in its picture of the nation's development millions of assimilated people of "foreign" extraction and more millions still in some phase of the Americanization process. What makes the United States what it is—what has always distinguished it—is the presence here of people of all the diverse races and cultures of the globe and the evidences in our culture of their contribution to our heritage and their participation in our daily life.

That heritage is not exclusively English. It was an Italian, Columbus, who discovered in the western ocean the islands that were first thought to be part of Asia. Cabot, whose voyage in 1497 made possible England's territorial claims in the New World, was born in Genoa and became a citizen of Venice. Amerigo Vespucci, an Italian navigator, gave the western hemisphere the name "America" in his treatise on geography. In 1513, Ponce de Leon discovered Florida, and Balboa, another Spaniard, discovered the Pacific Ocean. French explorers reached the coast of Canada as early as 1534. DeSoto, also a Spaniard, landed in Florida in 1539 and marched to the Mississippi River, possibly getting as far north as what is now Kentucky before he died. Estevanico, a Christian Negro who had been with Cabeza de Vaca in the Texas area for several years, in 1539 guided a Spanish expedition into what is now New Mexico. A year later Coronado, another Spaniard, led an expedition that probably reached the area of Oklahoma and Kansas. In Florida, Spaniards founded St. Augustine, the oldest city in North America, twenty years before Sir Walter Raleigh's ill-fated English colonists landed on Roanoke Island off the coast of North Carolina in 1585.

The colony at Jamestown, the first permanent English settlement in America, included in its population settlers who do not conform to the aristocratic image of romantic tradition. Among the laborers there in 1608 were Poles and Germans. Only two English women were present, one of whom, a lady's maid named Anne Buras, married that year another laborer, John Laydon, in the first wedding of Europeans on Virginia soil. No courtly dame and cavalier were they, Stephen Vincent Benét noted in *Western Star* (1943):

> And yet, while they lived (and they had not long to live),
> They were half of the first families in Virginia.

The sponsors of the colony came to understand the value of women to the enterprise and sent ninety English maidens to become settlers' wives in 1619, the same year in which a Dutch vessel landed the first Africans there. That was the year, too, when the House of Burgesses was convened. America's first representative assembly ruled that only English men had the right to vote, but Poles exerted pressure and were not long denied the franchise.

In 1620 the Pilgrims founded Plymouth, the first English colony in New England. Most of the passengers on the *Mayflower,* and on all the later Pilgrim ships, were not English Separatists seeking a place to worship as they pleased but "Strangers," as the Pilgrims called them, who came to better their economic lot. From the Pilgrim's friend Samoset, a man named John Brown bought 12,000 acres of Maine land for fifty beaver skins in 1625. A year later the Dutch bought Manhattan Island in exchange for trinkets worth twenty-four dollars. They encouraged in New Amsterdam a polyglot population symbolic of New York's later character; there were people of eighteen nationalities and several religions on hand when the English took over the colony less than thirty years later. Of course that population included blacks, for Africans were to be found in each of the thirteen original English colonies from the earliest years of settlement. The Massachusetts Bay Colony was established in 1630, and by the time these Puritans adopted Nathaniel Ward's *Body of Liberties* in 1641, making theirs the first English colony to give legal sanction to Negro slavery, 20,000 Europeans were in the New England area. Finns and Swedes established a permanent settlement in Delaware in 1636, two years after Catholics landed in Maryland. And all the while the original Americans, the Indians, were all over the land.

In any literature, aliens or minorities are likely to be depicted unfavorably when they are readily distinguishable by their appearance, language, costume, etc. If the benighted people are few in numbers, docile, useful, and no threat to vested interests, they may be shown as quaint or exotic. But if they are hostile or have potential power that threatens the status quo, they must expect to be demeaned, ridiculed, exploited, and persecuted in literature as well as in life. As the group moves toward accommodation with the dominant culture, or as the value judgments or the power structure of the society is transformed, the literary treatment the group receives will improve in range and quality, with a general decline in the use of denigrating stereotypes and an increase in the favorable portrayal of figures conforming most fully to majority values.

Two incidents in the early history and literature of the American people are relevant to the principles stated above and serve as starting points for the study of the literary expression of the minority presence. The first was reported somewhat belatedly by John Smith, notable for his achievement as leader of the colony at Jamestown. Captain Smith wrote of being captured by Indians who were about to beat his brains out when the chief's daughter Pocahontas, "got his head in her armes, and laid her owne upon his to save him from death." This famous story of an eponymous hero who is rescued from the enemy through the devotion of an attractive alien woman who prefers him to her own people fits the classic pattern of folk literature, fairy tales, and man's universal erotic dream. Later, when Pocahontas was visiting England, Smith wrote to recommend her to Queen Anne for risking her life to save his. For two or three years after that incident, he said, she had visited the Jamestown settlement and had been God's instrument "to preserve this Colonie from death, famine and utter confusion." He noted "her extraordinairie affection to our Nation" and praised her for marrying John Rolfe and "rejecting her barbarous condition." The Indian princess was, he said, "the first Christian ever of that Nation, the first Virginian ever spake English, or had a childe in marriage by an Englishman." It is not surprising that Londoners, admiring her hat and ruff and ladylike demeanor, approved of her or that generations of Virginians proudly acknowledged descent from the alliance of Rolfe and his Indian wife. A defector from her native culture, Pocahontas did more than adopt Christianity; she converted to white. A popular figure in

American literature, she has not been depicted in accordance with derogatory Indian stereotypes.

Another illuminating account is that in William Bradford's history of the Pilgrim settlement at Plymouth. After they landed late in 1620 the colonists suffered from severe weather, hunger, disease, and hostile natives. But to their astonishment, an Indian they met the following March spoke some English, was acquainted with European ways, and was disposed to be friendly. This man, Samoset, introduced them to Squanto, who had been to England and spoke even better English. Over the years the help of Samoset and Squanto did a great deal to make possible the survival of the colony. Expressing the conviction that Providence determined the colonists' fortunes, Bradford said that Squanto was a special instrument sent of God for their good. Calling his death a great loss, Bradford mourned for the colonists, not for Squanto.

The works of other colonial writers demonstrate that man is often motivated by self-interest and is prone to judge other humans by their relationship to himself, but there is evidence in this writing also of man's capacity for a more generous treatment of his fellows. Gradually there is an enlargement of the role of Indians and blacks and an increased understanding of minority experience. As cultural differences are blurred and intergroup associations assume more varied and intimate patterns the minority figures gain identity as persons. Once merely creatures notable for their divergence from established norms, they cease to be things and begin to acquire human rights that must be respected. Blacks and Indians are converted to Christianity. Miscegenation and intermarriage take place. The justice of slavery is challenged. And exceptional individuals prove by their achievement that people of all colors and creeds have creative intelligence as well as souls.

But a few individuals may deviate from a society's image of a subordinate group without greatly affecting that image. Many exceptions are needed to change the rule, to break the force of stereotypes rooted in bigotry and racism. The treatment of red men and black men in the literature of the English colonies relied on the assumption of their inferiority even as it advanced in range and gave some sympathetic representations of their character and their plight in a culture that exploited them. That culture became more complex

and the society increasingly multi-ethnic. When cries of independence and freedom filled the air, writers were inspired to think of
the rights of all—if only all white males. But the equalitarian ideals
that were proclaimed when the thirteen colonies established their
political independence from England and King George were not
conceived as extending to Indians and blacks, either slave or free.

The literary emancipation of a minority comes about when its
members are perceived as equals and as single and unique beings
who are more notable for their basic human qualities than for the
distinctions that set the group apart. When at last the minority is
seen and depicted in terms of its own culture, which is accepted as
having as much validity as any other, the literary artist—whatever
his own ethnic identity—will have broken free from the shackles of
King Prejudice.

II.
The Minority Presence Looms Larger
(1800–1865)

> Our fellow countrymen in chains!
> Slaves—in a land of light and law!
> Slaves—crouching on the very plains
> Where rolled the storm of Freedom's war!

WHITTIER.

Most early American writing dealt with the lives and concerns of Englishmen endeavoring to establish an outpost of European civilization in a new physical environment. What the writers of the nineteenth century found themselves obliged to record and interpret was the development of a new nation and a unique culture created by the interaction of American Indians, Africans, Asians, and assorted Europeans. Some of the diverse ingredients that went into the melting pot blended readily, while others made their contribution to the whole but kept distinct identities. The interaction was often a struggle and was frequently violent, with uprisings, raids, massacres, riots, and wars marking the course of the years from the opening of the century to its close. But there was an advance toward accommodation, with separate cultures fusing into new patterns and national and racial groups losing some of the sharp outlines of their alienation. It was a period of conflict and social change. And it was a time when the nation's literature became truly American in character.

As the century opened, Parson Weems published his *Life of Washington* and added the cherry tree fable to our tradition. At his death the year before, the victorious commander of the American forces, in what Whittier called "Freedom's war," had freed his slaves, having finally become "principalled against . . . traffic in the human species." In his late years he must also have seen the error of a youthful provincialism that led him to write in his journal at sixteen about some German immigrants he met on the frontier he was

11

surveying, "ignorante . . . they would never speak English but, when spoken too, they speak all Dutch." When he died, the nation Washington had done so much to create stretched from the Atlantic coast to the Mississippi River. Its territory doubled in 1803 with President Jefferson's Louisiana Purchase, reaching across the plains to the Rocky Mountains. In the next sixty years Americans would extend their control all the way to the Pacific Ocean and would establish the country's present continental borders.

This expansion meant making and breaking treaties with the Indians, driving them from their lands and steadily consolidating white victories and advances. Forty-eight million acres of Indian hunting grounds passed into white hands between 1795 and 1809. The Shawnee chief, Tecumseh, offered brilliant resistance to the conquest, and was perhaps the ablest leader the Americans faced in the War of 1812. General Andrew Jackson, whose military reputation was important to his rise to the presidency, first came to national attention when he defeated the Creeks at Horseshoe Bend in 1814. It took two wars to clear the Seminoles from Florida and Black Hawk's War of 1832 to dispossess the Indians of the Old Northwest. As trains of Conestoga wagons and prairie schooners carried the pioneers westward, the epic struggle shifted to the prairies and plains. The Manifest Destiny that justified the conquest of the Indians served to cover also the annexation of Texas and the thousands of acres that were the fruit of victory in the war the United States provoked with Mexico in 1848.

The "fellow countrymen" whose enslavement Whittier protested in his poem were in bondage in the South, since, by 1800, virtually all the North's Negroes had been freed. Once a tottering system given somewhat apologetic approval, slavery became of crucial importance to southern states following the perfection of the cotton gin that Eli Whitney produced in 1793; and soon a spirited defense was provided for the "peculiar institution" that let the cotton kingdom flourish. The black race, it was argued, was biologically inferior and slavery was the Negro's natural state. Southern leaders emphasized the Bible's endorsement of servitude and insisted that theirs were happy slaves contented with their lot. That claim lacks confirmation in the record of slave rebellions and the steady flow of blacks escaping to freedom in the North and Canada. There was the

Gabriel uprising in Virginia in 1800, the Denmark Vesey conspiracy in South Carolina in 1822, and, most important of all, Nat Turner's rebellion in Virginia in 1831. From that time to the Civil War, some 2,500 slaves made their escape to liberty each year by way of the underground railroad.

Opposition to slavery mounted as the plantation system strengthened its hold; internal traffic in human beings with Virginia and its neighbors kept the cotton fields of the deep South supplied with bondsmen; and the spread of slavery to new states threatened to alter the regional relationships of the nation's political structure. For thirty years before the war broke out between the states, slavery was the dominant issue in American public affairs. Garrison founded his *Liberator* in 1831, and the American Anti-Slavery Society was organized in 1833, the climactic year when Parliament abolished slavery in all lands under British control. As historian Benjamin Quarles has pointed out, "although practically all slaves were Negroes, not all Negroes were slaves." In 1830, when the black population was more than 2,300,000 and constituted 18.1 percent of the national total, the free proportion of the Negro population reached the all-time high of 13.7 percent. The census of 1860 reported 3,953,000 slaves and 488,000 free blacks. Free blacks were no inconsequential force in the antislavery struggle.

The literary war, engaging black writers and white, Northerners and Southerners, was waged with increasing vigor and reached its climax with the publication of Harriet Beecher Stowe's *Uncle Tom's Cabin* in 1852. Its dramatization added to sectional animosities. John Brown's insurrection in 1859 was followed in the next year by Lincoln's election to the presidency and South Carolina's secession from the Union. Whatever other conflicts of interest combined to bring on the Civil War of 1861–65, the issue of slavery was of crucial importance to both the Union and the Confederacy. If Lincoln's Emancipation Proclamation of 1863 was more rhetoric and military policy than an instrument to liberate the South's slaves, the victories of Northern troops did bring freedom to blacks throughout the land. They did not end the Negro's minority status.

Other minorities were in evidence now more than ever before, though Europeans of many nationalities had been arriving in the English colonies for decades and had played an important role in the war for independence. Colonists of non-English extraction were more than willing to sever the ties with King George III. Thousands of General Washington's troops were Germans, and sometimes his Irish soldiers amounted to about a third of his whole command. Blacks, of course, saw service in both the Continental army and navy, fighting side by side with whites. When independence was won, St. Jean de Crèvecoeur was not alone in seeing Americans as a new breed, "a mixture of English, Scotch, Irish, French, Dutch, Germans, and Swedes."

Though immigration lagged after the Revolution, it picked up early in the nineteenth century. More than 50,000 immigrants arrived from Ireland between 1820 and 1830, and more than 200,000 came in the following decade. The first federal census of the foreign-born reported in 1850 that nearly a million of them were of Irish descent. Another half million Irish, driven by the potato famine at home, joined them in the next ten years, when 90,000 new German immigrants also landed on American soil. Newcomers beset by poverty and language problems met with residential segregation, religious intolerance, and job exploitation. They were crowded into urban slums, restricted to manual labor, and victimized by riot mobs. "The Negro is black outside," agitators said, "the Irishman is black inside." When the Civil War came, more than 140,000 Irish and 175,000 Germans fought in Union ranks. So did more than 180,000 black volunteers. Shouldering heavy burdens in the crisis, the nation's largest minorities affirmed their commitment to its interests, their claims to American identity.

A clear sense of the national identity and a truly American literature were called for immediately after independence was achieved, but took time to develop. It was not until after the romantic period had begun that Americans could take pride in writers of really major stature. Irving and Cooper won both critical and popular approval at home and abroad for fiction that still has a hold on our imagination. Both wrote a good deal about the nation's minorities and had a part in conceiving the American image held by their countrymen and the world. In retrospect they seem deficient in appreciation for some of the minorities they depicted and guilty of contributing to the stereotypes that fastened themselves to our collective consciousness. Though they may be charged with racism, their guilt diminishes when it is remembered that contrived plots and patronizing humor suited the taste of their audience. Irving's minstrel blacks offend modern readers who fail to observe that he assigned similarly grotesque anatomy and stereotyped behavior to some white characters. Cooper is interesting for his use of interracial romances but annoying for his care in frustrating the lovers, whether the couples are Indian-white, white-black, or black-Indian. The tragedy of these alliances anticipates a multitude of arbitrarily blighted love affairs in fiction from Cooper's day to the present.

Poe wrote too little about the daily life of the real world to give much attention to the minority presence, and Hawthorne provides less material on blacks than might be expected of a man of public affairs and alert intelligence writing in the midst of the slavery controversy. But Melville balances Hawthorne's neglect with a wealth of provocative characters, incidents, and symbols, and an understanding of depths of human nature few writers have explored. Emerson and Thoreau, revered as speculative thinkers and proponents of transcendentalism, were more active participants in the struggles of the time and more important as social critics than literary textbooks generally indicate. But as sympathetic as they were to the plight of enslaved blacks, they shared indifference to the predicament of immigrants who were near at hand. Sometimes it is easier to love mankind than a neighbor, easier, too, to pity the slave, confront the aborigine, and open the door to the alien than to conceive of these diverse types as one's countrymen. But Whittier's compassion conceded that status to blacks, and Walt Whitman, professed champion of the common man, deliberately included all humanity in his catalogs of brotherhood. In the nation's literature, the minority presence, whether trite and wooden or infused with new humanity, was firmly established as the identifying ingredient.

III.
Old Blood and New: The Minority Presence from 1865 to 1900

> There is something in the contemplation of the mode in which America has been settled, that, in a noble breast, should forever extinguish the prejudices of national dislikes.
>
> Settled by the people of all nations, all nations may claim her for their own. You can not spill a drop of American blood without spilling the blood of the whole world.
>
> MELVILLE

From the surrender of the Confederacy at Appomatox to the end of the nineteenth century, black Americans found that they were not emancipated from the stigma of slavery and the burdens of subordination; they had not won full civil rights. Indians, the victims of continuing attrition, were the nation's enemies or its wards. And masses of European immigrants, marked by ethnic identities they could not efface for a generation or more, suffered the limitations of second-class citizenship in the promised land. People of minority status or alien origin discovered that being Americans did not make them white Anglo-Saxon Protestants.

The hopes of black citizens, both freedmen and freemen, were raised as the nation embarked on Reconstruction. Constitutional amendments affirmed their full citizenship, the Freedman's Bureau gave aid to the ailing and destitute, newly established systems of public education became available to them, and they achieved political representation in the South. But the benefits proved to be temporary or limited gains. Slavery was replaced by rigid segregation as the Jim Crow system built a wall that confined the Negro to "his place." The Ku Klux Klan, founded in 1866, became a powerful force for tyranny. Sharecropping doomed tenant farmers to poverty. Mob violence and lynchings assured white dominance. In 1866 mobs

16

burned schools and churches and killed or seriously wounded more than a hundred blacks in Memphis and New Orleans, and lynchings reached a peak of 235 victims for one year in 1892. The struggle for civil rights was lost in the courts and in the public forum as northern humanitarians fell silent or shifted their support from the ex-slave to other underprivileged groups. The twentieth century opened with white supremacists firmly in control of the solid South and enjoying the approval of most Americans everywhere, except for the 8,830,000 citizens (11.6 percent of the total population) whose African ancestry made them members of the country's largest racial minority.

A military campaign to "pacify" the Plains Indians was begun during the Civil War and continued for twenty-five years until they had been driven from the lands coveted for settlement, mining, or railroad development. The doctrine that "the only good Indian is a dead Indian" threatened their extermination. The final conquest of the West was marked by bloody and ignoble victories. Soldiers massacred hundreds of Cheyennes and Arapahos at Sand Creek in Colorado in 1864. General Custer's column was wiped out at the Battle of Little Big Horn in 1876, but the victory sealed the Indians' doom. Geronimo and his Apaches were finally defeated about the time the last buffalo herd was destroyed in 1884. The greatest victory for federal troops came in 1890 when some two hundred unarmed Sioux, women and children among them, were massacred at Wounded Knee in South Dakota. By 1900 the Indian population, ravaged by disease, assimilation, conquest, and oppression, was down to about 250,000, less than a third of what estimates say it was before Europeans arrived on their continent.

After the Civil War the same nationalities that had dominated the ranks of the nation's immigrants for decades continued to outnumber other new arrivals. Irish and Germans and Scandinavians flocked to America. Two million Germans landed here between 1870 and 1890, and 400,000 Swedes and many other Scandinavians came during the same period. But after 1880 immigration began to take on a different character. With people of northern European extraction well settled and advanced in the Americanization process, new peoples, more alien and less easily assimilated, began to constitute the bulk of the immigrants. They came largely from southern and eastern Europe: Italians, Greeks, Czechs, Slovaks, Russian Jews, Poles, Hungarians. These huddled masses seeking refuge bore unpronounceable names, spoke strange tongues, and might be identified by dark complexions and different profiles. On the west coast the tide of Chinese immigrants reached such a height that Congress passed the Chinese Exclusion Act in 1882, the first racist closing of America's golden door of opportunity.

The earliest immigrants had encountered some hostility, and many an ad for employment in the 1860s read "No Irish need apply," but now the new arrivals met with rising disfavor. They were herded into urban ghettos, and poorly paid for heavy labor. Still the immigrants came. By 1890 one third of the people of Boston were of alien birth. And in New York then there were twice as many Irish as in Dublin, half as many Italians as in Naples, as many Germans as in Hamburg, and two and a half times as many Jews as in Warsaw. Benjamin Franklin once argued that "white" should be reserved for Saxons and the English, Francis Parkman denied that the term included Mexicans, and later Americans often withheld that accolade from the Balkan and Mediterranean peoples. Persuaded that the Anglo-Saxon was superior to the Celt, the Chinese, and the southern Europeans, many American writers ignored the presence of these groups on the national scene, patronized them, or otherwise treated them in the stereotypical fashion reserved for minorities.

The status of any minority in the period can be determined by examining the representation of that group in jokes, cartoons, stage comedy, and other informal and often anonymous productions roughly classified as humor. The comic relief selections in American journals, even those in a magazine of the stature of *Scribner's Monthly*, can be as illuminating in regard to the image of a minority as is the serious treatment accorded that group elsewhere in the same periodicals.

Humor can be lighthearted or vicious. Human beings find it difficult, if not impossible, to resist the conclusion that persons who are different from themselves are laughable. Foreigners speak a funny language and wear preposterous clothes. We laugh *with* those whose condition or human frailty is of the sort to which we, too, are prone; we laugh *at* inferiors. We "poke fun" at those we would demean. Ridicule of unalterable liabilities of appearance or condition is at best thoughtless, at worst malicious.

The most frequent butt of amateur and professional humorists in America has been the black man, whose physical difference and cultural distance from the accepted norm made him exceedingly vulnerable. But other subordinate groups have also been subjected to abuse and mockery in the guise of humor, among them the Irish and the Chinese. Like other minorities, the Chinese were most ridiculed when their difference from the dominant group was exaggerated, in their case by pigeon-English and queue. Once it seemed that their prospects for full acceptance in American society had no better than "a Chinaman's chance," a popular expression meaning no chance at all.

The selection that follows appeared anonymously in *Scribner's Monthly* for January, 1871, but was revealed later as the work of Mary Mapes Dodge, a writer of juvenile fiction best known for *Hans Brinker: or, the Silver Skates.* Serious treatments of the "Chinese Question" appeared in articles in the same journal in March, May, and September of that year. An anonymous review in the May issue praised William Dean Howells for *Suburban Sketches,* without commenting on his allusion, in the selection from his book that is included in this volume, to the alleged threat to the nation's well-being from the Chinese immigrants in the West and the Irish immigrants in the East.

MISS MALONY ON THE CHINESE QUESTION

Och! don't be talkin'. Is it howld on, ye say? An' didn't I howld on till the heart of me was clane broke entirely, and me wastin' that thin you could clutch me wid yer two hands. To think o' me toilin' like a nager for the six year I've been in Ameriky—bad luck to the day I iver left the owld counthry! to be bate by the likes o' them! (faix an' I'll sit down when I'm ready, so I will, Ann Ryan, an' ye'd better be listnin' than drawin' your remarks) an' is it mysel, with five good charac'ters from respectable places, would be herdin' wid the haythens? The saints forgive me but I'd be buried alive sooner'n put up wid it a day longer. Sure an' I was the granehorn not be lavin' at onct when the missus kim into me kitchen wid her perlaver about the new waiter man which was brought out from Californy. "He'll

be here the night," says she, "and Kitty, it's meself looks to you to
be kind and patient wid him, for he's a furriner," says she, a kind
o'lookin' off. "Sure an' it's little I'll hinder nor interfare wid him nor
any other, mum," says I, a kind o' stiff, for I minded me how these
French waiters, wid their paper collars and brass rings on their fingers, isn't company for no gurril brought up dacint and honest. Och!
sorra a bit I knew what was comin' till the missus walked into me
kitchen smilin', and says kind o'shcared: "Here's Fing Wing, Kitty,
an' you'll have too much sinse to mind his bein' a little strange."
Wid that she shoots the doore, and I, misthrusting if I was tidied up
sufficient for me fine buy wid his paper collar, looks up and—Howly
fathers! may I niver brathe another breath, but there stud a rale
haythen Chineser a-grinnin' like he'd just come off a tay-box. If
you'll belave me, the crayture was that *yeller* it'ud sicken you to see
him; and sorra stitch was on him but a black night-gown over his
trowsers and the front of his head shaved claner nor a copper biler,
and a black tail a-hanging down from it behind, wid his two feet
stook into the heathenestest shoes you ever set eyes on. Och! but I
was up-stairs afore you could turn about, a givin' the missus warnin,' an' only stopt wid her by her raisin' me wages two dollars, and
playdin' wid me how it was a Christian's duty to bear wid haythens
and taitch'em all in our power—the saints save us! Well, the ways
and trials I had wid that Chineser, Ann Ryan, I couldn't be tellin'.
Not a blissed thing cud I do but he'd be lookin' on wid his eyes
cocked up'ard like two poomp-handles, an'he widdout a speck or
smitch o' whiskers on him, an' his finger nails full a yard long. But
it's dyin' you'd be to see the missus a'larnin him, and he grinnin' an'
waggin' his pig-tail (which was pieced out long wid some black
stoof, the haythen chate!) and gettin' into her ways wonderful quick,
I don't deny, imitatin' that sharp, you'd be shurprised, and ketchin'
an' copyin' things the best of us will be a-hurried wid work, yet
don't want comin' to the knowledge of the family—bad luck to him!

Is it ate wid him? Arrah, an' would I be sittin' wid a haythen an'
he a-atin' wid drum-sticks—yes, an' atin' dogs an' cats unknownst to
me, I warrant you, which it is the custom of them Chinesers, till the
thought made me that sick I could die. An' didn't the crayture prof-
fer to help me a wake ago come Toosday, an' me a foldin' down me
clane clothes for the ironin', and fill his haythin mouth wid water,
an' afore I could hinder squirrit it through his teeth stret over the
best linen table-cloth, and fold it up tight as innercent now as a
baby, the dirrity baste! But the worrest of all was the copyin' he'd be
doin' till ye'd be dishtracted. It's yersel' knows the tinder feet that's

on me since ever I've bin in this counthry. Well, owin' to that, I fell
into a way o' slippin' me shoes off when I'd be settin' down to pale
the praities or the likes o' that, and, do ye mind! that haythin would
do the same thing after me whinivir the missus set him to parin'
apples or tomaterses. The saints in heaven couldn't have made him
belave he cud kape the shoes on him when he'd be paylin' anything.

Did I lave fur that? Faix an' I didn't. Didn't he get me into trouble wid my missus, the haythin? You're aware yersel' how the
boondles comin' in from the grocery often contains more'n 'll go
into anything dacently. So, for that matter I'd now and then take out
a sup o'sugar, or flour, or tay, an' wrap it in paper and put it in me
bit of a box tucked under the ironin' blankit the how it cuddent be
bodderin' any one. Well, what shud it be, but this blessed Sathurday
morn the missus was a spakin' pleasant and respec'ful wid me in me
kitchen when the grocer boy comes in an' stands fornenst her wid
his boondles, an' she motions like to Fing Wing (which I never
would call him by that name ner any other but just haythin), she motions to him, she does, for to take the boondles an' empty out the
sugar an' what not where they belongs. If you'll belave me, Ann
Ryan, what did that blatherin' Chineser do but take out a sup o'
sugar, an' a handful o' tay, an' a bit o' chaze right afore the missus,
wrap them into bits o' paper, an' I spacheless wid shurprize, an' he
the next minute up wid the ironin' blankit and pullin' out me box
wid a show o' bein' sly to put them in. Och, the Lord forgive me,
but I clutched it, and the missus sayin', "O Kitty!" in a way that 'ud
cruddle your blood. "He's a haythin nager," says I. "I've found you
out," says she. "I'll arrist him," says I. "It's you ought to be arris-
ted," says she. "You won't," says I. "I will," says she—and so it went
till she give me such sass as I cuddent take from no lady—an' I give
her warnin' and' I left that instant, an' she a-point-in' to the doore.

"Miss Malony on the Chinese Question" shows very clearly the influence of local color, the literary movement of the 1870s and 1880s
brought on by Bret Harte's popular verses and stories about life in
the mining camps of the Far West. The genre featured racial, regional, occupational, and other minorities which might be depicted
as quaint and humorous. Every group and every section had its
spokesman, as writers staked claims to literary materials like
prospectors asserting their rights to the earth's minerals. The movement enriched our literature by adding new subjects and attitudes,

for often the author's intent was to gain favorable attention for some little-known people or place. Though the writer did not belong to the group and was prone to misrepresent its values and patronize his characters, at least one professed purpose of the work was to present a novel subject with sympathetic understanding. Some of this writing, like the best fiction of George W. Cable and Kate Chopin, moved on toward regionalism and realism, producing a gallery of notable minority characters.

When realism became the prevailing literary style in the United States, William Dean Howells set the model for close observation and careful reporting on the commonplaces of middle-class life. His incidental treatment of immigrants gives us insights into the reaction of Americans to newcomers whose inferiority was not attested by gross physical deviations from the dominant standard. For such supposedly disappearing minorities a full accommodation to the majority values might seem to promise early release from the handicaps that attend cultural difference. Howells's references to Jews, Irish, and urban blacks have the virtue of quiet directness. More impassioned is the work of Mark Twain, whose misanthropy grew as he pondered the abuse and persecution visited upon minorities and the underprivileged in all human societies. Twain's spirited defenses of the rights of blacks and Chinese are sometimes misunderstood by readers unable to identify irony or appreciate sophisticated humor. Although not all his work is equally admirable for its rendering of minority experience, his *Adventures of Huckleberry Finn* is rightly called a "hymn to freedom."

Stereotyping of minorities—races, nationalities, etc.—comes about when writers and readers generalize and oversimplify. The attainable task for the artist is to depict with fidelity, depth, and compassion a woman or certain particular women, not *everywoman;* a Navaho bride or modern Mohawk steelworkers, not *the* Indian. Writers should write about what they know about, whatever that may be, which is not to say either that only Chicanos should write about Chicanos, or that a Nisei author should write only about Nisei. Minority identity does not automatically confer artistic skill and profound understanding of human nature and human society. Genius may produce a brilliant representation of some condition or identity the writer does not share in his or her own person. But for the fullest expression of the minority presence in America there must be artists who are part of the culture they depict and products of the tradition they describe.

Unfortunately, literary genius is not on call and does not appear in response to every need. Accomplishment in belles lettres takes time and opportunity. Oppressed people must put their energies into the daily battle for life and freedom; formal art is obliged to wait. Yet by the beginning of the twentieth century, Theodore Dreiser, a second-generation American, had made the first of his several major contributions to the mainstream of our literature, and Abraham Cahan, born in Russia, was producing authoritative studies of life in the ghettos where the new immigrants were herded. Charles W. Chesnutt and Paul Laurence Dunbar, whose ancestry traced to African slaves, had attained national recognition for their interpretations of black experience. They were heralds of a multitude of twentieth century writers of many ethnic identities whose works have added the indispensible inside view to the representation of these Americans in the nation's literature.

The theme of many of these writers is the predicament of people who are torn between the customs and values of the culture of their birth and those of the dominant society of which they are a part. Often they see the melting pot as merely a metaphor and feel that the majority culture induces them to abandon their heritage but withholds full participation and an equal status in American life. They write of the frustrations of the outsider who may possibly attain material success and public recognition but not admission to an inner circle. Joseph P. Kennedy, the first man of Irish descent to serve as American ambassador to England, once remarked before his son became President, "I was born in the United States and so was my father. Yet my children are still called Irish. What the hell do we have to do to become Americans?" They write also of the ambivalence of members of minority groups that leads them, as did Ambassador Kennedy at the Court of St. James, to take pride in their ethnic identity and to measure their advance by the distance they have come from their origin. "Tell them we are rising" was the message the struggling freedmen sent to their well-wishers; "We're movin' on up" is the theme song of modern blacks who have left Harlem for Manhattan's East Side. Upward mobility remains enough of a possibility in American life to make the national dream a compelling force.

And the flow of immigrants seeking refuge and opportunity continues. More than forty million people have migrated to the United States since the first European settlers arrived. By 1930 there were more people of Italian birth living in New York than in Rome. In the midst of the racial turmoil of the 1960s, about 33,000 black immigrants, ranging from laborers to professionals, came each year from the West Indies and Africa. Ethnic confusion goes on unabated: there are about 7,000 black Jews in the United States—among them some who have been Jews for generations—and one might find at an American university a black student majoring, as a matter of course, in Hebrew Studies. The newest immigrants—Puerto Ricans, Cubans, Mexicans, Hungarians, Koreans, Vietnamese—repeat the patterns experienced by their predecessors.

If each group advances in status as its members gain economic toeholds and make accommodations and contributions to the dominant culture, there are also penalties for whatever degree of alienation or identification persists. If some minorities have made dramatic progress up the ladder, it is yet true that there is a long way to go before all have a fair share of the rewards of American life. Discrimination and exploitation are meted out in heavy doses for some groups, while others experience them in lesser measure. In top corporations in Chicago in the early 1970s the number of black directors was only 0.4 percent, but those of Polish or Hispanic identity were even fewer. The number of people in Pittsburgh with incomes under $3,500 per year was twice as great for the foreign stock as for blacks. Indians, their numbers increased to almost 800,000 by the time of the 1970 census, constituted the most economically and educationally deprived minority in the nation, more than half of them living on reservations.

The cries of "Black Power" that dominated headlines of a decade ago have been followed by shouts of "Chicano Power" and "Women's Liberation," and virtually all the nation's minority groups have become vocal in protests and in formal literature. The study of their image becomes increasingly, but by no means exclusively, the study of works by ethnic writers. But these are, of course, also American writers, whose products are contributions to the growth and development of our national literature. The ever growing minority presence, a test and a challenge, remains central to the American experience.

WALT WHITMAN
(1819–1892)

Whitman's attitude toward minorities incorporates the contradictions he claimed as the privilege of one large enough to "contain multitudes." All the poetry below comes from *Leaves of Grass,* his manifesto and *magnum opus.* The selections from *Song of Myself* (1855) have been entitled "Myself and Others" for this volume, while those from *Salut au Monde* (1856) are called "The Menials of the Earth." "Ethiopia Saluting the Colors" dates from 1871. Whitman's eminence as "the Good Gray Poet" obscures the significance of his prose, much of which is relevant to the study of the minority presence in the nation's literature.

26

MYSELF AND OTHERS

10

... I saw the marriage of the trapper in the open air in
the far west, the bride was a red girl,
Her father and his friends sat near cross-legged and
dumbly smoking, they had moccasins to their feet
and large thick blankets hanging from their
shoulders,
On a bank lounged the trapper, he was drest mostly in
skins, his luxuriant beard and curls protected his
neck, he held his bride by the hand,
She had long eyelashes, her head was bare, her coarse
straight locks descended upon her voluptuous limbs
and reach'd to her feet.

The runaway slave came to my house and stopt outside,
I heard his motions crackling the twigs of the woodpile,
Through the swung half-door of the kitchen I saw him
limpsy and weak,
And went where he sat on a log and led him in and
assured him,
And brought water and fill'd a tub for his sweated body
and bruis'd feet,
And gave him a room that enter'd from my own, and
gave him some coarse clean clothes,
And remember perfectly well his revolving eyes and his
awkwardness,
And remember putting plasters on the galls of his neck
and ankles;
He staid with me a week before he was recuperated and
pass'd north,
I had him sit next me at table, my fire-lock lean'd in the
corner.

o   o   o   o   o

13

The negro holds firmly the reins of his four horses, the
    block swags underneath on its tied-over chain,
The negro that drives the long dray of the stone-yard,
    steady and tall he stands pois'd on one leg on the
    string-piece,
His blue shirt exposes his ample neck and breast and
    loosens over his hip-band,
His glance is calm and commanding, he tosses the slouch
    of his hat away from his forehead,
The sun falls on his crispy hair and mustache, falls on the
    black of his polish'd and perfect limbs.

I behold the picturesque giant and love him, and I do not
    stop there,
I go with the team also.

In me the caresser of life wherever moving, backward as
    well as forward sluing,
To niches aside and junior bending, not a person or
    object missing,
Absorbing all to myself and for this song. . . .

o   o   o   o   o

15

The pure contralto sings in the organ loft,
The carpenter dresses his plank, the tongue of his
    foreplane whistles its wild ascending lisp,
The married and unmarried children ride home to their
    Thanksgiving dinner,
The pilot seizes the king-pin, he heaves down with a
    strong arm,
The mate stands braced in the whale-boat, lance and
    harpoon are ready,
The duck-shooter walks by silent and cautious stretches,

The deacons are ordain'd with cross'd hands at the altar,
The spinning-girl retreats and advances to the hum of
the big wheel,
The farmer stops by the bars as he walks on a First-day
loafe and looks at the oats and rye,
The lunatic is carried at last to the asylum a confirm'd
case,
(He will never sleep any more as he did in the cot in his
mother's bed-room;)
The jour printer with gray head and gaunt jaws works at
his case,
He turns his quid of tobacco while his eyes blurr with the
manuscript;
The malform'd limbs are tied to the surgeon's table,
What is removed drops horribly in a pail;
The quadroon girl is sold at the auction-stand, the
drunkard nods by the bar-room stove,
The machinist rolls up his sleeves, the policeman travels
his beat, the gate-keeper marks who pass,
The young fellow drives the express-wagon, (I love him,
though I do not know him;)
The half-breed straps on his light boots to compete in
the race,
The western turkey-shooting draws old and young, some
lean on their rifles, some sit on logs,
Out from the crowd steps the marksman, takes his
position, levels his piece;
The groups of newly-come immigrants cover the wharf
or levee,
As the woolly-pates hoe in the sugar-field, the overseer
views them from his saddle,
The bugle calls in the ball-room, the gentlemen run for
their partners, the dancers bow to each other,
The youth lies awake in the cedar-roof'd garret and harks
to the musical rain,
The Wolverine sets traps on the creek that helps fill the
Huron,
The squaw wrapt in her yellow-hemm'd cloth is offering

moccasins and bead-bags for sale,

The connoisseur peers along the exhibition-gallery with half-shut eyes bent sideways,

As the deck-hands make fast the steamboat the plank is thrown for the shore-going passengers,

The young sister holds out the skein while the elder sister winds it off in a ball, and stops now and then for the knots,

The one-year wife is recovering and happy having a week ago borne her first child,

The clean-hair'd Yankee girl works with her sewing-machine or in the factory or mill,

The paving-man leans on his two-handed rammer, the reporter's lead flies swiftly over the note-book, the sign-painter is lettering with blue and gold,

The canal boy trots on the tow-path, the book-keeper counts at his desk, the shoemaker waxes his thread,

The conductor beats time for the band and all the performers follow him,

The child is baptized, the convert is making his first professions,

The regatta is spread on the bay, the race is begun, (how the white sails sparkle!)

The drover watching his drove sings out to them that would stray,

The pedler sweats with his pack on his back, (the purchaser higgling about the odd cent;)

The bride unrumples her white dress, the minute-hand of the clock moves slowly,

The opium-eater reclines with rigid head and just-open'd lips,

The prostitute draggles her shawl, her bonnet bobs on her tipsy and pimpled neck,

The crowd laugh at her blackguard oaths, the men jeer and wink to each other,

(Miserable! I do not laugh at your oaths nor jeer you;)

The President holding a cabinet council is surrounded by the great Secretaries,

On the piazza walk three matrons stately and friendly
    with twined arms,
The crew of the fish-smack pack repeated layers of
    halibut in the hold,
The Missourian crosses the plains toting his wares and
    his cattle,
As the fare-collector goes through the train he gives
    notice by the jingling of loose change,
The floor-men are laying the floor, the tinners are
    tinning the roof, the masons are calling for mortar,
In single file each shouldering his hod pass onward the
    laborers;
Seasons pursuing each other the indescribable crowd is
    gather'd, it is the fourth of Seventh-month, (what
    salutes of cannon and small arms!)
Seasons pursuing each other the plougher ploughs, the
    mower mows, and the winter-grain falls in the
    ground;
Off on the lakes the pike-fisher watches and waits by the
    hole in the frozen surface,
The stumps stand thick round the clearing, the squatter
    strikes deep with his axe,
Flatboatmen make fast towards dusk near the cotton-
    wood or pecan-trees,
Coon-seekers go through the regions of the Red river or
    through those drain'd by the Tennessee, or through
    those of the Arkansas,
Torches shine in the dark that hangs on the Chatta-
    hooche or Altamahaw,
Patriarchs sit at supper with sons and grandsons and
    great-grandsons around them,
In walls of adobie, in canvas tents, rest hunters and
    trappers after their day's sport,
The city sleeps and the country sleeps,
The living sleep for their time, the dead sleep for their
    time,
The old husband sleeps by his wife and the young
    husband sleeps by his wife;

And these tend inward to me, and I tend outward to
   them,
And such as it is to be of these more or less I am,
And of these one and all I weave the song of myself.

o   o   o   o   o

19

This is the meal equally set, this the meat for natural
   hunger,
It is for the wicked just the same as the righteous, I make
   appointments with all,
I will not have a single person slighted or left away,
The kept-woman, sponger, thief, are hereby invited,
The heavy-lipp'd slave is invited, the venerealee is
   invited;
There shall be no difference between them and the
   rest. . . .

o   o   o   o   o

33

. . . The disdain and calmness of martyrs,
The mother of old, condemn'd for a witch, burnt with
   dry wood, her children gazing on,
The hounded slave that flags in the race, leans by the
   fence, blowing, cover'd with sweat,
The twinges that sting like needles his legs and neck, the
   murderous buckshot and the bullets,
All these I feel or am.

I am the hounded slave, I wince at the bite of the dogs,
Hell and despair are upon me, crack and again crack the
   marksmen,

I clutch the rails of the fence, my gore dribs, thinn'd with
    the ooze of my skin,
I fall on the weeds and stones,
The riders spur their unwilling horses, haul close,
Taunt my dizzy ears and beat me violently over the head
    with whip-stocks.

Agonies are one of my changes of garments,
I do not ask the wounded person how he feels, I myself
    become the wounded person,
My hurts turn livid upon me as I lean on a cane and
    observe. . . .

THE MENIALS OF THE EARTH

... I see all the menials of the earth, laboring,
I see all the prisoners in the prisons,
I see the defective human bodies of the earth,
The blind, the deaf and dumb, idiots, hunchbacks,
    lunatics,
The pirates, thieves, betrayers, murderers, slave-makers
    of the earth,
The helpless infants, and the helpless old men and
    women.

I see male and female everywhere,
I see the serene brotherhood of philosophs,
I see the constructiveness of my race,
I see the results of the perseverance and industry of my
    race,
I see ranks, colors, barbarisms, civilizations, I go among
    them, I mix indiscriminately,
And I salute all the inhabitants of the earth.

11

You whoever you are!
You daughter or son of England!
You of the might Slavic tribes and empires! you Russ in
    Russia!
You dim-descended, black, divine-soul'd African, large,
    fine-headed, nobly-form'd, superbly destin'd, on
    equal terms with me!
You Norwegian! Swede! Dane! Icelander! you Prussian!
You Spaniard of Spain! you Portuguese!
You Frenchwoman and Frenchman of France!

You Belge! you liberty-lover of the Netherlands! (you
    stock whence I myself have descended;)
You sturdy Austrian! you Lombard! Hun! Bohemian!
    farmer of Styria!
You neighbor of the Danube!
You working-man of the Rhine, the Elbe, or the Weser!
    you working-woman too!
You Sardinian! you Bavarian! Swabian! Saxon!
    Wallachian! Bulgarian!
You Roman! Neapolitan! you Greek!
You lithe matador in the arena at Seville!
You mountaineer living lawlessly on the Taurus or
    Caucasus!
You Bokh horse-herd watching your mares and stallions
    feeding!
You beautiful-bodied Persian at full speed in the saddle
    shooting arrows to the mark!
You Chinaman and Chinawoman of China! you Tartar of
    Tartary!
You women of the earth subordinated at your tasks!
You Jew journeying in your old age through every risk to
    stand once on Styrian ground!
You other Jews waiting in all lands for your Messiah!
You thoughtful Armenian pondering by some stream of
    the Euphrates! you peering amid the ruins of
    Nineveh! you ascending mount Ararat!
You foot-worn pilgrim welcoming the far-away sparkle
    of the minarets of Mecca!
You sheiks along the stretch from Suez to Bab-el-mandeb
    ruling your families and tribes!
You olive-grower tending your fruit on fields of
    Nazareth, Damascus, or lake Tiberias!
You Thibet trader on the wide inland or bargaining in
    the shops of Lassa!
You Japanese man or woman! you liver in Madagascar,
    Ceylon, Sumatra, Borneo!
All you continentals of Asia, Africa, Europe, Australia,
    indifferent of place!

All you on the numberless islands of the archipelagoes of
    the sea!
And you of centuries hence when you listen to me!
And you each and everywhere whom I specify not, but
    include just the same!
Health to you! good will to you all, from me and
    America sent!

Each of us inevitable,
Each of us limitless—each of us with his or her right
    upon the earth,
Each of us allow'd the eternal purports of the earth,
Each of us here as divinely as any is here.

12

You Hottentot with clicking palate! you woolly-hair'd
    hordes!
You own'd persons dropping sweat-drops or blood-
    drops!
You human forms with the fathomless ever-impressive
    countenances of brutes!
You poor koboo whom the meanest of the rest look
    down upon for all your glimmering language and
    spirituality!
You dwarf'd Kamtschatkan, Greenlander, Lapp!
You Austral negro, naked, red, sooty, with protrusive lip,
    groveling, seeking your food!
You Caffre, Berber, Soudanese!
You haggard, uncouth, untutor'd Bedowee!
You plague-swarms in Madras, Nankin, Kaubul, Cairo!
You benighted roamer of Amazonia! you Patagonian!
    you Feejee-man!
I do not prefer others so very much before you either,
I do not say one word against you, away back there
    where you stand,
(You will come forward in due time to my side.)

13

My spirit has pass'd in compassion and determination
    around the whole earth,
I have look'd for equals and lovers and found them ready
    for me in all lands.
I think some divine rapport has equalized me with
    them . . . .

ETHIOPIA SALUTING
THE COLORS

Who are you dusky woman, so ancient hardly human,
With your woolly-white and turban'd head, and bare
    bony feet?
Why rising by the roadside here, do you the colors greet?

('Tis while our army lines Carolina's sands and pines,
Forth from thy hovel door thou Ethiopia com'st to me,
As under doughty Sherman I march toward the sea.)

Me master years a hundred since from my parents
    sunder'd,
A little child, they caught me as the savage beast is
    caught,
Then hither me across the sea the cruel slaver brought.

No further does she say, but lingering all the day,
Her high-borne turban'd head she wags, and rolls her
    darkling eye,
And courtesies to the regiments, the guidons moving by.

What is it fateful woman, so blear, hardly human?
Why wag your head with turban bound, yellow, red and
    green?
Are the things so strange and marvelous you see or have
    seen?

SUGGESTED ADDITIONAL READINGS

Franklin Evans
The Half-Breed: A Tale of the Western Frontier
"Tomb Blossoms"
"Says"
"The Bowery"
"Prohibition of Colored Persons"

SELECTED REFERENCES

Andrews, Thomas F. "Walt Whitman and Slavery: A Reconsideration of One Aspect of His Concept of the American Common Man." *CLA Journal,* 9 (1966), 225-33.

Clark, Leadie M. *Walt Whitman's Concept of the American Common Man* (1955).

Cox, James M. "Walt Whitman, Mark Twain, and the Civil War." *Sewanee Review,* 49 (1961), 185-204.

Davis, Charles T. "Walt Whitman and the Problem of an American Tradition." *CLA Journal,* 5 (1961), 1-16.

Ford, Nick Aaron. "Walt Whitman's Conception of Democracy." *Phylon,* 11 (1950), 201-206.

Gibson, Donald B. "The Good Black Poet and the Good Gray Poet: The Poetry of Hughes and Whitman." *Langston Hughes, Black Genius: A Critical Evaluation* (1971), ed. by Therman B. O'Daniel.

Glicksberg, Charles I. "Walt Whitman and the Negro." *Phylon,* 9 (1948), 326-31.

Rahv, Philip. "Paleface and Redskin." *Kenyon Review,* 1 (1939), 251-56.

Turner, Lorenzo Dow. "Walt Whitman and the Negro." *Chicago Jewish Forum,* 15 (1956), 5-11.

Warfel, Harry R. "Whitman's *Salut au Monde:* The Ideal of Human Brotherhood." *Phylon,* 19 (1958), 154-56.

PROJECTS AND PROBLEMS

Compare the aged black widow in "Tomb Blossoms" with Margaret, the glamorous slave woman in *Franklin Evans.* Which of these early pieces is more credible? Does each agree with prevailing stereotypes?

Are Whitman's references to Jews, Germans, and other immigrants fully in accord with the equalitarian doctrine he pronounced? Is there evidence that he had a personal antipathy for blacks that ran counter to the pronouncements in his poetry?

Compare Whitman's treatment of the fugitive slave with that offered in "The Fugitive Slave" by Jones Very. Comment on the different styles of the poets as well as their posture in regard to the fugitives.

Examine *Franklin Evans* and *The Half-Breed* for Whitman's views (or the conventional views of the period) on miscegenation. Did he adhere fully to the stereotypes for his characterization of blacks and Indians?

Compare Whitman's treatment of blacks and slavery in *Leaves of Grass* with the opinions he expressed in some of his earlier prose contributions to Brooklyn newspapers. Explain the differences.

JAMES P. BECKWOURTH
(1798-1866)

The advance guard of Europeans on the frontier was always composed of hunters and trappers. Some became renegades, while others remained loyal to their heritage and served the whites as guides and army scouts. In the Far West, Kit Carson and Jim Bridger became famous for their exploits. Less celebrated today but widely known in his own time was Jim Beckwourth, whose mother was of African ancestry and may have been a slave.

As a young man, Beckwourth left St. Louis and made his way westward, soon becoming an able frontiersman. Mistaken identity led to his adoption by the Crow Indians in 1824, and eventually he became a chief of the tribe. Later adventures after he left the Crows included army service against the Seminoles in Florida and trapping and prospecting in the West. An important pass that he discovered in the Sierra Nevadas and a town nearby still bear his name.

Thomas D. Bonner, to whom Beckwourth dictated his memoirs, was a journalist and justice of the peace in California gold camps. Their collaboration produced *The Life and Adventures of James P. Beckwourth, Mountaineer, Scout, and Pioneer, and Chief of the Crow Nation of Indians* in 1856. There was an English edition in the same year, a French translation appeared in 1860, and there have been several American printings.

The book is a stirring representative of the many works purporting to be inside accounts of life among the Indians, a genre, related to the Indian captivity narrative, that has enjoyed popular favor. Beckwourth's memoirs run true to type, showing carelessness with dates, an affection for exaggeration, and self-glorification. His claims of enemy casualties fit an American tradition that runs from John Smith's reports to the dispatches from the Vietnam War. But the book also provides insights into Indian life and some appreciation for the values of Indian culture. The first part of the selection is taken from Chapter XIII.

A MOUNTAIN MAN AMONG
THE CROWS

... Visiting at my father's lodge one day, he asked me why I did not head a party myself, and go on some expedition as leader. By so doing, he informed me, I stood a better chance of gaining promotion. "Your medicine is good," said he, "and the medicine of both will bring you great success."

I replied that I had been domiciliated there so short a time that I did not wish to be too precipitate in pushing myself forward, and that I preferred to fight a while longer as a brave, rather than risk the responsibility of being leader.

He replied, "Here is your brother-in-law, take him; also your brothers will go with you. If they all get killed, so be it; I will cheerfully submit to old age without them, and die alone."

I reflected that, in order to advance by promotion, I must risk everything; so I consented to follow his advice.

"Black Panther," my brother-in-law, was anxious to follow me, and there were seven young striplings, from ten to eighteen years old, that my father called his sons, though, in fact, half of them were what I called nephews. I put myself forward as the leader, the party comprising only two men and the above-mentioned seven boys.

We departed from the village, and pressed on to the head-waters of the Arkansas, coming directly to the Arrap-a-ho and I-a-tan villages. At night we drove off one hundred and eighteen fine horses, with which we moved on in all possible haste toward home. We were then about three hundred miles from our village, and two hundred from the Crow country. In passing through the Park we discovered three Indians coming toward us, driving a small drove of horses. We concealed ourselves from their view by dropping back over the brow of a small hill directly in their route, until they had approached within ten steps of us. We raised the war-hoop, and rushed out on them, killing two of the three; the third was at a greater distance, driving the cattle, and when he saw the fate of his companions he mounted one of the fleetest, and was soon beyond pursuit. My company had achieved a great victory, the spoils of

43

which were fourteen horses, in addition to those already in our possession, two scalps, one gun, two battle-axes, one lance, bow, quiver, etc. This trivial affair exalted my young brothers in their own esteem higher than the greatest veteran their village contained. During their return home they were anticipating with untiring tongues the ovation that awaited them.

We fell in with no more enemies on our way to the village. The horses we had captured from the three Indians had been stolen by them from the Crows, and as a recovery of lost horses is a greater achievement in Indians' eyes than the original acquisition, our merit was in proportion. We entered singing, with our faces blackened, bearing two scalps and other trophies, and driving one hundred and thirty-two fine horses before us. The whole village resounded with the shouts with which our brethren and kindred welcomed us. I was hailed bravest of the brave, and my promotion appeared certain.

My father and all his family rose greatly in popular favor. The Antelope's distinguished skill and bravery were reflected in lucent rays upon their names. "Great is the Antelope," was chanted on all sides, "the lost son of Big Bowl; their medicine is good and prosperous."

There is one trait in Indian character which civilized society would derive much profit by imitating. Envy is a quality unknown to the savages. When a warrior has performed any deed of daring, his merit is freely accorded by all his associate braves; his deeds are extolled in every public and private reunion, and his name is an incentive to generous emulation. I never witnessed any envious attempt to derogate from the merit of a brave's achievement. No damning with faint praise; none

"Willing to wound and yet afraid to strike;"

no faltering innuendoes that the man has not accomplished so much, after all. The same way with the women. When a woman's husband has distinguished himself, her neighbors, one and all, take a pride in rejoicing with her over her happiness. If a woman displays more ingenuity than common in ornamenting her husband's war dress, or in adding any fancy work to her own habiliments, she at once becomes the pattern of the neighborhood. You see no flaws picked in her character because of her rising to note; no aspersions cast upon her birth or present standing. Such and such is her merit, and it is deserving of our praise; the fact perceived, it receives full acknowledgement. This leads to the natural conclusion that civilization, in introducing the ostentation of display which is too frequently affected without sufficient ground to stand upon, warps the mind from the charity that is natural to it, and leads to all the petty strifes, and scandalous tales, and heartburnings that imbitter the lives of so many in civilized life . . . .

In the month of March (1826), a small war-party of twenty men left our village on an excursion, and not one of them ever came back, their pack-dogs (used for carrying extra moccasins when a party goes to war) alone returning to intimate their fate. Another party was quickly dispatched, of whom I was appointed leader, and we soon came upon the remains of the massacred party, which yet bore the marks of the weapons that had laid them low. There were also many fresh Indian tracks about the place, which led us to the inference that there were enemies near. We made immediate search for them, and had only marched about six miles when we came upon a village of nine lodges, which we instantly assaulted, killing every man but two. These were on a hill near by, and as they made off we did not follow them. My personal trophies in this encounter were one scalp and the equipments of its wearer; one young girl of about fourteen years, and a little boy. We killed forty-eight of the enemy, and took six women prisoners, together with a large drove of horses, and a valuable stock of beaver, otter, and other skins, with which we returned to the village. There was great rejoicing again (not one of our party was scratched), and the beaver-skins, to the number of one hundred and sixty-three, were bestowed upon me for my skill in command.

Before we made the assault we felt convinced that this was the party who had killed our missing friends, and our convictions were substantiated subsequently by recognizing several weapons in their possession which had formerly belonged to our braves; indeed, some of our women prisoners acknowledged that our departed brethren had killed many of their people.

The Crows treat the women whom they take prisoners much better than other tribes do. They do not impose upon them a harder lot than their own women endure, and they allow them to marry into the tribe, after which they are in equal fellowship with them. On finding themselves captives, they generally mourn a day or two, but their grief quickly subsides, and they seem to care no farther for their violent removal from their own people.

At this time the Crows were incessantly at war with all the tribes within their reach, with the exception of the Snakes and the Flat Heads; and they did not escape frequent ruptures with them, brought about by the Indians' universal obtuseness as to all law relating to the right of property in horses.

The Crows could raise an army of sixteen thousand warriors, and, although there were tribes much more numerous, there were none could match them in an open fight. The Camanches and Apaches have tilted lances with them repeatedly, and invariably to their discomfiture. If the Crows ever suffered defeat, it was when overwhelmed by numbers. One principal cause of their marked superiority was their plentiful supply of guns and ammunition, which the whites always more readily exchanged to them on account of their well-proved fidelity to the white man. When other tribes were constrained to leave their fire-arms in their lodges for want of ammunition, the Crows would have plenty, and could use their arms with great effect against an enemy which had only bow and arrows to shoot with. Farther, they were the most expert horsemen of any Indian tribe, notwithstanding the great name bestowed upon the Camanches and Apaches—those two great terrors of northern Mexico. I have seen them all, and consider myself in a position to judge, although some, perhaps, will say that I am prejudiced in favor of the Crows, seeing that I am one *myself.*

o   o   o   o   o

CHAPTER XXXVII

Mistakes regarding the Character of the Indian.—Extent of the Western Tribes.—Their Character.—How a War against them should be conducted.—Reflections.—Closing Address to the Indian Heroine.

As an American citizen, a friend of my race, and a sincere lover of my country, and also as one well acquainted with the Indian character, I feel that I can not properly conclude the record of my eventful life without saying something for the Red Man. It should be remembered, when judging of their acts, that they consider the country they inhabit as the gift of the "Great Spirit," and they resent in their hearts the invasion of the immigrant just as much as any civilized people would, if another nation, without permission, should cross their territory. It must also be understood, that the Indians believe the buffalo to be theirs by inheritance, not as game, but in the light of ownership, given to them by Providence for their support and comfort, and that, when an immigrant shoots a buffalo, the Indian looks upon it exactly as the destruction by a stranger of so much private property.

With these ideas clearly in the mind of the reader, it can be understood why the Indian, in destroying a cow belonging to white people, or stealing a horse, considers himself as merely retaliating for injuries received, repaying himself, in fact, for what he has lost. For this act on the part of the Red Man, the United States troops are often turned indiscriminately upon his race; the innocent generally suffer, and those who have raised the storm can not understand of what crime they can be guilty.

But if the government is determined to make war upon the Western tribes, let it be done intelligently, and so effectually that mercy will temper justice. To attempt to chastise Indians with United States troops is simply ridiculous; the expense of such campaigns is only surpassed by their inefficiency. The Indians live on horseback, and they can steal and drive off the government horses faster than it can bring them together. The Indians having no stationary villages, they can travel faster, even with the incumbrance of their lodges, women, and children, subsisting themselves on buffalo slain on the way, than any force, however richly appointed, the country could send against them. An army must tire out in such a chase before summer is gone, while the Indians will constantly harass it with their sharp-shooters, and, should several powerful tribes unite—not an unusual occurrence—many thousand men would make no impression.

It should also be recollected by our officers sent to fight in the Rocky Mountains, that the Indians have a mode of telegraphing by

the aid of robes and mirrors, and thus, by having their spies sta-
tioned at convenient distances, they convey intelligence of the
movements of their enemies at great distances and in a very few
minutes, thus informing villages whether it would be best to retreat
or not. Some tribes telegraph by fires at night, and by smoke in the
daytime. An officer might hear of a band of warriors encamped at a
certain place; he immediately makes a forced march, and when his
troops arrive at their destination, those same warriors may be many
miles in his rear, encamped on his trail.

A village of three hundred lodges of Crows or Cheyennes could,
within thirty minutes after receiving an order to move, have all their
lodges struck, the poles attached to the horses, and their men,
women, and children going at full speed, and could thus outstrip the
best dragoons sent in their pursuit.

I have seen enough of Indian treaties and annuities to satisfy me
that their effects for good are worse than fruitless. The idea formed
by the Indians is that the annuities are sent to them by the great
white chief because he is afraid of them, and wishes to purchase
their friendship. There are some of the tribes—a very few—who
would keep a treaty sacred; but the majority would not be bound by
one, for they can not understand their nature. When caught at a dis-
advantage, and reduced to enter into a compact, they would agree
to any proposals that were offered; but when the controlling power
is withdrawn, and they can repeat their depredations with apparent
impunity, no moral obligation would restrain them, and the treaty
that was negotiated at so much cost to the country proves a mere
delusion.

The officer having charge of an expedition against the Indians
should rightly understand which *band* of a tribe he is commissioned
to punish. The Siouxs, for instance, which, a few years ago, could
raise thirty thousand warriors, are divided into many bands, which,
at times, are hundreds of miles apart. One band of that tribe may
commit a depredation on the emigrant road, and the other bands not
even have heard of it: they do not hold themselves amenable for the
misdeeds of another body totally distinct from them in social relations, and to inflict chastisement upon them in such a case would be
a manifest injustice. But in a case of extreme danger all these bands
coalesce . . . .

The Western Indians have no hummocks or everglades to fight among, but they have their boundless prairies to weary an army in, and the fastnesses of the Rocky Mountains to retreat to. Should a majority of those powerful nations coalesce in defense against one common enemy, it would be the worst Indian war—the most costly in blood and treasure that the national government has ever entered into. The coalition tribes could bring two hundred and fifty thousand warriors against any hostile force, and I know I am greatly within the limits of truth in assigning that number to them.

If it is the policy of government to utterly exterminate the Indian race, the most expeditious manner of effecting this ought to be the one adopted. The introduction of whisky among the Red Men, under the connivance of government agents, leads to the demoralization and consequent extermination, by more powerful races, of thousands of Indians annually. Still, this infernal agent is not effectual; the Indians diminish in numbers, but with comparative slowness. The most direct and speedy mode of clearing the land of them would be by the simple means of starvation—by depriving them of their hereditary sustenance, the buffalo. To effect this, send an army of hunters among them, to root out and destroy, in every possible manner, the animal in question. They can shoot them, poison them, dig pit-falls for them, and resort to numberless other contrivances to efface the devoted animal, which serves, it would seem, by the wealth of his carcass, to preserve the Indian, and thus impede the expanding development of civilization.

To fight the Indians *vi et armis*, the government could employ no such effectual means as to take into its service five hundred mountaineers for the space of one year, and any one tribe of Indians that they should fall foul of could never survive the contest. Such men, employed for that purpose, would have no encumbrance from superfluous baggage to impede them in a pursuit or a retreat over their illimitable plains. The mode of life of a mountaineer just fits him for an Indian fighter, and if he has to submit to privation, and put up with an empty commissariat, he has the means of support always at hand. He is so much an Indian from habit that he can fight them in their own way: if they steal his horses, he can steal theirs in return; if they snatch a hasty repose in the open air, it is all he asks for himself, and his health and spirits are fortified with such regimen. It is only by men possessing the qualities of the white hunter, combined with Indian habits, that the Indians can be effectually and economically conquered.

SELECTED REFERENCES

Durham, Philip and Everett L. Jones. *The Negro Cowboys* (1965).

Katz, William Loren. Introduction to *The Life and Adventures of James P. Beckwourth,* by T. D. Bonner (1969).

Oswald, Delmont R. Introduction and epilogue to *The Life and Adventures of James P. Beckwourth,* as told to Thomas D. Bonner (1972).

PROJECTS AND PROBLEMS

In his copy of Beckwourth's book, Francis Parkman wrote, "Beckwourth is a fellow of bad character—a compound of white and black blood." Does this suggest that Parkman's derogatory comments about Beckwourth in Chapter X of *The Oregon Trail* may be dismissed as racism?

Notice Beckwourth's succession of wives. Do these alliances add to the ambivalence shown in his relations with Indians and whites? Speculate on the explanation for Beckwourth's failure to make any reference to his mother.

Oswald's scholarly edition of Beckwourth's memoirs establishes the inaccuracy of the work in many instances. Does this seriously affect the value of the book as an inside report on Indian life? Does it distinguish Beckwourth's biography from others of the genre?

Compare Beckwourth's attitudes and experiences with those reported in *Belden, The White Chief: Or Twelve Years Among the Wild Indians of the Plain* (1870), based on the diaries and manuscripts of George Belden.

HARRIET BEECHER STOWE
(1811–1896)

Stirred by her religious training and the antislavery movement, Mrs. Stowe produced in *Uncle Tom's Cabin* (1852) a work of tremendous value to that cause. In 1856 she published her second antislavery novel, *Dred, A Tale of the Great Dismal Swamp,* from which this selection is taken. In the story Harry Gordon is forced by his white half-brother to flee to the swamp where he is protected by Dred, a black religious fanatic rather resembling Nat Turner. The sensational success of Mrs. Stowe's antislavery writing made her later career seem anticlimactic. But several of her books after *Dred* won quiet favor and have continuing appeal, among them two works on the woman's rights to a career: *My Wife and I* (1871) and *We and Our Neighbors* (1875).

DRED, A FREE MAN

... Nothing is more vexatious to an active and enterprising person than to be thrown into a state of entire idleness; and Harry, after lounging about for a short time in the morning, found his indignation increased by every moment of enforced absence from the scene of his daily labors and interests. Having always enjoyed substantially the privileges of a free man in the ability to regulate his time according to his own ideas, to come and go, to buy and sell, and transact business unfettered by any felt control, he was the more keenly alive to the degradation implied in his present position.

"Here I must skulk around," said he to himself, "like a partridge in the bushes, allowing everything to run at loose ends, preparing the way for my being found fault with for a lazy fellow by and by; and all for what? Because my younger brother chooses to come, without right or reason, to domineer over me, to insult my wife; and because the laws will protect him in it, if he does it! Ah! ah! that's it. They are all leagued together! No matter how right I am—no matter how bad he is! Everybody will stand up for him, and put me down; all because my grandmother was born in Africa, and his grandmother was born in America. Confound it all, I won't stand it! Who knows what he'll be saying and doing to Lisette while I am gone? I'll go back and face him, like a man! I'll keep straight about my business, and if he crosses me, let him take care! He hasn't got but one life, any more than I have. Let him look out!"

And Harry jumped upon his horse, and turned his head homeward. He struck into a circuitous path, which led along that immense belt of swampy land to which the name of Dismal has been given. As he was riding along immersed in thought, the clatter of horses' feet was heard in front of him. A sudden turn of the road brought him directly facing to Tom Gordon and Mr. Jekyl, who had risen early and started off on horseback, in order to reach a certain stage depot before the heat of the day. There was a momentary pause on both sides; when Tom Gordon, like one who knows his power, and is determined to use it to the utmost, broke out scornfully:—

"Stop, you d—d nigger, and tell your master where you are going!"

52

"You are not my master!" said Harry, in words whose concentrated calmness conveyed more bitterness and wrath than could have been given by the most violent outburst.

"You d—d whelp!" said Tom Gordon, striking him across the face twice with his whip, "take that, and that! We'll see if I'm not your master! There, now, help yourself, won't you? Isn't that a master's mark?"

It had been the lifelong habit of Harry's position to repress every emotion of anger within himself. But at this moment his face wore a deadly and frightful expression. Still, there was something majestic and almost commanding in the attitude with which he reined back his horse, and slowly lifted his hand to heaven. He tried to speak, but his voice was choked with repressed passion. At last he said:—

"You may be sure, Mr. Gordon, this mark will *never* be forgotten!"

There are moments of high excitement, when all that is in a human being seems to be roused, and to concentrate itself in the eye and the voice. And in such moments *any* man, apparently by virtue of his mere humanity, by the mere awfulness of the human soul that is in him, gains power to overawe those who in other hours scorn him. There was a minute's pause in which neither spoke; and Mr. Jekyl, who was a man of peace, took occasion to touch Tom's elbow, and say:—

"It seems to me this isn't worth while—we shall miss the stage." And as Harry had already turned his horse and was riding away, Tom Gordon turned his, shouting after him, with a scornful laugh:—

"I called on your wife before I came away this morning, and I liked her rather better the second time than I did the first!"

This last taunt flew like a Parthian arrow backward, and struck into the soul of the bondman with even a keener power than the degrading blow. The sting of it seemed to rankle more bitterly as he rode along, till at last he dropped the reins on his horse's neck, and burst into a transport of bitter cursing.

"Aha! aha! it has come nigh thee, has it? It toucheth thee, and thou faintest!" said a deep voice from the swampy thicket beside him.

Harry stopped his horse and his imprecations. There was a crackling in the swamp, and a movement among the copse of briers; and at last the speaker emerged, and stood before Harry. He was a tall black man, of magnificent stature and proportions. His skin was intensely black, and polished like marble. A loose shirt of red flannel, which opened very wide at the breast, gave a display of a neck and chest of herculean strength. The sleeves of the shirt, rolled up nearly to the shoulders, showed the muscles of a gladiator. The head, which rose with an imperial air from the broad shoulders, was large and massive, and developed with equal force both in the reflective and perceptive department. The perceptive organs jutted like dark ridges over the eyes, while that part of the head which phrenologists attribute to the moral and intellectual sentiments rose like an ample dome above them. The large eyes had that peculiar and solemn effect of unfathomable blackness and darkness which is often a striking characteristic of the African eye. But there burned in them, like tongues of flame in a black pool of naphtha, a subtle and restless fire that betokened habitual excitement to the verge of insanity. If any organs were predominant in the head, they were those of ideality, wonder, veneration, and firmness; and the whole combination was such as might have formed one of the wild old warrior prophets of the heroic ages. He wore a fantastic sort of turban, apparently of an old scarlet shawl, which added to the outlandish effect of his appearance. His nether garments, of coarse negro-cloth, were girded round the waist by a strip of scarlet flannel, in which were thrust a bowie-knife and hatchet. Over one shoulder he carried a rifle, and a shot-pouch was suspended to his belt. A rude game-bag hung upon his arm. Wild and startling as the apparition might have been, it appeared to be no stranger to Harry; for after the first movement of surprise, he said in a tone of familiar recognition, in which there was blended somewhat of awe and respect:—

"Oh, it is you, then, Dred! I didn't know that you were hearing me!"

"Have I not heard?" said the speaker, raising his arm, and his eyes gleaming with wild excitement. "How long wilt thou halt between two opinions? Did not Moses refuse to be called the son of Pharaoh's daughter? How long wilt thou cast in thy lot with the oppressors of Israel, who say unto thee, 'Bow down that we may walk over thee'? Shall not the Red Sea be divided? 'Yea,' saith the Lord, 'it shall.' "

"Dred! I know what you mean!" said Harry, trembling with excitement.

"Yea, thou dost!" said the figure. "Yea, thou dost! Hast thou not eaten the fat and drunk the sweet with the oppressor, and hid thine eyes from the oppression of thy people? Have not our wives been for a prey, and thou hast not regarded? Hath not our cheek been given to the smiter? Have we not been counted as sheep for the slaughter? But thou saidst, 'Lo! I knew it not,' and didst hide thine eyes! Therefore, the curse of Meroz is upon thee, saith the Lord. And thou shalt bow down to the oppressor, and his rod shall be upon thee; and thy wife shall be for a prey!"

"Don't talk in that way!—don't," said Harry, striking out his hands with a frantic gesture, as if to push back the words. "You are raising the very devil in me!"

"Look here, Harry," said the other, dropping from the high tone he at first used to that of common conversation, and speaking in bitter irony, "did your master strike you? It's sweet to kiss the rod, isn't it? Bend your neck and ask to be struck again!—won't you? Be meek and lowly! that's the religion for you! You are a slave, and you wear broadcloth, and sleep soft. By and by he will give you a fip to buy salve for those cuts! Don't fret about your wife! Women always like the master better than the slave! Why shouldn't they? When a man licks his master's foot, his wife scorns him,—serves him right. Take it meekly, my boy! 'Servants, obey your masters.' Take your master's old coats—take your wife when he's done with her—and bless God that brought you under the light of the gospel! Go! you are a slave! But as for me," he said, drawing up his head, and throwing back his shoulders with a deep inspiration, "*I* am a free man! Free by this," holding out his rifle. "Free by the Lord of hosts, that numbereth the stars, and calleth them forth by their names. Go home—that's all I have to say to you! You sleep in a curtained bed.—I sleep on the ground, in the swamps! You eat the fat of the land. I have what the ravens bring me! But no man whips me!—no man touches my wife!— no man says to me, 'Why do ye so?' Go! you are a slave!—I am free!" And with one athletic bound, he sprang into the thicket, and was gone.

SUGGESTED ADDITIONAL READINGS

Uncle Tom's Cabin
A Key to Uncle Tom's Cabin

SELECTED REFERENCES

Baldwin, James. "Everybody's Protest Novel." *Partisan Review,* 16 (1949), 578–85.

Haley, Alex. "In Uncle Tom Are Our Guilt and Hope." *New York Times Magazine,* March 1, 1964, pp. 23, 90.

Hill, Herbert. " 'Uncle Tom,' An Enduring American Myth." *Crisis,* May, 1965, pp. 289–95, 325.

Lebedun, Jean. "Harriet Beecher Stowe's Interest in Sojourner Truth, Black Feminist." *American Literature,* 46 (1974), 359–63.

Levin, David. "American Fiction as Historical Evidence: Reflections on *Uncle Tom's Cabin.*" *Negro American Literature Forum,* 5 (1971), 132–36; 154.

McDowell, Tremaine, "The Use of Negro Dialect by Harriet Beecher Stowe." *American Speech,* 6 (1931), 322–26.

Nichols, Charles. "The Origin of *Uncle Tom's Cabin.*" *Phylon,* 19 (1958), 328–34.

Ward, John William. "*Uncle Tom's Cabin,* As a Matter of Historical Fact." *Columbia University Forum,* 9 (1966), 42–47.

Wyman, Margaret. "Harriet Beecher Stowe's Topical Novel on Woman Suffrage." *New England Quarterly,* 25 (1952), 383–91.

PROJECTS AND PROBLEMS

Discuss the validity of these lines Oliver Wendell Holmes wrote in tribute to Mrs. Stowe:

All through the conflict, up and down
Marched Uncle Tom and Old John Brown,
    One ghost, one form ideal;
And which was false and which was true,

And which was mightier of the two,
The wisest sibyl never knew,
    For both alike were real.

Develop the thesis that Mrs. Stowe's antislavery efforts were inspired by her sense of Christian duty rather than by a commitment to the doctrine of racial equality. Comment on Cuff in "The Parson's Horse-Race," one of the tales in *Sam Lawson's Oldtown Fireside Stories*. Consider also Milly in *Dred* and Candace in *The Minister's Wooing*.

Compare Lydia Maria Child's picture of rebellious slaves in "The Black Saxons," in this volume, with the treatment of similar figures in Mrs. Stowe's *Dred*.

Is Vachel Lindsay's "A Negro Sermon: Simon Legree" more effective as a poetic tribute to the impact of Mrs. Stowe's major antislavery novel than it is as a "Negro sermon"? Is Lindsay's interpretation of Legree based on the novel or on the dramatizations?

Compare Cassy, the quadroon in *Uncle Tom's Cabin*, with her counterpart in Mayne Reid's *The Quadroon*, Lydia Maria Child's "The Quadroons," William Wells Brown's *Clotel*, or Dion Boucicault's *The Octoroon*. In considering Mrs. Stowe's use of a stock character, see David W. Levy, "Racial Stereotypes in Anti-slavery Fiction," *Phylon*, 31 (1970), 265–79.

JOSIAH HENSON
(1789–1883)

From slavery in Maryland and Kentucky, Henson
escaped to Canada and a career as preacher, community
leader, and Underground Railroad agent. Fame came
when Harriet Beecher Stowe disclosed that in creating
Uncle Tom, the leading figure in her antislavery novel,
she had used what she had read of Henson's life and what
he had told her in two conversations. The selection
below is from his expanded autobiography, *Father
Henson's Story of His Own Life* (1858). That book and a
later version make it clear that Henson deserves the
scorn some modern students have bestowed on him even
less than does Mrs. Stowe's much abused fictional
character.

UNCLE TOM'S OWN STORY

The story of my life, which I am about to record, is one full of striking incident. Keener pangs, deeper joys, more singular vicissitudes, few have been led in God's providence to experience. As I look back on it through the vista of more than sixty years, and scene on scene it rises before me, an ever fresh wonder fills my mind. I delight to recall it. I dwell on it as did the Jews on the marvellous history of their rescue from the bondage of Egypt. Time has touched with its mellowing fingers its sterner features. The sufferings of the past are now like a dream, and the enduring lessons left behind make me to praise God that my soul has been tempered by him in so fiery a furnace and under such heavy blows.

I was born June 15th, 1789, in Charles county, Maryland, on a farm belonging to Mr. Francis Newman, about a mile from Port Tobacco. My mother was a slave of Dr. Josiah McPherson, but hired to the Mr. Newman to whom my father belonged. The only incident I can remember, which occurred while my mother continued on Mr. Newman's farm, was the appearance one day of my father with his head bloody and his back lacerated. He was beside himself with mingled rage and suffering. The explanation I picked up from the conversation of others only partially explained the matter to my mind; but as I grew older I understood it all. It seemed the overseer had sent my mother away from the other field hands to a retired place, and after trying persuasion in vain, had resorted to force to accomplish a brutal purpose. Her screams aroused my father at his distant work, and running up, he found his wife struggling with the man. Furious at the sight, he sprung upon him like a tiger. In a moment the overseer was down, and, mastered by rage, my father would have killed him but for the entreaties of my mother, and the overseer's own promise that nothing should ever be said of the matter. The promise was kept—like most promises of the cowardly and debased—as long as the danger lasted.

The laws of slave states provide means and opportunities for revenge so ample, that miscreants like him never fail to improve them. "A nigger has struck a white man"; that is enough to set a whole county on fire; no question is asked about the provocation.

59

The authorities were soon in pursuit of my father. The fact of the sacrilegious act of lifting a hand against the sacred temple of a white man's body—a profanity as blasphemous in the eye of a slave-state tribunal as was among the Jews the entrance of a Gentile dog into the Holy of Holies—this was all it was necessary to establish. And the penalty followed: one hundred lashes on the bare back, and to have the right ear nailed to the whipping-post, and then severed from the body. For a time my father kept out of the way, hiding in the woods, and at night venturing into some cabin in search of food. But at length the strict watch set baffled all his efforts. His supplies cut off, he was fairly starved out, and compelled by hunger to come back and give himself up.

The day for the execution of the penalty was appointed. The negroes from the neighboring plantations were summoned, for their moral improvement, to witness the scene. A powerful blacksmith named Hewes laid on the stripes. Fifty were given, during which the cries of my father might be heard a mile, and then a pause ensued. True, he had struck a white man, but as valuable property he must not be damaged. Judicious men felt his pulse. Oh! he could stand the whole. Again and again the thong fell on his lacerated back. His cries grew fainter and fainter, till a feeble groan was the only response to the final blows. His head was then thrust against the post, and his right ear fastened to it with a tack; a swift pass of a knife, and the bleeding member was left sticking to the place. Then came a hurra from the degraded crowd, and the exclamation, "That's what he's got for striking a white man." A few said, "it's a damned shame"; but the majority regarded it as but a proper tribute to their offended majesty.

It may be difficult for you, reader, to comprehend such brutality, and in the name of humanity you may protest against the truth of these statements. To you, such cruelty inflicted on a man seems fiendish. Ay, on a *man;* there hinges the whole. In the estimation of the illiterate, besotted poor whites who constituted the witnesses of such scenes in Charles County, Maryland, the man who did not feel rage enough at hearing of "a nigger" striking a white to be ready to burn him alive, was only fit to be lynched out of the neighborhood. A blow at one white man is a blow at all; is the muttering and upheaving of volcanic fires, which underlie and threaten to burst forth and utterly consume the whole social fabric. Terror is the fiercest nurse of cruelty. And when, in this our day, you find tender English women and Christian English divines fiercely urging that India should be made one pool of Sepoy blood, pause a moment before you lightly refuse to believe in the existence of such ferocious passions in the breasts of tyrannical and cowardly slave-drivers.

Previous to this affair my father, from all I can learn, had been a good-humored and light-hearted man, the ringleader in all fun at corn-huskings and Christmas buffoonery. His banjo was the life of the farm, and all night long at a merry-making would he play on it while the other negroes danced. But from this hour he became utterly changed. Sullen, morose, and dogged, nothing could be done with him. The milk of human kindness in his heart was turned to gall. He brooded over his wrongs. No fear or threats of being sold to the *far south*—the greatest of all terrors to the Maryland slave—would render him tractable. So off he was sent to Alabama. What was his after fate neither my mother nor I have ever learned; the great day will reveal all. This was the first chapter in my history.

SELECTED REFERENCES

Fisher, Walter. Introduction to *Father Henson's Story of His Own Life* (1962).

Furnas, J. C. *Goodbye to Uncle Tom* (1956).

Gysin, Brion. *To Master, A Long Goodnight* (1946).

Nichols, Charles H. *Many Thousand Gone: The Ex-Slaves' Account of Their Bondage and Freedom* (1963).

Stowe, Harriet Beecher. *A Key to Uncle Tom's Cabin* (1853).

PROJECTS AND PROBLEMS

The first version of Henson's life story was a pamphlet issued in 1849. Compare this with the full autobiography published in 1858, or later editions, noting any differences in style and attitude as well as content.

Henson and Frederick Douglass were both born in slavery in Maryland and escaped to become influential in the struggle for freedom. Search their autobiographies for parallels in their experience as victims of the South's "Peculiar Institution."

Discuss the relationship between Henson's life and character, as presented in the autobiography, and the use Harriet Beecher Stowe made of them in *Uncle Tom's Cabin*.

DION BOUCICAULT
(1822?–1890)

Born in Dublin, Boucicault achieved prominence in London as both actor and dramatist. A prolific writer, he was adept in the use of stage tricks. In 1859, a few years after he had come to New York with the wife who was leading lady for many of his productions, they created a sensation with *The Octoroon*, a melodrama adapted from Mayne Reid's *The Quadroon*. It opened three days after the execution of John Brown, when national excitement over the slavery issue was intense.

When the play begins, George Peyton, nephew of the late owner of Plantation Terrebonne in Louisiana, has arrived from Paris as heir to the estate. Unfamiliar with the South, he does not know that Zoe is a free octoroon. Scudder, one of the plantation's overseers, has invented a camera which is important later in identifying a murderer. Before the curtain rises on Act II, Paul, a slave boy, and Wahnotee, his Indian companion, have been sent to fetch mailbags which contain a letter that McClosky, a villainous overseer, is anxious to intercept so he may acquire Zoe and the plantation.

THE OCTOROON

Act Two

*The wharf with goods, boxes, and bales scattered about—
a camera on a stand;* DORA *being photographed by* Scudder, *who is arranging photographic apparatus,* GEORGE
and PAUL *looking on at back.*

SCUDDER. Just turn your face a leetle this way—fix your—let's see—
look here.

DORA. So?

SCUDDER. That's right. (*Putting his head under the darkening
apron*) It's such a long time since I did this sort of thing, and this old
machine has got so dirty and stiff, I'm afraid it won't operate. That's
about right. Now don't stir.

PAUL. Ugh! She looks as though she war gwine to have a tooth
drawed!

SCUDDER. I've got four plates ready, in case we miss the first shot.
One of them is prepared with a *self-developing* liquid that I've invented. I hope it will turn out better than most of my notions. Now
fix yourself. Are you ready?

DORA. Ready!

SCUDDER. Fire!—one, two, three. (SCUDDER *takes out watch.*)

PAUL. Now it's cooking; laws mussey! I feel it all inside, as if I was
at a lottery.

SCUDDER. So! (*Throws down apron.*) That's enough. (*Withdrawing
slide, turns and sees* PAUL.) What! what are you doing there, you
young varmint! Ain't you took them bags to the house yet?

PAUL. Now, it ain't no use trying to get mad, Mas'r Scudder. I'm
gwine! I only come back to find Wahnotee; whar is dat ign'ant In-
giun?

SCUDDER. You'll find him scenting round the rum store, hitched
up by the nose. (*Goes into the room.*)

PAUL (*calling at the door*). Say, Mas'r Scudder, take me in dat telescope?

64

SCUDDER. *(inside the room)*. Get out, you cub! Clar out!

PAUL. You got four of dem dishes ready. Gosh, wouldn't I like to hab myself took! What's de charge, Mas'r Scudder? *(He runs off.)*

SCUDDER. *(enters from the room)*. Job had none of them critters on his plantation, else he'd never ha' stood through so many chapters. Well, that has come out clear, ain't it? *(Showing the plate.)*

DORA. O, beautiful! Look, Mr. Peyton.

GEORGE. *(looking)*. Yes, very fine!

SCUDDER. The apparatus can't mistake. When I travelled round with this machine, the homely folks used to sing out, "Hillo, mister, this ain't like me!" "Ma'am," says I, "the apparatus can't mistake." "But, mister, that ain't my nose." "Ma'am, your nose drawed it. The machine can't err—you may mistake your phiz but the apparatus don't." "But, sir, it ain't agreeable." "No, ma'am, the truth seldom is."

PETE. *(enters, puffing)*. Mas'r Scudder! Mas'r Scudder!

SCUDDER. Hillo! What are you blowing about like a steamboat with one wheel for?

PETE. *You* blow, Mas'r Scudder, when I tole you: Dere's a man from Noo Aleens just arriv'd at de house, and he's stuck up two papers on de gates: "For sale—dis yer property," and a heap of oder tings—an he seen missus, and arter he shown some papers she burst out crying—I yelled; den de corious of little niggers dey set up, den de hull plantation children—de live stock reared up and created a purpiration of lamentation as did de ole heart good to har.

DORA. What's the matter?

SCUDDER. He's come.

PETE. Dass it—I saw 'm!

SCUDDER. The sheriff from New Orleans has taken possession— Terrebonne is in the hands of the law.

ZOE. *(enters)*. O, Mr. Scudder! Dora! Mr. Peyton! come home— there are strangers in the house.

DORA. Stay, Mr. Peyton: Zoe, a word! *(She leads her forward— aside)* Zoe, the more I see of George Peyton the better I like him; but he is too modest—that is a very impertinent virtue in a man.

ZOE. I'm no judge, dear.

DORA. Of course not, you little fool; no one ever made love to you, and you can't understand; I mean, that George knows I am an heiress; my fortune would release this estate from debt.

ZOE. O, I see!

DORA. If he would only propose to marry me I would accept him, but he don't know that, and he will go on fooling, in his slow European way, until it is too late.

ZOE. What's to be done?

DORA. You tell him.

ZOE. What? that he isn't to go on fooling in his slow—

DORA. No, you goose! twit him on his silence and abstraction—I'm sure it's plain enough, for he has not spoken two words to me all day; then joke round the subject, and at last speak out.

SCUDDER. Pete, as you came here, did you pass Paul and the Indian with the letter-bags?

PETE. No, sar; but dem vagabonds neber take the 'specable straight road, dey goes by de swamp. (*Exits up the path.*)

SCUDDER. Come, sir!

DORA (*to* ZOE). Now's your time.—(*Aloud*) Mr. Scudder, take us with you—Mr. Peyton is so slow, there's no getting him on. (*Exit* DORA *and* SCUDDER.)

ZOE. They are gone!—(*Glancing at* GEORGE) Poor fellow, he has lost all.

GEORGE. Poor child! how sad she looks now she has no resource.

ZOE. How shall I ask him to stay?

GEORGE. Zoe, will you remain here? I wish to speak to you.

ZOE. (*aside*). Well, that saves trouble.

GEORGE. By our ruin you lose all.

ZOE. O, I'm nothing; think of yourself.

GEORGE. I can think of nothing but the image that remains face to face with me; so beautiful, so simple, so confiding, that I dare not express the feelings that have grown up so rapidly in my heart.

ZOE (*aside*). He means Dora.

GEORGE. If I dared to speak!

ZOE. That's just what you must do, and do it at once, or it will be too late.

GEORGE. Has my love been divined?

ZOE. It has been more than suspected.

GEORGE. Zoe, listen to me, then. I shall see this estate pass from me without a sigh, for it possesses no charm for me; the wealth I covet is the love of those around me—eyes that are rich in fond looks, lips that breathe endearing words; the only estate I value is the heart of one true woman, and the slaves I'd have are her thoughts.

ZOE. George, George, your words take away my breath!

GEORGE. The world, Zoe, the free struggle of minds and hands is before me; the education bestowed on me by my dear uncle is a noble heritage which no sheriff can seize; with that I can build up a fortune, spread a roof over the heads I love, and place before them the food I have earned; I will work—

ZOE. Work! I thought none but colored people worked.

GEORGE. Work, Zoe, is the salt that gives savor to life.

ZOE. Dora said you were slow; if she could hear you now—

GEORGE. Zoe, you are young; your mirror must have told you that you are beautiful. Is your heart free?

ZOE. Free? of course it is!

GEORGE. We have known each other but a few days, but to me those days have been worth all the rest of my life. Zoe, you have suspected the feeling that now commands an utterance—you have seen that I love you.

ZOE. Me! you love *me?*

GEORGE. As my wife—the sharer of my hopes, my ambitions, and my sorrows; under the shelter of your love I could watch the storms of fortune pass unheeded by.

ZOE. *My* love! *My* love? George, you know not what you say! *I* the sharer of your sorrows—your wife! Do you know what I am?

GEORGE. Your birth—I know it. Has not my dear aunt forgotten it —she who had the most right to remember it? You are illegitimate, but love knows no prejudice.

ZOE. *(aside).* Alas! he does not know, he does not know! and will despise me, spurn me, loathe me, when he learns who, what, he has so loved.—*(Aloud)* George, O, forgive me! Yes, I love you—I did not know it until your words showed me what has been in my heart; each of them awoke a new sense, and now I know how unhappy— how very unhappy I am.

GEORGE. Zoe, what have I said to wound you?

ZOE. Nothing; but you must learn what I thought you already knew. George, you cannot marry me; the laws forbid it!

GEORGE. Forbid it?

ZOE. There is a gulf between us, as wide as your love, as deep as my despair; but, O, tell me, say you will pity me! that you will not throw me from you like a poisoned thing!

GEORGE. Zoe, explain yourself—your language fills me with shapeless fears.

ZOE. And what shall I say? I—my mother was—no, no—not her! Why should I refer the blame to her? George, do you see that hand you hold? look at these fingers; do you see the nails are of a bluish tinge?

GEORGE. Yes, near the quick there is a faint blue mark.

ZOE. Look in my eyes; is not the same color in the white?

GEORGE. It is their beauty.

ZOE. Could you see the roots of my hair you would see the same dark, fatal mark. Do you know what that is?

GEORGE. No.

ZOE. That is the ineffaceable curse of Cain. Of the blood that feeds my heart, one drop in eight is black—bright red as the rest may be, that one drop poisons all the flood; those seven bright drops give me love like yours—hope like yours—ambition like yours—life hung with passions like dewdrops on the morning flowers; but the one black drop gives me despair, for I'm an unclean thing—forbidden by the laws—I'm an Octoroon!

GEORGE. Zoe, I love you none the less; this knowledge brings no revolt to my heart, and I can overcome the obstacle.

ZOE. But *I* cannot.

GEORGE. We can leave this country, and go far away where none can know.

ZOE. And your mother, she who from infancy treated me with such fondness, she who, as you said, has most reason to spurn me, can she forget what I am? Will she gladly see you wedded to the child of her husband's slave? No! She would revolt from it, as all but you would; and if I consented to hear the cries of my heart, if I did not crush out my infant love, what would she say to the poor girl on whom she had bestowed so much? No, no!

GEORGE. Zoe, must we immolate our lives on her prejudice?

ZOE. Yes, for I'd rather be black than ungrateful! Ah, George, our race has at least one virtue—it knows how to suffer!

GEORGE. Each word you utter makes my love sink deeper into my heart.

ZOE. And I remained here to induce you to offer that heart to Dora!

GEORGE. If you bid me do so I will obey you—

ZOE. No, no! if you cannot be mine, O, let me not blush when I think of you.

GEORGE. Dearest Zoe! *(Exit* GEORGE *and* ZOE. *As they exit,* M'CLOSKY *rises from behind a rock and looks after them.)*

M'CLOSKY. She loves him! I felt it—and how she can love! *(Advances.)* That one black drop of blood burns in her veins and lights up her heart like a foggy sun. O, how I lapped up her words, like a thirsty bloodhound! I'll have her, if it costs me my life! Yonder the boy still lurks with those mailbags; the devil still keeps him here to tempt me, darn his yellow skin! I arrived just too late, he had grabbed the prize as I came up. Hillo! He's coming this way, fighting with his Injiun. *(Conceals himself.)*

PAUL *(enters, wrestling with* WAHNOTEE). It ain't no use now: you got to gib it up!

WAHNOTEE. Ugh!

PAUL. It won't do! You got dat bottle of rum hid under your blanket—gib it up now, you—. Yar! *(Wrenching it from him)* You nasty, lying Injiun! It's no use you putting on airs; I ain't gwine to sit up wid you all night and you drunk. Hillo! war's de crowd gone? And dar's de 'paratus—O, gosh, if I could take a likeness ob dis child! Uh—uh, let's have a peep. *(Looking through camera)* O, golly! yar, you Wahnotee! You stan' dar, I see you. Ta demine usti. *(He looks at* WAHNOTEE *through the camera;* WAHNOTEE *springs back with an expression of alarm.)*

WAHNOTEE. No tue Wahnotee.

PAUL. Ha, ha! he tinks it's a gun. You ign'ant Injiun, it can't hurt you! Stop, here's dem dishes—plates—dat's what he call 'em, all fix; I see Mas'r Scudder do it often—tink I can take likeness—stay dere, Wahnotee.

WAHNOTEE. No, carabine tue.

PAUL. I must operate and take my own likeness too—how debbel I do dat? Can't be ober dar an' here too—I ain't twins. Ugh! 'Top; you look, you Wahnotee; you see dis rag, eh? Well when I say go, den lift dis rag like dis, see! den run to dat pine tree up dar *(Points.)* and back ag'in, and den pull down de rag so, d'ye see?

WAHNOTEE. Hugh!

PAUL. Den you hab glass ob rum.

WAHNOTEE. Rum!

PAUL. Dat wakes him up. Coute, Wahnotee in omenee dit go Wahnotee, poina la fa, comb a pine tree, la revieut sala, la fa.

WAHNOTEE. Firewater!

PAUL. Yes, den a glass ob firewater; now den. *(Throwing mailbags down and sitting on them)* Pret, now den go.

(WAHNOTEE *raises the apron and runs off.* PAUL *sits for his picture—* M'CLOSKY *appears.)*

M'CLOSKY. Where are they? Ah, yonder goes the Indian!

PAUL. De time he gone just 'bout enough to cook dat dish plate.

M'CLOSKY. Yonder is the boy—now is my time! What's he doing; is he asleep? *(Advancing)* He is sitting on my prize! Darn his carcass! I'll clear him off there—he'll never know what stunned him. *(He takes Indian's tomahawk and steals to* Paul.*)*

PAUL. Dam dat Injiun! is dat him creeping dar? I daren't move fear to spile myself. (M'CLOSKY *strikes him on the head—he falls dead.)*

M'CLOSKY. Hooraw; the bags are mine—now for it!—*(Opening the mailbags)* What's here? Sunnyside, Pointdexter, Jackson, Peyton; here it is—the Liverpool postmark, sure enough!—*(Opening letter— reads.)* "Madam, we are instructed by the firm of Mason and Co. to inform you that a dividend of forty per cent is payable on the first proximo, this amount in consideration of position, they send herewith, and you will find enclosed by draft to your order, on the Bank of Louisiana, which please acknowledge—the balance will be paid in full, with interest, in three, six, and nine months—your drafts on Mason Brothers at those dates will be accepted by La Palisse and Compagnie, N. O., so that you may command immediate use of the whole amount at once, if required. Yours, etc., James Brown." What a find! this infernal letter would have saved all. *(During the reading of the letter, he remains nearly motionless under the focus of the camera.)* But now I guess it will arrive too late—these darned U.S. mails are to blame. The Injiun! He must not see me. *(Exits rapidly.)*

(WAHONTEE *runs on, and pulls down the apron. He sees* PAUL, *lying on the ground, and speaks to him, thinking that he is shamming sleep. He gesticulates and jabbers to him and moves him with his feet, then kneels down to rouse him. To his horror he finds him dead. Expressing great grief he raises his eyes and they fall upon the camera. Rising with a savage growl, he seizes the tomahawk and smashes the camera to pieces. Going to* PAUL *he expresses in pantomime grief, sorrow, and fondness, and takes him in his arms to carry him away.)*

SELECTED REFERENCES

Faulkner, Sheldon. "The Octoroon War." *Educational Theatre Journal,* 15 (1963), 33–38.

Hogan, Robert. *Dion Boucicault* (1969).

Kaplan, Sidney. *"The Octoroon:* Early History of the Drama of Miscegenation." *Journal of Negro Education,* 20 (1951), 215–22.

——. "100-Year-Old Drama Still Speaks." *New York Times,* January 22, 1961.

PROJECTS AND PROBLEMS

Mayne Reid's novel, which was Boucicault's major source for his play, did not emphasize the conflict between the North and South. Why did Boucicault stress it? Was this theme or the sensational plot of the melodrama more important to its success?

In the version of *The Octoroon* that played in London, Boucicault eliminated Zoe's suicide, and at the close of the drama she and George embrace and declare they will go abroad to "solemnize a lawful union." This follows the pattern set by Aurore and Rutherford in Reid's *The Quadroon.* Compare the ending of the novel and the two versions of the play and speculate on the reasons for offering the American ending when the play was revived in New York in 1961.

Compare Boucicault's use of a photographic plate to identify a murderer and save an innocent man with Mark Twain's use of fingerprints in *Pudd'nhead Wilson.*

The miscegenation treated in this drama is characteristic of the slave system, which gave white male owners easy access to slave women. But extensive black-white matings also took place between blacks and white indentured servants. Why is this earlier type of miscegenation largely ignored in our literature while the other, especially when it involves a beautiful octoroon, is exploited in many works? Give literary as well as other explanations. See Cheesman A. Herrick, *White Servitude in Pennsylvania* (1969) and Charles F. Marden and Gladys Meyer, *Minorities in American Society*, fourth ed. (1973).

OLIVER WENDELL HOLMES
(1809–1894)

Physician, scientist, novelist, essayist, and poet, Holmes was the very embodiment of the literary and cultural elite that he described in *Elsie Venner* as the Brahmin Caste of New England. A witty, urbane man, his talents found expression in many forms, but he is remembered mainly for his poems, especially those written for special occasions. The poem below, called "The Beni-Israel" when it first appeared in 1859, was revised and titled "At the Pantomime" when it was published in 1875 in *Songs of Many Seasons*.

AT THE PANTOMIME

The house was crammed from roof to floor,
Heads piled on heads at every door;
Half dead with August's seething heat
I crowded on and found my seat,
My patience slightly out of joint,
My temper short of boiling-point,
Not quite at *Hate mankind as such,*
Nor yet at *Love them overmuch.*

Amidst the throng the pageant drew
Were gathered Hebrews not a few,
Black-bearded, swarthy,—at their side
Dark, jewelled women, orient-eyed:
If scarce a Christian hopes for grace
Who crowds one in his narrow place
What will the savage victim do
Whose ribs are kneaded by a Jew?

Next on my left a breathing form
Wedged up against me, close and warm;
The beak that crowned the bistred face
Betrayed the mould of Abraham's race,—
That coal-black hair, that smoke-brown hue,—
Ah, curséd, unbelieving Jew!
I started, shuddering, to the right,
And squeezed—a second Israelite!

Then woke the evil brood of rage
That slumber, tongueless, in their cage;
I stabbed in turn with silent oaths
The hook-nosed kite of carrion clothes,
The snaky usurer, him that crawls
And cheats beneath the golden balls,
Moses and Levi, all the horde,
Spawn of the race that slew its Lord.

Up came their murderous deeds of old,
The grisly story Chaucer told,
And many an ugly tale beside
Of children caught and crucified;
I heard the ducat-sweating thieves
Beneath the Ghetto's slouching eaves,
And, thrust beyond the tented green,
The lepers cry, "Unclean! Unclean!"

The show went on, but, ill at ease,
My sullen eye it could not please,
In vain my conscience whispered, "Shame!
Who but their Maker is to blame?"
I thought of Judas and his bribe,
And steeled my soul against their tribe:
My neighbors stirred; I looked again
Full on the younger of the twain.

A fresh young cheek whose olive hue
The mantling blood shows faintly through;
Locks dark as midnight, that divide
And shade the neck on either side;
Soft, gentle, loving eyes that gleam
Clear as a starlit mountain stream;—
So looked that other child of Shem,
The Maiden's Boy of Bethlehem!

—And thou couldst scorn the peerless blood
That flows unmingled from the Flood,—
Thy scutcheon spotted with the stains
Of Norman thieves and pirate Danes!
The New World's foundling, in thy pride
Scowl on the Hebrew at thy side,
And lo! the very semblance there
The Lord of Glory deigned to wear!

I see that radiant image rise,
The flowing hair, the pitying eyes,

The faintly crimsoned cheek that shows
The blush of Sharon's opening rose,—
Thy hands would clasp his hallowed feet
Whose brethren soil thy Christian seat,
Thy lips would press his garment's hem
That curl in wrathful scorn for them!

A sudden mist, a watery screen,
Dropped like a veil before the scene;
The shadow floated from my soul,
And to my lips a whisper stole,—
"Thy prophets caught the Spirit's flame,
From thee the Son of Mary came,
With thee the Father deigned to dwell,—
Peace be upon thee, Israel!"

SUGGESTED ADDITIONAL READINGS-

"Brother Jonathan's Lament for Sister Caroline"
"To Canaan"
"Hymn After the Emancipation Proclamation"
"Two Poems to Harriet Beecher Stowe"

SELECTED REFERENCE-

Small, Miriam Rossiter. *Oliver Wendell Holmes* (1962).

PROJECTS AND PROBLEMS -

Compare "At the Pantomime" with Longfellow's "The Jewish Cemetery at Newport." Are the poets' generous intentions adversely affected by their emphasis on the Jew's religious difference and cultural distance?

Is the stress in "At the Pantomime" on the contemporary or the legendary and Biblical Jew? Consider that the story by Chaucer alluded to in the poem is the tale told by the Prioress about a widow's son whose throat was cut when he passed through the Jewish ghetto singing "O alma Redemptoris mater."

ANN S. STEPHENS
(1813–1886)

Mrs. Stephens was a successful practitioner of the art of the popular novel. She wrote some twenty-five books, mostly romantic fiction based on history. Her most notable work, which sold around 300,000 copies, was *Malaeska: The Indian Wife of the White Hunter* (1860), the first dime novel. This genre, to which she made other contributions, is of limited literary value, but it is a form of popular culture that may both express and influence the prevailing attitudes towards minorities. The selection below is from the final chapter of *Malaeska*. Mrs. Stephens also wrote *Mahaska, the Indian Princess* and *The Indian Queen*.

HIS INDIAN MOTHER

But we are describing subsequent things, rather than the scenery as it existed at the time of our story. Then, the hillside and all the broad plain was a forest of heavy timbered land, but the bank of the creek was much in its present condition. The undergrowth throve a little more luxuriantly, and the "Hoppy Nose" shot out from it covered with a thick coating of grass, but shrubless, with the exception of two or three saplings and a few clumps of wild-flowers.

As the moon arose on the night after Sarah Jones' interview with the Indian woman, that singular being stood upon the "Hoppy Nose," waiting the appearance of young Danforth. More than once she went out to the extreme verge of the projection, looked eagerly up and down the stream, then back into the shadow again, with folded arms, continued her watch as before.

At length a slight sound came from the opposite side; she sprang forward, and supporting herself by a sapling, bent over the stream, with one foot just touching the verge of the projection, her lips slightly parted, and her left hand holding back the hair from her temples, eager to ascertain the nature of the sound. The sapling bent and almost snapped beneath her hold, but she remained motionless, her eyes shining in the moonlight with a strange, uncertain luster, and fixed keenly on the place whence the sound proceeded.

A canoe cut out into the river, and made toward the spot where she was standing.

"It is he!" broke from her parted lips, as the moonlight fell on the clear forehead and graceful form of a young man, who stood upright in the little shallop, and drawing a deep breath, she settled back, folded her arms, and waited his approach.

The sapling had scarcely swayed back to its position, when the youth curved his canoe round to a hollow in the bank, and climbing along the ascent, he drew himself up the steep side of the "Hoppy Nose" by the brushwood, and sprang to the Indian woman's side.

"Malaeska," he said, extending his hand with a manner and voice of friendly recognition; "my good, kind nurse, believe me, I am rejoiced to have found you again."

Malaeska did not take his hand, but after an intense and eager gaze into his face, flung herself on his bosom, sobbing aloud, murmuring soft, broken words of endearment, and trembling all over with a rush of unconquerable tenderness.

The youth started back, and a frown gathered on his haughty forehead. His prejudices were offended, and he strove to put her from his bosom; even gratitude for all her goodness could not conquer the disgust with which he recoiled from the embrace of a savage.

"Malaeska," he said, almost sternly, attempting to unclasp her arms from his neck, "You forget—I am no longer a boy—be composed, and say what I can do for you?"

But she only clung to him the more passionately, and answered with an appeal that thrilled to his very heart.

"Put not your mother away—she has waited long—my son! my son!"

The youth did not comprehend the whole meaning of her words. They were more energetic and full of pathos than he had ever witnessed before; but she had been his nurse, and he had been long absent from her, and the strength of her attachment made him, for a moment, forgetful of her race. He was affected almost to tears.

"Malaeska," he said kindly, "I did not know till now how much you loved me. Yet it is not strange—I can remember when you were almost a mother to me."

"*Almost!*" she exclaimed, throwing back her head till the moonlight revealed her face. "Almost! William Danforth, as surely as there is a God to witness my words, you are my own son!"

The youth started, as if a dagger had been thrust to his heart. He forced the agitated woman from his bosom, and, bending forward, gazed sternly into her eyes.

"Woman, are you mad? Dare you assert this to *me?*"

He grasped her arm almost fiercely, and seemed as if tempted to offer some violence, for the insult her words had conveyed; but she lifted her eyes to his with a look of tenderness, in painful contrast with his almost insane gaze.

"Mad, my son?" she said, in a voice that thrilled with a sweet and broken earnestness on the still air. "It was a blessed madness—the madness of two warm young hearts that forgot every thing in the sweet impulse with which they clung together; it was madness which led your father to take the wild Indian girl to his bosom, when in the bloom of early girlhood. Mad! oh, I could go mad with very tenderness, when I think of the time when your little form was first placed in my arms; when my heart ached with love to feel your little hand upon my bosom, and your low murmur fill my ear. Oh, it was a sweet madness. I would die to know it again."

The youth had gradually relaxed his hold on her arm, and stood looking upon her as one in a dream, his arms dropping helpless as if they had been suddenly paralyzed; but when she again drew toward him, he was aroused to frenzy.

"Great God!" he almost shrieked, dashing his hand against his forehead. "No, no! it cannot—I, an Indian? a half-blood? the grandson of my father's murderer? Woman, speak the truth; word for word, give me the accursed history of my disgrace. If I am your son, give me proof—proof, I say!"

When the poor woman saw the furious passion she had raised, she sunk back in silent terror, and it was several minutes before she could answer his wild appeal. When she did speak, it was gaspingly and in terror. She told him all—of his birth; his father's death; of her voyage to Manhattan; and of the cruel promise that had been wrung from her, to conceal the relationship between herself and her child. She spoke of her solitary life in the wigwam, of the yearning power which urged her mother's heart to claim the love of her only child, when that child appeared in her neighborhood. She asked not to be acknowledged as his parent, but only to live with him, even as a bond servant, if he willed it, so as to look upon his face and to claim his love in private, when none should be near to witness it.

He stood perfectly still, with his pale face bent to hers, listening to her quick gasping speech, till she had done. Then she could see that his face was convulsed in the moonlight, and that he trembled and grasped a sapling which stood near for support. His voice was that of one utterly overwhelmed and broken-hearted.

"Malaeska," he said, "unsay all this, if you would not see me die at your feet. I am young, and a world of happiness was before me. I was about to be married to one so gentle—so pure—I, an Indian—was about give my stained hand to a lovely being of untainted blood. I, who was so proud of lifting her to my lofty station. Oh, Malaeska!" he exclaimed, vehemently grasping her hand with a clutch of iron, "say that this was a story—a sad, pitiful story got up to punish my pride; say but this, and I will give you all I have on earth—every farthing. I will love you better than a thousand sons. Oh, if you have mercy, contradict the wretched falsehood!" His frame shook with agitation, and he gazed upon her as one pleading for his life.

When the wretched mother saw the hopeless misery which she had heaped upon her proud and sensitive child, she would have laid down her life could she have unsaid the tale which had wrought such agony, without bringing a stain of falsehood on her soul.

But words are fearful weapons, never to be checked when once put in motion. Like barbed arrows they enter the heart, and can not be withdrawn again, even by the hand that has shot them. Poisoned they are at times, with a venom that clings to the memory forever. Words are, indeed, fearful things! The poor Indian mother could not recall hers, but she tried to soothe the proud feelings which had been so terribly wounded.

"Why should my son scorn the race of his mother? The blood which she gave him from her heart was that of a brave and kingly line, warriors and chieftains, all———"

The youth interrupted her with a low, bitter laugh. The deep prejudices which had been instilled into his nature—pride, despair, every feeling which urges to madness and evil—were a fire in his heart.

"So I have a patent of nobility to gild my sable birthright, an ancestral line of dusky chiefs to boast of. I should have known this, when I offered my hand to that lovely girl. She little knew the dignity which awaited her union. Father of heaven, my heart will break —I am going mad!"

He looked wildly around as he spoke, and his eyes settled on the dark waters, flowing so tranquilly a few feet beneath him. Instantly he became calm, as one who had found an unexpected resource in his affliction. His face was perfectly colorless and gleamed like marble as he turned to his mother, who stood in a posture of deep humility and supplication a few paces off, for she dared not approach him again either with words of comfort or tenderness. All the sweet hopes which had of late been so warm in her heart, were utterly crushed. She was a heart-broken, wretched woman, without a hope on this side the grave. The young man drew close to her, and taking both her hands, looked sorrowfully into her face. His voice was tranquil and deep-toned, but a slight husky sound gave an unnatural solemnity to his words.

"Malaeska," he said, raising her hands toward heaven, "swear to me by the God whom we both worship, that you have told me nothing but the truth; I would have no doubt."

There was something sublime in his position, and in the solemn calmness which had settled upon him. The poor woman had been weeping, but the tears were checked in her eyes, and her pale lips ceased their quivering motion and became firm, as she looked up to the white face bending over her.

"As I hope to meet you, my son, before that God, I have spoken nothing but the truth."

"Malaeska!"

"Will you not call me mother?" said the meek woman, with touching pathos. "I know that I am an Indian, but your father loved me."

"Mother? Yes, God forbid that I should refuse to call you mother; I am afraid that I have often been harsh to you, but I did not know your claim on my love. Even now, I have been unkind."

"No, no, my son."

"I remember you were always meek and forgiving—you forgive me now, my poor mother?"

Malaeska could not speak, but she sank to her son's feet, and covered his hand with tears and kisses.

"There is one who will feel this more deeply than either of us. You will comfort her, Mala—mother, will you not?"

Malaeska rose slowly up, and looked into her son's face. She was terrified by his child-like gentleness; her breath came painfully. She knew not why it was, but a shudder ran through her frame, and her heart grew heavy, as if some terrible catastrophe were about to happen. The young man stepped a pace nearer the bank, and stood, motionless, gazing down into the water. Malaeska drew close to him, and laid her hand on his arm.

"My son, why do you stand thus? Why gaze so fearfully upon the water?"

He did not answer, but drew her to his bosom, and pressed his lips down upon her forehead. Tears sprang afresh to the mother's eyes, and her heart thrilled with an exquisite sensation, which was almost pain. It was the first time he had kissed her since his childhood. She trembled with mingled awe and tenderness as he released her from his embrace, and put her gently from the brink of the projection. The action had placed her back toward him. She turned—saw him clasp his hands high over his head, and spring into the air. There was a plunge; the deep rushing sound of waters flowing back to their place, and then a shriek, sharp and full of terrible agony, rung over the stream like the death-cry of a human being.

The cry broke from the wretched mother, as she tore off her outer garments and plunged after the self-murderer. Twice the moonlight fell upon her pallid face and her long hair, as it streamed out on the water. The third time another marble face rose to the surface, and with almost superhuman strength the mother bore up the lifeless body of her son with one arm, and with the other struggled to the shore. She carried him up the steep bank where, at another time, no woman could have clambered even without incumbrance, and laid him on the grass. She tore open his vest, and laid her hand upon the heart. It was cold and pulseless. She chafed his palms, rubbed his marble forehead, and stretching herself on his body, tried to breathe life into his marble lips from her own cold heart. It was in vain. When convinced of this, she ceased all exertion; her face fell forward to the earth, and, with a low sobbing breath, she lay motionless by the dead.

The villagers heard that fearful shriek, and rushed down to the stream. Boats were launched, and when their crews reached the "Hoppy Nose," it was to find two human beings lying upon it.

The next morning found a sorrowful household in Arthur Jones' dwelling. Mrs. Jones was in tears, and the children moved noiselessly around the house, and spoke in timid whispers, as if the dead could be aroused. In the "out-room" lay the body of William Danforth, shrouded in his winding-sheet. With her heavy eyes fixed on the marble features of her son, sat the wretched Indian mother. Until the evening before, her dark hair had retained the volume and gloss of youth, but now it fell back from her hollow temples profusely as ever, but perfectly gray. The frost of grief had changed it in a single night. Her features were sunken, and she sat by the dead, motionless and resigned. There was nothing of stubborn grief about her. She answered when spoken to, and was patient in her suffering; but all could see that it was but the tranquility of a broken heart, mild in its utter desolation. When the villagers gathered for the funeral, Malaeska, in a few gentle words, told them of her relationship to the dead, and besought them to bury him by the side of his father.

The coffin was carried out, and a solemn train followed it through the forest. Women and children all went forth to the burial.

When the dead body of her affianced husband was brought home, Sarah Jones had been carried senseless to her chamber. The day wore on, the funeral procession passed forth, and she knew nothing of it. She was falling continually from one fainting fit to another, murmuring sorrowfully in her intervals of consciousness, and dropping gently away with the sad words on her lips, like a child mourning itself to sleep. Late in the night, after her lover's interment, she awoke to a consciousness of misfortune. She turned feebly upon her pillow, and prayed earnestly and with a faith which turned trustingly to God for strength. As the light dawned, a yearning wish awoke in her heart to visit the grave of her betrothed. She arose, dressed herself, and bent her way with feeble step toward the forest. Strength returned to her as she went forward. The dew lay heavily among the wild-flowers in her path, and a squirrel, which had made her walk cheerful two days before, was playing among the branches overhead. She remembered the happy feeling with which she had witnessed his gambols then, and covered her face as if a friend had attempted to comfort her.

The wigwam was desolate, and the path which led to the grave lay with the dew yet unbroken on its turf. The early sunshine was playing among the wet, heavy branches of the hemlock, when she reached the inclosure. A sweet fragrance was shed over the trampled grass from the white rose-tree which bent low beneath the weight of its pure blossoms. A shower of damp petals lay upon the chieftain's grave, and the green leaves quivered in the air as it sighed through them with a pleasant and cheering motion. But Sarah saw nothing but a newly-made grave, and stretched upon its fresh sods the form of a human being. A feeling of awe came over the maiden's heart. She moved reverently onward, feeling that she was in the sanctuary of the dead. The form was Malaeska's. One arm fell over the grave, and her long hair, in all its mournful change of color, had been swept back from her forehead, and lay tangled amid the rank grass. The sod on which her head rested was sprinkled over with tiny white blossoms. A handful lay crushed beneath her cheek, and sent up a faint odor over the marble face. Sarah bent down and touched the forehead. It was cold and hard, but a tranquil sweetness was there which told that the spirit had passed away without a struggle. Malaeska lay dead among the graves of her household, the heartbroken victim of an unnatural marriage.

SELECTED REFERENCES

Curti, Merle. "Dime Novels and the American Tradition." *Yale Review*, 26 (1937), 761–78.

Nye, Russel. *The Unembarrassed Muse: The Popular Arts in America* (1970).

O'Brien, Frank P. Introduction to *Malaeska: The Indian Wife of the White Hunter* (1971), by Ann S. Stephens.

PROJECTS AND PROBLEMS

Mrs. Stephens wrote with sympathy about the Senecas of New York. Might her work have been different had she been treating the Plains Indians?

Compare the behavior of Malaeska's son when he learns of his Indian ancestry with that of Tom in Mark Twain's *Pudd'nhead Wilson* when Roxy reveals that he is her child and was born a slave.

Like the heroines of two later dime novels, Malaeska was the daughter of a chief. Note the parallels with the Pocahontas-John Rolfe alliance. Why did Malaeska fail to win the acceptance accorded Pocahontas when she married Rolfe?

Discuss the popularity of miscegenation as a theme in both serious and popular literature. Note that the alliances almost invariably feature as the minority figure a woman, generally one of distinguished lineage, high character, and physical beauty. Do these qualities outweigh the blemish of her racial identity and raise her to equality with her white lover?

Compare the treatment of interracial romance in *Malaeska* with that in another early dime novel, Metta V. Victor's *Maum Guinea and her Plantation "Children"; or, Holiday Week on a Louisiana Estate* (1861). See Michael K. Simmons, "*Maum Guinea*: or A Dime Novelist Looks at Abolition," *Journal of Popular Culture*, 10 (1976), 81–87.

JOHN GREENLEAF WHITTIER (1807–1892)

The poetry of this staunch abolitionist treats virtually all the important incidents of the campaign waged against slavery during his time. His early antislavery poems were collected in *Voices of Freedom* in 1846, and he continued to write tracts and poetry in support of this cause during the years before and after the Civil War. His reputation in American literature, on the decline in recent years, rests largely on *Snowbound* and other rustic idylls and simple narratives. His tributes to John Brown and Union General Oliver Otis Howard, for whom Howard University is named, are characteristic of his humanitarian spirit and his commitment to Quaker principles.

BROWN OF OSSAWATOMIE

John Brown of Ossawatomie spake on his dying day:
"I will not have to shrive my soul a priest in Slavery's
pay.
But let some poor slave-mother whom I have striven to
free,
With her children, from the gallows-stair put up a prayer
for me!"

John Brown of Ossawatomie, they led him out to die;
And lo! a poor slave-mother with her little child pressed
nigh.
Then the bold, blue eye grew tender, and the old harsh
face grew mild,
As he stooped between the jeering ranks and kissed the
negro's child!

The shadows of his stormy life that moment fell apart;
And they who blamed the bloody hand forgave the
loving heart.
That kiss from all its guilty means redeemed the good
intent,
And round the grisly fighter's hair the martyr's aureole
bent!

Perish with him the folly that seeks through evil good!
Long live the generous purpose unstained with human
blood!
Not the raid of midnight terror, but the thought which
underlies;
Not the borderer's pride of daring, but the Christian's
sacrifice.

Nevermore may yon Blue Ridges the Northern rifle hear,
Nor see the light of blazing homes flash on the negro's
spear.

But let the free-winged angel Truth their guarded passes
    scale,
To teach that right is more than might, and justice more
    than mail!

So vainly shall Virginia set her battle in array;
In vain her trampling squadrons knead the winter snow
    with clay.
She may strike the pouncing eagle, but she dares
    not harm the dove;
And every gate she bars to Hate shall open wide
    to Love!

HOWARD AT ATLANTA

Right in the track where Sherman
  Ploughed his red furrow,
Out of the narrow cabin,
  Up from the cellar's burrow,
Gathered the little black people,
  With freedom newly dowered,
Where, beside their Northern teacher,
  Stood the soldier, Howard.

He listened and heard the children
  Of the poor and long-enslavéd
Reading the words of Jesus,
  Singing the songs of David.
Behold!—the dumb lips speaking,
  The blind eyes seeing!
Bones of the Prophet's vision
  Warmed into being!

Transformed he saw them passing
  Their new life's portal!
Almost it seemed the mortal
  Put on the immortal.
No more with the beasts of burden,
  No more with stone and clod,
But crowned with glory and honor
  In the image of God!

There was the human chattel
  Its manhood taking;
There, in each dark, brown statue.
  A soul was waking!
The man of many battles,
  With tears his eyelids pressing,
Stretched over those dusky foreheads
  His one-armed blessing.

And he said: "Who hears can never
    Fear for or doubt you;
What shall I tell the children
    Up North about you?"
Then ran round a whisper, a murmur,
    Some answer devising;
And a little boy stood up: "Massa,
    Tell 'em we're rising!"

O black boy of Atlanta!
    But half was spoken:
The slave's chain and the master's
    Alike are broken.
The one curse of the races
    Held both in tether:
They are rising,—all are rising,
    The black and white together!

O brave men and fair women!
    Ill comes of hate and scorning:
Shall the dark faces only
    Be turned to morning?—
Make Time your sole avenger,
    All-healing, all-redressing;
Meet Fate half-way, and make it
    A joy and blessing!

SUGGESTED ADDITIONAL READINGS

"Mogg Megone"
Voices of Freedom
"Stanzas for the Times"
"A Sabbath Scene"
"At Port Royal"
"Laos Deo!"
"Nauhaught, the Deacon"

"The Jubilee Singers"
"Abram Morrison"
"How the Robin Came"

SELECTED REFERENCES

Currier, Thomas F. "Whittier and the Amesbury-Salisbury Strike." *New England Quarterly,* 8 (1935), 105–12.

Griswold, M. J. "American Quaker History in the Works of Whittier, Hawthorne and Longfellow." *Americana,* 34 (1940), 220–63.

Holmes, J. Welfred. "Whittier and Sumner: A Political Friendship." *New England Quarterly,* 30 (1957), 58–72.

————."Whittier's Friends Among the Lowly." *Whittier Memorabilia* (1968), ed. by John B. Pickard.

Pollard, J. A. "Whittier on Labor Unions." *New England Quarterly,* 12 (1939), 99–102.

Smallwood, O. T. "The Historical Significance of Whittier's Anti-Slavery Poems." *Journal of Negro History,* 35 (1950), 150–73.

PROJECTS AND PROBLEMS

Is "Mogg Megone" a romantic picture of Indian character? What did Whittier say about his models and the subject of the poem? See also "Nauhaught, the Deacon" and "How the Robin Came."

Discuss *Justice and Expedience,* Whittier's antislavery tract, in comparison with Lydia Maria Child's *Appeal in Favor of That Class of Americans Called Africans* or David Walker's *Appeal in Four Articles Together with a Preamble to the Colored Citizens of the World, but in Particular and Very Expressly to Those of the United States.*

Compare Whittier's attitude toward black slaves with his response to the "wage slaves" of New England factory towns.

Longfellow's talents as a poet were not inferior to those of Whittier. Why are Longfellow's antislavery poems less effective than Whittier's?

Does Whittier's record of friendship with Charlotte Forten, Charles L. Remond, and other notable blacks distinguish him from other New England writers who opposed slavery?

Discuss Whittier's role as editor for slave narratives such as those of Josiah Henson and James Williams.

Does Whittier depict Abram Morrison entirely in the tradition of the Irish stereotype? Is Morrison a comic figure?

HARRIET BRENT JACOBS
(1818–1896)

When she narrated her life as a slave, Harriet Brent Jacobs called herself Linda Brent and used fictitious names for everyone in her story. Her account was edited by Lydia Maria Child and published in 1861 as *Incidents in the Life of a Slave Girl,* from which the selection below is taken. Hundreds of narratives describing the experience of ex-slaves, the testimony of the victims of the South's Peculiar Institution, found their way into print and swelled the ranks of the abolitionists. Mrs. Jacobs' work was a late addition to the popular genre, a useful weapon in the arsenal of the antislavery forces.

LUST AND THE FEMALE SLAVE

... I now entered on my fifteenth year—a sad epoch in the life of a slave girl. My master began to whisper foul words in my ear. Young as I was, I could not remain ignorant of their import. I tried to treat them with indifference or contempt. The master's age, my extreme youth, and the fear that his conduct would be reported to my grandmother, made him bear this treatment for many months. He was a crafty man, and resorted to many means to accomplish his purposes. Sometimes he had stormy, terrific ways, that made his victims tremble; sometimes he assumed a gentleness that he thought must surely subdue. Of the two, I preferred his stormy moods, although they left me trembling. He tried his utmost to corrupt the pure principles my grandmother had instilled. He peopled my young mind with unclean images, such as only a vile monster could think of. I turned from him with disgust and hatred. But he was my master. I was compelled to live under the same roof with him—where I saw a man forty years my senior daily violating the most sacred commandments of nature. He told me I was his property; that I must be subject to his will in all things. My soul revolted against the mean tyranny. But where could I turn for protection? No matter whether the slave girl be as black as ebony or as fair as her mistress. In either case, there is no shadow of law to protect her from insult, from violence, or even from death; all these are inflicted by fiends who bear the shape of men. The mistress, who ought to protect the helpless victim, has no other feelings toward her but those of jealousy and rage. The degradation, the wrongs, the vices, that grow out of slavery, are more than I can describe. They are greater than you would willingly believe. Surely, if you credited one-half the truths that are told you concerning the helpless millions suffering in this cruel bondage, you at the north would not help to tighten the yoke. You surely would refuse to do for the master, on your own soil, the mean and cruel work which trained bloodhounds and the lowest class of whites do for him at the south.

Every where the years bring to all enough of sin and sorrow; but in slavery the very dawn of life is darkened by these shadows. Even the little child, who is accustomed to wait on her mistress and her children, will learn, before she is twelve years old, why it is that her mistress hates such and such a one among the slaves. Perhaps the child's own mother is among those hated ones. She listens to violent outbreaks of jealous passion, and cannot help understanding what is the cause. She will become prematurely knowing in evil things. Soon she will learn to tremble when she hears her master's footfall. She will be compelled to realize that she is no longer a child. If God has bestowed beauty upon her, it will prove her greatest curse. That which commands admiration in the white woman only hastens the degradation of the female slave. I know that some are too much brutalized by slavery to feel the humiliation of their position; but many slaves feel it most acutely, and shrink from the memory of it. I cannot tell how much I suffered in the presence of these wrongs, nor how I am still pained by the retrospect. My master met me at every turn, reminding me that I belonged to him, and swearing by heaven and earth that he would compel me to submit to him. If I went out for a breath of fresh air, after a day of unwearied toil, his footsteps dogged me. If I knelt by my mother's grave, his dark shadow fell on me even there. The light heart which nature had given me became heavy with sad forebodings. The other slaves in my master's house noticed the change. Many of them pitied me; but none dared to ask the cause. They had no need to inquire. They knew too well the guilty practices under that roof; and they were aware that to speak of them was an offence that never went unpunished.

I longed for someone to confide in. I would have given the world to have laid my head on my grandmother's faithful bosom, and told her all my troubles. But Dr. Flint swore he would kill me, if I was not as silent as the grave. Then, although my grandmother was all in all to me, I feared her as well as loved her. I had been accustomed to look up to her with a respect bordering upon awe. I was very young, and felt shamefaced about telling her such impure things, especially as I knew her to be very strict on such subjects. Moreover, she was a woman of a high spirit. She was usually very quiet in her demeanor; but if her indignation was once roused, it was not very easily quelled. I had been told that she once chased a white gentleman with a loaded pistol, because he insulted one of her daughters. I dreaded the consequences of a violent outbreak; and both pride and fear kept me silent. But though I did not confide in my grandmother, and even evaded her vigilant watchfulness and inquiry, her presence in the neighborhood was some protection to me. Though she had been a slave, Dr. Flint was afraid of her. He dreaded her scorching rebukes. Moreover, she was known and patronized by many people; and he did not wish to have his villainy made public. It was lucky for me that I did not live on a distant plantation, but in a town not so large that the inhabitants were ignorant of each other's affairs. Bad as are the laws and customs in a slaveholding community, the doctor, as a professional man, deemed it prudent to keep up some outward show of decency.

O, what days and nights of fear and sorrow that man caused me! Reader, it is not to awaken sympathy for myself that I am telling you truthfully what I suffered in slavery. I do it to kindle a flame of compassion in your hearts for my sisters who are still in bondage, suffering as I once suffered.

I once saw two beautiful children playing together. One was a fair white child; the other was her slave, and also her sister. When I saw them embracing each other, and heard their joyous laughter, I turned sadly away from the lovely sight. I foresaw the inevitable blight that would fall on the little slave's heart. I knew how soon her laughter would be changed to sighs. The fair child grew up to be a still fairer woman. From childhood to womanhood her pathway was blooming with flowers, and overarched by a sunny sky. Scarcely one day of her life had been clouded when the sun rose on her happy bridal morning.

How had those years dealt with her slave sister, the little playmate of her childhood? She, also, was very beautiful; but the flowers and sunshine of love were not for her. She drank the cup of sin, and shame, and misery, whereof her persecuted race are compelled to drink.

SELECTED REFERENCES

Nichols, Charles H. *Many Thousand Gone: The Ex-Slaves' Account of Their Bondage and Freedom* (1963).

——. "The Slave Narrative and the Plantation Legend." *Phylon*, 10 (1949), 201–10.

PROJECTS AND PROBLEMS

Compare this work with the narratives of Ellen Craft or Harriet Tubman. Discuss the merits and limitations of the slave narrative as both literature and propaganda.

Does the fact that Lydia Maria Child edited Harriet Jacobs' story explain the dispute about whether it should be classified as autobiography or fiction? Discuss the problems of attribution and authenticity for slave narratives in general.

Compare Linda Brent as a character with Samuel Richardson's Pamela or Walt Whitman's Margaret in *Franklin Evans*.

Chapter 21 of *Incidents in the Life of a Slave Girl* gives a vivid account of the effects of Nat Turner's Insurrection on slave communities. Compare this material with the references to that uprising in William Wells Brown's *Clotel* and other nineteenth century fiction.

DAVID ROSS LOCKE
(1833–1888)

An itinerant journalist, Locke joined the ranks of the
professional funny fellows when he created Petroleum V.
Nasby, a country preacher whose arguments in support
of slavery made the Confederate cause seem ridiculous.
The Nasby letters made their first appearance in an Ohio
newspaper in 1861. Like his colleagues Charles Farrar
Browne ("Artemus Ward") and Henry W. Shaw ("Josh
Billings"), Locke resorted to "eye dialect" to emphasize
the illiteracy of his comic figure. When slavery ended
after the Civil War, the satiric letters were devoted to
other public issues.

PETROLEUM V. NASBY ON THE DIVERSITY OF THE RACES

September the 24th, 1865.
Whenever yoo ask the people to adopt any given line uv ackshen, yoo hev got to give em a tolable good reason therefor. Troo, this never hez bin so nessary in the Dimekratik party, whose members hev alluz follered their leeders, without askin the why or wherefore, with a fidelity beautiful to behold. But people, ginrally, are inquisitive, and wun reason why we hev never succeeded with the slavery question, is becoz we never hev yet given a good reason why the nigger shood be held in slavery.

Wunst it wuz sought to be defended on the ground that the nigger wuz inferior to the white man, but it woodent do. Why? Becoz the full–blown Dimekrat thot to hisself to wunst, "Ef the stronger shel own the weaker—ef the intellectooally sooperior shel hold in slavery the intellectooally inferior, LORD HELP ME! Why, I might ez well go into a Ablishn township and select my master to wunst."

The same argument won't do ez to nigger equality. Why shood we say that the nigger shan't vote, on the skore uv his not bein fitted by eddicashen or intelligence, when the fust and cheefest qualificashen uv a strate Dimekrat is his not knowin how to read? Why, to-day, in my county, ef a Dimekrat kin rite his name without runnin his tongue out, we alluz refooze to elect him a delegate in the county convenshun. It exposes him to the suspishun uv knowin too much.

I hev quit all these shaller dodges, long ago. We must hev the nigger, for jest at this time there ain't no uther cappitle for us to run on; but he must be put on maintainable ground. I put my foot on him, on the ground uv the DIVERSITY UV THE RACES! He is not wun uv us. He is not a descendant uv Adam. Goddlemity probably made him, ez he did the ox, and the ass, and the dorg, and the babboon, but not at the same time, nor for the same purposes. He is not, in enny sence uv

100

the word, a MAN! His kulor is different, the size uv his head is diffrent, his foot is longer, and his hand is bigger. He wuz created a beast, and the fiat uv the Almity give us dominion over him, the same ez over other beasts.

Does the theologian say that this doctrine undermines the Christian religion? I to wunst reply, that that don't matter to us. Dimokrasy and religion shook hands and bid each other a affekshunate farewell, years ago. Uv what comparison is religion to a Dimekratik triumph?

Doth the ethnologist say that the diffrence atween the Caucassian and Afrikin is no greater than atween the Caucassian and Mongolian? I anser to wunst that he is rite—that the Mongolian is likewise a beest; becoz, don't yoo see there ain't no Mongolians in this seckshun uv country to disprove it.

Doth the Ablishnist pint to a nigger who kin read and rite, and figure through to division, and in sich other partickelers show hisself sooperior to the majority uv Dimekrats? I alluz draw myself up to my full hite, assoom a virchusly indignant look, and exclaim, "He's nuthin but a d--d nigger, anyhow!" which is the only effective argument we hev hed for ten years.

Doth the besotted nigger-lover pint to the mulatter, and say, "What will yoo do with him, who is half beest and half man, who hez half a sole that is to be saved—for one-half uv whom Christ died?" I anser at wunst, that I don't deal in abstrackshuns, and git out ez soon ez possible, for there is a weak pint there, that I hevent ez yit bin able to git over.

This wun weak pint is no argument agin my theory, for happy is the Dimekrat who kin propound a theory that hezent a skore, instid uv wun, weak places in it.

This doctrine kivers the whole ground. Ef the nigger is a beest, Dimekrats hev a good excuse for not givin to mishnary sosieties, for uv what use is it to undertake to Christianize beests, who hev no soles to save and no interest in the blood uv Christ? It gives us a perfek rite to re-establish slavery, for doth not Blackstun, who wuz supposed to know ez much law ez a Noo Gersey justis uv the peece, say that we hev a rite to ketch and tame the wild beest, and bend him to our uses?

Also, he can't vote; for wood the lowest white man consent to vote alongside uv a beest, even ef he did walk on 2 legs? Not enny.

Let this doctrine be vigerusly preechd, and I hev no doubt suthin will result from it.

PETROLEUM V. NASBY,
Lait Paster Uv The Church Uv The Noo Dispensashun.

SUGGESTED ADDITIONAL READING

Swingen Round the Circle

SELECTED REFERENCES

Blair, Walter. *Native American Humor* (1937).

Rubin, Louis D., Jr., ed. *The Comic Imagination in American Literature* (1973).

PROJECTS AND PROBLEMS

Compare the work of such northern newspaper humorists as Locke, Charles Farrar Browne, and Henry W. Shaw with that of humorists of the southwestern frontier, such as George Washington Harris and Johnson Jones Hooper.

Distinguish between dialect and eye-dialect, using illustrations from the works of Locke and Finley Peter Dunne.

JOHN W. DeFOREST
(1826-1906)

DeForest grew up in Connecticut, visited Europe, and spent some time in South Carolina before joining the Union Army. As commander of a company of Connecticut volunteers he had recruited, he served under General Benjamin F. Butler in the capture and occupation of New Orleans. By that time he had published several books, among them a scholarly history of the Indians of his native state.

Miss Ravenel's Conversion from Secession to Loyalty (1867), from which the selection below is taken, is regarded as one of the best novels about the Civil War period and a classic of American realism. This incident involves Lillie Ravenel; her spirited young aunt, Mrs. Larue, a Louisiana lady "not quite as good as she should be"; and Edward Colburne, a Union officer.

"An Independent Ku Klux," was published in *The Galaxy*, April, 1872. DeForest's later works include fiction treating a variety of subjects and autobiographical works notable for their documentary value.

THE WHITE COLORED PEOPLE OF NEW ORLEANS

... There is a geographical fable of civilized white negroes in the centre of Africa, somewhere near the Mountains of the Moon. This fable is realized in the Crescent City and in some of the richest planting districts of Louisiana, where you will find a class of colored people, who are not black people at all, having only the merest fraction of negro blood in their veins, and who are respectable in character, numbers of them wealthy, and some of them accomplished. These Creoles, as they call themselves, have been free for generations, and until Anglo-Saxon law invaded Louisiana, enjoyed the same rights as other citizens. They are good Catholics; they marry and are given in marriage; their sons are educated in Paris on a perfect level with young Frenchmen; their daughters receive the strict surveillance which is allotted to girls in most southern countries. In the street many of them are scarcely distinguishable from the unmixed descendants of the old French planters. But there is a social line of demarkation drawn about them, like the sanitary cordon about an infected district. The Anglo-Saxon race, the proudest race of modern times, does not marry nor consort with them, nor of late years does the pure French Creole, driven to join in this ostracism by the brute force of Henghist and Horsa prejudice. The New Orleanois who before the war should have treated these white colored people on terms of equality, would have shared in their opprobrium, and perhaps have been ridden on a rail by his outraged fellow-citizens of northern descent.

Now these white negroes from the Mountains of the Moon constituted the sole loyal class, except the slaves, which Butler found in Louisiana. They and their black cousins of the sixteenth degree were the only people who, as a body, came forward with joy to welcome the drums and tramplings of the New England Division; and when the commanding General called for regiments of free blacks to uphold the Stars and Stripes, he met a patriotic response as enthusiastic as that of Connecticut or Massachusetts. Foremost in this military uprising were two brothers of the name of Meurice, who poured out their wealth freely to meet those incidental expenses, never acknowledged by Government, which attend the recruiting of volunteer regiments. They gave dinners and presented flags; they advanced uniforms, sabres and pistols for officers; they trusted the families of private soldiers. The youngest Meurice became Major of one of the regiments, which I take to be the nearest approach to a miracle ever yet enacted in the United States of America. Their entertainments became so famous that invitations to them were gratefully accepted by officers of Anglo-Saxon organizations. At their profuse yet elegant table, where Brillât-Savarin would not have been annoyed by a badly cooked dish or an inferior wine, and where he might have listened to the accents of his own Parisian, Colburne had met New Englanders, New Yorkers, and even stray Marylanders and Kentuckians. There he became acquainted (ignorant Baratarian that he was!) with the *tasse de cafe noir* and the *petit verre de cognac* which close a French dinner. There he smoked cigars which gave him new ideas concerning the value of Cuba. For these pleasures he was now to suffer at the Caucasian hands of Madame Larue.

"I am afraid that we are doomed to lose you, Captain Colburne," she said with a smile which expressed something worse than good-natured raillery. "I hear that you have made some fascinating acquaintances in New Orleans. I never myself had the pleasure of knowing the Meurices. They are very charming, are they not?"

Colburne's nerves quivered under this speech, not because he was conscious of having done any thing unbecoming a gentleman, but because he divined the clever malice of the attack. To gentle spirits the consciousness that they are the objects of spite, is a dolorous sensation.

"It is a very pleasant and intelligent family," he replied bravely.

"Who are they?" smilingly asked Miss Ravenel, who inferred from her aunt's manner that Colburne was to be charged with a flirtation.

"Ce sont des métis, ma chère," laughed Mrs. Larue.

"Il y a diné plusieurs fois. Ces abolitionistes oût leur gonts a eux."

Lillie colored crimson with amazement, with horror, with downright anger. To this New Orleans born Anglo-Saxon girl, full of the pride of lineage and the prejudices of the slaveholding society in which she had been nurtured, it seemed a downright insult that a gentleman who called on her, should also call on a *métis*, and admit it and defend it. She glanced at Colburne to see if he had a word to offer of apology or explanation. It might be that he had visited these mixed bloods in the performance of some disagreeable but unavoidable duty as an officer of the Federal army. She hoped so, for she liked him too well to be willing to despise him.

"Intelligent? But without doubt," assented Madame, "if they had been stupid, you would not have dined with them four or five times."

"Three times, to be exact, Mrs. Larue," said Colburne. He had formed his line of battle, and could be not merely defiant but ironically aggressive. But the lady was master of the southern tactics; she had taken the initiative, and she attacked audaciously; although, I must explain, without the slightest sign of irritation.

"Which do you find the most agreeable," she asked, "the white people of New Orleans, or the brown?"

Colburne was tempted to reply that he did not see much difference, but refrained on account of Miss Ravenel; and, dropping satire, he entered on a calm defence, less of himself than of the mixed race in question. He affirmed their intelligence, education, good breeding, respectability of character, and exceptional patriotism in a community of rebels.

"You, Mrs. Larue, think something of the elegancies of society as an element of civilization," he said. "Now then, I am obliged to confess that these people can give a finer dinner, better-selected, better-cooked, better-served, than I ever saw in my own city of New Boston, notwithstanding that we are as white as they are and—can't speak French. These Meurices, for example, have actually given me new ideas of hospitality, as something which may be plenteous without being coarse, and cordial without being boreous. I don't hesitate to call them nice people. As for the African blood in their veins (if that is a reproach) I can't detect a trace of it. I shouldn't have believed it if they hadn't assured me of it. There is a little child there, a cousin, with blue eyes and straight flaxen hair. She has the honor, if it is one, of being whiter than I am."

It will be remembered here that any one who was whiter than Colburne was necessarily much whiter than Mrs. Larue.

"When I first saw the eldest Meurice," he proceeded, "I supposed from his looks that he was a German. The Major bears a striking re-

semblance to the first Napoleon, and is certainly one of the handsomest men that I have seen in New Orleans. His manners are
charming, as I suppose they ought to be, seeing that he has lived in
Paris since he was a child."

Mrs. Larue had never transgressed the borders of Louisiana.

"When this war broke out he came home to see if he might be
permitted to fight for his race, and for his and my country. He now
wears the same uniform that I do, and he is my superior officer."

"It is shameful," broke out Lillie.

"It is the will of authority," answered Colburne,—"of authority
that I have sworn to respect."

"A southern gentleman would resign," said Mrs. Larue.

"A northern gentleman keeps his oath and stands by his flag," retorted Colburne.

AN INDEPENDENT KU-KLUX

"Say," observed Selnarten Bowen to his wife, Nan Bowen, "these niggers is gone in for stealin' worse 'n ever. Hev we lost anythin'?"

Nan Bowen drew herself up the full height of her five feet nine inches, grappled her mighty hips with her large sinewy hands as if she were about to throw herself at somebody's head, ground her quid of tobacco with a cowlike opening of the mouth and twisting of the lower jaw, and hit a sapling ten feet away with nicotine enough to poison a rattlesnake.

Having thus got her mind in trim and cleared her upper decks for action, she proceeded to fire the following contemptuous queries at her "old man," meanwhile not once turning her clear gray eyes upon his diminutive figure, but staring fixedly and with a curiously blank expression at the rotten roof of her log cabin.

"What hev we got to lose?" said Nan Bowen in a slow, hard, scornful monotone, and with long pauses between her sentences. "What did we ever own? What did you ever own? What is there in our house? Anythin' that niggers would steal? Not as I knows on."

"I've arned as much as you hev," retorted Selnarten, meanwhile sidling away from his partner, who was the better man of the two.

"Who said you didn't?" answered Nan, still speaking with icy deliberation, and still eyeing her rack-o'-bones dwelling.

"An' I've done some shootin'," continued Selnarten.

"Yes, shot rich folkses' hogs, jest like these niggers," commented Nan.

"Wild hogs," put in Selnarten. "I allays allowed them hogs was wild. An' who said anythin' agin it? Did you? You et yer part, I reckon."

It must be explained that Selnarten Bowen was very suspicious of wildness in hogs. He hardly ever saw a porker anywhere or under any conditions, not even when shut up in a pen, but what he was ready to impute wildness to him, and wanted to shoot or otherwise slay him; and not only slay him, but tote him home, and not only tote him home, but eat him. If he had encountered a pig in the shape of spareribs and slices of bacon and strings of sausages, he would have been disposed to pronounce them wild spareribs and

108

wild slices of bacon and wild sausages, and to lay appropriating hands upon them accordingly. It is hardly too much to assert that, had a pig come to him in a black dress coat and white neckchoker, and exhorted him to attend a camp-meeting, he would still have been inclined to fall upon him for a wild pig, and proceed to butcher. One wonders, by the way, what would have become of Selnarten had swine been thus inimical to wildness in men, and felt it to be their mission to put an end to it. There would surely have been a drove after him intent upon civilizing him by picking his bones.

"Nobody ever complained," continued Selnarten. "Nobody ever said hogs to *me*. Now, as for these yere niggers, they're complained of. Folks want to put 'em down. An' I go for it."

"*I* don't keer what you do to niggers," responded Nan, still speaking with an air and tone of uttermost scorn, as if there were nothing in creation that she did not despise, beginning with negroes and ending with her husband. "You can go for 'em ef you like. Only ef you get yourself in a muss don't come howlin' around me. I won't hev it."

"They're settin' up for white folks," resumed Selnarten in a grunting undertone, as if in his much chasing of wild hogs he had caught the swine pronunciation. "Folks gen'rally is gwine in for to put 'em down. Square Anderson an' Rarry Saxton, an' a lot more, has jined the Ku-Klux. I'm gwine to try to git to jine."

"Jine away!" answered Nan, with her habitual air of sarcastic and bitter indifference.

"I'll start for Saxonburg now," decided Selnarten, turning on his heels and striking out without further good-bye.

"Take care yerself," said Nan, which was her usual adieu when she did not say "Go to the devil!"

In the next breath she turned toward her husband and called sharply, "Say! When you comin' back?"

"Some time before sun-up," responded Selnarten, rather wondering that she should care.

"Fetch home somethin'," added Nan. "Thar ain't much in the barl."

"If I see ary wild hog," promised Selnarten, and pushed on with a rapid, slouching lope, not even looking over his shoulder.

We positively cannot attend further to Selnarten's adventures without first pausing to consider his extraordinary name. Bowen is well enough; there have been other people in the world entitled Bowen; we can accept Bowen without an effort. But Selnarten is a puzzler, and one might almost say, in the phrase of Mr. Boffin, a "scarer." The man himself could give no sort of information upon the subject, as indeed he never thought of giving any or asking any. Why he was christened thus, or whether he was christened at all, he could no more tell than he could tell the origin of the word christened, or of any other word connected with the Christian religion, or with any other religion. All he knew about it was that ever since he could remember anything, people had addressed him as Selnarten, and he had answered "Yere," or to that effect. As the mind refuses to concede that any native American of Anglo-Saxon stock could really lay claim to such a nomenclature, we have spent more thought on this philological riddle than it deserves, and have ended by guessing that the word Selnarten began life as Elnathan, and got warped into its present shape by some hostile influence, perhaps fever and ague.

Selnarten's person, like his cognomen, had a made-over look. In build and features and expression he was not so much a natural human being as a sort of shabby work of art, like a totem or a fetish. That Rembrandt of the spirits of the air, that grotesque and malicious sculptor and painter, Malaria, had taken him in hand from the days of his doughy infancy, and had moulded and colored him in accordance with its wayward taste. He could not show a limb nor a muscle which had not been scraped down and withered and distorted by this indefatigable and pitiless carver. Malaria had hollowed his abdomen and gouged out his cheeks and sunk his eyes and pinched his temples. Then, laying aside the chisel, it had gone at him with the brush; staining him from within outwards, as if he were a meerschaum pipe; cramming him to reeking with all the monotonous tints of dumb ague; taking a fresh dab at him every time it got him around to a new swamp; using up on him the richness of acres of decaying trees and of creeks full of oozing vegetable mud; running the pencil along every surface vein and into the whites of his eyes and the roots of his hair; spotting him here and stippling him there, and streaking him in other places; in short, giving him the finish of a masterpiece.

Even the long, thin, and dry locks (seemingly dry enough to rustle) that hung short over his narrow forehead and long behind his grimy ears, were of a dead-and-alive yellow, which could only have come from the palette of Malaria. When he combed them, which happened perhaps once a quarter, or when he took off his hat, which he generally did on going to bed, he must have dispensed fever-and-ague spores through the atmosphere. If he had been a side of leather, and had passed his regulation seven years in a vat, he could not have been tanned more thoroughly than he was. It seemed also as if Malaria had not stopped with his person, but had gone over his very garments and taken extra pains with them. His broad-brimmed wool hat was as ragged as though it had shaken itself to pieces in "cold fits"; and its varnished, spotted, bistred drab complexion appeared very much like a continuation of Selnarten's countenance; much as if his head had spread out at the top, after the fashion of a toadstool. Same tint in his short-waisted, short-sleeved, buttonless frock coat, inadequate vest, wizened trousers, and gaping shoes. Butternut and gray and black had all alike become foxy. His entire wardrobe looked as if it needed a course of quinine.

Thus haggard, and warped, and stained, and threadbare, he favored the scarecrow species rather than the human; and a scarecrow, for that matter, who had fallen from his first estate—a scarecrow badly impoverished, out at elbows, and faded—a scarecrow broken down by the "agur." A spectator with a bold imagination and a keen eye for color might also have been reminded by him of one of those barkless logs which may be seen floating on the mud or sticking in the edging reeds of a southern creek, dark yellow with wet rot and light yellow with dry rot, whimsically carved by peckings of birds and gnawings of the atmosphere, unwholesome and ugly and dismally picturesque. A white man he sometimes proudly called himself; but an unprejudiced observer would sooner have classed him as a Malay; and philology, bending its mind to the subject, might ask, Why not a Malay when so malarious?

Through the wintry sloughs of one of those roads whose mission it is to render travelling difficult, Selnarten Bowen tramped out the five lonesome miles which lay between his cabin and the straggling, rusty village of Saxonburg.

The first person whom he addressed was Squire John Calhoun Rawson. Squire Jack, as he was commonly styled, had been useful in

other days to Selnarten, having brought him clear of a charge of
hog-stealing, the defence being wildness in the hog. He was a man of
not more than thirty-five, but already so corpulent that it seemed as
if it would be a comfort to him to disembowel him, and a still
greater comfort to hang him up by the heels in a breeze, with perhaps a cob in his mouth. Even the unimaginative Selnarten could
hardly look at his legal friend without thinking of an enticing
porker. His face was large and flattened and pasty, reminding one of
a batch of dough set away to rise. His eyes were slightly yellowish,
for Malaria had given him a touch or two; but, for all that, they
were not disagreeable eyes to meet; there was both kindness and
drollery in them. His expression, too, was good-humored, and he was
almost always smiling quietly, as if his mind ran upon jokes for
casters.

It was dull times with Squire Jack Rawson. Since the war everybody in and around Saxonburg had gone more or less bankrupt, and
"lawing" had fallen into disrepute, with other luxuries. Squire Jack
did little but stand in his office door, like Giant Pope in the mouth
of his cave, and survey the passersby; only, instead of biting his nails
at them, he smiled upon them and cheered them with puns and illu-
minated them with views on politics. At intervals, finding the winter
dampness too shrewish, he retreated into his sanctum, threw a small
green stick on a sulky fire which smoked and spit against the sooty
back of a cracked Franklin stove, drew himself up to the same in a
willow-bottomed arm-chair, clapped his puffy feet patronizingly on
the stove's shoulders, read anew the local items of the Saxonburg
"Banner," found them stupid and yawned in their faces. Then out he
would sally again, like a restless dog out of his kennel, to lean
against the door-post with hands in pockets, to talk if there was a
talker at hand, and if not, to smile vaguely.

"Evenin', Squire," was the salutation of Selnarten. In Saxonburg,
by the way, it was morning until twelve o'clock, and after that it was
evening.

"How are you, Mr. Bowen?" nodded the lawyer, with that civility
which a Southerner habitually accords to a white fellow citizen, no
matter how poor and ignorant. "Anything stirring your way?"

"Nary," replied Mr. Bowen, who could not remember that he had
seen a hog loose. After pondering a moment, he sidled up to Squire

Jack, taking a circuitous course, so as to get a little behind him, and muttered in his ear, "Want to see ye."

"Well, what is it, Mr. Bowen? Another wild hog case?"

"Nary," whispered Selnarten. "But how about jinin' the Ku-Klux?"

Squire Jack meditated; then his dreamy smile brightened; then a merry twinkle lighted up his moist eyes. This stupid, unlettered vagabond wanted to join the Ku-Klux, undoubtedly with a view to robbing nigger pig-pens with impunity. It was a good joke, and it might be worked up into something capital; and Squire Jack reflected no further. He was not himself a Ku-Klux, and in fact, he called himself since the war a Union man, though meanwhile he abominated a carpet-bagger. A good-hearted creature, with honorable instincts, he abhorred the extremists of both parties who were disgracing and ruining South Carolina. It seemed to him equally dreadful that the carpet-bag adventurers should plunder the State treasury, and that the reactionist desperadoes who opposed them should bushwhack and maltreat the poor "niggers." Still, he was not a deeply reflective man, and it was not in his nature to take things violently to heart, and he never could resist the temptation of a joke. Without a thought of the consequences, he determined to have some sport out of Selnarten.

"What am I to understand, Mr. Bowen?" he asked. "Do you wish to join the Ku-Klux?"

"Yes," mumbled Selnarten, while a tremor of anxiety shook his ill-covered skeleton, as if his life-long master, the "agur," had come for him.

"Walk into my office, Mr. Bowen," continued Squire Jack. "Walk in and sit. I'll get together some of the leading members of the order. We'll have you on the gridiron directly. By the way, how about whiskey? Could you raise a quart?"

"I hain't got no whiskey, and I hain't got no money," confessed Selnarten.

"Oh well, never mind," answered Squire Jack, looking, however, a little disappointed, as if the joke were drier than he had hoped. "It isn't absolutely necessary, though it's always best to have it."

He turned Selnarten into his office and locked the door on him to keep out intruders. Then he trundled his broad face and load of an

abdomen into two or three neighboring sanctums of brother lawyers, and soon brought together half a dozen gentlemen as out of
work and as in for fun as himself. Whether any one of the six were a
Ku-Klux Squire Jack did not and could not know, and light-mindedly
did not care. But as head-centers and high joint commissioners and
grand sojourners of the famous order, he ceremoniously introduced
them to Selnarten.

"Gentlemen, take seats," bowed Squire Jack, forcing his obese
thumbs into the pockets of his over-crowded waistcoat, and slowly
turning his jolly smile, like a lantern, from face to face of the company. "This chapter will now come to order," he proceeded, assuming an elocutionary manner, "for the purpose of receiving into the
bosom of Ku-Kluxery and all other luxery a most acceptable candidate, Mr. Selnarten Bowen. Gentlemen, we all know this candidate;
he was born and brought up in our very midst; we know him as Nor-
val knew the Grampian Hills. We know who his mother was; we
have reason to believe that we know who his grandmother was; and,
gentlemen, if we had lived long enough ago, I venture to say that we
might have known who his great-grandmother was; and, gentlemen,
it would not surprise me in the least to learn that that great-grandmother was a continental dam."

Here Squire Jack looked blandly and steadily into the saffron eyes
of Selnarten, who, being in a state of extreme intimidation and confusion, responded meekly, "That's so!" much to the delight of the
counterfeit Ku-Klux.

But we have not space to report Squire Jack's oratory. For ten
minutes he ran a stream of extravagances; it was a grotesque imitation of the so-called spread-eagle style of eloquence; it was a farrago
of hifalutin which would have charmed an Arkansas jury. He ended
by demanding in a voice of thunder that whoever objected to the reception of *this* candidate into the holy alliance and brotherhood of
Ku-Kluxery should now set forth cause for his opposition, or else
forever thereafter hold his peace.

"We all seem to assent to the nomination," observed Colonel
Gallop of the ex-Confederate army. "Let the neophyte be inducted
into the mysteries."

"Stand up, neophyte," ordained Squire Jack.

"Me?" inquired Selnarten.

"Yes," said Squire Jack.

Selnarten rose to his feet.

"Now stand on your head."

The poor ignoramus tried to obey, and naturally fell in a heap. Next he was mounted on a table, then made to crawl under it on his hands and knees, and so on through a variety of ridiculous gymnastics, the ceremony ending with seating him cross-legged on the Franklin stove, which fortunately was in a lukewarm condition, as it generally was. At last the jokers were tired of their poor fun, and put an end to it.

"Mr. Bowen, you are now a Ku-Klux," said Squire Jack. "You are now a free and accepted member of our great order. All that remains is to instruct you in your new responsibilities and duties, which consist in being at peace and amity with all men, and in bearing enmity and hate toward wild hogs. In the words of our classic founder *Quousque tandem, Catilina, abutere patientia nostra?*—that is to say, how long shall these wild hogs abuse our patience? Go, Brother Ku-Klux; go, Brother Selnarten Bowen—take care of yourself. And if, in the performance of what shall come to pass, you get into trouble, come to me."

Out of the presence of these jesters went Selnarten, much in the dark as to what a Ku-Klux was bound or permitted to do, but not in the least doubting that he was a Ku-Klux.

How should he doubt it? All his life he had looked up to "high-tone gentlemen" for instruction and direction. He was simple, he was profoundly ignorant, and he was the child of simplicity and ignorance from untold generations, inheriting simplicity and ignorance as he inherited the name of Bowen. He could not read; his father before him could not read; he was sprung from a race of illiterate low-downers; they, probably, from illiterate convicts deported to the Virginias; they, probably, from illiterate tramps or hinds in Old England. All the way back to the days of the Heptarchy, it may be; all the way back to the pirate keels of Hengist and Horsa; all the way through the Germanic forests and the Scythian steppes; all the way back across to the Indo-European cradle in Aryana; there is no certainty that a Bowen of this stock ever did read—no certainty that a Bowen of this stock was ever anything but illiterate and stupid. With the inherited, accumulated, and concentrated ignorance of so

many generations in his brain and his very marrow, how should Selnarten fail to be the bubble of every high-toned gentleman who
chose to puff him out with a breath of nonsense, and shake him
loose for folly or mischief?

"What did they tell me I oughter do?" queried this American
freeman and elector, as he trudged homeward through clinging mire
and gathering darkness. "Said suthin' about peace with all men.
That means white men, reckon. Of course don't mean niggers; can't
mean niggers. Anyhow, said I mought go for hogs, wild hogs.
Reckon I will. Reckon I will *now*. Nan tole me to fetch home
suthin'."

On the road, or rather a quarter of a mile off the road, lived a
fellow-citizen and elector who was as simple and ignorant as Selnarten himself, but who in the matter of wealth had considerably the
advantage of him, being the owner of a pig. Ham Irvine was a one-
legged negro, pretty well advanced in middle life, but otherwise a
stout and hearty "chunk of a man." Being unfitted for field work
through his infirmity, he had picked up the art of cobbling, and
gained a meagre living by mending brogans for his colored brethren,
and putting new vitality into old harnesses, etc., for white farmers.
He was often seen in the village, stumping grimly about in search of
jobs or dues, his solid figure draped to the heels in the greasy azure
of a cast-off military overcoat, underneath which were other garments vastly in need of a washtub.

Notwithstanding his fifty years and his deficiency in members,
Ham was a fervent seeker after the gentle sex, and much in the habit
of matrimony. He had had nobody knows how many wives; in fact,
there never was a more marrying man in a monogamous country;
and this saint's perseverance was needed to keep him spliced, for his
better halves were addicted to absconding. Ham, you see, believed
in loving and chastening; if a woman was what he called foolish, he
used to "lam" her; and if a hickory wouldn't answer, he laid on with
his wooden leg. The result was that his hymeneal bliss was subject to
frequent interruptions, and that he spent about as much time in
hunting wives, old or new, as in looking up jobs of cobbling.

The last prize which he had drawn at the altar was a fat, lazy, ragged, fatherless and motherless young offscouring of the earth, known
to Saxonburg by the unsupported name of Phillis. This offscouring

had married Ham, as whiter ladies have married more numerously-legged men, for the sake of getting a home. Her opinion of said home may be inferred from the fact that at the end of a week she decided to dispense with the rest of the honeymoon, took an early start for parts unknown, and ran clean away from her old man, who of course had not a high turn of speed. Ham, who never gave up a spouse willingly, stumped after her as far as the village, left messages of mercy or of threatening for her with all her acquaintance, and in short did his dull best to get her back. While engaged in pegging to and fro on this labor of love, he had been observed by his brother elector, the candidate for Ku-Klux. Selnarten at once conceived the suspicion that Ham's pig had gone wild, and resolved to look into the animal's moral status on his way home.

"Wonder if he's back," mused the cracker, as he came to a turn in the miry road, whence diverged a still mirier path leading to the cobbler's cabin. "Reckon not yet. Wooden legs can't travel much. Reckon I'll see after his shoat."

He had his gun with him—a gun that had been dropped on more than one battle-field—a gun that had seen service, and showed it, yet not quite a cripple. With his rusty Enfield under his arm, its lock shielded from the dripping of dank branches by his ragged coat, Selnarten struck through a slip of swampy wood (with Malaria painting away at him) and came out upon a bare, sandy old field, the passe-partout of Ham's cabin. No dog barking, he guessed that the negro was still absent, and boldly approached the lonely dwelling. The shoat, he knew, pastured by day at his own sweet will, but at night was always housed with his master for safety, and probably now would not be far distant. Selnarten hunted and Selnarten grunted; but piggy neither appeared nor answered.

"Dog gone the critter!" muttered our Ku-Klux. "He's run wild, sure pop; an' I'll cut his durned throat. Reckon he's inside. That's it. Ham shet him up afore he put out."

It was not difficult to enter the cabin. The only lock was a wooden latch pulled by a string which hung outside. After a little fumbling and listening, Selnarten crossed the teetering threshold, closed the door after him, and began a game of blind man's buff among Ham's benches, barrels, and other rude furniture, his object of course being to find the shoat. He was quite easy about it; in other days he had hunted pork with an evil conscience, but now he had not the least idea that he was committing a crime. Holding himself to be a true member of the Ku-Klux society, and supposing that every Ku-Klux had a right to "go for niggers" in any way that pleased him, he had no more scruples of conscience about his person than if he had been a sheriff duly provided with a search-warrant.

The shoat, too, was there. He could hear him snuffling and grunting and capering in a most appetizing manner, fairly making a cracker's mouth water. But catch him he could not; the animal had a surprising aptitude for blind man's buff; he was like the famous pig who was too spry to be counted. After falling down several times, Selnarten decided to have a light; he turned over the smouldering back-log, threw on some bits of pitch pine, and roused a blaze. Now he had a clear view of the cobbler's interior; and we also cannot do better than take a look at it. A sketch of Ham's cabin will be doubly useful, as it will give us a tolerably exact idea of Selnarten's cabin, and of the cabin of many another negro and low-downer.

It was a log house, and not a very fine one of the kind, and not ending its career so fine as it had begun it. The logs had gone into the job in such a hurry that they had not taken time to get themselves seasoned or squared, or even to pull off their jackets; and the consequence was that they were now in a lamentably shrunken, warped, deformed, knock-kneed, bow-legged condition; leaning apart as if they were mutually afraid of catching the dry rot of each other; their remnants of bark peeling up in worm-eaten tatters; neither clothed nor in their right minds. Originally they had been chinked in with clay; but this filling had been soaked out by rains or nibbled out by winds or poked out by rampaging outsiders; and now the gaps had either nothing at all in them, or only some crumbling edgings of common earth. Thus the walls had become a sort of open-work, or trellis, more fitted for vines to clamber upon than useful as a protection against the weather. If the man in the moon, surveying the house with his best telescope, had taken it for a hen-coop, or a squirrel cage with the wheel off, he would not thereby have incurred a just charge of lunacy. Counting from top to bottom and all around the four sides, there must have been something like two or three hundred drafts in this residence. The roof was of a piece with the rest; the unpainted boards of which it was constructed had been blown apart so much and put together again so little that they were all at sixes and sevens; and there were any number of openings to let the glory of the heavens through. Standing inside, you could see any constellation you liked; and standing in any constellation you liked, you could see inside.

The floor was much the same with the roof. Every board in it had its own mind as to the way it wanted to lie, and also as to whether it wanted to lie down or get up. Some of them had both extremities aloft, as if they were sticking up their heads to see whether their toes were covered. Some were fastened at one end and some at the other, and some in the middle, each according to his luck. You could not walk across this floor without producing a succession of slams and clatters, and other ligneous grumblings, as if it were complaining of your awkwardness and wanting to know when you would get off it. It was a dreadful floor for a stranger to venture upon in the dark, being always ready to make a sly grab at his toes and a vicious spring at his nose, as Selnarten Bowen by this time well knew. In one spot there were no boards at all, but a man trap or quadruped trap in the shape of a large hole, the result of a short and easy method of manufacturing kindlings. This hole did not precipitate you into a cellar, but into something in the way of open country between the cabin and the earth, where the wind and Ham's shoat were accustomed to root among straws, feathers, bones, and other refuse, and where Ham's successive pickaninnies had disported themselves until they were carried away by their absquatulating mammies.

Selnarten took no note of all these picturesque details. Neither did he pause to examine the rough furniture of the cabin, the homemade cobbler's bench, the one low stool, the two limping chairs, the pot and frying pan. His mind, the whole of it, what little there was of it, was bent upon the pig. At last he discovered his game. The cunning little beast (a forty-pounder or thereabouts) had sought refuge behind Ham's bed. This bed was not on a bedstead, but on the floor in one corner. It was a rabble of old straw mattress, ragged empty sacks, tatters of carpeting and greasy coverlets, all lying in tangled confusion, as if they had got drunk, gone to fighting, and fallen in a heap. In the rear of this rampart appeared the shoat, his spine bristling, his snout twitching, and his eyes twinkling.

Selnarten stood his gun in one corner, drew and opened his large jack-knife, and made a rush. There was a wonderful chase; the shoat dodged, galloped, grunted, and squealed; the rheumatic boards of the floor jumped about in an agony; the cracker ran and stumbled and rolled and rose and ran again. A complete account of the ups and downs of that hunt, of all its adventures, horizontal and perpendicular, would make too long a story. We must cut the matter short by stating, with brutal brevity, that Selnarten killed the pig.

And now came new excitement. Just as the suffering innocent gave forth his last gurgle the door of the cabin flew open with a bang, and its owner stumped in. Ham Irvine, returning wifeless from the village, had discovered a light in his domicile, and, suspecting danger to his shoat, had hurried to the rescue. Mr. Bowen was disagreeably surprised, but he was unnaturally intelligent in whatever related to pig-stealing, and he showed himself equal to the emergency. Snatching a piece of carpeting from Ham's miscellany of a bed, he flung it upon the blazing light-wood and produced darkness.

"Who's yere?" demanded Ham.

"The Ku-Klux," responded Mr. Bowen, suddenly recollecting that he belonged to that noble society, and claiming its lawful privileges.

"Somebody's been worryin' my shoat," continued Ham, either not hearing the awful name, or not caring for it.

"You better clar!" advised Mr. Bowen, who by this time had got hold of his gun.

"You clar yourself," retorted Ham. "Whoever you is, you no business inside my do', when I ain't yere."

Then came a fight in the dark. Ham, who was very muscular, and much more lively on his badly-matched supporters than one might imagine, got a grip of Selnarten's baggy clothing, floored him at the first jerk, and fell across him. For a minute there was an amazing clatter, the loose boards floundering and bouncing as if they were determined to get out from under, and the wooden leg joining in the uproar with extraordinary emphasis, rapping and tapping as if it were carrying on a scuffle of its own. At last the combatants separated in three divisions, one being the cracker, another the negro, and another the negro's spare limb. This last was a weapon which Ham well knew how to use. He caught it up, gave it a vicious swing in the direction of his antagonist, and laid him prostrate.

And now the gun came into play. Under ordinary circumstances

Selnarten would not have ventured to carry out a job of mere pig-stealing by shooting a human being, even though that human being were no more than a "nigger." But this evening he believed that he was a Ku-Klux, and that as such he had a right to kill whosoever resisted him. He seized his Enfield, aimed it at a dark something which he knew must be Ham, aimed it with intent to take life, and fired. When he left the cabin, with the defunct shoat upon his shoulder, he was not only a pig-stealer and a burglar, but a murderer.

Weeks later, when martial law was declared in his district, when troopers in blue jackets arrived to trample out a silly and savage reign of terror, when high-toned and low-toned members of the famous order were confessing their atrocities and surrendering themselves for trial, this almost incredibly ignorant creature came into military headquarters and gave himself up as a Ku-Klux, revealing for the first time who it was that had killed Ham Irvine.

SUGGESTED ADDITIONAL READINGS

History of the Indians of Connecticut
Overland
Kate Beaumont
The Bloody Chasm
A Volunteer's Adventures: A Union Captain's Record of the Civil War
A Union Officer in the Reconstruction

SELECTED REFERENCES

"John William DeForest (1826–1906): A Critical Bibliography of Secondary Comment." Compiled by the editors. *American Literary Realism, 1870–1910*, No. 4 (1968), 2–56.
Light, James F. *John William DeForest* (1965).
Stone, Albert E., Jr. "Reading, Writing, and History: Best Novel of the Civil War." *American Heritage*, 13, No. 4 (1962), 84–88.

PROJECTS AND PROBLEMS -

Compare DeForest's treatment of race relations in the South after the Civil War with Albion W. Tourgée's *A Fool's Errand* or *Bricks Without Straw.*

Does *Overland*, DeForest's novel set in Apache country, show the same authority and objectivity as his history of the Connecticut Indians? Is *Overland* an attack on racism?

Does DeForest's treatment of the South in his fiction support his assertion: "I have written from life and have been a realist"?

Compare DeForest's poor whites in "An Independent Ku-Klux" with those of Joel Chandler Harris in "Free Joe and the Rest of the World." Take into account DeForest's "The Low-Down People," first published in *Putnam's Magazine* in June, 1868, and collected in *A Union Officer in the Reconstruction.* For a description of California's "Low-downers," see Robert Louis Stevenson's "The Silverado Squatters," in *Century Magazine*, December, 1883.

BRET HARTE
(1836–1902)

Harte's short stories and verse in San Francisco's *Overland Monthly* are often credited with beginning the local color movement, with its emphasis on a picturesque setting and quaint or exotic characters. The novelty of his western materials and his skillful blend of sentiment and melodrama made him a sensation in 1870, following the publication of "Plain Language from Truthful James" (also known as "The Heathen Chinee") and *The Luck of Roaring Camp and Other Stories,* which included "John Chinaman." "The Latest Chinese Outrage" and "Wan Lee, the Pagan" appeared in 1875, after Harte had returned to the East.

On the death of retail merchant A. T. Stewart, the Grand Union Hotel at Saratoga Springs passed into the management of lawyer Henry Hilton, who ordered that no Jews be accommodated there. Harte wrote "That Ebrew Jew" in protest. The poem first appeared in newspapers in 1877.

PLAIN LANGUAGE FROM TRUTHFUL JAMES
(Table Mountain , 1870)

Which I wish to remark,
   And my language is plain,
That for ways that are dark
   And for tricks that are vain,
The heathen Chinee is peculiar,
   Which the same I would rise to explain.

Ah Sin was his name;
   And I shall not deny,
In regard to the same,
   What that name might imply;
But his smile it was pensive and childlike,
   As I frequent remarked to Bill Nye.

It was August the third,
   And quite soft was the skies;
Which it might be inferred
   That Ah Sin was likewise;
Yet he played it that day upon William
   And me in a way I despise.

Which we had a small game,
   And Ah Sin took a hand:
It was Euchre. The same
   He did not understand;
But he smiled as he sat by the table,
   With the smile that was childlike and bland.

Yet the cards they were stocked
   In a way that I grieve,
And my feelings were shocked
   At the state of Nye's sleeve,

Which was stuffed full of aces and bowers,
    And the same with intent to deceive.

But the hands that were played
    By that heathen Chinee,
And the points that he made,
    Were quite frightful to see,—
Till at last he put down a right bower,
    Which the same Nye had dealt unto me.

Then I looked up at Nye,
    And he gazed upon me;
And he rose with a sigh,
    And said, "Can this be?
We are ruined by Chinese cheap labor,"—
    And he went for that heathen Chinee.

In the scene that ensued
    I did not take a hand,
But the floor it was strewed
    Like the leaves on the strand
With the cards that Ah Sin had been hiding,
    In the game "he did not understand."

In his sleeves, which were long,
    He had twenty-four packs,—
Which was coming it strong,
    Yet I state but the facts;
And we found on his nails, which were taper,
    What is frequent in tapes,—that's wax.

Which is why I remark,
    And my language is plain,
That for ways that are dark
    And for tricks that are vain,
The heathen Chinee is peculiar,—
    Which the same I am free to maintain.

JOHN CHINAMAN

The expression of the Chinese face in the aggregate is neither cheerful nor happy. In an acquaintance of half a dozen years, I can only recall one or two exceptions to this rule. There is an abiding consciousness of degradation,—a secret pain or self-humiliation visible in the lines of the mouth and eye. Whether it is only a modification of Turkish gravity, or whether it is the dread Valley of the Shadow of the Drug through which they are continually straying, I cannot say. They seldom smile, and their laughter is of such an extraordinary and sardonic nature—so purely a mechanical spasm, quite independent of any mirthful attribute—that to this day I am doubtful whether I ever saw a Chinaman laugh. A theatrical representation by natives, one might think, would have set my mind at ease on this point; but it did not. Indeed, a new difficulty presented itself,—the impossibility of determining whether the performance was a tragedy or farce. I thought I detected the low comedian in an active youth who turned two somersaults, and knocked everybody down on entering the stage. But, unfortunately, even this classic resemblance to the legitimate farce of our civilization was deceptive. Another brocaded actor, who represented the hero of the play, turned three somersaults, and not only upset my theory and his fellow-actors at the same time, but apparently run a-muck behind the scenes for some time afterward. I looked around at the glinting white teeth to observe the effect of these two palpable hits. They were received with equal acclamation, and apparently equal facial spasms. One or two beheadings which enlivened the play produced the same sardonic effect, and left upon my mind a painful anxiety to know what was the serious business of life in China. It was noticeable, however, that my unrestrained laughter had a discordant effect, and that triangular eyes sometimes turned ominously toward the "Fanqui devil"; but as I retired discreetly before the play was finished, there were no serious results. I have only given the above as an instance of the impossibility of deciding upon the outward and superficial expression of Chinese mirth. Of its inner and deeper existence I have some private doubts. An audience that will view with a serious aspect the hero, after a frightful and agonizing death, get up and quietly walk off the stage cannot be said to have remarkable perceptions of the ludicrous.

I have often been struck with the delicate pliability of the Chinese expression and taste, that might suggest a broader and deeper criticism than is becoming these pages. A Chinaman will adopt the American costume, and wear it with a taste of color and detail that will surpass those "native, and to the manner born." To look at a Chinese slipper, one might imagine it impossible to shape the original foot to anything less cumbrous and roomy, yet a neater-fitting boot than that belonging to the Americanized Chinaman is rarely seen on this side of the Continent. When the loose sack or paletot takes the place of his brocade blouse, it is worn with a refinement and grace that might bring a jealous pang to the exquisite of our more refined civilization. Pantaloons fall easily and naturally over legs that have known unlimited freedom and bagginess, and even garrote collars meet correctly around sun-tanned throats. The new expression seldom overflows in gaudy cravats. I will back my Americanized Chinaman against any neophyte of European birth in the choice of that article. While in our own State, the Greaser resists one by one the garments of the Northern invader, and even wears the livery of his conqueror with a wild and buttonless freedom, the Chinaman, abused and degraded as he is, changes by correctly graded transition to the garments of Christian civilization. There is but one article of European wear that he avoids. These Bohemian eyes have never yet been pained by the spectacle of a tall hat on the head of an intelligent Chinaman.

My acquaintance with John has been made up of weekly interviews, involving the adjustment of the washing accounts, so that I have not been able to study his character from a social view-point or observe him in the privacy of the domestic circle. I have gathered enough to justify me in believing him to be generally honest, faithful, simple, and painstaking. Of his simplicity let me record an instance where a sad and civil young Chinaman brought me certain shirts with most of the buttons missing and others hanging on delusively by a single thread. In a moment of unguarded irony I informed him that unity would at least have been preserved if the buttons were removed altogether. He smiled sadly and went away. I thought I had hurt his feelings, until the next week when he brought me my

shirts with a look of intelligence, and the buttons carefully and totally erased. At another time, to guard against his general disposition
to carry off anything as soiled clothes that he thought could hold
water, I requested him to always wait until he saw me. Coming
home late one evening, I found the household in great consternation, over an immovable Celestial who had remained seated on the
front door-step during the day, sad and submissive, firm but also patient, and only betraying any animation or token of his mission when
he saw me coming. This same Chinaman evinced some evidences of
regard for a little girl in the family, who in her turn reposed such
faith in his intellectual qualities as to present him with a preter-
naturally uninteresting Sunday-School book, her own property. This
book John made a point of carrying ostentatiously with him in his
weekly visits. It appeared usually on the top of the clean clothes,
and was sometimes painfully clasped outside of the big bundle of
soiled linen. Whether John believed he unconsciously imbibed some
spiritual life through its pasteboard cover, as the Prince in the Ara-
bian Nights imbibed the medicine through the handle of the mallet,
or whether he wished to exhibit a due sense of gratitude, or whether
he hadn't any pockets, I have never been able to ascertain. In his
turn he would sometimes cut marvelous imitation roses from carrots
for his little friend. I am inclined to think that the few roses strewn
in John's path were such scentless imitations. The thorns only were
real. From the persecutions of the young and old of a certain class,
his life was a torment. I don't know what was the exact philosophy
that Confucius taught, but it is to be hoped that poor John in his
persecution is still able to detect the conscious hate and fear with
which inferiority always regards the possibility of even-handed justice, and which is the keynote to the vulgar clamor about servile and
degraded races.

THE LATEST CHINESE OUTRAGE

It was noon by the sun; we had finished our game,
And was passin' remarks goin' back to our claim;
Jones was countin' his chips, Smith relievin' his mind
Of ideas that a "straight" should beat "three of a kind,"
When Johnson of Elko came gallopin' down,
With a look on his face 'twixt a grin and a frown,
And he calls, "Drop your shovels and face right about,
For them Chinees from Murphy's are cleanin' us out—

> With their ching-a-ring-chow
> And their chic-colorow
> They're bent upon making
> No slouch of a row."

Then Jones—my own pardner—looks up with a sigh;
"It's your wash bill," sez he, and I answers, "You lie!"
But afore he could draw or the others could arm,
Up tumbles the Bates boys, who heard the alarm.
And a yell from the hilltop and roar of a gong,
Mixed up with remarks like "Hi! yi! Chang-a-wong,"
And bombs, shells, and crackers, that crashed through
    the trees,
Revealed in their war-togs four hundred Chinees!

> Four hundred Chinee;
> We are eight, don't ye see!
> That made a square fifty
> To just one o' we.

They were dressed in their best, but I grieve that that
    same
Was largely made up of our own, to their shame;
And my pardner's best shirt and his trousers were hung
On a spear, and above him were tauntingly swung;
While that beggar, Chey Lee, like a conjurer sat

Pullin' out eggs and chickens from Johnson's best hat;
And Bates' game rooster was part of their "loot,"
And all of Smith's pigs were skyugled to boot;
But the climax was reached and I like to have died
When my demijohn, empty, came down the hillside, —

        Down the hillside—
        What once held the pride
        Of Robertson County
        Pitched down the hillside!

Then we axed for a parley. When out of the din
To the front comes a-rockin' that heathen, Ah Sin!
"You owe flowty dollee—me washee you camp,
You catchee my washee—me catchee no stamp;
One dollar hap dozen, me no catchee yet,
Now that flowty dollee—no hab?—how can get?
Me catchee you pigee—me sellee for cash,
It catchee me licee—you catchee no 'hash';
Me belly good Sheliff—me lebbee when can,
Me allee same halp pin as Melican man!

        But Melican man
        He washee him pan
        On *bottom* side hillee
        And catchee—how can?"

"Are we men?" says Joe Johnson, "and list to this jaw,
Without process of warrant or color of law?
Are we men or—a-chew!"—here he gasped in his speech,
For a stink-pot had fallen just out of his reach.
"Shall we stand here as idle, and let Asia pour
Her barbaric hordes on this civilized shore?
Has the White Man no country? Are we left in the lurch?
And likewise what's gone of the Established Church?
One man to four hundred is great odds, I own,
But this 'yer's a white man—I plays it alone!
And he sprang up the hillside—to stop him none dare—
Till a yell from the top told a "white man was there!"

        A White Man was there!

We prayed he might spare
Those misguided heathens
The few clothes they wear.

They fled, and he followed, but no matter where;
They fled to escape him,—the "White Man was there,"—
Till we missed first his voice on the pine-wooded slope,
And we knew for the heathen henceforth was no hope;
And the yells they grew fainter, when Petersen said,
"It simply was human to bury his dead."
　　　And then, with slow tread,
　　　We crept up, in dread,
　　　But found nary mortal there,
　　　Living or dead.

But there was his trail, and the way that they came,
And younder, no doubt, he was bagging his game.
When Jones drops his pickaxe, and Thompson says
　　"Shoo!"
And both of 'em points to a cage of bamboo
Hanging down from a tree, with a label that swung
Conspicuous, with letters in some foreign tongue,
Which, when freely translated, the same did appear
Was the Chinese for saying, "A White Man is here!"
　　　And as we drew near,
　　　In anger and fear,
　　　Bound hand and foot, Johnson
　　　Looked down with a leer!

In his mouth was an opium pipe—which was why
He leered at us so with a drunken-like eye!
They had shaved off his eyebrows, and tacked on a cue,
They had painted his face of a coppery hue,
And rigged him all up in a heathenish suit,
And softly departed, each man with his "loot."
　　　Yes, every galoot,
　　　And Ah Sin, to boot,
　　　Had left him hanging
　　　Like ripening fruit.

At a mass meeting held up at Murphy's next day
There were seventeen speakers and each had his say;
There were twelve resolutions that instantly passed,
And each resolution was worse than the last;
There were fourteen petitions, which, granting the same,
Will determine what Governor Murphy's shall name;
And the man from our district who goes up next year
Goes up on one issue—that's patent and clear:

"Can the work of a mean,
Degraded, unclean
Believer in Buddah
Be held as a lien?"

WAN LEE, THE PAGAN

As I opened Hop Sing's letter there fluttered to the ground a square strip of yellow paper covered with hieroglyphics, which at first glance I innocently took to be the label from a pack of Chinese fire-crackers. But the same envelope also contained a smaller strip of rice paper, with two Chinese characters traced in India ink, that I at once knew to be Hop Sing's visiting card. The whole, as afterwards literally translated, ran as follows:

To the stranger the gates of my house are not closed; the rice-jar is on the left, and the sweetmeats on the right, as you enter.
Two sayings of the Master:
Hospitality is the virtue of the son and the wisdom of the ancestor.
The superior man is light-hearted after the crop-gathering; he makes a festival.
When the stranger is in your melon patch observe him not too closely; inattention is often the highest form of civility.
Happiness, Peace, and Prosperity.   HOP SING.

Admirable, certainly, as was this morality and proverbial wisdom, and although this last axiom was very characteristic of my friend Hop Sing, who was that most sombre of all humorists, a Chinese philospher, I must confess that, even after a very free translation, I was at a loss to make any immediate application of the message. Luckily I discovered a third inclosure in the shape of a little note in English and Hop Sing's own commercial hand. It ran thus:—

The pleasure of your company is requested at No. —. Sacramento Street, on Friday evening at eight o'clock. A cup of tea at nine—sharp.   HOP SING.

This explained all. It meant a visit to Hop Sing's warehouse, the opening and exhibition of some rare Chinese novelties and curios, a chat in the back office, a cup of tea of a perfection unknown beyond

133

these sacred precincts, cigars, and a visit to the Chinese Theater or Temple. This was in fact the favorite programme of Hop Sing when he exercised his functions of hospitality as the chief factor or superintendent of the Ning Foo Company.

At eight o'clock on Friday evening I entered the warehouse of Hop Sing. Here was that deliciously commingled mysterious foreign odor that I had so often noticed; there was the old array of uncouth-looking objects, the long procession of jars and crockery, the same singular blending of the grotesque and the mathematically neat and exact, the same endless suggestions of frivolity and fragility, the same want of harmony in colors that were each, in themselves, beautiful and rare. Kites in the shape of enormous dragons and gigantic butterflies; kites so ingeniously arranged as to utter at intervals, when facing the wind, the cry of a hawk; kites so large as to be beyond any boy's power of restraint—so large that you understood why kite-flying in China was an amusement for adults; gods of china and bronze so gratuitously ugly as to be beyond any human interest or sympathy from their very impossibility; jars of sweetmeats covered all over with moral sentiments from Confucius; hats that looked like baskets, and baskets that looked like hats; silk so light that I hesitate to record the incredible number of square yards that you might pass through the ring on your little finger—these and a great many other indescribable objects were all familiar to me. I pushed my way through the dimly lighted warehouse until I reached the back office or parlor, where I found Hop Sing waiting to receive me.

Before I describe him I want the average reader to discharge from his mind any idea of a Chinaman that he may have gathered from the pantomime. He did not wear beautifully scalloped drawers fringed with little bells—I never met a Chinaman who did; he did not habitually carry his forefinger extended before him at right angles with his body, nor did I ever hear him utter the mysterious sentence, "Ching a ring a ring chaw," nor dance under any provocation. He was, on the whole, a rather grave, decorous, handsome gentleman. His complexion, which extended all over his head except where his long pig-tail grew, was like a very nice piece of glazed brown paper-muslin. His eyes were black and bright, and his eyelids set at an angle of 15°; his nose straight and delicately formed, his mouth small, and his teeth white and clean. He wore a dark blue silk blouse, and in the streets on cold days a short jacket of Astrakhan fur. He wore also a pair of drawers of blue brocade gathered tightly over his calves and ankles, offering a general sort of suggestion that he had forgotten his trousers that morning, but that, so gentlemanly were his manners, his friends had forborne to mention the fact to him. His manner was urbane, although quite serious. He spoke French and English fluently. In brief, I doubt if you could have found the equal of this Pagan shopkeeper among the Christian traders of San Francisco.

There were a few others present: a Judge of the Federal Court, an editor, a high government official, and a prominent merchant. After we had drunk our tea, and tasted a few sweetmeats from a mysterious jar, that looked as if it might contain a preserved mouse among its other nondescript treasures, Hop Sing arose, and gravely beckoning us to follow him, began to descend to the basement. When we got there, we were amazed at finding it brilliantly lighted, and that a number of chairs were arranged in a half-circle on the asphalt pavement. When he had courteously seated us, he said,—

"I have invited you to witness a performance which I can at least promise you no other foreigners but yourselves have ever seen. Wang, the court juggler, arrived here yesterday morning. He has never given a performance outside of the palace before. I have asked him to entertain my friends this evening. He requires no theatre, stage, accessories, or any confederate—nothing more than you see here. Will you be pleased to examine the ground yourselves, gentlemen."

Of course we examined the premises. It was the ordinary basement or cellar of the San Francisco storehouse, cemented to keep out the damp. We poked our sticks into the pavement and rapped on the walls to satisfy our polite host, but for no other purpose. We were quite content to be the victims of any clever deception. For myself, I knew I was ready to be deluded to any extent, and if I had been offered an explanation of what followed, I should have probably declined it.

Although I am satisfied that Wang's general performance was the first of that kind ever given on American soil, it has probably since become so familiar to many of my readers that I shall not bore them with it here. He began by setting to flight, with the aid of his fan, the usual number of butterflies made before our eyes of little bits of tissue-paper, and kept them in the air during the remainder of the performance. I have a vivid recollection of the judge trying to catch one that had lit on his knee, and of its evading him with the pertinacity of a living insect. And even at this time Wang, still plying his fan, was taking chickens out of hats, making oranges disappear, pulling endless yards of silk from his sleeve, apparently filling the whole area of the basement with goods that appeared mysteriously from the ground, from his own sleeves, from nowhere! He swallowed knives to the ruin of his digestion for years to come; he dislocated every limb of his body; he reclined in the air, apparently upon nothing. But his crowning performance, which I have never yet seen repeated, was the most weird, mysterious, and astounding. It is my apology for this long introduction, my sole excuse for writing this article, the genesis of this veracious history.

He cleared the ground of its encumbering articles for a space of about fifteen feet square, and then invited us all to walk forward and again examine it. We did so gravely; there was nothing but the cemented pavement below to be seen or felt. He then asked for the loan of a handkerchief, and, as I chanced to be nearest him, I offered mine. He took it and spread it open upon the floor. Over this he spread a large square of silk, and over this again a large shawl covering the space he had cleared. He then took a position at one of the points of this rectangle, and began a monotonous chant, rocking his body to and fro in time with the somewhat lugubrious air.

We sat still and waited. Above the chant we could hear the striking of the city clocks, and the occasional rattle of a cart in the street overhead. The absolute watchfulness and expectation, the dim, mysterious half-light of the cellar, falling in a gruesome way upon the misshapen bulk of a Chinese diety in the background, a faint smell of opium smoke mingling with spice, and the dreadful uncertainty of what we were really waiting for, sent an uncomfortable thrill down our backs, and made us look at each other with a forced and unnatural smile. This feeling was heightened when Hop Sing slowly rose, and, without a word, pointed with his finger to the centre of the shawl.

There was something beneath the shawl! Surely—and something

that was not there before. At first a mere suggestion in relief, a faint outline, but growing more and more distinct and visible every moment. The chant still continued, the perspiration began to roll from the singer's face, gradually the hidden object took upon itself a shape and bulk that raised the shawl in its centre some five or six inches. It was now unmistakably the outline of a small but perfect human figure, with extended arms and legs. One or two of us turned pale; there was a feeling of general uneasiness, until the editor broke the silence by a gibe that, poor as it was, was received with spontaneous enthusiasm. Then the chant suddenly ceased, Wang arose, and, with a quick, dexterous movement, stripped both shawl and silk away, and discovered, sleeping peacefully upon my handkerchief, a tiny Chinese baby!

The applause and uproar which followed this revelation ought to have satisfied Wang, even if his audience was a small one; it was loud enough to awaken the baby—a pretty little boy about a year old, looking like a Cupid cut out of sandalwood. He was whisked away almost as mysteriously as he appeared. When Hop Sing returned my handkerchief to me with a bow, I asked if the juggler was the father of the baby. "No sabe!" said the imperturbable Hop Sing, taking refuge in that Spanish form of noncommittalism so common in California.

"But does he have a new baby for every performance?" I asked.

"Perhaps; who knows?"

"But what will become of this one?"

"Whatever you choose, gentlemen," replied Hop Sing, with a courteous inclination; "it was born here—you are its godfathers."

There were two characteristic peculiarities of any Californian assemblage in 1856; it was quick to take a hint, and generous to the point of prodigality in its response to any charitable appeal. No matter how sordid or avaricious the individual, he could not resist the infection of sympathy. I doubled the points of my handkerchief into a bag, dropped a coin into it, and, without a word, passed it to the judge. He quietly added a twenty-dollar gold-piece, and passed it to the next; when it was returned it contained over a hundred dollars. I knotted the money in the handkerchief, and gave it to Hop Sing.

"For the baby, from its godfathers."

"But what name?" said the judge. There was a running fire of "Erebus," "Nox," "Plutus," "Terra Cotta," "Antaeus,"etc., etc. Finally the question was referred to our host.

"Why not keep its own name," he said quietly,—"Wan Lee?" and he did.

And thus was Wan Lee, on the night of Friday the 5th of March, 1856, born into this veracious chronicle.

The last form of the "Northern Star" for the 19th of July, 1865,— the only daily paper published in Klamath County,—had just gone to press, and at three A.M. I was putting aside my proofs and manuscripts, preparatory to going home, when I discovered a letter lying under some sheets of paper which I must have overlooked. The envelope was considerably soiled, it had no postmark, but I had no difficulty in recognizing the hand of my friend Hop Sing. I opened it hurriedly, and read as follows:—

MY DEAR SIR,—I do not know whether the bearer will suit you, but unless the office of "devil" in your newspaper is a purely technical one, I think he has all the qualities required. He is very quick, active, and intelligent; understands English better than he speaks it, and makes up for any defect by his habits of observation and imitation. You have only to show him how to do a thing once, and he will repeat it, whether it is an offense or a virtue. But you certainly know him already; you are one of his godfathers, for is he not Wan Lee, the reputed son of Wang the conjurer, to whose performances I had the honor to introduce you? But perhaps you have forgotten it.

I shall send him with a gang of coolies to Stockton, thence by express to your town. If you can use him there, you will do me a favor, and probably save his life, which is at present in great peril from the hands of the younger members of your Christian and highly civilized race who attend the enlightened schools in San Francisco.

He has acquired some singular habits and customs from his experience of Wang's profession, which he followed for some years, until he became too large to go in a hat, or be produced from his father's sleeve. The money you left with me has been expended on his education; he has gone through the Tri-literal Classics, but, I think, without much benefit. He knows but little of Confucius, and absolutely nothing of Mencius. Owing to the negligence of his father, he associated, perhaps, too much with American children.

I should have answered your letter before, by post, but I thought that Wan Lee himself would be a better messenger for this.

Yours respectfully,
HOP SING.

And this was the long-delayed answer to my letter to Hop Sing. But where was "The bearer"? How was the letter delivered? I summoned hastily the foreman, printers, and office boy, but without eliciting anything; no one had seen the letter delivered, nor knew anything of the bearer. A few days later I had a visit from my laundryman, Ah Ri.

"You wantee debbil? All lightee; me catchee him."

He returned in a few moments with a bright-looking Chinese boy, about ten years old, with whose appearance and general intelligence I was so greatly impressed that I engaged him on the spot. When the business was concluded, I asked his name.

"Wan Lee," said the boy.

"What! Are you the boy sent out by Hop Sing? What the devil do you mean by not coming here before, and how did you deliver that letter?"

Wan Lee looked at me and laughed. "Me pitchee in top side window."

I did not understand. He looked for a moment perplexed, and then, snatching the letter out of my hand, ran down the stairs. After a moment's pause, to my great astonishment, the letter came flying in at the window, circled twice around the room, and then dropped gently like a bird upon my table. Before I had got over my surprise Wan Lee reappeared, smiled, looked at the letter and then at me, said, "So, John," and then remained gravely silent. I said nothing further, but it was understood that this was his first official act.

His next performance, I grieve to say, was not attended with equal success. One of our regular paper-carriers fell sick, and, at a pinch,

Wan Lee was ordered to fill his place. To prevent mistakes he was shown over the route the previous evening, and supplied at about daylight with the usual number of subscribers' copies. He returned after an hour, in good spirits and without the papers. He had delivered them all he said.

Unfortunately for Wan Lee, at eight o'clock indignant subscribers began to arrive at the office. They had received their copies; but how? In the form of hardpressed cannon-balls, delivered by a single shot and a mere *tour de force* through the glass of bedroom windows. They had received them full in the face, like a baseball, if they happened to be up and stirring; they had received them in quarter sheets, tucked in at separate windows; they had found them in the chimney, pinned against the door, shot through the attic windows, delivered in long slips through convenient keyholes, stuffed into ventilators, and occupying the same can with the morning's milk. One subscriber, who waited for some time at the office door, to have a personal interview with Wan Lee (then uncomfortably locked in my bedroom), told me, with tears of rage in his eyes, that he had been awakened at five o'clock by a most hideous yelling below his windows; that on rising, in great agitation, he was startled by the sudden appearance of the "Northern Star" rolled hard and bent into the form of a boomerang or East Indian club, that sailed into the window, described a number of fiendish circles in the room, knocked over the light, slapped the baby's face, "took" him (the subscriber) "in the jaw," and then returned out of the window, and dropped helplessly in the area. During the rest of the day wads and strips of soiled paper, purporting to be copies of the "Northern Star" of that morning's issue, were brought indignantly to the office. An admirable editorial on "The Resources of Humboldt County," which I had constructed the evening before, and which, I have reason to believe, might have changed the whole balance of trade during the ensuing year, and left San Francisco bankrupt at her wharves, was in this way lost to the public.

It was deemed advisable for the next three weeks to keep Wan Lee closely confined to the printing-office and the purely mechanical part of the business. Here he developed a surprising quickness and adaptability, winning even the favor and good will of the printers and foreman, who at first looked upon his introduction into

the secrets of their trade as fraught with the gravest political significance. He learned to set type readily and neatly, his wonderful skill
in manipulation aiding him in the mere mechanical act, and his ignorance of the language confining him simply to the mechanical effort—confirming the printer's axiom that the printer who considers
or follows the ideas of his copy makes a poor compositor. He would
set up deliberately long diatribes against himself, composed by his
fellow printers, and hung on his hook as copy, and even such short
sentences as "Wan Lee is the devil's own imp," "Wan Lee is a Mongolian rascal," and bring the proof to me with happiness beaming
from every tooth and satisfaction shining in his huckleberry eyes.

It was not long, however, before he learned to retaliate on his
mischievous persecutors. I remember one instance in which his re-
prisal came very near involving me in a serious misunderstanding.
Our foreman's name was Webster, and Wan Lee presently learned
to know and recognize the individual and combined letters of his
name. It was during a political campaign, and the eloquent and fiery
Colonel Starbottle of Siskiyou had delivered an effective speech,
which was reported especially for the "Northern Star." In a very
sublime peroration Colonel Starbottle had said, "In the language of
the godlike Webster, I repeat"—and here followed the quotation,
which I have forgotten. Now, it chanced that Wan Lee, looking
over the galley after it had been revised, saw the name of his chief
persecutor, and, of course, imagined the quotation his. After the
form was locked up, Wan Lee took advantage of Webster's absence
to remove the quotation, and substitute a thin piece of lead, of the
same size as the type, engraved with Chinese characters, making a
sentence which, I had reason to believe, was an utter and abject confession of the incapacity and offensiveness of the Webster family
generally, and exceedingly eulogistic of Wan Lee himself personally.

The next morning's paper contained Colonel Starbottle's speech
in full, in which it appeared that the "godlike" Webster had on one
occasion uttered his thoughts in excellent but perfectly enigmatical
Chinese. The rage of Colonel Starbottle knew no bounds. I have a
vivid recollection of that admirable man walking into my office and
demanding a retraction of the statement.

"But, my dear sir," I asked, "are you willing to deny, over your own signature, that Webster never uttered such a sentence? Dare you deny that, with Mr. Webster's well-known attainments, a knowledge of Chinese might not have been among the number? Are you willing to submit a translation suitable to the capacity of our readers, and deny, upon your honor as a gentleman, that the late Mr. Webster ever uttered such a sentiment? If you are, sir, I am willing to publish your denial."

The Colonel was not, and left, highly indignant.

Webster, the foreman, took it more coolly. Happily he was unaware that for two days after, Chinamen from the laundries, from the gulches, from the kitchens, looked in the front office door with faces beaming with sardonic delight; that three hundred extra copies of the "Star" were ordered for the wash-houses on the river. He only knew that during the day Wan Lee occasionally went off into convulsive spasms, and that he was obliged to kick him into consciousness again. A week after the occurrence I called Wan Lee into my office.

"Wan," I said gravely, "I should like you to give me, for my own personal satisfaction, a translation of that Chinese sentence which my gifted countryman, the late godlike Webster, uttered upon a public occasion." Wan Lee looked at me intently, and then the slightest possible twinkle crept into his black eyes. Then he replied, with equal gravity,—

"Mishtel Webstel,—he say: 'China boy makee me belly much foolee. China boy makee me heap sick.'" Which I have reason to think was true.

But I fear I am giving but one side, and not the best, of Wan Lee's character. As he imparted it to me, his had been a hard life. He had known scarcely any childhood —he had no recollection of a father or mother. The conjurer Wang had brought him up. He had spent the first seven years of his life in appearing from baskets, in dropping out of hats, in climbing ladders, in putting his little limbs out of joint in posturing. He had lived in an atmosphere of trickery and deception; he had learned to look upon mankind as dupes of their senses; in fine, if he had thought at all, he would have been a skeptic; if he had been a little older, he would have been a cynic; if he had been older still, he would have been a philosopher. As it was, he was a little imp! A good-natured imp it was, too,— an imp whose moral nature had never been awakened, an imp up for a holiday, and willing to try virtue as a diversion. I don't know that he had any spiritual nature; he was very superstitious; he carried about with him a hideous little porcelain god, which he was in the habit of alternately reviling and propitiating. He was too intelligent for the commoner Chinese vices of stealing or gratuitous lying. Whatever discipline he practiced was taught by his intellect.

I am inclined to think that his feelings were not altogether unimpressible,—although it was almost impossible to extract an expression from him,—and I conscientiously believe he became attached to those who were good to him. What he might have become under more favorable conditions than the bondsman of an overworked, underpaid literary man, I don't know; I only know that the scant, irregular, impulsive kindnesses that I showed him were gratefully received. He was very loyal and patient—two qualities rare in the average American servant. He was like Malvolio, "sad and civil" with me; only once, and then under great provocation, do I remember of his exhibiting any impatience. It was my habit, after leaving the office at night, to take him with me to my rooms, as the bearer of any supplemental or happy afterthought in the editorial way, that might occur to me before the paper went to press. One night I had been scribbling away past the usual hour of dismissing Wan Lee, and had become quite oblivious of his presence in a chair near my door, when suddenly I became aware of a voice saying, in plaintive accents, something that sounded like "Chy Lee."

I faced around sternly.

"What did you say?"

"Me say, 'Chy Lee.' "

"Well?" I said impatiently.

"You sabe, 'How do, John'?"

"Yes."

"You sabe, 'So long, John'?"

"Yes."

"Well, 'Chy Lee' allee same!"

I understood him quite plainly. It appeared that "Chy Lee" was a form of "good-night," and that Wan Lee was anxious to go home. But an instinct of mischief which I fear I possessed in common with him, impelled me to act as if oblivious of the hint. I muttered some-

thing about not understanding him, and again bent over my work. In
a few minutes I heard his wooden shoes pattering pathetically over
the floor. I looked up. He was standing near the door.

"You no sabe, 'Chy Lee'?"

"No," I said sternly.

"You sabe muchee big foolee!—allee same!"

And with this audacity upon his lips he fled. The next morning,
however, he was as meek and patient as before, and I did not recall
his offense. As a probable peace-offering, he blacked all my boots,—
a duty never required of him,—including a pair of buff deerskin slip-
pers and an immense pair of horseman's jack-boots, on which he in-
dulged his remorse for two hours.

I have spoken of his honesty as being a quality of his intellect
rather than his principle, but I recall about this time two exceptions
to the rule. I was anxious to get some fresh eggs, as a change to the
heavy diet of a mining town, and knowing that Wan Lee's countrymen were great poultry-raisers, I applied to him. He furnished me
with them regularly every morning, but refused to take any pay, saying that the man did not sell them,—a remarkable instance of self-
abnegation, as eggs were then worth half a dollar apiece. One morning, my neighbor, Foster, dropped in upon me at breakfast, and took
occasion to bewail his own ill fortune, as his hens had lately stopped
laying, or wandered off in the bush. Wan Lee, who was present during our colloquy, preserved his characteristic sad taciturnity. When
my neighbor had gone, he turned to me with a slight chuckle—
"Floster's hens—Wan Lee's hens—allee same!" His other offense
was more serious and ambitious. It was a season of great irregulari-
ties in the mails, and Wan Lee had heard me deplore the delay in
the delivery of my letters and newspapers. On arriving at my office
one day, I was amazed to find my table covered with letters, evidently just from the post-office, but unfortunately not one addressed
to me. I turned to Wan Lee, who was surveying them with a calm
satisfaction, and demanded an explanation. To my horror he pointed
to an empty mail-bag in the corner, and said, "Postman he say, 'No
lettee, John—no lettee, John.' Postman plentee lie! Postman no
good. Me catchee lettee last night—allee same!" Luckily it was still
early; the mails had not been distributed; I had a hurried interview
with the postmaster, and Wan Lee's bold attempt at robbing the

U.S. Mail was finally condoned, by the purchase of a new mail-bag, and the whole affair thus kept a secret.

If my liking for my little pagan page had not been sufficient, my duty to Hop Sing was enough to cause me to take Wan Lee with me when I returned to San Francisco, after my two years' experience with the "Northern Star." I do not think he contemplated the change with pleasure. I attributed his feelings to a nervous dread of crowded public streets—when he had to go across town for me on an errand, he always made a long circuit of the outskirts; to his dislike for the dicipline of the Chinese and English school to which I proposed to send him; to his fondness for the free, vagrant life of the mines; to sheer willfulness! That it might have been a superstitious premonition did not occur to me until long after.

Nevertheless it really seemed as if the opportunity I had lⁱ..g looked for and confidently expected had come,—the opportunity of placing Wan Lee under gently restraining influences, of subjecting him to a life and experience that would draw out of him what good my superficial care and ill-regulated kindness could not reach. Wan Lee was placed at the school of a Chinese missionary,—an intelligent and kindhearted clergyman, who had shown great interest in the boy, and who, better than all, had a wonderful faith in him. A home was found for him in the family of a widow, who had a bright and interesting daughter about two years younger than Wan Lee. It was this bright, cheery, innocent, and artless child that touched and reached a depth in the boy's nature that hitherto had been unsuspected—that awakened a moral susceptibility which had lain for years insensible alike to the teachings of society or the ethics of the theologian.

These few brief months, bright with a promise that we never saw fulfilled, must have been happy ones to Wan Lee. He worshiped his little friend with something of the same superstition, but without any of the caprice, that he bestowed upon his porcelain Pagan god. It was his delight to walk behind her to school, carrying her books,— a service always fraught with danger to him from the little hands of his Caucasian Christian brothers. He made her the most marvelous toys; he would cut out of carrots and turnips the most astonishing roses and tulips; he made lifelike chickens out of melon-seeds; he constructed fans and kites, and was singularly proficient in the making of dolls' paper dresses. On the other hand she played and sang to him; taught him a thousand little prettinesses and refinements only known to girls; gave him a yellow ribbon for his pigtail, as best suiting his complexion; read to him; showed him wherein he was original and valuable; took him to Sunday-school with her, against the precedents of the school, and, small-womanlike, triumphed. I wish I could add here, that she effected his conversion, and made him give up his porcelain idol, but I am telling a true story, and this little girl was quite content to fill him with her own Christian goodness, without letting him know that he was changed. So they got along very well together—this little Christian girl, with her shining cross hanging around her plump, white, little neck, and this dark little Pagan, with his hideous porcelain god hidden away in his blouse.

There were two days of that eventful year which will long be remembered in San Francisco,—two days when a mob of her citizens set upon and killed unarmed, defenseless foreigners, because they were foreigners and of another race, religion, and color, and worked for what wages they could get. There were some public men so timid that, seeing this, they thought that the end of the world had come; there were some eminent statesmen, whose names I am ashamed to write here, who began to think that the passage in the Constitution which guarantees civil and religious liberty to every citizen or foreigner was a mistake. But there were also some men who were not so easily frightened, and in twenty-four hours we had things so arranged that the timid men could wring their hands in safety, and the eminent statesmen utter their doubts without hurting anybody or anything. And in the midst of this I got a note from Hop Sing, asking me to come to him immediately.

I found his warehouse closed and strongly guarded by the police against any possible attack of the rioters. Hop Sing admitted me through a barred grating with his usual imperturbable calm, but, as it seemed to me, with more than his usual seriousness. Without a word he took my hand and led me to the rear of the room, and thence downstairs into the basement. It was dimly lighted, but there was something lying on the floor covered by a shawl. As I approached, he drew the shawl away with a sudden gesture, and revealed Wan Lee, the Pagan, lying there dead!

Dead, my reverend friends, dead! Stoned to death in the streets of

San Francisco, in the year of grace, eighteen hundred and sixty-nine, by a mob of half-grown boys and Christian school-children!

As I put my hand reverently upon his breast, I felt something crumbling beneath his blouse. I looked inquiringly at Hop Sing. He put his hand between the folds of silk, and drew out something with the first bitter smile I had ever seen on the face of that Pagan gentleman.

It was Wan Lee's porcelain god, crushed by a stone from the hands of those Christian iconoclasts!

THAT EBREW JEW

There once was a tradesman, renowned as a screw,
Who sold pins and needles, and calicoes, too,
Till he built up a fortune—the which, as it grew,
Just ruined small traders the whole city through.
    Yet one thing he knew
    Between me and you:
    There was a distinction
    'Twixt Christian and Jew.

Till he died in his mansion a great millionaire,
The owner of thousands, but nothing to spare
For the needy and poor who from hunger might drop,
And only a pittance to clerks in his shop,
    But left it all to
    A lawyer who knew
    A subtle distinction
    'Twixt Ebrew and Jew.

This man was no trader, but simply a friend
Of this gent who kept shop, and who, nearing his end,
Handed over a million—'twas only his due,
Who discovered this contrast 'twixt Ebrew and Jew.
    For he said, "If you view
    This case as I do,
    There *is* a distinction
    'Twixt Ebrew and Jew."

"For the Jew is a man who will make money through
His skill, his *finesse,* and his capital, too.
And an Ebrew's a man that we Gentiles can 'do.'
So you see there's a contrast 'twixt Ebrew and Jew.
    Ebrew and Jew,
    Jew and Ebrew—
    There's a subtle distinction
    'Twixt Ebrew and Jew.

So he kept up his business of needles and pins,
But always one day he atoned for his sins,
But never the same day (for that wouldn't do)
That the Jew faced his God with the awful Ebrew.
    For this man he knew,
    Between me and you,
    There was a distinction
    'Twixt Ebrew and Jew.

So he sold soda water and shut up the fount
Of the druggist whose creed was the Speech on the
    Mount;
And he trafficked in gaiters, and ruined the trade
Of a German whose creed was by great Luther made.
    But always he knew,
    Between me and you,
    A subtle distinction
    'Twixt Ebrew and Jew.

Then he kept a hotel—here his trouble began—
In a fashion unknown to his primitive plan.
For the rule of his house to his manager ran:
"Don't give entertainment to Israelite man."
    Yet the manager knew,
    Between me and you,
    No other distinction
    'Twixt Ebrew and Jew.

"You may give to John Morrissey supper and wine,
And Madame N.N. to your care I resign;
You will see that those Jenkins from Missouri Flat
Are properly cared for, but recollect that
    Never a Jew
    Who's not an Ebrew,
    Shall take up his lodgings
    Here at the Grand U.

"You'll allow Miss McFlimsey her diamonds to wear,
You'll permit the Van Dams at the waiters to swear,
You'll allow Miss Decollete to flirt on the stair,
But, as to an Israelite, pray have a care.
    For, between me and you
    Though the doctrine is new,
    There's a business distinction
    'Twixt Ebrew and Jew.

Now, how shall we know? Prophet, tell us, pray do,
Where the line of the Hebrew fades into the Jew?
Shall we keep out Disraeli and take Rothschild in?
Or snub Meyerbeer and think Verdi[1] a sin?
    What shall we do?
    Oh give us a few
    Points to distinguish
    'Twixt Ebrew and Jew.

There was One—Heaven help us!—who died in man's
    place,
With thorns on his forehead, but love in his face;
And when "foxes had holes," and the birds of the air
Had their nests in the trees, there was no spot to spare
    For this "King of the Jews."
    Did the Romans refuse
    This right to the Ebrews,
    Or only to Jews?

SUGGESTED ADDITIONAL READINGS

    "Chu Chu"
    "The Passing of Enriquez"
    "The Devotion of Enriquez"

[1]Giuseppe Verdi was not a Jew.

"An Episode of Fiddletown'
"See Yup"
"Two Men from Sandy Bar"
"Three Vagabonds from Trinidad"

SELECTED REFERENCES

Duckett, Margaret. "Bret Harte's Portrayal of Half-Breeds."
American Literature, 25 (1953), 193–212.
——. *Mark Twain and Bret Harte* (1964).
Fenn, William Purviance. *Ah Sin and His Brethren in American Literature* (1933).

PROJECTS AND PROBLEMS

Did Harte create the stereotyped characterization of the Chinese that was popular during his time? Is stereotyped characterization an inevitable ingredient of local color fiction? Compare Harte's treatment of Chinese and Mexican characters.

Judge the importance of Harte's strain of Jewish ancestry to his relationship with Mark Twain.

Notice the use of Israelite, Hebrew, and Jew in "That Ebrew Jew" and determine the differences between these designations. Compare the distinctions suggested in the poem with those evident in the selection from "The Impressions of a Cousin," by Henry James, in this volume.

Compare Harte's doggerel protest against anti-Semitism with the anonymous "No Irish Need Apply" that was popular at about this time. One version of the poem is in Wayne Miller's *A Gathering of Ghetto Writers* (1972). Find other expressions of the minority presence in popular verse of the period, including pieces by Charles Follen Adams.

For a later treatment of California's Chinese than that of Harte and Mark Twain, see Chester B. Fernald's *The Cat and the Cherub* and *Chinatown Stories*, both published in 1896. Do Fernald's stories simply bring the stereotypes up to date or break away from them.

WILLIAM DEAN HOWELLS
(1837–1920)

Born in Ohio where he had a very limited formal education, Howells became the dean of American letters for the last decades of the nineteenth century. He used his enormous influence to champion realism and to encourage neglected writers whose promise he recognized. His many books constitute a portrait of the manners of his time, offering insights into the prevailing attitudes toward minorities and marking the limits of his equalitarian and humanitarian principles. The first selection below comes from "Mrs. Johnson" and the second is taken from "A Pedestrian Tour," both of which were published in *Suburban Sketches* in 1871. "Memories of an Ohio Boyhood" is extracted from *A Boy's Town* (1890).

MRS. JOHNSON

... Our last Irish girl went with the last snow, and on one of those midsummer-like days that sometimes fall in early April to our yet bleak and desolate zone, our hearts sang of Africa and golden joys. A Libyan longing took us, and we would have chosen, if we could, to bear a strand of grotesque beads, or a handful of brazen gauds, and traffic them for some sable maid with crisped locks, whom, uncoffling from the captive train beside the desert, we should make to do our general housework forever, through the right of lawful purchase. But we knew that this was impossible, and that, if we desired colored help, we must seek it at the intelligence office, which is in one of those streets chiefly inhabited by the orphaned children and grandchildren of slavery. To tell the truth these orphans do not seem to grieve much for their bereavement, but lead a life of joyous and rather indolent oblivion in their quarter of the city. They are often to be seen sauntering up and down the street by which the Charles-bridge[1] cars arrive,—the young with a harmless swagger, and the old with the generic limp which our Autocrat has already noted as attending advanced years in their race. They seem the natural human interest of a street so largely devoted to old clothes; and the thoughtful may see a felicity in their presence where the pawnbrokers' windows display the forfeited pledges of improvidence, and subtly remind us that we have yet to redeem a whole race, pawned in our needy and reckless national youth, and still held against us by the Uncle of Injustice, who is also the Father of Lies. How gayly are the young ladies of this race attired, as they trip up and down the sidewalks, and in and out through the pendent garments at the shop doors! They are the black pansies and marigolds and dark-blooded dahlias among womankind. They try to assume something of our colder race's demeanor, but even the passer on the horsecar can see that it is not native with them, and is better pleased when they forget us, and ungenteelly laugh in encountering friends, letting their white teeth glitter through the generous lips that open to their ears. In the streets branching upwards from this avenue, very little colored men and maids play with broken or enfeebled toys, or sport on the wooden pavements of the entrances to the inner courts. Now

[1]Cambridge, Massachusetts.

153

and then a colored soldier or sailor—looking strange in his uniform, even after the custom of several years—emerges from those passages; or, more rarely, a black gentleman, stricken in years, and cased in shining broadcloth, walks solidly down the brick sidewalk, cane in hand,—a vision of serene self-complacency, and so plainly the expression of virtuous public sentiment that the great colored louts, innocent enough till then in their idleness, are taken with a sudden sense of depravity, and loaf guiltily up against the house-walls. At the same moment, perhaps, a young damsel, amorously scuffling with an admirer through one of the low open windows, suspends the strife, and bids him, "Go along now, do!" More rarely yet than the gentleman described, one may see a white girl among the dark neighbors, whose frowzy head is uncovered, and whose sleeves are rolled up to her elbows, and who, though no doubt quite at home, looks as strange there as that pale anomaly which may sometimes be seen among a crew of blackbirds.

An air not so much of decay as of unthrift, and yet hardly of unthrift, seems to prevail in the neighborhood, which has none of the aggressive and impudent squalor of an Irish quarter, and none of the surly wickedness of a low American street. A gayety not born of the things that bring its serious joy to the true New England heart—a ragged gayety, which comes of summer in the blood, and not in the pocket or the conscience, and which affects the countenance and the whole demeanor, setting the feet to some inward music, and at times bursting into a line of song or a child-like and irresponsible laugh—gives tone to the visible life, and wakens a very friendly spirit in the passer, who somehow thinks there of a milder climate, and is half persuaded that the orange-peel on the sidewalks came from fruit grown in the soft atmosphere of those back courts.

It was in this quarter, then, that we heard of Mrs. Johnson; and it was from a colored boarding-house there that she came out to Charlesbridge to look at us, bringing her daughter of twelve years with her. She was a matron of mature age and portly figure, with a complexion like coffee soothed with the richest cream; and her manners were so full of a certain tranquility and grace, that she charmed away all our will to ask for references. It was only her barbaric laughter and her lawless eye that betrayed how slightly her New England birth and breeding covered her ancestral traits, and bridged the gulf of a thousand years of civilization that lay between her race and ours. But in fact, she was doubly estranged by descent; for, as we learned later, a sylvan wildness mixed with that of the desert in her veins: her grandfather was an Indian, and her ancestors on this side had probably sold their lands for the same value in trinkets that bought the original African pair on the other side.

The first day that Mrs. Johnson descended into our kitchen, she conjured from the malicious disorder in which it had been left by the flitting Irish kobold a dinner that revealed the inspirations of genius, and was quite different from a dinner of mere routine and laborious talent. Something original and authentic mingled with the accustomed flavors; and, though vague reminiscences of canal-boat travel and woodland camps arose from the relish of certain of the dishes, there was yet the assurance of such power in the preparation of the whole, that we knew her to be merely running over the chords of our appetite with preliminary savors, as a musician acquaints his touch with the keys of an unfamiliar piano before breaking into brilliant and triumphant execution. Within a week she had mastered her instrument; and thereafter there was no faltering in her performances, which she varied constantly, through inspiration or from suggestion. She was so quick to receive new ideas in her art, that, when the Roman statuary who stayed a few weeks with us explained the mystery of various purely Latin dishes, she caught their principle at once; and visions of the great white cathedral, the Coliseum, and the "dome of Brunelleschi" floated before us in the exhalations of the Milanese *risotto*, Roman *stufadino*, and Florentine *stracotto* that smoked upon our board. But, after all, it was in puddings that Mrs. Johnson chiefly excelled. She was one of those cooks—rare as men of genius in literature—who love their own dishes; and she had, in her personally child-like simplicity of taste, and the inherited appetites of her savage forefathers, a dominant passion for sweets. So far as we could learn, she subsisted principally upon puddings and tea. Through the same primitive instincts, no doubt, she loved praise. She openly exulted in our artless flatteries of her skill; she waited jealously at the head of the kitchen stairs to hear what was said of her work, especially if there were guests; and she was never too weary to attempt emprises of cookery.

While engaged in these, she wore a species of sightly handker-

chief like a turban upon her head, and about her person those mysti-
cal swathings in which old ladies of the African race delight. But she
most pleasured our sense of beauty and moral fitness when, after the
last pan was washed and the last pot was scraped, she lighted a po-
tent pipe, and, taking her stand at the kitchen door, laded the soft
evening air with its pungent odors. If we surprised her at these supreme moments, she took the pipe from her lips, and put it behind
her, with a low, mellow chuckle, and a look of half-defiant consciousness; never guessing that none of her merits took us half so
much as the cheerful vice which she only feigned to conceal.

Some things she could not do so perfectly as cooking, because of
her failing eyesight; and we persuaded her that spectacles would
both become and befriend a lady of her years, and so bought her a
pair of steel-bowed glasses. She wore them in some great emergen-
cies at first, but had clearly no pride in them. Before long she laid
them aside altogether, and they had passed from our thoughts, when
one day we heard her mellow note of laughter and her daughter's
harsher cackle outside our door, and, opening it, beheld Mrs. Johnson in gold-bowed spectacles of massive frame. We then learned
that their purchase was in fulfillment of a vow made long ago, in the
life-time of Mr. Johnson, that, if ever she wore glasses, they should
be gold-bowed; and I hope the manes of the dead were half as happy
in these votive spectacles as the simple soul that offered them.

She and her late partner were the parents of eleven children, some
of whom were dead, and some of whom were wanderers in unknown
parts. During his life-time she had kept a little shop in her native
town; and it was only within a few years that she had gone into service. She cherished a natural haughtiness of spirit, and resented control, although disposed to do all she could of her own motion. Being
told to say when she wanted an afternoon, she explained that when
she wanted an afternoon she always took it without asking, but always planned so as not to discommode the ladies with whom she
lived. These, she said, had numbered twenty-seven within three
years, which made us doubt the success of her system in all cases,
though she merely held out the fact as an assurance of her faith in
the future, and a proof of the ease with which places were to be
found. She contended, moreover, that a lady who had for thirty years
had a house of her own, was in nowise bound to ask permission to

receive visits from friends where she might be living, but that they ought freely to come and go like other guests. In this spirit she once invited her son-in-law, Professor Jones of Providence, to dine with her; and her defied mistress, on entering the dining room, found the Professor at pudding and tea there,—an impressively respectable figure in black clothes, with a black face rendered yet more effective by a pair of green goggles. It appeared that this dark professor was a light of phrenology in Rhode Island, and that he was believed to have uncommon virtue in his science by reason of being blind as well as black.

I am loath to confess that Mrs. Johnson had not a flattering opinion of the Caucasian race in all respects. In fact, she had very good philosophical and Scriptural reasons for looking upon us as an upstart people of new blood, who had come into their whiteness by no creditable or pleasant process. The late Mr. Johnson, who had died in the West Indies, whither he voyaged for his health in quality of cook upon a Down-East schooner, was a man of letters, and had written a book to show the superiority of the black over the white branches of the human family. In this he held that, as all islands have been at their discovery found peopled by blacks, we must needs believe that humanity was first created of that color. Mrs. Johnson could not show us her husband's work (a sole copy in the library of an English gentleman at Port au Prince is not to be bought for money), but she often developed its arguments to the lady of the house; and one day, with a great show of reluctance, and many protests that no personal slight was meant, let fall the fact that Mr. Johnson believed the white race descended from Gehazi the leper, upon whom the leprosy of Naaman fell when the latter returned by Divine favor to his original blackness. "And he went out from his presence a leper as white as snow," said Mrs. Johnson, quoting irrefutable Scripture. "Leprosy, leprosy," she added thoughtfully,— "nothing but leprosy bleached you out."

It seems to me much in her praise that she did not exult in our taint and degradation, as some white philosophers used to do in the opposite idea that a part of the human family were cursed to lasting blackness and slavery in Ham and his children, but even told us of a remarkable approach to whiteness in many of her own offspring. In a kindred spirit of charity, no doubt, she refused ever to attend church with people of her elder and wholesomer blood. When she went to church, she said, she always went to a white church, though while with us I am bound to say she never went to any. She professed to read her Bible in her bedroom on Sundays; but we suspected, from certain sounds and odors which used to steal out of this sanctuary, that her piety more commonly found expression in dozing and smoking.

I would not make a wanton jest here of Mrs. Johnson's anxiety to claim honor for the African color, while denying this color in many of her own family. It afforded a glimpse of the pain which all her people must endure, however proudly they hide it or light-heartedly forget it, from the despite and contumely to which they are guiltlessly born; and when I thought how irreparable was this disgrace and calamity of a black skin, and how irreparable it must be for ages yet, in this world where every other shame and all manner of wilful guilt and wickedness may hope for covert and pardon, I had little heart to laugh. Indeed, it was so pathetic to hear this poor old soul talk of her dead and lost ones, and try, in spite of all Mr. Johnson's theories and her own arrogant generalizations, to establish their whiteness, that we must have been very cruel and silly people to turn her sacred fables even into matter of question. I have no doubt that her Antoinette Anastasia and her Thomas Jefferson Wilberforce —it is impossible to give a full idea of the splendor and scope of the baptismal names in Mrs. Johnson's family—have as light skins and as golden hair in heaven as her reverend maternal fancy painted for them in our world. There, certainly, they would not be subject to tanning, which had ruined the delicate complexion, and had knotted into black woolly tangles the once wavy blonde locks of our little maid-servant Naomi; and I would fain believe that Toussaint Washington Johnson, who ran away to sea so many years ago, has found some fortunate zone where his hair and skin keep the same sunny and rosy tints they wore to his mother's eyes in infancy. But I have no means of knowing this, or of telling whether he was the prodigy of intellect that he was declared to be. Naomi could no more be taken in proof of the one assertion than of the other. When she came to us, it was agreed that she should go to school; but she overruled her mother in this as in everything else, and never went. Except Sunday-school lessons, she had no other instruction than that her mistress gave her in the evenings, when a heavy day's play and the natural influences of the hour conspired with original causes to render her powerless before words of one syllable.

The first week of her service she was obedient and faithful to her duties; but, relaxing in the atmosphere of a house which seems to demoralize all menials, she shortly fell into disorderly ways of lying in wait for callers out of doors, and, when people rang, of running up the front steps, and letting them in from the outside. As the season expanded, and the fine weather became confirmed, she modified even this form of service, and spent her time in the fields, appearing at the house only when nature importunately craved molasses. She had a parrotlike quickness, so far as music was concerned, and learned from the Roman statuary to make the groves and half-finished houses resound,

> "Camicia rossa,
> Ove t' ascondi?
> T' appella Italia,—
> Tu non respondi!"

She taught the Garibaldi song, moreover, to all the neighboring children, so that I sometimes wondered if our street were not about to march upon Rome in a body.

In her untamable disobedience, Naomi alone betrayed her sylvan blood, for she was in all other respects negro and not Indian. But it was of her aboriginal ancestry that Mrs. Johnson chiefly boasted,— when not engaged in argument to maintain the superiority of the African race. She loved to descant upon it as the cause and explanation of her own arrogant habit of feeling; and she seemed indeed to have inherited something of the Indian's hauteur along with the Ethiop's supple cunning and abundant amiability. She gave many instances in which her pride had met and overcome the insolence of employers, and the kindly old creature was by no means singular in her pride of being reputed proud.

She could never have been a woman of strong logical faculties, but she had in some things a very surprising and awful astuteness. She seldom introduced any purpose directly, but bore all about it, and then suddenly sprung it upon her unprepared antagonist. At other times she obscurely hinted a reason, and left a conclusion to be inferred; as when she warded off reproach for some delinquency by saying in a general way that she had lived with ladies who used to come scolding into the kitchen after they had taken their bitters. "Quality ladies took their bitters regular," she added, to remove any sting of personality from her remark; for, from many things she had let fall, we knew that she did not regard us as quality. On the contrary, she often tried to overbear us with the gentility of her former places; and would tell the lady over whom she reigned, that she had lived with folks worth their three and four hundred thousand dollars, who never complained as she did of the ironing. Yet she had a sufficient regard for the literary occupations of the family, Mr. Johnson having been an author. She even professed to have herself written a book, which was still in manuscript, and preserved somewhere among her best clothes.

It was well, on many accounts, to be in contact with a mind so original and suggestive as Mrs. Johnson's. We loved to trace its intricate yet often transparent operations, and were perhaps too fond of explaining its peculiarities by facts of ancestry,—of finding hints of the Powwow or the Grand Custom in each grotesque development. We were conscious of something warmer in this old soul than in ourselves, and something wilder, and we chose to think it the tropic and the untracked forest. She had scarcely any being apart from her affection; she had no morality, but was good because she neither hated nor envied; and she might have been a saint far more easily than far more civilized people.

There was that also in her sinuous yet malleable nature, so full of guile and so full of goodness, that reminded us pleasantly of lowly folk in elder lands, where relaxing oppressions have lifted the restraints of fear between master and servant, without disturbing the familiarity of their relation. She advised freely with us upon all household matters, and took a motherly interest in whatever concerned us. She could be flattered or caressed into almost any service, but no threat or command could move her. When she erred, she never acknowledged her wrong in words, but handsomely expressed her regrets in a pudding, or sent up her apologies in a favorite dish secretly prepared. We grew so well used to this form of exculpation, that, whenever Mrs. Johnson took an afternoon at an inconvenient season, we knew that for a week afterwards we should be feasted like princes. She owned frankly that she loved us, that she never had done half so much for people before, and that she never had been nearly so well suited in any other place; and for a brief and happy time we thought that we never should part.

One day, however, our dividing destiny appeared in the basement, and was presented to us as Hippolyto Thucydides, the son of Mrs. Johnson, who had just arrived on a visit to his mother from the State of New Hampshire. He was a heavy and loutish youth, standing upon the borders of boyhood, and looking forward to the future with a vacant and listless eye. I mean that this was his figurative attitude; his actual manner, as he lolled upon a chair beside the kitchen window, was so eccentric, that we felt a little uncertain how to regard him, and Mrs. Johnson openly described him as peculiar. He was so deeply tanned by the fervid suns of the New Hampshire winter, and his hair had so far suffered from the example of the sheep lately under his charge, that he could not be classed by any stretch of compassion with the blonde and straight-haired members of Mrs. Johnson's family.

He remained with us all the first day until late in the afternoon, when his mother took him out to get him a boarding-house. Then he departed in the van of her and Naomi, pausing at the gate to collect his spirits, and, after he had sufficiently animated himself by clapping his palms together, starting off down the street at a hand-gallop, to the manifest terror of the cows in the pastures, and the confusion of the less demonstrative people of our household. Other characteristic traits appeared in Hippolyto Thucydides within no very long period of time, and he ran away from his lodgings so often during the summer that he might be said to board round among the outlying corn-fields and turnip-patches of Charlesbridge. As a check upon this habit, Mrs. Johnson seemed to have invited him to spend his whole time in our basement; for whenever we went below we found him there, balanced—perhaps in homage to us, and perhaps as a token of extreme sensibility in himself—upon the low window-sill, the bottoms of his boots touching the floor inside, and his face buried in the grass without.

We could formulate no very tenable objection to all this, and yet the presence of Thucydides in our kitchen unaccountably oppressed

our imaginations. We beheld him all over the house, a monstrous ei-
dolon, balanced upon every window-sill; and he certainly attracted
unpleasant notice to our place, no less by his furtive and hang-dog
manner of arrival than by the bold displays with which he celebrated
his departures. We hinted this to Mrs. Johnson, but she could not
enter into our feeling. Indeed, all the wild poetry of her maternal
and primitive nature seemed to cast itself about this hapless boy;
and if we had listened to her we should have believed there was no
one so agreeable in society, or so quick-witted in affairs, as Hippolyto, when he chose. She used to rehearse us long epics concerning his industry, his courage, and his talent; and she put fine
speeches in his mouth with no more regard to the truth than if she
had been a historian, and not a poet. Perhaps she believed that he
really said and did the things she attributed to him: it is the destiny
of those who repeatedly tell great things either of themselves or others; and I think we may readily forgive the illusion to her zeal and
fondness. In fact, she was not a wise woman, and she spoiled her
children as if she had been a rich one.

At last, when we said positively that Thucydides should come to
us no more, and then qualified the prohibition by allowing him to
come every Sunday, she answered that she never would hurt the
child's feelings by telling him not to come where his mother was;
that people who did not love her children did not love her; and that,
if Hippy went, she went. We thought it a master-stroke of firmness
to rejoin that Hippolyto must go in any event; but I am bound to
own that he did not go, and that his mother stayed, and so fed us
with every cunning propitiatory dainty, that we must have been Pa-
gans to renew our threat. In fact, we begged Mrs. Johnson to go into
the country with us, and she, after long reluctation on Hippy's account, consented, agreeing to send him away to friends during her
absence.

We made every preparation, and on the eve of our departure Mrs.
Johnson went into the city to engage her son's passage to Bangor,
while we awaited her return in untroubled security.

But she did not appear till midnight, and then responded with but
a sad "Well, sah!" to the cheerful "Well, Mrs. Johnson!" that
greeted her.

"All right, Mrs. Johnson?"

Mrs. Johnson made a strange noise, half chuckle and half death-rattle, in her throat. "All wrong, sah. Hippy's off again; and I've been all over the city after him."

"Then you can't go with us in the morning?"

"How *can* I, sah?"

Mrs. Johnson went sadly out of the room. Then she came back to the door again, and, opening it, uttered, for the first time in our service, words of apology and regret: "I hope I ha'n't put you out any. I *wanted* to go with you, but I ought to *knowed* I couldn't. All is, I loved you too much."

A NEIGHBORHOOD IN
TRANSITION

...I sometimes go upon a pedestrian tour, which is of no great extent in itself, and which I moreover modify by keeping always within sound of the horse-car bells, or easy reach of some steam-car station.

I fear that I should find these rambles dull, but that their utter lack of interest amuses me. I will be honest with the reader, though, and any Master Pliable is free to forsake me at this point; for I cannot promise to be really livelier than my walk. There is a Slough of Despond in full view, and not a Delectable Mountain to be seen, unless you choose so to call the high lands about Waltham, which we shall behold dark blue against the western sky presently. As I sally forth upon Benicia Street, the whole suburb of Charlesbridge stretches about me,—a vast space upon which I can embroider any fancy I like as I saunter along. I have no associations with it, or memories of it, and, at some seasons, I might wander for days in the most frequented parts of it, and meet hardly any one I know. It is not, however, to these parts that I commonly turn, but northward, up a street upon which a flight of French-roof houses suddenly settled a year or two since, with families in them, and many outward signs of permanence, though their precipitate arrival might cast some doubt upon this. I have to admire their uniform neatness and prettiness, and I look at their dormer-windows with the envy of one to whose weak sentimentality dormer-windows long appeared the supreme architectural happiness. But, for all my admiration of the houses, I find a variety that is pleasanter in the landscape, when I reach, beyond them, a little bridge which appears to span a small stream. It unites banks lined with a growth of trees and briers nodding their heads above the neighboring levels, and suggesting a quiet water-course; though in fact it is the Fitchburg Railroad that purls between them, with rippling freight and passenger trains and ever-gurgling locomotives. The banks take the earliest green of spring upon their southward slope, and on a Sunday morning of May, when the bells are lamenting the Sabbaths of the past, I find

164

their sunny tranquility sufficient to give me a slight heart-ache for I know not what. If I descend them and follow the railroad westward half a mile, I come to vast brick-yards, which are not in themselves exciting to the imagination, and which yet, from an irresistible association of ideas, remind me of Egypt, and are forever newly forsaken of those who made bricks without straw; so that I have no trouble in erecting temples and dynastic tombs out of the kilns; while the mills for grinding the clay serve me very well for those sad-voiced *sakias* or wheel-pumps which the Howadji Curtis heard wailing at their work of drawing water from the Nile. A little farther on I come to the boarding-house built at the railroad side for the French Canadians who have by this time succeeded the Hebrews in the toil of the brick-yards, and who, as they loiter in windy-voiced, good-humored groups about the doors of their lodgings, insist upon bringing before me the town of St. Michel at the mouth of the great Mont Cenis tunnel, where so many peasant folk like them are always amiably quarreling before the *cabarets* when the diligence comes and goes. Somewhere, there must be a gendarme with a cocked hat and a sword on, standing with folded arms to represent the Empire and Peace among that rural population; if I looked in-doors, I am sure I should see the neatest of landladies and landladies' daughters and nieces in high black silk caps, bearing hither and thither smoking bowls of *bouillon* and *café-au-lait*. Well, it takes as little to make one happy as miserable, thank Heaven! and I derive a cheerfulness from this scene which quite atones to me for the fleeting desolation suffered from the sunny verdure on the railroad bank. With repaired spirits I take my way up through the brick-yards toward the Irish settlement on the north, passing under the long sheds that shelter the kilns. The ashes lie cold about the mouths of most, and the bricks are burnt to the proper complexion; in others these are freshly arranged over flues in which the fire has not been kindled; but in whatever state I see them, I am reminded of brick-kilns of boyhood. They were then such palaces of enchantment as any architect should now vainly attempt to rival with bricks upon the most desirable corner lot of the Back Bay, and were the homes of men truly to be envied: men privileged to stay up all night; to sleep, as it were, out of doors; to hear the wild geese as they flew over in the darkness; to be waking in time to shoot the early ducks that visited the neighboring ponds; to roast corn upon the ends of sticks; to tell and to listen to stories that never ended, save in some sudden impulse to rise and dance a happy hoe-down in the ruddy light of the kiln-fires. If by day they were seen to have the redness of eyes of men that looked upon the whiskey when it was yellow and gave its color in the flask; if now and then the fragments of a broken bottle strewed the scene of their vigils, and a head broken to match appeared among those good comrades, the boyish imagination was not shocked by these things, but accepted them merely as the symbols of a free virile life. Some such life no doubt is still to be found in the Dublin to which I am come by the time my repertory of associations with brick-kilns is exhausted; but, oddly enough, I no longer care to encounter it.

It is perhaps in a pious recognition of our mortality that Dublin is built around the Irish grave-yard. Most of its windows look out upon the sepulchral monuments and the pretty constant arrival of the funeral trains with their long lines of carriages bringing to the celebration of the sad ultimate rites those gay companies of Irish mourners. I suppose that the spectacle of such obsequies is not at all depressing to the inhabitants of Dublin; but that, on the contrary, it must beget in them a feeling which, if not resignation to death, is, at least, a sort of subacute cheerfulness in his presence. None but a Dubliner, however, would have been greatly animated by a scene which I witnessed during a stroll through this cemetery one afternoon of early spring. The fact that a marble slab or shaft more or less sculptured, and inscribed with words more or less helpless, is the utmost that we can give to one whom once we could caress with every tenderness of speech and touch; and that, after all, the memorial we raise is rather to our own grief, and is a decency, a mere conventionality,—this is a dreadful fact on which the heart breaks itself with such a pang, that it always seems a desolation never recognized, an anguish never felt before. Whilst I stood revolving this thought in my mind, and reading the Irish names upon the stones and the black head-boards,—the latter adorned with pictures of angels, once gilt, but now weather-worn down to the yellow paint,—a wail of intolerable pathos filled the air: "O my darling, O my darling! O—O—O!" with sobs and groans and sighs; and, looking about, I saw two women, one standing upright beside another that had cast herself upon a grave, and lay clasping it with her comfortless arms, uttering these cries. The grave was a year old at least, but the grief seemed of yesterday or of that morning. At times the friend that stood beside the prostrate woman stooped and spoke a soothing word to her, while she wailed out her woe; and in the midst some little ribald Irish boys came scuffling and quarreling up the pathway, singing snatches of an obscene song; and when both the wailing and the singing had died away, an old woman, decently clad, and with her many-wrinkled face softened by the old-fashioned frill running round the inside of her cap, dropped down upon her knees beside a very old grave, and clasped her hands in a silent prayer above it.

If I had beheld all this in some village *campo santo* in Italy, I should have been much more vividly impressed by it, as an aesthetical observer; whereas I was now merely touched as a human being, and had little desire to turn the scene to literary account. I could not help feeling that it wanted the atmosphere of sentimental association; the whole background was a blank or worse than a blank. Yet I have not been able to hide from myself so much as I would like certain points of resemblance between our Irish and the poorer classes of Italians. The likeness is one of the first things that strikes an American in Italy, and I am always reminded of it in Dublin. So much of the local life appears upon the street; there is so much gossip from house to house, and the talk is always such a resonant clamoring; the women, bareheaded, or with a shawl folded over the head and caught beneath the chin with the hand, have such a contented down-at-heel aspect, shuffling from door to door, or lounging, arms akimbo, among the cats and poultry at their own thresholds, that one beholding it all might well fancy himself upon some Italian *calle* or *vicolo*. Of course the illusion does not hold good on a Sunday, when the Dubliners are coming home from church in their best, —their extraordinary best bonnets and their prodigious silk hats. It does not hold good in any way or at any time, except upon the surface, for there is beneath all this resemblance the difference that must exist between a race immemorially civilized and one which has lately emerged from barbarism "after six centuries of oppression." You are likely to find a polite pagan under the mask of the modern Italian; you feel pretty sure that any of his race would, with a little washing and skillful manipulation, *restore*, like a neglected painting, into something genuinely graceful and pleasing; but if one of these Yankee-fied Celts were scraped, it is but too possible that you might find a kern, a Whiteboy, or a Pikeman. The chance of discovering a scholar or a saint of the period when Ireland was the centre of learning, and the favorite seat of the Church, is scarcely one in three.

Among the houses fronting on the main street of Dublin, every other one—I speak in all moderation—is a grocery, if I may judge by a tin case of cornballs, a jar of candy, and a card of shirt-buttons, with an under layer of primers and ballads, in the windows. You descend from the street by several steps into these haunts, which are contrived to secure the greatest possible dampness and darkness; and if you have made an errand inside, you doubtless find a lady before the counter in the act of putting down a guilty-looking tumbler with one hand, while she neatly wipes her mouth on the back of the other. She has that effect, observable in all tippling women of low degree, of having no upper garment on but a shawl, which hangs about her in statuesque folds and lines. She slinks out directly, but the lady behind the counter gives you good evening with

"The affectation of a bright-eyed ease,"

intended to deceive if you chance to be a State constable in disguise, and to propitiate if you are a veritable customer: "Who was that woman, lamenting so, over in the grave-yard?" "O, I don't know, sir," answered the lady, making change for the price of a ballad. "Some Irish folks. They ginerally cries that way."

In yet earlier spring walks through Dublin, I found a depth of mud appalling even to one who had lived three years in Charlesbridge. The streets were passable only to pedestrians skilled in shifting themselves along the sides of fences and alert to take advantage of every projecting doorstep. There were no dry places, except in front of the groceries, where the ground was beaten hard by the broad feet of loafing geese and the coming and going of admirably small children making purchases there. The number of the little ones was quite as remarkable as their size, and ought to have been even more interesting, if, as sometimes appears probable, such increase shall—together with the well-known ambition of Dubliners to rule the land—one day make an end of us poor Yankees as a dominant plurality.

The town was somewhat tainted with our architectural respectability, unless the newness of some of the buildings gave illusion of this; and, though the streets of Dublin were not at all cared for, and though every house on the main thoroughfare stood upon the brink of a slough, without yard, or any attempt at garden or shrubbery, there were many cottages in the less aristocratic quarters inclosed in palings, and embowered in the usual suburban pear–trees and currant-bushes. These, indeed, were dwellings of an elder sort, and had clearly been inherited from a population now as extinct in that region as the Pequots, and they were not always carefully cherished. On the border of the hamlet is to be seen an old farm-house of the poorer sort, built about the beginning of this century, and now thickly peopled by Dubliners. Its gate is thrown down, and the great wild-grown lilac hedge, no longer protected by a fence, shows skirts bedabbled by the familiarity of lawless poultry, as little like the steady-habited poultry of other times, as the people of the house are like the former inmates, long since dead or gone West. I offer the poor place a sentiment of regret as I pass, thinking of its better days. I think of its decorous, hard-working, cleanly, school-going, church-attending life, which was full of the pleasure of duty done, and was not without its own quaint beauty and grace. What long Sabbaths were kept in that old house, what scanty holidays! Yet from this and such as this came the dominion of the whole wild continent, the freedom of a race, the greatness of the greatest people. It may be that I regretted a little too exultantly, and that out of this particular house came only peddling of innumerable clocks and multitudinous tin-ware. But as yet, it is pretty certain that the general character of the population has not gained by the change. What is in the future, let the prophets say; any one can see that something not quite agreeable is in the present; something that takes the wrong side, as by instinct, in politics; something that mainly helps to prop up tottering priestcraft among us; something that one thinks of with dismay as destined to control so largely the civil and religious interests of the country. This, however, is only the aggregate aspect. Mrs. Clannahan's kitchen, as it may be seen by the desperate philosopher when he goes to engage her for the spring house-cleaning, is a strong argument against his fears. If Mrs. Clannahan, lately of an Irish cabin, can show a kitchen so capably appointed and so neatly kept as that, the country may yet be an inch or two from the brink of ruin, and the race which we trust as little as we love may turn out no more spendthrift than most heirs. It is encouraging, moreover, when any people can flatter themselves upon a superior prosperity and virtue, and we may take heart from the fact that the French Canadians, many of whom have lodgings in Dublin, are not well seen by the higher classes of the citizens there. Mrs. Clannahan, whose house stands over against the main gate of the grave-yard, and who may, therefore, be considered as moving in the best Dublin society, hints, that though good Catholics, the French are not thought perfectly honest,—"things have been missed" since they came to blight with their crimes and vices the once happy seat of integrity. It is amusing to find Dublin fearful of the encroachment of the French, as we, in our turn, dread the advance of the Irish. We must make a jest of our own alarms, and even smile—since we cannot help ourselves—at the spiritual desolation occasioned by the settlement of an Irish family in one of our suburban neighborhoods. The householders view with fear and jealousy the erection of any dwelling of less than a stated cost, as portending a possible advent of Irish; and when the calamitous race actually appears, a mortal pang strikes to the bottom of every pocket. Values tremble throughout that neighborhood, to which the new-comers communicate a species of moral dry-rot. None but the Irish will build near the Irish; and the infection of fear spreads to the elder Yankee homes about, and the owners prepare to abandon them,—not always, however, let us hope, without turning, at the expense of the invaders, a Parthian penny in their flight. In my walk from Dublin to North Charlesbridge, I saw more than one token of the encroachment of the Celtic army, which had here and there invested a Yankee house with besieging shanties on every side, and thus given to its essential and otherwise quite hopeless ugliness a touch of the poetry that attends failing fortunes, and hallows decayed gentility of however poor a sort originally. The fortunes of such a house are, of course, not to be retrieved. Where the Celt sets his foot, there the Yankee (and it is perhaps wholesome if not agreeable to know that the Irish citizen whom we do not always honor as our equal in civilization loves to speak of us scornfully as Yankees) rarely, if ever, returns. The place remains to the intruder and his heirs forever. We gracefully retire before him even in politics, as the metropolis—if it is the metropolis—can witness; and we wait with an anxious curiosity the encounter of the Irish and the Chinese, now rapidly approaching each other from opposite shores of the continent. Shall we be crushed in the collision of these superior races? Every intelligence-office will soon be ringing with the cries of combat, and all our kitchens strewn with pig-tails and bark chignons. As yet we have gay hopes of our Buddhistic brethren; but how will it be when they begin to quarter the Dragon upon the Stars and Stripes, and buy up all the best sites for temples, and burn their joss-sticks, as it were, under our very noses? . . .

MEMORIES OF AN OHIO BOYHOOD

... The Smith-house neighborhood was a famous place ... both because there were lots of boys, and because there were so many sheds and stables where you could hide, and everything. There was a town-pump there for you, so that you would not have to go into the house for a drink when you got thirsty, and perhaps be set to doing something; and there were plenty of boards for teeter and see-saw; and somehow that neighborhood seemed to understand boys, and did not molest them in any way. In a vacant lot behind one of the houses there was a whirligig, that you could ride on and get sick in about a minute; it was splendid. There was a family of German boys living across the street, that you could stone whenever they came out of their front gate, for the simple and sufficient reason that they were Dutchmen, and without going to the trouble of a quarrel with them ....

o   o   o   o   o

Besides the town-drunkards there were other persons in whom the boys were interested, like the two or three dandies, whom their splendor in dress had given a public importance in a community of carelessly dressed men. Then there were certain genteel loafers, young men of good families, who hung about the principal hotel, and whom the boys believed to be fighters of singular prowess. Far below these in the social scale, the boys had yet other heroes, such as the Dumb Negro and his family. Between these and the white people, among whom the boys knew of no distinctions, they were aware that there was an impassable gulf; and it would not be easy to give a notion of just the sort of consideration in which they held them. But they held the Dumb Negro himself in almost superstitious regard as one who, though a deaf-mute, knew everything that was going on, and could make you understand anything he wished. He was, in fact, a master of most eloquent pantomime; he had gestures

172

that could not be mistaken, and he had a graphic dumb-show for persons and occupations and experiences that was delightfully vivid. For a dentist, he gave an upward twist of the hand from his jaw, and uttered a howl which left no doubt that he meant tooth-pulling; and for what would happen to a boy if he kept on misbehaving, he crossed his fingers before his face and looked through them in a way that brought the jail-window clearly before the eyes of the offender.

The boys knew vaguely that his family helped runaway slaves on their way North, and in a community that was for the most part bitterly pro-slavery these negroes were held in a sort of respect for their courageous fidelity to their race. The men were swarthy, handsome fellows, not much darker than Spaniards, and they were so little afraid of the chances which were often such fatal mischances to colored people in that day that one of them travelled through the South, and passed himself in very good company as a Cherokee Indian of rank and education.

SUGGESTED ADDITIONAL READINGS

Annie Kilburn
A Hazard of New Fortunes
An Imperative Duty
"The Albany Depot"
"Out of the Question"

SELECTED REFERENCES

Amacher, Anne Ward. "The Genteel Primitivist and the Semi-Tragic Octoroon." *New England Quarterly,* 29 (1956), 216–27.

Becker, H. G. "William Dean Howells: The Awakening Social Conscience." *College English,* 19 (1958), 283–91.

Belcher, H. G. "Howells's Opinions on the Religious Conflicts of His Age as Exhibited in Magazine Articles." *American Literature,* 15 (1943), 262–78.

Cecil, L. Moffitt. "William Dean Howells and the South." *Mississippi Quarterly,* 20 (1966), 13–24.

Ford, Thomas W. "Howells and the American Negro." *Texas Studies in Literature and Language,* 5 (1964), 530–37.

Hough, Robert L. *The Quiet Rebel: William Dean Howells as a Social Commentator* (1959).

Inge, W. Thomas. "William Dean Howells on Southern Literature." *Mississippi Quarterly,* 21 (1968), 291–304.

Kirk, Clara and Rudolf. "William Dean Howells, George William Curtis, and the 'Haymarket Affair.'" *American Literature,* 40 (1969), 487–98.

Parks, E. W. "A Realist Avoids Reality: W. D. Howells and the Civil War Years." *South Atlantic Quarterly,* 52 (1953), 93–97.

Stronks, J. B. "Paul Laurence Dunbar and William Dean Howells." *Ohio Historical Quarterly,* 67 (1958), 95–108.

Turaj, Frank. "The Social Gospel in Howells' Novels." *South Atlantic Quarterly,* 66 (1967), 449–64.

PROJECTS AND PROBLEMS

Did Howells's boyhood in an Ohio town prepare him to deal generously with members of minority groups? See *A Boy's Town.*

Compare the treatment of miscegenation and the "tragic octoroon" in *An Imperative Duty* with that in George W. Cable's *Madame Delphine.*

In "A Romance of Real Life" one character says that mistreating Dutch, Spaniards, Chinese, and Portuguese "ain't like abusing a white man." In other works of fiction some of Howells's characters speak disparagingly of various racial and national groups. Do these characters speak for Howells? Do they express his opinions about some minorities but not about others?

Compare Longfellow's *Poems on Slavery* with Howells's "The Pilot's story," reprinted in *William Dean Howells, Representative Selections* (1961), ed. by Clara Marburg Kirk and Rudolph Kirk.

Compose a list of individual blacks about whom Howells wrote comments. Note his remarks about Harriet Tubman in "The Smiling Aspects of American Life" (in *Criticism and Fiction*), his evaluation of Charles W. Chesnutt's stories in *Atlantic Monthly* for May, 1900, and his words on William Stanley Braithwaite in the December,

1917, *Harper's*. Was W. E. B. Du Bois correct in calling him "a friend of the Colored Man" in the Boston *Evening Transcript*, February 24, 1912?

The serial version of *The Rise of Silas Lapham* in *Century Magazine* in 1884 included allusions to the impact on property values when Jews moved into Boston neighborhoods. Howells was induced to delete this material from the book version of his novel. Was he less sympathetic in his treatment of Jews and the Irish than of blacks? Consider his critical reaction to the ghetto fiction of Stephen Crane and Abraham Cahan, and see his portrait of the Lower East Side, "An East Side Ramble," in his *Impressions and Experiences* (1896).

The role of the loyal retainer at a New England mountain resort described in *The Landlord at Lion's Head* (1896) is held by Jombateeste, a French Canadian, who later finds work in a Cambridge brickyard. Explain the hero's uncertainty late in the novel about his ability to pick out Jombateeste "among all those Canucks."

MARK TWAIN
(Samuel L. Clemens)
(1835–1910)

Mark Twain's lifelong concern for man's inhumanity to man made him especially sensitive to the plight of minorities at home and abroad, and much of his writing includes minority characters or treats their problems and circumstances. A talented journalist who rose to fame as practitioner of the tall tale and southwestern humor, he was still thought of as merely a humorist when he wrote the chapter about the Chinese in Virginia City, Nevada, that appeared in *Roughing It,* the amusing account of his western years that was published in 1872.

"A True Story Repeated Word for Word as I Heard It," his first contribution to the prestigious *Atlantic Monthly* (November, 1874), helped to transform him from a popular writer to a serious author. The underlying misanthropic spirit of much of his work, apparent in "Disgraceful Persecution of a Boy," published in *Sketches New and Old* in 1875, was to increase as the years passed.

The short scene featuring Jim, one of the outstanding characters in American literature, is from *Adventures of Huckleberry Finn* (1885). That novel is Twain's masterpiece, an acknowledged world classic. His many portrayals of life in the Missouri town of his boyhood and on the Mississippi River in the great steamboat days before the Civil War are among the triumphs of American writing.

A colorful public figure whose career often seemed to epitomize American values, Mark Twain became a legend in his own time.

THE GENTLE, INOFFENSIVE CHINESE

Of course there was a large Chinese population in Virginia—it is the case with every town and city on the Pacific coast. They are a harmless race when white men either let them alone or treat them no worse than dogs; in fact, they are almost entirely harmless anyhow, for they seldom think of resenting the vilest insults or the cruelest injuries. They are quiet, peaceable, tractable, free from drunkenness, and they are as industrious as the day is long. A disorderly Chinaman is rare, and a lazy one does not exist. So long as a Chinaman has strength to use his hands he needs no support from anybody; white men often complain of want of work, but a Chinaman offers no such complaint; he always manages to find something to do. He is a great convenience to everybody—even to the worst class of white men, for he bears the most of their sins, suffering fines for their petty thefts, imprisonment for their robberies, and death for their murders. Any white man can swear a Chinaman's life away in the courts, but no Chinaman can testify against a white man. Ours is the "land of the free"—nobody denies that—nobody challenges it. [Maybe it is because we won't let other people testify.][1] As I write, news comes that in broad daylight in San Francisco, some boys have stoned an inoffensive Chinaman to death, and that although a large crowd witnessed the shameful deed, no one interfered.

There are seventy thousand (and possibly one hundred thousand) Chinamen on the Pacific coast. There were about a thousand in Virginia. They were penned into a "Chinese quarter"—a thing which they do not particularly object to, as they are fond of herding together. Their buildings were of wood; usually only one story high, and set thickly together along streets scarcely wide enough for a wagon to pass through. Their quarter was a little removed from the rest of the town. The chief employment of Chinamen in towns is to wash clothing. They always send a bill pinned to the clothes. It is mere ceremony, for it does not enlighten the customer much. Their

[1]Twain's brackets.

price for washing was $2.50 per dozen—rather cheaper than white people could afford to wash for at that time. A very common sign on the Chinese houses was: "See Yup, Washer and Ironer"; "Hong Wo, Washer"; "Sam Sing & Ah Hop, Washing." The house-servants, cooks, etc., in California and Nevada, were chiefly Chinamen. There were few white servants and no Chinawomen so employed. Chinamen make good house-servants, being quick, obedient, patient, quick to learn, and tirelessly industrious. They do not need to be taught a thing twice, as a general thing. They are imitative. If a Chinaman were to see his master break up a center-table, in a passion, and kindle a fire with it, that Chinaman would be likely to resort to the furniture for fuel forever afterward.

All Chinamen can read, write, and cipher with easy facility—pity but all our petted *voters* could. In California they rent little patches of ground and do a deal of gardening. They will raise surprising crops of vegetables on a sand-pile. They waste nothing. What is rubbish to a Christian, a Chinaman carefully preserves and makes useful in one way or another. He gathers up all the old oyster and sardine cans that white people throw away, and procures marketable tin and solder from them by melting. He gathers up old bones and turns them into manure. In California he gets a living out of old mining claims that white men have abandoned as exhausted and worthless—and then the officers come down on him once a month with an exorbitant swindle to which the legislature has given the broad, general name of "foreign" mining tax, but it is usually inflicted on no foreigners but Chinamen. This swindle has in some cases been repeated once or twice on the same victim in the course of the same month—but the public treasury was not additionally enriched by it, probably.

Chinamen hold their dead in great reverence—they worship their departed ancestors, in fact. Hence, in China, a man's front yard, back yard, or any other part of his premises, is made his family burying–ground, in order that he may visit the graves at any and all times. Therefore that huge empire is one mighty cemetery; it is ridged and wrinkled from its center to its circumference with graves —and inasmuch as every foot of ground must be made to do its utmost, in China, lest the swarming population suffer for food, the very graves are cultivated and yield a harvest, custom holding this to

be no dishonor to the dead. Since the departed are held in such wor-
shipful reverence, a Chinaman cannot bear that any indignity be offered the places where they sleep. Mr. Burlingame said that herein
lay China's bitter opposition to railroads; a road could not be built
anywhere in the empire without disturbing the graves of their ancestors or friends.

A Chinaman hardly believes he could enjoy the hereafter except
his body lay in his beloved China; also, he desires to receive, himself, after death, that worship with which he has honored his dead
that preceded him. Therefore, if he visits a foreign country, he
makes arrangements to have his bones returned to China in case he
dies; if he hires to go to a foreign country on a labor contract, there
is always a stipulation that his body shall be taken back to China if
he dies; if the government sells a gang of coolies to a foreigner for
the usual five-year term, it is specified in the contract that their
bodies shall be restored to China in case of death. On the Pacific
coast the Chinamen all belong to one or another of several great
companies or organizations, and these companies keep track of their
members, register their names, and ship their bodies home when
they die. The See Yup Company is held to be the largest of these.
The Ning Yeong Company is next, and numbers eighteen thousand
members on the coast. Its headquarters are at San Francisco, where
it has a costly temple, several great officers (one of whom keeps
regal state in seclusion and cannot be approached by common humanity), and a numerous priesthood. In it I was shown a register of
its members, with the dead and the date of their shipment to China
duly marked. Every ship that sails from San Francisco carries away a
heavy freight of Chinese corpses—or did, at least, until the legislature, with an ingenious refinement of Christian cruelty, forbade the
shipments, as a neat underhanded way of deterring Chinese immigration. The bill was offered, whether it passed or not. It is my
impression that it passed. There was another bill—it became a law—
compelling every incoming Chinaman to be vaccinated on the wharf
and pay a duly-appointed quack (no decent doctor would defile himself with such legalized robbery) ten dollars for it. As few importers
of Chinese would want to go to an expense like that, the lawmakers
thought this would be another heavy blow to Chinese immigration.

What the Chinese quarter of Virginia was like—or, indeed, what

the Chinese quarter of any Pacific coast town was and is like—may
be gathered from this item which I printed in the *Enterprise* while
reporting for that paper:

CHINATOWN.—Accompanied by a fellow-reporter, we made a
trip through our Chinese quarter the other night. The Chinese have built their portion of the city to suit themselves;
and as they keep neither carriages nor wagons, their streets
are not wide enough, as a general thing, to admit the passage
of vehicles. At ten o'clock at night the Chinaman may be
seen in all his glory. In every little cooped-up, dingy cavern
of a hut, faint with the odor of burning Josh-lights and with
nothing to see the gloom by save the sickly, guttering tallow
candle, were two or three yellow, long-tailed vagabonds,
coiled up on a sort of short truckle-bed, smoking opium, motionless and with their lusterless eyes turned inward from ex-
cess of satisfaction— or rather the recent smoker looks thus,
immediately after having passed the pipe to his neighbor—
for opium-smoking is a comfortless operation, and requires
constant attention. A lamp sits on the bed, the length of the
long pipe-stem from the smoker's mouth; he puts a pellet of
opium on the end of a wire, sets it on fire, and plasters it into
the pipe much as a Christian would fill a hole with putty;
then he applies the bowl to the lamp and proceeds to smoke
—and the stewing and frying of the drug and the gurgling of
the juices in the stem would well-nigh turn the stomach of a
statue. John likes it, though; it soothes him; he takes about
two dozen whiffs, and then rolls over to dream, Heaven only
knows what, for we could not imagine by looking at the
soggy creature. Possibly in his visions he travels far away
from the gross world and his regular washing, and feasts on
succulent rats and birds'-nests in Paradise.

Mr. Ah Sing keeps a general grocery and provision store at
No. 13 Wang Street. He lavished his hospitality upon our
party in the friendliest way. He had various kinds of colored
and colorless wines and brandies, with unpronounceable
names, imported from China in little crockery jugs, and
which he offered to us in dainty little miniature wash-basins
of porcelain. He offered us a mess of birds'-nests; also, small,
neat sausages, of which we could have swallowed several
yards if we had chosen to try, but we suspected that each link
contained the corpse of a mouse, and therefore refrained. Mr.

Sing had in his store a thousand articles of merchandise, curious to behold, impossible to imagine the uses of, and beyond our ability to describe.

His ducks, however, and his eggs, we could understand; the former were split open and flattened out like codfish, and came from China in that shape, and the latter were plastered over with some kind of paste which kept them fresh and palatable through the long voyage.

We found Mr. Hong Wo, No. 37 Chow-chow Street, making up a lottery scheme—in fact, we found a dozen others occupied in the same way in various parts of the quarter, for about every third Chinaman runs a lottery, and the balance of the tribe "buck" at it. "Tom," who speaks faultless English, and used to be chief and only cook to the *Territorial Enterprise,* when the establishment kept bachelor's hall two years ago, said that "Sometime Chinaman buy ticket one dollar hap, ketch um two tree hundred, sometime no ketch um anyting; lottery like one man fight um seventy—maybe he whip, maybe he get whip heself, welly good." However, the percentage being sixty-nine against him, the chances are, as a general thing, that "he get whip heself." We could not see that these lotteries differed in any respect from our own, save that the figures being Chinese, no ignorant white man might ever hope to succeed in telling "t'other from which"; the manner of drawing is similar to ours.

Mr. See Yup keeps a fancy store on Live Fox Street. He sold us fans of white feathers, gorgeously ornamented; perfumery that smelled like Limburger cheese, Chinese pens, and watch-charms made of a stone unscratchable with steel instruments, yet polished and tinted like the inner coat of a sea-shell.[1] As tokens of his esteem, See Yup presented the party with gaudy plumes made of gold tinsel and trimmed with peacocks' feathers.

We ate chow-chow with chop-sticks in the celestial restaurants; our comrade chided the moon-eyed damsels in front of the houses for their want of feminine reserve; we received protecting Josh-lights from our hosts and "dickered" for a pagan god or two. Finally, we were impressed with the ge-

[1] A peculiar species of the "jade-stone"—to a Chinaman peculiarly precious. [Twain's note.]

nius of a Chinese bookkeeper; he figured up his accounts on a machine like a gridiron with buttons strung on its bars; the different rows represented units, tens, hundreds, and thousands. He fingered them with incredible rapidity—in fact, he pushed them from place to place as fast as a musical professor's fingers travel over the keys of a piano."

They are a kindly-disposed, well-meaning race, and are respected and well treated by the upper classes, all over the Pacific coast. No Californian *gentleman* or *lady* ever abuses or oppresses a Chinaman, under any circumstances, an explanation that seems to be much needed in the East. Only the scum of the population do it—they and their children; they, naturally and consistently, the policemen and politicians, likewise, for these are the dust-licking pimps and slaves of the scum, there as well as elsewhere in America.

A TRUE STORY REPEATED WORD FOR WORD AS I HEARD IT

It was summer-time, and twilight. We were sitting on the porch of the farmhouse, on the summit of the hill, and "Aunt Rachel" was sitting respectfully below our level, on the steps—for she was our servant, and colored. She was of mighty frame and stature; she was sixty years old, but her eye was undimmed and her strength unabated. She was a cheerful, hearty soul, and it was no more trouble for her to laugh than it is for a bird to sing. She was under fire now, as usual when the day was done. That is to say, she was being chaffed without mercy, and was enjoying it. She would let off peal after peal of laughter, and then sit with her face in her hands and shake with throes of enjoyment which she could no longer get breath enough to express. At such a moment as this a thought occurred to me, and I said:

"Aunt Rachel, how is it that you've lived sixty years and never had any trouble?"

She stopped quaking. She paused, and there was a moment of silence. She turned her face over her shoulder toward me, and said, without even a smile in her voice:

"Misto C——, is you in 'arnest?"

It surprised me a good deal; and it sobered my manner and my speech, too. I said:

"Why, I thought—that is, I meant—why, you *can't* have had any trouble. I've never heard you sigh, and never seen your eye when there wasn't a laugh in it."

She faced fairly around now, and was full of earnestness.

"Has I had any trouble? Misto C——, I's gwyne to tell you, den I leave it to you. I was bawn down 'mongst de slaves; I knows all 'bout slavery, 'case I ben one of 'em my own se'f. Well, sah, my ole man—dat's my husban'—he was lovin' an' kind to me, jist as kind as you is to yo' own wife. An' we had chil'en—seven chil'en—an' we loved dem chil'en jist de same as you loves yo' chil'en. Dey was black, but de Lord can't make no chil'en so black but what dey mother loves 'em an' wouldn't give 'em up, no, not for anything dat's in dis whole world.

"Well, sah, I was raised in ole Fo'ginny, but my mother she was raised in Maryland; an' my *souls!* she was turrible when she'd git started! My *lan'!* but she'd make de fur fly! When she'd git into dem tantrums, she always had one word dat she said. She'd straighten herse'f up an' put her fists in her hips an' say, 'I want you to understan' dat I wa'n't bawn in the mash to be fool' by trash! I's one o' de ole Blue Hen's Chickens, *I* is!' 'Ca'se, you see, dat's what folks dat's bawn in Maryland calls deyselves, an' dey's proud of it. Well, dat was her word. I don't ever forgit it, beca'se she said it so much, an' beca'se she said it one day when my little Henry tore his wris' awful, and most busted his head, right up at de top of his forehead, an' de niggers didn't fly aroun' fas' enough to 'tend to him. An' when dey talk' back at her, she up an' she says, 'Look-a-heah!' she says, 'I want you niggers to understan' dat I wa'n't bawn in de mash to be fool' by trash! I's one o' de ole Blue Hen's Chickens, *I* is!' an' den she clar' dat kitchen an' bandage' up de chile herse'f. So I says dat word, too, when I's riled.

"Well, bymeby my ole mistis say she's broke, an' she got to sell all de niggers on de place. An' when I heah dat dey gwyne to sell us all off at oction in Richmon', oh, de good gracious! I know what dat mean!"

Aunt Rachel had gradually risen, while she warmed to her subject, and now she towered above us, black against the stars.

"Dey put chains on us an' put us on a stan' as high as dis po'ch—twenty foot high—an' all de people stood aroun', crowds an' crowds. An' dey'd come up dah an' look at us all roun', an' squeeze our arm, an' make us git up an' walk, an' den say, 'Dis one too ole,' or 'Dis one lame,' or 'Dis one don't 'mount to much.' An' dey sole my ole man, an' took him away, an' dey begin to sell my chil'en an' take *dem* away, an' I begin to cry; an' de man say, 'Shet up yo' damn blubberin',' an' hit me on de mouf wid his han'. An' when de las' one was gone but my little Henry, I grab' *him* clost up to my breas' so, an' I ris up an' says, 'You sha'n't take him away,' I says; 'I'll kill de man dat tetches him!' I says. But my little Henry whisper an' say, 'I gwyne to run away, an' den I work an' buy yo' freedom.' Oh, bless de chile, he always so good! But dey got him—dey got him, de men did;

but I took and tear de clo'es mos' off of 'em an' beat 'em over de head wid my chain; an' *dey* give it to *me*, too, but I didn't mine dat.

"Well, dah was my ole man gone, an' all my chil'en, all my seven chil'en—an' six of 'em I hain't set eyes on ag'in to dis day, an' dat's twenty-two year ago las' Easter. De man dat bought me b'long' in Newbern, an' he took me dah. Well, bymeby de years roll on an' de waw come. My marster he was a Confedrit colonel, an' I was his family's cook. So when de Unions took dat town, dey all run away an' lef' me all by myse'f wid de other niggers in dat mons'us big house. So de big Union officers move in dah, an' dey ask me would I cook for *dem*. 'Lord bless you,' says I, 'dat's what I's *for.*'

"Dey wa'n't no small-fry officers, mine you, dey was de biggest dey *is;* an' de way dey made dem sojers mosey roun'! De Gen'l he tole me to boss dat kitchen; an' he say, 'If anybody come meddlin' wid you, you jist make 'em walk chalk; don't you be afeared,' he say; 'you's 'mong frens now.'

"Well, I thinks to myse'f, if my little Henry ever got a chance to run away, he'd make to de Norf, o' course. So one day I comes in dah whar de big officers was, in de parlor, an' I drops a kurtchy, so, an' I up an' tole 'em 'bout my Henry, dey a-listenin' to my troubles jist de same as if I was white folks; an' I says, 'What I come for is beca'se if he got away and got up Norf whar you gemmen comes from, you might 'a' seen him, maybe, an' could tell me so as I could fine him ag'in; he was very little, an' he had a sk-yar on his lef' wris' an' at de top of his forehead,' Den dey look mournful, an' de Gen'l says, 'How long sence you los' him?' an' I say, 'Thirteen year.' Den de Gen'l say, 'He wouldn't be little no mo' now—he's a man!'

"I never thought o' dat befo'! He was only dat little feller to *me* yit. I never thought 'bout him growin' up an' bein' big. But I see it den. None o' de gemmen had run acrost him, so dey couldn't do nothin' for me. But all dat time, do' *I* didn't know it, my Henry *was* run off to de Norf, years an' years, an' he was a barber, too, an' worked for hisse'f. An' bymeby, when de waw come he ups an' he says: 'I's done barberin',' he says, 'I's gwyne to fine my ole mammy, less'n she's dead.' So he sole out an' went to whar dey was recruitin', an' hired hisse'f out to de colonel for his servant; an' den he went all froo de battles everywhah, huntin' for his ole mammy; yes, indeedy, he'd hire to fust one officer an' den another, tell he'd ransacked de whole Souf; but you see *I* didn't know nuffin 'bout *dis*. How was *I* gwyne to know it?

"Well, one night we had a big sojer ball; de sojers dah at Newbern was always havin' balls an' carryin' on. Dey had 'em in my kitchen, heaps o' times, 'ca'se it was so big. Mine you, I was *down* on sich doin's; beca'se my place was wid de officers, an' it rasp me to have dem common sojers cavortin' roun' my kitchen like dat. But I alway' stood aroun' an' kep' things straight, I did; an' sometimes dey'd git my dander up, an' den I'd make 'em clar dat kitchen, mine I *tell* you!

"Well, one night—it was a Friday night—dey comes a whole platoon f'm a *nigger* ridgment dat was on guard at de house—de house was headquarters, you know—an' den I was jist a-*bilin'*! Mad? I was jist a-*boomin'*! I swelled aroun', an' swelled aroun'; I jist was a-itchin' for 'em to do somefin for to start me. *An'* dey was a-waltzin' an' a-dancin'! *my!* but dey was havin' a time! an' I jist a-swellin' an' a-swellin' up! Pooty soon, 'long comes *sich* a spruce young nigger a-sailin' down de room wid a yaller wench roun' de wais'; an' roun' an' roun' an' roun' dey went, enough to make a body drunk to look at 'em; an' when dey got abreas' o' me, dey went to kin' o' balacin' aroun' fust on one leg an' den on t'other, an' smilin' at my big red turban, an' makin' fun, an' I ups an' says '*Git* along wid you!—rubbage!' De young man's face kin' o' changed, all of a sudden, for 'bout a second, but den he went to smilin' ag'in, same as he was befo'. Well, 'bout dis time, in comes some niggers dat played music and b'long' to de ban', an' dey *never* could git along widout puttin' on airs. An' de very fust air dey put on dat night, I lit into 'em! Dey laughed, an' dat made me wuss. De res' o' de niggers got to laughin', an' den my soul *alive* but I was hot! My eye was jist a-blazin'! I jist straightened myself up so—jist as I is now, plum to de ceilin', mos'— an' I digs my fists into my hips, an' I says, 'Look-a-heah!' I says, 'I want you niggers to understan' dat I wa'n't bawn in de mash to be fool' by trash! I's one o' de ole Blue Hen's Chickens, *I* is!' an' den I see dat young man stan' a-starin' an' stiff, lookin' kin' o' up at de ceilin' like he fo'got somefin, an' couldn't 'member it no mo'. Well, I jist march' on dem niggers—so, lookin' like a gen'l—an' dey jist cave' away befo' me an' out at de do'. An' as dis young man was a-goin' out, I heah him say to another nigger, 'Jim,' he says, 'you go

'long an' tell de cap'n I be on han' 'bout eight o'clock in de mawnin';
dey's somefin on my mine,' he says; 'I don't sleep no mo' dis night.
You go 'long,' he says, 'an' leave me by my own se'f.'

"Dis was 'bout one o'clock in de mawnin'. Well, 'bout seven, I
was up an' on han', gittin' de officers' breakfast. I was a-stoopin'
down by de stove—jist so, same as if yo' foot was de stove—an' I'd
opened de stove do' wid my right han'—so, pushin' it back, jist as I
pushes yo' foot—an' I'd jist got de pan o' hot biscuits in my han' an'
was 'bout to raise up, when I see a black face come aroun' under
mine, an' de eyes a-lookin' up into mine, jist as I's a-lookin' up clost
under yo' face now; an' I jist stopped *right dah*, an' never budged!
jist gazed an' gazed so; an' de pan begin to tremble, an' all of a sudden I *knowed!* De pan drop' on de flo' an' I grab his lef' han' an'
shove back his sleeve—jist so, as I's doin' to you—an' den I goes for
his forehead an' push de hair back so, an' 'Boy!' I says, 'if you an't my
Henry, what is you doin' wid dis welt on yo' wris' an' dat sk-yar on
yo' forehead? De Lord God ob heaven be praise', I got my own
ag'in!'

"Oh no, Misto C-----, *I* hain't had no trouble. An' no *joy!*"

DISGRACEFUL
PERSECUTION OF A BOY

In San Francisco, the other day, "A well-dressed boy, on his way to Sunday-school, was arrested and thrown into the city prison for stoning Chinamen."

What a commentary is this upon human justice! What sad prominence it gives to our human disposition to tyrannize over the weak! San Francisco has little right to take credit to herself for her treatment of this poor boy. What had the child's education been? How should he suppose it was wrong to stone a Chinaman? Before we side against him, along with outraged San Francisco, let us give him a chance—let us hear the testimony for the defense.

He was a "well-dressed" boy, and a Sunday-school scholar, and therefore the chances are that his parents were intelligent, well-to-do people, with just enough natural villainy in their composition to make them yearn after the daily papers, and enjoy them; and so this boy had opportunities to learn all through the week how to do right, as well as on Sunday.

It was in this way that he found out that the great commonwealth of California imposes an unlawful mining-tax upon John the foreigner, and allows Patrick the foreigner to dig gold for nothing—probably because the degraded Mongol is at no expense for whiskey, and the refined Celt cannot exist without it.

It was in this way that he found out that a respectable number of the taxgatherers—it would be unkind to say all of them—collect the tax twice, instead of once; and that, inasmuch as they do it solely to discourage Chinese immigration into the mines, it is a thing that is much applauded, and likewise regarded as being singularly facetious.

It was in this way that he found out that when a white man robs a sluice-box (by the term white man is meant Spaniards, Mexicans, Portuguese, Irish, Hondurans, Peruvians, Chileans, etc., etc.), they make him leave the camp; and when a Chinaman does that thing, they hang him.

It was in this way that he found out that in many districts of the

188

vast Pacific coast, so strong is the wild, free love of justice in the
hearts of the people, that whenever any secret and mysterious crime
is committed, they say, "Let justice be done, though the heavens
fall," and go straightway and swing a Chinaman.

It was in this way that he found out that by studying one-half of
each day's "local items," it would appear that the police of San
Francisco were either asleep or dead, and by studying the other half
it would seem that the reporters were gone mad with admiration of
the energy, the virtue, the high effectiveness, and the dare-devil in-
trepidity of that very police—making exultant mention of how "the
Argus-eyed officer So-and-so," captured a wretched knave of a
Chinaman who was stealing chickens, and brought him gloriously to
the city prison; and how "the gallant officer Such-and-such-a-one,"
quietly kept an eye on the movements of an "unsuspecting, almond-
eyed son of Confucius" (your reporter is nothing if not facetious),
following him around with that far-off look of vacancy and uncon-
sciousness always so finely affected by that inscrutable being, the
forty-dollar policeman, during a waking interval, and captured him
at last in the very act of placing his hands in a suspicious manner
upon a paper of tacks, left by the owner in an exposed situation; and
how one officer performed this prodigious thing, and another officer
that, and another the other—and pretty much every one of these performances having for a dazzling central incident a Chinaman guilty
of a shilling's worth of crime, an unfortunate, whose misdemeanor
must be hurrahed into something enormous in order to keep the
public from noticing how many really important rascals went un-
captured in the meantime, and how overrated those glorified policemen actually are.

It was in this way that the boy found out that the legislature,
being aware that the Constitution has made America an asylum for
the poor and the oppressed of all nations, and that, therefore, the
poor and oppressed who fly to our shelter must not be charged a dis-
abling admission fee, made a law that every Chinaman, upon landing, must be *vaccinated* upon the wharf, and pay to the State's appointed officer *ten dollars* for the service, when there are plenty of
doctors in San Francisco who would be glad enough to do it for him
for fifty cents.

It was in this way that the boy found out that a Chinaman had no rights that any man was bound to respect; that he had no sorrows that any man was bound to pity; that neither his life nor his liberty was worth the purchase of a penny when a white man needed a scapegoat; that nobody loved Chinamen, nobody befriended them, nobody spared them suffering when it was convenient to inflict it; everybody, individuals, communities, the majesty of the State itself, joined in hating, abusing, and persecuting these humble strangers.

And, therefore, what *could* have been more natural than for this sunny-hearted boy, tripping along to Sunday-school, with his mind teeming with freshly-learned incentives to high and virtuous action, to say to himself:

"Ah, there goes a Chinaman! God will not love me if I do not stone him."

And for this he was arrested and put in the city jail.

Everything conspired to teach him that it was a high and holy thing to stone a Chinaman, and yet he no sooner attempts to do his duty than he is punished for it—he, poor chap, who has been aware all his life that one of the principal recreations of the police, out toward the Gold Refinery, is to look on with tranquil enjoyment while the butchers of Brannan Street set their dogs on unoffending Chinamen, and make them flee for their lives.[1]

Keeping in mind the tuition in the humanities which the entire "Pacific coast" gives its youth, there is a very sublimity of incongruity in the virtuous flourish with which the good city fathers of San Francisco proclaim (as they have lately done) that "The police are positively ordered to arrest all boys, of every description and wherever found, who engage in assaulting Chinamen."

Still, let us be truly glad they have made the order, notwithstanding its inconsistency; and let us rest perfectly confident the police are glad, too. Because there is no personal peril in arresting boys,

[1] I have many such memories in my mind, but am thinking just at present of one particular one, where the Brannan Street butchers set their dogs on a Chinaman who was quietly passing with a basket of clothes on his head; and while the dogs mutilated his flesh, a butcher increased the hilarity of the occasion by knocking some of the Chinaman's teeth down his throat with half a brick. This incident sticks in my memory with a more malevolent tenacity, perhaps, on account of the fact that I was in the employ of a San Franciso journal at the time, and was not allowed to publish it because it might offend some of the peculiar element that subscribed for the paper. [Twain's note.]

provided they be of the small kind, and the reporters will have to laud their performances just as loyally as ever, or go without items.

The new form for local items in San Francisco will now be: "The ever vigilant and efficient officer So-and-so succeeded, yesterday afternoon, in arresting Master Tommy Jones, after a determined resistance," etc., etc., followed by the customary statistics and final hurrah, with its unconscious sarcasm: "We are happy in being able to state that this is the forty-seventh boy arrested by this gallant officer since the new ordinance went into effect. The most extraordinary activity prevails in the police department. Nothing like it has been seen since we can remember."

A REMORSEFUL FATHER

I went to sleep, and Jim didn't call me when it was my turn. He often done that. When I waked up, just at day-break, he was setting there with his head down betwixt his knees, moaning and mourning to himself. I didn't take notice, nor let on. I knowed what it was about. He was thinking about his wife and his children, away up yonder, and he was low and homesick; because he hadn't ever been away from home before in his life; and I do believe he cared just as much for his people as white folks does for their'n. It don't seem natural, but I reckon it's so. He was often moaning and mourning that way, nights, when he judged I was asleep, and saying, "Po' little 'Lizabeth! po' little Johnny! its mighty hard; I spec' I ain't ever gwyne to see you no mo', no mo'!" He was a mighty good nigger, Jim was.

But this time I somehow got to talking to him about his wife and young ones; and by-and-by he says:

"What makes me feel so bad dis time, 'uz bekase I hear sumpn over yonder on de bank like a whack, er a slam, while ago, en it mine me er de time I treat my little 'Lizabeth so ornery. She warn't on'y 'bout fo' year ole, en she tuck de sk'yarlet-fever, en had a powful rough spell; but she got well, en one day she was a-stannin' aroun', en I says to her, I says:

" 'Shet de do'.'

"She never done it; jis' stood dah, kiner smilin' up at me. It make me mad; en I says agin, mighty loud, I says:

" 'Doan' you hear me?—shet de do'!'

"She jis' stood de same way, kiner smilin' up. I was a-bilin'! I says:

" 'I lay I *make* you mine!'

"En wid dat I fetch' her a slap side de head dat sont her a-sprawlin'. Den I went into de yuther room, en 'uz gone 'bout ten minutes; en when I come back, dah was dat do' a-stannin' open *yit*, en dat chile stannin' mos' right in it, a-lookin' down and mournin', en de tears runnin' down. My, but I *wuz* mad, I was agwyne for de child, but jis' den—it was a do' dat open innerds—jis' den, 'long come de wind en slam it to, behine de chile, ker-*blam!*—en my lan', de chile never move'! My breff mos' hop outer me; en I feel so—so— I

192

doan' know *how* I feel. I crope out, all a-tremblin', en crope aroun' en open de do' easy en slow, en poke my head in behine de chile, sof' en still, en all uv a sudden, I says *pow!* jis' as loud as I could yell. *She never budge!* Oh, Huck, I bust out a-cryin' en grab her up in my arms, en say, 'Oh, de po' little thing! de Lord God Amighty fogive po' ole Jim, kaze he never gwyne to fogive hisself as long's he live!' Oh, she was plumb deef en dumb, Huck, plumb deef en dumb—en I'd ben a-treat'n her so!"

SUGGESTED ADDITIONAL READINGS

"John Chinaman in New York"
"Goldsmith's Friend Abroad Again"
The Adventures of Tom Sawyer
"The Quarles Farm"
"The Noble Red Man"
The Tragedy of Pudd'nhead Wilson
"The Man That Corrupted Hadleyburg"
"Concerning the Jews"
"The United States of Lyncherdom"

SELECTED REFERENCES

Altenbernd, Lynn. "Huck Finn, Emancipator." *Criticism,* 1 (1959), 298–307.

Budd, Louis J. *Mark Twain: Social Philosopher* (1962).

———. "Twain, Howells, and the Boston Nihilists." *New England Quarterly,* 32 (1959), 351–71.

Butcher, Philip. "Mark Twain's Installment on the National Debt." *Southern Literary Journal,* 1, No. 2 (1969), 48–55.

———. "Mark Twain Sells Roxy Down the River." *CLA Journal,* 8 (1965), 225–33.

DeVoto, Bernard. "Mark Twain About the Jews." *Jewish Frontier,* 6 (1939), 7–9.

Fiedler, Leslie. " 'Come Back to the Raft Ag'in Huck Honey!' " *Partisan Review,* 15 (1948), 664–71.

194   THE MINORITY PRESENCE IN AMERICAN LITERATURE

Ford, Thomas W. "The Miscegenation Theme in Pudd'nhead Wilson." *Mark Twain Journal,* 10 (1955), 13–14.

Hansen, Chadwick. "The Character of Jim and the Ending of *Huckleberry Finn.*" *Massachusetts Review,* 5 (1963), 45–66.

Harris, Helen L. "Mark Twain's Response to the Native American." *American Literature,* 46 (1975), 495–505.

Hoffman, Daniel G. "Jim's Magic: Black or White?" *American Literature,* 32 (1960), 1–10.

Lorch, Fred W. "Mark Twain's Early Views on Western Indians." *Twainian,* 4 (1945), 1–2.

Mattson, J. Stanley. "Mark Twain on War and Peace: The Missouri Rebel and 'The Campaign That Failed.'" *American Quarterly,* 20 (1968), 783–94.

Sidnell, M. J. "Huck Finn and Jim: Their Abortive Freedom Ride." *Cambridge Quarterly,* 2 (1966), 203–11.

Stewart, Herbert L. "Mark Twain on the Jewish Problem." *Dalhousie Review,* 14 (1935), 455–58.

Tidwell, J. N. "Mark Twain's Representation of Negro Speech." *American Speech,* 17 (1942), 174–76.

Turner, Arlin. "Mark Twain and the South: An Affair of Love and Anger." *Southern Review,* 4 (1968), 493–519.

Wecter, Dixon. "Mark Twain and the West." *Huntington Library Quarterly,* 8 (1945), 359–77.

West, Victor Royse. "Folklore in the Works of Mark Twain." *Studies in Language, Literature, and Criticism,* 10 (1939), 1–87.

PROJECTS AND PROBLEMS-

Because some readers find it difficult to identify irony and to respond to some kinds of humor, *Adventures of Huckleberry Finn* is not always recognized as the "hymn to freedom" that it is. Study carefully the characterization of Jim and use this as a major support for the view that the novel is an attack both on slavery and on the racist practices and principles of the time when it was written.

Compare Twain's treatment of the Mormons in *Roughing It* with the attitude he offers toward Christian Scientists in *Christian Science.*

Study Twain's autobiographical works and compile an account of his relationship with individual blacks. Exclude prominent men such as Booker T. Washington and Frederick Douglass.

Discuss the theory that *A Connecticut Yankee in King Arthur's Court* is in part an expression of Twain's understanding of racism in America.

Compare Twain's picture of the Chinese with that of Bret Harte.

Twain's hostility toward the Indian found expression in his frequent use of derogatory stereotypes and references. What experiences in his life may account for this exception to his generally enlightened treatment of minorities?

Discuss Twain's treatment of octoroons in *Pudd'nhead Wilson,* "The Man That Corrupted Hadleyburg," and elsewhere. Does his work deviate from the stereotype?

In claiming an absence of discourteous references to Jews in his works, Twain wrote in *Harper's Magazine,* September, 1899, "I am quite sure that I have no race prejudices, and I think I have no color prejudices nor caste prejudices nor creed prejudices. . . . All that I care to know is that a man is a human being—that is enough for me; he can't be any worse." Does his major fiction confirm his claim or reveal that there were exceptions to his tolerance?

LAFCADIO HEARN
(1850–1904)

Of Irish-Greek parentage, Hearn was born in the Ionian Islands and educated in England and France. After he entered the United States in 1869 he worked as a journalist in Cincinnati and New Orleans and then spent two years in Martinique. After a brief stay in New York he spent the rest of his life in Japan. He married a Japanese, became a citizen, wrote books about his adopted country, and taught at the Imperial University. His contributions to American literature are in the local color tradition. The following selection is from an article Hearn published in the *Cincinnati Commercial* on August 22, 1875.

THE RACIAL MÉLANGE IN BUCKTOWN

... The inimity ordinarily concomitant with the admixture of race ceases to exist on the confines of Bucktown; whites and blacks are forced into a species of criminal fraternization; all are Ishmaels bound together by fate, by habit, by instinct, and by the iron law and never cooling hate of an outraged society. The harlot's bully, the pimp, the prostitute, the thief, the procuress, the highway robber,—white, tawny, brown and black—constitute the mass of the population. But there are two other classes—very small indeed, yet still well worth notice. The first is composed of those who have lost caste by miscegenation; the second, that of levee hands, who live in a state of concubinage with mistresses who remain faithful to them. Of the former class it is scarcely necessary to say that white women wholly compose it—women who have conceived strange attachments for black laborers, and live with them as mistresses; also, women who boast black pimps for their masters, and support them by prostitution. Of the other class referred to, we may observe that it constitutes but a part of the floating population of Bucktown, inasmuch as the levee hands and their women are the most honest portion of this extraordinary community. Consequently, they live there only because their poverty, not their will, consents, and whenever opportunity offers, they will seek quarters up town, in some alley building or tenement-house.

As the violation of nature's laws begets deformity and hideousness, and as the inhabitants of Bucktown are popularly supposed to be great violators of nature's laws, they are vulgarly supposed to be all homely, if not positively ugly or monstrously deformed. "A Bucktown hag," and "an ugly old Bucktown wench," are expressions commonly used in the narration by uninformed gossips of some Bucktown incident. This idea is, however, for the most part fallacious. The really hideous and deformed portion of the Bucktown population is confined to a few crippled or worn-out, honest ragpickers, and perhaps two or more ancient harlots, superannuated in their degrading profession, and compelled at last to resort to the

197

dumps for a living. The majority of the darker colored women are muscular, well-built people, who would have sold at high prices in a Southern slave market before the war; the lighter tinted are, in some instances, remarkably well favored; and among the white girls one occasionally meets with an attractive face, bearing traces of what must have been uncommon beauty. Gigantic negresses, stronger than men, whose immense stature and phenomenal muscularity bear strong witness to the old slave custom of human stock breeding; neatly built mulatto girls, with the supple, pantherish strength peculiar to half-breeds; slender octoroons, willowy and graceful of figure, with a good claim to the qualification pretty,—will all be found among the crowd of cotton-turbaned and ebon-visaged throng, who talk alike and think alike and all live and look alike. To a philosophical or even fair-minded observer the viciousness and harlotry of this class are less shocking than the sins of Sixth street, or even than the fashionable vice of Broadway; when it is considered how many of the former have been begotten in vice, reared in vice, know of none but vicious associations, have never been taught the commonest decencies of life, and are ignorant of the very rudiments of education.

Desiring to see the inner life of Bucktown the writer, some evenings since, accompanied a couple of police officers in the search for a female thief, who had been shortly before observed fleeing to this city of refuge. Bucktown by day is little more than a collection of shaky and soot-begrimed frames, blackened old brick dwellings, windowless and tenantless wooden cottages, all gathered about the great, mouse-colored building where the congregation of Allen Temple once worshipped, but which has long since been unused, as its score of shattered windows attests. But by night this odd district has its picturesque points. Bucktown is nothing if not seen by gaslight. Then it presents a most striking effect of fantastic *chiar'-oscuro;* its frames seem to own doresque façades—a mass of many-angled shadows in the background, relieved in front by long gleams of light on some obtruding post or porch or wooden stairway; its doorways yawn in blackness, like entrances to some interminable labyrinth; the jagged outline of its dwellings against the sky seems the part of some mighty wreck; its tortuous ways are filled with long shadows of the weirdest goblin form. The houses with lighted windows appear to possess an animate individuality, a character, a sentient consciousness, a face; and to stare with pale-yellow eyes and hungry door-mouth all agape at the lonely passer-by, as though desiring to devour him. The silent frames with nailed-up entrances, and roof jagged with ruin, seem but long specters of dwelling-places, mockeries in shadow of tenanted houses, ghosts, perhaps, of dwellings long since sacrificed to Progress by the philosophical Board of Improvements. The gurgling gutter-water seems blacker than ink with the filth it is vainly attempting to carry away; the air is foul with the breath of nameless narrow alleys; and the more distant lights seem to own a phosphorescent glow suggesting foul marasmal exhalation and ancient decay.

Following the guide down the sloping sidewalk of broken brick pavement from Broadway on Sixth street east, all along in the shadow figures in white or black are visible, flitting to and fro in a half-ghostly way, or congregated in motley groups at various doorways; and the sounds of gossip and laughter are audible at a great distance, owing to the stillness of the night. The figures vanish and the laughter ceases as the heavy tread of the patrolmen approaches —even the tap of a police-club on the pavement hushes the gossip and scatters the gossips. These are the owls, the night hawks, the Sirens of Bucktown, the wayside phantoms of this Valley of the Shadow of moral Death. They walk abroad at all hours of the tepid summer night, disappearing from view by day into their dens. Dens, indeed, is the only term which can with propriety be applied to many of their dwellings, whereof the roofs are level with the street, and the lower floors are thirty feet under ground, like some of those hideous haunts described in the Mysteries of Paris. For while some old rookeries have been raised, others have been fairly covered up by the fills of Culvert, Harrison, and lower Sixth streets; houses that once stood on stilts and to which access was only obtained by ladders, are now under the roadway and can only be entered by crawling on hands and knees. Fancy a lonely policeman struggling with a muscular and desperate murderer, thirty or forty feet under ground, in a worse than Egyptian darkness! There are many reasons, however, why such noisome, darksome, miasmatic dens should be forthwith destroyed, or at least why leasing or renting them to tenants should be prohibited by law. It was found necessary, in Paris, some years since, to wall up certain dark arches under the ramparts, which had been used for dwelling places by the poorest of the poor; nearly all the children born there were deformed, hideous monsters.

"These," observed the patrolman, pointing with his club to the buildings between the corner drugstore and the first alley east of Broadway, "are occupied by people who claim to be respectable. They never give us trouble. East of this there is scarcely a dwelling that is not occupied by the worst kind of people." Nevertheless, this alley can not be said to mark the boundary between two classes, as it is lined with evil haunts. It is foul with slime, black with slime, and is haunted by odors peculiarly unsavory. Passing by its entrance, and subsequently by some three or four well known "ranches," as the patrolman terms them, we enter the house of Mary Williams, a mongrel building, half brick, half frame.

This place is notorious as a panel den, a hive of thieves, a resort for criminals and roughs of the lowest grade. The door is wide open, and the room within lighted by the rays of a lamp with a very smoky chimney. A bed with a dirty looking comfort, a battered bureau, a very dilapidated rocking chair with a hole in its bottom, a rickety table, and a mirror, constitute all the furniture of the apartment. The walls have not been whitewashed or repaired for years; and the plaster has fallen away here and there, in great leprous patches, baring the lath framework beneath. Mary Williams and a black girl, with a red bandana turban, receive the patrolman with a smile and a nod of recognition. Mary is on her best behavior, having escaped a long sentence but a week before through the failure of a prosecuting witness to appear. A very ordinary looking woman is Mary—bright mulatto, with strongly Irish features, slight form, apparently thirty-five years of age. This blood seems to predominate strongly in the veins of half the mulattoes of Bucktown. The dreamy Sphinx-face with well-molded pouting lips, and large solemn eyes, and wide brows—the face that recalls old Egyptian paintings, and is not without a charm of its own—is never seen in Bucktown, although not an infrequent type of physiognomy in respectable colored circles. The solemn, calm, intelligent thought, quiet will, dormant strength of the Sphinx-face is never associated with vice.

Mary swore "to her just God" that no one was concealed about the premises; but the policemen lighted their candles and proceeded to examine every nook and corner of the building, under beds and tables, behind doors, and in shadowy places where giant spiders had spun gray webs of appalling size and remarkable tenacity. The rear room of the ground floor was a dark and shaky place—dark even in daylight, being beneath the level of the alley. The creaking of the boards under one's feet suggests unpleasant fancies about the facile disposal of a body beneath. A hundred robberies have taken place there. The fly once fairly in the trap, the lights are blown out, and he is left to make his exit as best he can, while the wily decoys, "thridding tortuous ways," are soon beyond pursuit. Above is the equally notorious establishment of Jennett Stewart, now, indeed, partially robbed of its old terrors by the committal of some half a dozen of its old denizens to the Work-house. Here Officer Sissmann once narrowly escaped being murdered. There was a tremendous fight going on in the third story, and the patrolman had mounted the creaky staircase to the scene of action, when he was suddenly pounced upon by the belligerent crowd of harlots and ruffians. Out went the candles; the treacherous club split in twain at the first blow; and before he could draw his revolver Sissmann was thrown over the balusters of the top floor, to which he still managed to cling for life. While hanging there the women slashed at him in the dark with razors, and the men kicked at his clinging hands in the endeavor to force him to let go. But the officer's muscles were iron, and he held on bravely, though covered with blood from random razor-slashes, until his partner rushed up in time to turn the tide of warfare. The recollection of this incident conjured up some decidedly unpleasant sensations on the occasion of our visit, while wending our way up the steep ascent of black and rotting stairs, fitfully illumed by gleams from Patrolman Tighe's candle. A double rap with the hickory club on a plank door at the summit, causes its almost instantaneous opening, and shows a group within of three colored women and two men, the former clad only in night-wrapper and chemise, the latter in shirt and pants. A tall, good-looking mulatto girl, with long, black, wavy hair and handsome eyes, but who smokes a very bad stoga and squirts saliva between her teeth like an old tobacco-chewer, answers the patrolmen's queries:

"What are you doing here, Annie?"

"I was hiding."

"Who are you hiding from at 2 o'clock in the morning?"

"Chestine Clark, Mr. Martin; for Christ's sake don't tell him I'm here—he swears he'll kill me."

Chestine is something of a dandy ruffian in Bucktown—a tall and sinewy mulatto, who always resists officers when opportunity offers; and is altogether a very unpleasant customer. Clark's father is a respectable and well-to-do old man, and has helped his son out of several very ugly scrapes. Annie is "his girl," and the officer evidently puts faith in her statement, for he promises secrecy. Having looked under the beds and examined every corner, the patrolmen descend, to emerge by a door on the second floor out on the noisome alley in the rear. This alley used to be a frightful place of a summer night, being crowded with thieves and harlots like Sausage Row on a June evening. But Anne Russell, Belle Bailey and Rose Lawson having been sent to the penitentiary, for cutting or passing counterfeit money; while Ann Stickley, Annie Moore, Annie Fish, Jennie Scott, Matt. Adams, Addie Stone, Molly Brown, Annie Jordan, Gabriella Wilson, and a hundred other notorious females, have been shipped off to the Work-house. "I always made it a rule," said Sissmann, "to keep the greater part of those women in the Work-house during the time I ran that beat. Otherwise the life of a patrolman would not be worth a hill of blue beans there. Where the prostitutes collect the thieves always gather. There are now between one hundred and fifty and two hundred women from Bucktown in the Work-house."

There were two women in white dresses sitting on doorsteps a little further on down the alley—one a bright quadroon, with curly hair, twisted into ringlets, and a plump, childish face; the other a tall white girl, with black hair and eyes, and a surprisingly well cut profile. Both are notorious; the former as a Sausage Row belle; the latter as the mistress of a black loafer, whom she supports by selling herself. Her sister, once quite a pretty woman, leads a similar existence when not in the Work-house. The patrolmen point them out, and pass into a doorway on the south side of the alley, leading to the upper story of the dwelling tenanted by John Ham, bar-keeper. Mrs. Ham, an obese negress, with immensely thick shoulders, comes forward to meet the patrolmen.

"Who's up stairs, Mrs. Ham?"

"Dey's no one only Molly, fo' God."

"Where's Long Nell?"

"In de Wuk-hus."

"And little Dolly?"

"Wuk-hus."

"And crooked-back Jim?"

"Wuk-hus."

"Ah, they've cleaned out these ranches since I used to run this beat before. Come up, gentlemen." Through a dark hall-way, over a creaking floor to a back room, and the patrolman's club plays the devil's tattoo upon the rickety planks. The door is unlocked and "Molly" makes her appearance.

Molly is the colored belle of this district. What her real name is neither her companions nor the police officers know. So far she has never been in the Work-house. She seemed to be about eighteen years old, of lithe and slender figure; complexion a Gypsy brown; hair long and dark with a slight wave; brows perfectly arched and delicately penciled; dreamy, brown eyes; nose well cut; mouth admirably molded; features generally pleasing. But Molly is said to be a "decoy" and a thief, and her apparent innocence a sham. The room is searched and found empty.

"Where did you get these?" exclaimed Tighe, picking up from the table a handsome pair of jet bracelets with heavy silver setting.

"They were made a present to me."

"That's too thin! Who gave them to you?"

"A man up town."

"What man?"

The officer lays down the trinkets with a frown; tells Molly that he has a good mind to lock her up "on suspicion;" and departs, looking unutterable things. "Did she steal them?" we ask.

"Oh, no," is the reply; "I only want to scare her a little, for I happen to know who gave them to her. It is a curious fact that business men and people of respectability get decoyed down here occasionally by girls like that, and get infatuated enough to bring them presents. She wouldn't tell, though, even if I locked her up."

Near here, a couple of doors away, is Joe Kite's place, concerning which horrid stories were once told; the old den kept by Addie Stone, a handsome but tigerish woman, now in the Work-house for cutting; and further on, the noisome underground den of Gilbert Page, who has lived in Bucktown for twenty-two years and has paid over five thousand dollars for fines to the Clerk of the Police Court. Here fish and bad whisky and pigs'-feet are sold three stories under ground; and here a police officer was nearly murdered while trying to arrest a prisoner in the labyrinth below. Over Joe Kite's lives a good-looking white girl, with some outward appearance of refinement, and who still retains that feminine charm soonest lost by a life of dissipation—a sweet voice. This is Dolly West, or "Detroit Dolly," as they call her, a colored man's woman, and one of the princesses of Bucktown. "Indian Maria," a yellow-skinned and hideous little woman from Michigan, with a little red blood in her veins, lives with others in the building once occupied by Addie Stone. Last week Matt. Lee, a mulatto girl, carved Indian Maria's ugly face with a razor, and was sent to the Work-house therefor. And not far from Culvert, in a two-story building known as Limber Jim's, lives a very peculiar-looking woman, Belle Bailey, just released from the Columbus Penitentiary. Belle is a West Indian, tall and gracefully built, with a complexion of ebony, but with beautiful hair, and features that are more than ordinarily attractive in their aquiline strength. Belle is not considered much of a thief, but she is dangerously quick with a knife. Indian Maria is not the only Indian here. There is also Pocahontas, a tall, hawk-nosed, yellow-skinned, superannuated sinner, who lives on Culvert street, back of the bar-room kept by the white desperado, Kirk, who has served a term in the Penitentiary. Pocahontas claims to be related to John Smith, of Virginia—"you know all about John Smith, of Virginia." Pocahontas, Indian Maria and a ghoulish-looking little woman without any nose, who lives over Greer's grocery, are all dump-pickers. So is Kate Miller, *alias* Hunnykut, who lives next to Kirk's, on the Sixth street side. We must not forget to mention Kate Hayes' den, the lowest thieves' hole in Bucktown, which is situated next to Pocahontas', and stands at the corner of Harrison and Culvert. Most of these buildings are two or three stories under ground. Culvert, between Sixth and Seventh, seems to mark the boundary line, east and west, between ignorant poverty, pure and simple, and ignorant vice of every description. On Culvert the population is about half and half of either sort; but from the fill up Seventh street north as far as Pruden's Barracks—a tenement house—for harlots, or to Mary Herron's den, still further up, wickedness reigns supreme all through the hours of darkness. On the south side of Seventh street matters are equally bad; and all along the nameless alleys and the tumble-down rookeries about the big factory in the heart of Bucktown, the sublimity of moral abomination abounds. The density of the population here is proportionately greater than in any other part of the city, although it is mostly a floating population—floating between the work-house or the penitentiary, and the dens in the filthy hollow. Ten, twelve, or even twenty inhabitants in one two-story underground den is common enough. At night even the roofs are occupied by sleepers, the balconies are crowded, and the dumps are frequently the scenes of wholesale debauchery the most degrading. How it is that sickness is not more common among this class, we confess ourselves unable to comprehend. The black hollows are foul, noisome, miasmatic; full of damp corruption, and often under water, or, better expressed, liquid filth. In the alley which runs by the old Allen Church, on Fifth and Culvert, some twenty feet below the fill, is a long, stagnant pool of execrable stench, which has become a horrible nuisance, and which never dries up. Insect life, the foulest and most monstrous, lurks in the dark underground shanties near by; and wriggling things, the most horrible, abound in the mud without. There is here a large field for both the Board of Health and the Board of Improvements to exercise talent. At the corner of Culvert and Sixth is a hole running into the sewer—a hole as deep as a well and as wide as a church door, and only covered with a few broken planks—splendid place to dispose of a body in. Then below the lots opposite Harrison and Culvert, where stands the ruins of Gordon's oil factory and of Woods & Carnahan's burnt out establishment, there is an immense well uncovered save by some charred beams. Here Buckton thieves congregate in packs at times, and highway robberies, rapes, and brutal fights have been committed time out of mind. That well should be filled up.

The search for the fugitive thief was continued by the officers until the sky became a pale gray in the east—down shaky ladders into cavernous underground dwellings, up rotten stair-cases into shaky frames, into hideous dens hidden away between larger buildings looking out on the alley. The sheepish humiliation of the debauchees, when the light from the officer's bull's-eye fell upon them, was sometimes pitiful. It was not uncommon to find white men of respectable appearance, and well dressed, sleeping in such dens. The police will seldom molest them while they "behave themselves;" but the well-known male thief, be he white or black, is allowed no place in Bucktown to hide his head, and if found in any den is at once kicked into the street. The first instance of this which came under our personal observation was in the brothel of a white woman, known as "Fatty Maria," who keeps on Sixth, near Culvert, opposite Kirk's. As a general rule no door is at any time closed against the police; but on this particular occasion, the women evidently knew what was coming, and all feigned slumber as long as they dared. Finally, repeated rappings and terrible threats caused a sudden opening of the door, and a fellow named Collison was found by the officers sleeping between two women, and at once ordered to vacate the premises. He first feigned sleep and drunken insensibility to the "nippers," and a wholesome tapping with a club; finally, he refused to depart. The women took part, and Fatty Maria attacked one of the officers like a wild cat. He received her with a backhanded slap in the face that sounded like the crack of a whip, when she sprang to the mantle-piece and seized a razor. Before she could use it, however, she was disarmed by another patrolman, and held down, powerless, on a chair, while Collison was fairly flung out of the room and kicked into the exterior darkness. "If that women did not harbor thieves," said the officer, "we could get along well enough with her, as she is generally quiet; but only this morning she pawned one of her beds and a bureau and a clock for $12, because she wanted to bail out a rascal from the Work-house."

During this episode at Fatty Maria's, a disgusting occurrence, which well illustrates the brutality of the Bucktown rough, occurred almost immediately across the way. There is a young white woman now in Bucktown, who spends the greater part of her existence in the Work-house for drunkenness, and whose degradation is such that she has even ceased to be known by name. On the day previous to our trip this wretched creature had been discharged from the Work-house, and returned to her old haunts. Some one had decoyed her into a low den, made her drunk and taken the most cowardly advantage of her condition, afterwards thrusting her into the street. Soon after some roughs half carried, half dragged her into Kirk's bar-room and poured some more poison down the poor creature's throat for similar purposes. When they heard the police approaching they dragged her out upon the sidewalk and propped her up in a sitting position upon some paving stones near the curb. Here she failed to attract attention while the officers passed down the other side, although in her drunken helplessness she fell sideways upon the stones, her hair streaming over the curb to mingle with the filth in the gutter. While the police were expelling Collison from Fatty Maria's a crowd of ruffians, white and black, lifted the unconscious woman, and carried her to a vacant lot in the hollow in rear of Kirk's, where they tore off part of her clothing. Before the police could reach the spot, the fellows fled beyond pursuit. The officers brought the wretched creature to a neighboring shanty, Kate Miller's. Kate agreed to take care of her, but expressed fears that the rowdies would return for their victim! It is comforting to think that in ten years hence Bucktown will have ceased to exist.

SUGGESTED ADDITIONAL READINGS

Chita
Two Years in The French West Indies
Youma
Children of the Levee (1957), ed. by O. W. Frost.

SELECTED REFERENCES

Tinker, Edward L. Lafcadio Hearn's American Days (1924).
Yu, Beongcheon. An Ape of Gods: The Art and Thought of Lafcadio Hearn (1964).

PROJECTS AND PROBLEMS

Was Hearn's attitude toward miscegenation affected by his brief marriage to Althea Foley, who was once a slave? Discuss the appeal of the exotic in his career and his attraction to "dark-tinted skins," mentioned by Van Wyck Brooks in his introduction to the 1961 edition of Chita.

A century has passed since Hearn's prediction that Bucktown would cease to exist in another decade. Do modern American cities have districts resembling Cincinnati's old Bucktown beat? Discuss the realistic and the romantic elements in Hearn's ghetto portrait.

Study Hearn's picture of the mélange of races he observed during his sojourn in New Orleans. Compare his treatment of Creoles with his representation of other minorities in the Cincinnati sketches assembled in *Children of the Levee*. Or compare his portrayal of black experience in antebellum Cincinnati with that in *North Into Freedom: The Autobiography of John Malvin, Free Negro, 1795–1880* (1966), ed. by Allan Peskin.

Summarize the relationship of Hearn and George W. Cable, giving special attention to their interest in folklore in New Orleans. Use as one reference Hearn's "The Scenes of Cable's Romances," in *Century Magazine*, November, 1883.

ALBION W. TOURGÉE
(1838–1905)

A Union officer who was seriously wounded in the Civil War, Tourgée settled his family in North Carolina, where he practiced law and entered politics. The novels he turned out were vehement in their support of the slaves and freedmen and in their condemnation of the nation's failure to make blacks real citizens with full civil rights. Judge Tourgée was not deterred by charges that he produced tracts rather than belles lettres. The failure of his southern sojourn is recorded in the autobiographical novel, *A Fool's Errand* (1879), from which the selection below is taken. Some later editions include Tourgée's supplement, "The Invisible Empire," which documents his charges against the Ku Klux Klan. After he left the South, Tourgée continued his campaign in books and articles. Probably the climax of his career came in 1896 when the Supreme Court ruled against his arguments in the *Plessy* vs. *Ferguson* case, thus sanctioning the reign of Jim Crow under the guise of "separate but equal."

THE FREEDMEN AND THE KLAN

There had been rumors in the air, for some months, of a strangely mysterious organization, said to be spreading over the Southern States, which added to the usual intangibility of the secret society an element of grotesque superstition unmatched in the history of any other.

It was at first regarded as farcical, and the newspapers of the North unwittingly accustomed their readers to regard it as a piece of the broadest and most ridiculous fun. Here and there throughout the South, by a sort of sporadic instinct, bands of ghostly horsemen, in quaint and horrible guise, appeared, and admonished the lazy and trifling of the African race, and threatened the vicious. They claimed to the affrighted negroes, it was said, to be the ghosts of departed Confederates who had come straight from the confines of hell to regulate affairs about their former homes.

All this was a matter of infinite jest and amusement to the good and wise people of the North. What could be funnier, or a more appropriate subject of mirth, than that the chivalric but humorous and jocose Southrons should organize a ghostly police to play upon the superstitious fears of the colored people, who were no doubt very trifling, and needed a good deal of regulation and restraint? So the Northern patriot sat back in his safe and quiet home, and laughed himself into tears and spasms at the grotesque delineations of ghostly K. K. K.'s and terrified darkies, for months before any idea of there being any impropriety therein dawned on his mind or on the minds of the wise men who controlled the affairs of the nation. That a few hundreds, a few thousands, or even millions, of the colored race, should be controlled and dominated by their superstitious fears, deprived of their volition, and compelled to follow the behests of others, was not regarded as at all dangerous in a republic, and as worthy of remark only from its irresistibly amusing character.

It was in the winter of 1868–69, therefore, when the wise men were jubilant over the success of the Great Experiment; when it was said that already Reconstruction had been an approved success, the

210

traces of the war been blotted out, and the era of the millennium anticipated,—that a little company of colored men came to the Fool one day; and one of them, who acted as spokesman, said,—

"What's dis we hear, Mars Kunnel, bout de Klux?"

"The what?" he asked.

"De Klux—de Ku-Kluckers dey calls demselves."

"Oh! the Ku-Klux, Ku-Klux-Klan, K. K. K.'s, you mean."

"Yes: dem folks what rides about at night a-pesterin' pore colored people, an' a-pertendin' tu be jes from hell, or some of de battle-fields ob ole Virginny."

"Oh, that's all gammon! There is nothing in the world in it,—nothing at all. Probably a parcel of boys now and then take it into their heads to scare a few colored people; but that's all. It is mean and cowardly, but nothing more. You needn't have any trouble about it, boys."

"An' you tink dat's all, Kunnel?"

"All? Of course it is! What else should there be?"

"I dunno, Mars Kunnel," said one.

"You don't think dey's ghostses, nor nothin' ob dat sort?" asked another.

"Think! I know they are not."

"So do I," growled one of their number who had not spoken before, in a tone of such meaning that it drew the eyes of the Fool upon him at once.

"So your mind's made up on that point too, is it, Bob?" he asked laughingly.

"I know dey's not ghosts, Kunnel. I wish ter God dey was!" was the reply.

"Why, what do you mean, Bob?" asked the colonel in surprise.

"Will you jes help me take off my shirt, Jim?" said Bob meaningly, as he turned to one of those with him.

The speaker was taller than the average of his race, of a peculiarly jetty complexion, broad-shouldered, straight, of compact and powerful build. His countenance, despite its blackness, was sharply cut; his head well shaped; and his whole appearance and demeanor marked him as a superior specimen of his race. Servosse had seen him before, and knew him well as an industrious and thrifty blacksmith, living in a distant part of the county, who was noted as being one of the most independent and self-reliant of his people in all political as well as pecuniary matters,—Bob Martin by name.

When his clothing had been removed, he turned his back towards the Fool, and, glancing over his shoulder, said coolly,—

"What d'ye tink ob dat, Kunnel?"

"My God!" exclaimed the Fool, starting back in surprise and horror. "What does this mean, Bob?"

"Seen de Kluckers, sah," was the grimly-laconic answer.

The sight which presented itself to the Fool's eyes was truly terrible. The broad muscular back, from the nape down to and below the waist, was gashed and marked by repeated blows. Great furrows were plowed in the black integument, whose greenly-livid lips were drawn back, while the coagulated fibrine stretched across, and mercifully protected the lacerated flesh. The whole back was livid and swollen, bruised as if it had been brayed in a mortar. Apparently, after having cut the flesh with closely-laid welts and furrows, sloping downward from the left side towards the right, with the peculiar skill in castigation which could only be obtained through the abundant opportunity for severe and deliberate flagellation which prevailed under the benign auspices of slavery, the operator had changed his position, and scientifically cross-checked the whole. That he was an expert whose skill justified Bob's remark—"Nobody but an ole oberseer ebber dun dat, Kunnel"—was evident even on a casual inspection. The injury which the man had sustained, though extensive and severe, was not dangerous to one of his constitution and hardened physique. To the eye of the Northern man who gazed at it, however, unused as are all his compeers to witness the effects of severe whipping, it seemed horrible beyond the power of words to express. He did not reflect that the African could have had none of that sense of indignity and degradation with which the Caucasian instinctively regards the application of the emblem of servility, and that he was but fulfilling the end of his dusky being in submitting to such castigation. He was filled with anger, surprise, and horror.

"What?—Who?—How?—My God! Tell me all about it. Can't I do something for you, my man?"

"Thank ye, Kunnel, nothing," said Bob seriously. "It's been washed in salt an' water. Dat's de bes' ting dere is to take out de soreness; an' it's doin as well as can be expected, I s'pose. I don't know much 'bout sech matters, Boss. I'se bin a slave goin' on forty-three years, but never hed a lash on my back sence I was a waitin'-boy till las' night."

His face was working with passion, and his eyes had a wicked fire in them, which clearly showed that he did not take this visitation in such a subdued and grateful spirit as his position properly demanded that he should. When his clothing had been resumed, he sat down and poured into the wondering ears of the Fool this story:—

BOB'S EXPERIENCE.

"Yer see, I'se a blacksmith at Burke's Cross-Roads. I've been thar ever sence a few days arter I heer ob de surrender. I rented an ole house dar, an' put up a sort of shop, an' got togedder a few tools, an' went to work. It's a right good stan'. Never used ter be ob any count, coz all de big plantations roun' dar hed der own smifs. But now de smifs hez scattered off, an' dey hev ter pay fer der work, dey finds it cheaper ter come ter my shop dan ter hire a blacksmif when dey's only half work fer him to do. So I'se been doin' right well, an' hev bought de house an' lot, an' got it all paid fer, tu. I've allers tended to my own business. 'Arly an' late Bob's bin at his shop, an' allers at work. I 'llowed to get me a snug home fer myself an' de ole 'ooman afore we got tu old ter work; an' I wanted to give de boys an' gals a little eddication, an' let em hev a fa'r start in life wid de rest ob de worl', if I could. Dat's what Bob's bin wukkin' fer; an' der ain't no man ner woman, black ner white, can say he hain't wukked honestly and fa'rly,—honestly an' fa'rly, ebbery day sence he's bin his own master.

"Long a while back—p'raps five er six months—I refused ter du some work fer Michael Anson or his boy, 'cause they'd run up quite a score at de shop, an' allers put me off when I wanted pay. I couldn't work jes fer de fun ob scorin' it down: so I quit. It made smart ob talk. Folks said I waz gettin' too smart fer a nigger, an' sech like; but I kep right on; tole em I waz a free man,—not born free, but made free by a miracle,—an' I didn't propose ter do any man's work fer noffin'. Most everybody hed somefin' to say about it; but it didn't seem ter hurt my trade very much. I jes went on gittin' all I could do, an' sometimes moah. I s'pose I acted pretty independent: I felt so, anyhow. I staid at home, an' axed nobody any favors. I know'd der wa'n't a better blacksmif in de country, an' thought I hed things jes' ez good ez I wanted 'em. When ther come an election, I sed my say, did my own votin', an' tole de other colored people dey waz free, an' hed a right ter du de same. Thet's bad doctrine up in our country. De white folks don't like ter hear it, and 'specially don't like ter hear a nigger say it. Dey don't mind 'bout our gettin' on ef dey hev a mortgage, so't de 'arnin's goes into ther pockets; nor 'bout our votin', so long ez we votes ez dey tells us. Dat's dare idea uv liberty fer a nigger.

"Well, here a few weeks ago, I foun' a board stuck up on my shop one mornin', wid dese words on to it:—

"'BOB MARTIN,—You're gettin' too dam smart! The white folks round Burke's Cross-Roads don't want any sech smart niggers round thar. You'd better git, er you'll hev a call from the

"'K. K. K.'

"I'd heerd 'bout the Klux, an' 'llowed jes' ez you did, Kunnel,—dat dey waz some triflin' boys dat fixed up an' went round jes' ter scare pore ignorant niggers, an' it made me all the madder ter think dey should try dat ar game on me. So I sed boldly, an' afore everybody, thet ef the Kluckers wanted enny thin' uv Bob Martin, they'd better come an' git it; thet I didn't 'bleve any nonsense about ther comin' straight from hell, an' drinkin' the rivers dry, an' all that: but, ef they'd come ter meddle with me, I 'llowed some on 'em mout go to hell afore it was over.

"I worked mighty hard an' late yesterday, an', when I went into de house, I was so tired thet I jes' fell down on de trundle–bed dat hed bin pulled out in front ob de souf do'. When my ole 'ooman got supper ready, an' called me, I jes' turned over, an' was that beat out an' sleepy, that I tole her to let me alone. So I lay thar, an' slep'. She put away de supper-tings, an' tuk part ob de chillen into bed wid her; an' de rest crawled in wid me, I s'pose. I dunno nothin' about it, fer I nebber woke up till some time in de night. I kinder remember hearin' de dog bark, but I didn't mind it; an', de fust ting I knew, de do' was bust in, an' fell off de hinges ober on de trundle–bed whar I was lyin'. It's a mercy I was thar. I don't s'pose I've lain down on it fer a year afore, an', ef de chillen hed all been thar alone, it's mor'n likely they'd all been killed. They hed taken a house–log I hed got (tinkin' ter put up a kitchen arter Christmas), an' free or four of 'em hed run wid it endwise agin de do'. So, when I woke from de crash, I hed do' an' house–log bofe on me, an' de ole 'ooman an' chillen screamin', so't I couldn't make out fer a minnit what it was, er whar I was. De moon was a-shinin bright, an' I 'spect de rascals t'ought I'd run, an' dey would shoot me as I come out. But, as soon as dey saw me heavin' an' strugglin' under de do', two on 'em run in, an' got on top of it. It was no use fer me to struggle any more under dat load. Besides dat, I was feared dey'd kill de chillen. So I tole 'em ef dey'd get off, an spar' de chillen, I'd surrender. Dey wouldn't bleve me, dough, till dey'd tied my han's. Den dey got off de do', an' I riz up, an' kind o' pushed it an' de house-log off de trundle-bed. Den dey pulled me out o' do's. Dar was 'bout tirty of 'em standin' dar in de moonlight, all dressed in black gowns thet come down to ther boots, an' some sort of high hat on, dat come down ober der faces, jes' leavin' little holes ter see fru, an' all trimmed wid different colored cloth, but mos'ly white.

"I axed 'em what dey wanted o' me. Dey sed I was gittin tu dam smart, an' dey'd jes' come roun' ter teach me some little manners. Den dey tied me tu a tree, an' done what you've seen. Dey tuk my wife an' oldes' gal out ob de house, tore de close nigh about off 'em, an' abused 'em shockin' afore my eyes. After tarin' tings up a heap in de house, dey rode off, tellin' me dey reckoned I'd larn to be 'spectful to white folks herearter, an' not refuse to work unless I hed pay in advance, an' not be so anxious 'bout radical votes. Den my ole woman cut me loose, an' we went into de house ter see what devilment dey'd done dar. We called de chillen. Dar's five on 'em,—de oldes' a gal 'bout fifteen, an' de younges' only little better'n a year ole. We foun' 'em all but de baby. I don' tink he ebber breaved arter de do' fell on us."

The tears stood in the eyes of the poor man as he finished. The Fool looked at him in a glamour of amazement, pity, and shame. He could not help feeling humiliated, that, in his own Christian land, one should be so treated by such a cowardly-seeming combination, simply for having used the liberty which the law had given him to acquire competence and independence by his own labor.

"Why have you not complained of this outrage to the authorities? " he asked after a moment.

"I tole Squire Haskins an' Judge Thompson what I hev tole you," answered Bob.

"And what did they say?"

"Dat dey couldn't do noffin' unless I could sw'ar to de parties."

"Did you not recognize any of them?"

"Not to say recognize; dat is, not so dat I could tell you so dat you could know de persons as de ones I named. I'm nigh 'bout sartin, from a lot of little tings, who dey was; but I couldn't sw'ar."

"Did you not know the voices of any of them?"

"Yes, I did. But de judge says I would jes' be makin' trouble fer myself to no 'count; fer he says no jury would convict on sech evidence when unsupported."

"I suppose he is right," mused the Colonel. "And there does not seem to be any way for you to get redress for what has been done to you, unless you can identify those who did the injury so clearly that no jury can resist a conviction. I suppose the vast majority of jurymen will be disinclined even to do justice. Perhaps some of the very men who were engaged in the act may be on the jury, or their brothers, fathers, or friends. So it would be useless for you to attempt a prosecution unless you had the very strongest and clearest testimony. I doubt not the judge was right in the advice he gave you."

"And do you tink der is any chance o' my gittin' sech testimony?" asked Bob.

"I confess," answered the Fool, "that I see very little. Time and care might possibly enable you to get it."

"Der's no hope o' dat,—no hope at all," answered the freedman sadly.

There was a moment's silence. Then the colored man asked,—

"Isn't dere no one else, Kunnel, dat could do any ting? Can't de President or Congress do somefin'? De gov'ment sot us free, an' it 'pears like it oughtn't to let our old masters impose on us in no sech way now. I ain't no coward, Kunnel, an' I don't want to brag; but I ain't 'feared of no man. I don't min' sufferin' nor dyin' ef I could see any good to come from it. I'd be willin' ter fight fer my liberty, er fer de country dat give me liberty. But I don't tink liberty was any favor ef we are to be cut up an' murdered jes' de same as in slave

times, an' wuss too. Bob'll take keer of himself, an' his wife an' chillen too, ef dey'll only give him a white man's chance. But ef men can
come to his house in de middle ob de night, kill his baby, an' beat
an' abuse him an' his family ez much ez dey please, jes' by puttin' a
little black cloth ober der faces, I may ez well give up, an' be a slave
agin."

"If it keeps on, and grows general," responded the Caucasian,
"the government will have to interfere. The necessity will be such
that they can not resist it. I don't quite see how it can be done, now
that these States are restored; but the government *must* protect the
lives of its citizens, and it *ought* to protect their liberties. I don't
know how it may be done. It may declare such acts treasonable, and
outlaw the offenders, authorizing any man to kill them when engaged in such unlawful acts."

"If dey would only do dat, Kunnel, we'd soon put an end to de Ku-
Kluckers. We'd watch de roads, an', ebery time dey rode frue de
bushes, dere'd be some less murderin' Kluckers dan when dey started
out. Hav' 'em du dat, Kunnel, an' we's all right. Jes' gib us a fa'r
chance, an' de culled men'll tak' keer o' dersel's. We ain't cowards.
We showed dat in de wah. I'se seen darkeys go whar de white troops
wa'n't anxious to foller 'em, mor'n once."

"Where was that, Bob?"

"Wal, at Fo't Wagner, for one."

"How did you know about that?"

"How did I know 'bout dat? Bress yer soul, Kunnel, I was dar!"

"How did that happen? I thought you were raised in the up country here?"

"So I was, Kunnel; but, when I heerd dat Abram Linkum had gib
us our freedom, I made up my mine I'd go an' git my sheer, an', ef
dar was any ting I could do to help de rest of my folks to git dars, I
was gwine ter du it. So I managed to slip away, one wayer 'nother,
an' got fru de lines down 'bout Charleston, an' jined de Fifty-fo'
Massachusetts Culled, Kunnel. Dat's how I come to be at Wagner."

"That explains, in part, the feeling against you, I suppose," said
Servosse.

"It s'plains annudder ting tu, Kunnel," said the colored man dog-
gedly.

"What is that?" asked the white ex-soldier.

"It s'plains why, ef dere's any mo' Kluckers raidin' roun' Burke's Corners, dar'll be some funerals tu," was the grim reply. . . .

SUGGESTED ADDITIONAL READINGS

A Royal Gentleman
Bricks Without Straw
An Appeal to Caesar
Pactolus Prime

SELECTED REFERENCES

Bowman, Sylvia E. "Judge Tourgée's Fictional Presentation of the Reconstruction." *Journal of Popular Culture*, 3 (1969), 307–23.

Franklin, John Hope. Introduction, "Albion Tourgée, Social Critic," *A Fool's Errand* (1961), by Albion Tourgée.

Gross, Theodore L. *Albion W. Tourgée* (1963).

———. "The Negro in the Literature of Reconstruction." *Phylon*, 22 (1961), 5–14.

Kaplan, Sidney. "Albion W. Tourgée: Attorney for the Segregated." *Journal of Negro History*, 49 (1964), 128–33.

Olsen, Otto H. *Carpetbagger's Crusade: The Life of Albion Winegar Tourgée* (1965).

PROJECTS AND PROBLEMS

Tourgée's books were often dismissed by critics as tracts lacking any substantial literary values. In considering the justice of this judgment, discuss in detail some of Tourgée's fugitive writing. See, in particular, "The South as a Field for Fiction," *Forum*, December, 1888, and "The Literary Quality of 'Uncle Tom's Cabin,'" *Independent*, August 20, 1896.

Compare one of Tourgée's Reconstruction novels with a work on the same subject by Thomas Dixon, John W. DeForest, or Joel Chandler Harris.

Compare Tourgée's position on education for the freedmen as it is presented in *Bricks Without Straw* and *Pactolus Prime*. Discuss the significance of Tourgée's brief to the Supreme Court in the historic *Plessy* v. *Ferguson* case on school desegregation, in which he wrote: "Justice is pictured blind and her daughter, the Law, ought at least to be color-blind."

Discuss the relationship between Tourgée's work and that of George W. Cable, and compare their achievements in the movement for civil rights. Give detailed attention to one topic, such as public education or the franchise.

Is *A Royal Gentleman* a substantial improvement over the earlier version, *Toinette?* Discuss.

HELEN HUNT JACKSON
(1830–1885)

The author of poetry, children's books, travel accounts, and novels, Helen Hunt Jackson published "The Wards of the United States Government," from which this selection is taken, in *Scribner's Monthly*, March, 1880. She extended her indictment of the nation for its mistreatment of the Indian in *A Century of Dishonor* (1881), which led to her appointment as a government investigator in California. *Ramona,* her romance about the Mission Indians of the southwest, won wide attention when it appeared in 1884.

CHIEF JOSEPH AND
GENERAL HOWARD

The story of the Nez Percé war, consequent on the attempt of the United States Government to "remove" this tribe from their homes, is still fresh in the minds of the American people, and is not yet complete on the official records of the Government. It is one of the few cases in which the Indian's side of the story has been told, and it is, therefore, one of the few cases which can be cited with anything like fairness.

The three chief sources of information in regard to the experiences of these Nez Percé "wards" of the United States Government are the official reports of Commissioners of Indian Affairs, a remarkable paper written by Chief Joseph of the Wal-lam-wat-kin band of Nez Percés, called "An Indian's Views of Indian Affairs," and published in the "North American Review" for April, 1879, and a reply to that article, written by General O. O. Howard, called "The True Story of the Wallowa Campaign," and published in the "North American Review" for July, 1879. It seems an oversight on the part of General Howard to call his paper "The True Story of the Wallowa Campaign," when, in fact, it speaks only of the events preceding the battles of that campaign, of the councils, agreements and final decisions in the matter of the removal of the Nez Percés, and only alludes in a few words, near the close, to the fact of the fights and the surrender of the Indians. He says that some of the Indians "treacherously escaped after the terms of surrender had been agreed upon," and thus did "break and make void the said terms of surrender." Is this the law of nations at war? If a few soldiers contrive to run away, after an army has surrendered, does that invalidate the conditions on which the generals of the two armies had agreed? General Howard expressly omits to state what those "terms of surrender" were; and by this omission, he gives the strongest proof that Chief Joseph, in his article, did not misrepresent them.

The beginning of the Nez Percé trouble was in the appointment, at Washington, of "a commission to visit the Nez Percé and other roving bands of Indians in Idaho, Oregon, and Washington Territory." [See Report of Ind., Com. for 1877, p. 211.] This word "rov-ing" is one of the many current phrases of misrepresentation about the Indians. "Roving Bands," "nomadic tribes," are catch-words for popular contempt and popular fear. In the true sense of the word, there is no such thing among our Indians as a "nomadic tribe."

Of these same Nez Percé Indians, this same official report (p. 80) says, they "seldom leave their homes except when called away on business. ° ° They do their trading semi-annually, in the spring and fall, returning home as soon as they have got through with their business!" and in the Report of the Indian Commissioner for 1874, p. 12, we find this statement:

> "Experience shows that no effort is more unsuccessful with an Indian than that which proposes to remove him from the place of his birth and the graves of his fathers. Though a barren plain without wood or water, he will not voluntarily exchange it for any prairie or woodland, however inviting."

Between the accounts given by General Howard, and by Chief Joseph, of the events preceding the Nez Percé war, there are notice-able discrepancies.

General Howard says that he listened to the "oft-repeated Dreamer nonsense of the chief, 'Too-hool-hool-suit,' with no impa-tience, but finally said to him:

"Twenty times over I hear that the earth is your mother, and about the chieftainship of the earth. I want to hear it no more."

Chief Joseph says:

"General Howard lost his temper and said 'Shut up! I don't want to hear any more of such talk.' Too-hool-hool-suit answered, 'Who are you, that you ask us to talk, and then tell me I shan't talk? Are you the Great Spirit? Did you make the world?' "

General Howard, quoting from his record at the time, says:

"The rough old fellow, in his most provoking tone, says some-thing in a short sentence, looking fiercely at me. The interpreter quickly says: 'He demands what person pretends to divide this land, and put me on it?' In the most decided voice, I said, 'I am the man. I stand here for the President, and there is no spirit, bad or good, that will hinder me. My orders are plain, and will be executed.' "

Chief Joseph says: "General Howard replied, 'You are an impudent fellow, and I will put you in the guard-house,' and then ordered a soldier to arrest him."

General Howard says: "After telling the Indians that this bad advice would be their ruin, I asked the chiefs to go with me to look at their land. 'The old man (Too-hool-hool-suit) shall not go. I will leave him with Colonel Perry.' He says, 'Do you want to scare me with reference to my body?' I said, 'I will leave your body with Colonel Perry.' I then arose and led him out of the council, and gave him into the charge of Colonel Perry."

Chief Joseph says: "Too-hool-hool-suit made no resistance. He asked General Howard, 'Is that your order? I don't care. I have expressed my heart to you. I have nothing to take back. I have spoken for my country. You can arrest me, but you cannot change me, or make me take back what I have said.' The soldiers came forward and seized my friend, and took him to the guard-house. My men whispered among themselves whether they should let this thing be done. I counseled them to submit. ° ° Too-hool-hool-suit was prisoner for five days before he was released."

General Howard, it will be observed, does not use the word "arrested," but as he says, later, "Too-hool-hool-suit was released on the pledge of Looking Glass and White Bird, and on his own earnest promise to behave better," it is plain that Chief Joseph did not misstate the facts. This Indian chief, therefore, was put under military arrest, and confined for five days, for uttering what General Howard calls a "tirade" in a council to which the Indians had been asked to come for the purpose of consultation and expression of sentiment.

Does not Chief Joseph speak common sense, as well as natural feeling, in saying,

"I turned to my people and said, 'The arrest of Too-hool-hool-suit was wrong, but we will not resent the insult. We were invited to this council to express our hearts, and we have done so.' "

If such and so swift penalty as this, for "tirades" in council, were the law of our land, especially in the District of Columbia, it would be "no just cause of complaint" when Indians suffer it. But considering the frequency, length and safety of "tirades" in all parts of America, it seems unjust not to permit Indians to deliver them. However, they do come under the head of "spontaneous productions of the soil": and an Indian on a reservation is "invested with no such proprietorship" in anything which comes under that head.— [Annual Report of the Indian Com. for 1878, p. 69.]

Chief Joseph and his band consented to move. Chief Joseph says:

"I said in my heart that rather than have war I would give up my country. I would give up my father's grave. I would give up everything rather than have the blood of white men upon the hands of my people."

It was not easy for Joseph to bring his people to consent to move. The young men wished to fight. It has been told that, at this time, Chief Joseph rode one day through his village, with a revolver in each hand, saying he would shoot the first one of his warriors that resisted the Government. Finally, they gathered all the stock they could find, and began the move. A storm came, and raised the river so high that some of the cattle could not be taken across. Indian guards were put in charge of the cattle left behind. White men attacked these guards and took the cattle. After this Joseph could no longer restrain his men, and the warfare began, which lasted over two months. It was a masterly campaign on the part of the Indians. They were followed by General Howard; they had General Crook on their right, and General Miles in front, but they were not once hemmed in; and, at last, when they surrendered at Bear Paw Mountain, in the Montana Hills, it was not because they were beaten, but because, as Joseph says, "I could not bear to see my wounded men and women suffer any longer; we had lost enough already." ° ° "We could have escaped from Bear Paw Mountain if we had left our wounded, old women and children, behind. We were unwilling to do this. We had never heard of a wounded Indian recovering while in the hands of white men. ° ° I believed General Miles, or I never would have surrendered. I have heard that he has been censured for making the promise to return us to Lapwai. He could not have made any other terms with me at that time. I could have held him in check until my friends came to my assistance, and then neither of the generals nor their soldiers would ever have left Bear Paw Mountain alive. On the fifth day I went to General Miles and gave up my gun, and said, 'From where the sun now stands, I will fight no more.' My people needed rest—we wanted peace."

The terms of this surrender were shamefully violated. Joseph and his band were taken first to Fort Leavenworth and then to the Indian Territory. At Leavenworth they were placed in the river bottom, with no water but the river water to drink.

"Many of my people sickened and died, and we buried them in this strange land," says Joseph. "I cannot tell how much my heart suffered for my people while at Leavenworth. The Great Spirit Chief who rules above seemed to be looking some other way, and did not see what was being done to my people."

Yet with a marvelous magnanimity, and a clear-headed sense of justice of which few men would be capable under the circumstances, Joseph says:

"I believe General Miles would have kept his word if he could have done so. I do not blame him for what we have suffered since the surrender. I do not know who is to blame. We gave up all our horses, over eleven hundred, and all our saddles, over one hundred, and we have not heard from them since. Somebody has got our horses."

This narrative of Chief Joseph's is profoundly touching; a very Iliad of tragedy, of dignified and hopeless sorrow; and it stands supported by the official records of the Indian Bureau.

SUGGESTED ADDITIONAL READINGS

A Century of Dishonor
Ramona

SELECTED REFERENCES

Beal, Merrill D. *"I Will Fight No More Forever": Chief Joseph and the Nez Perce War* (1963).

Byers, John R., Jr. "Helen Hunt Jackson (1830–1885)." *American Literary Realism, 1870–1910*, 2 (1969), 143–48.

Byers, John R., Jr. and Elizabeth S. "Helen Hunt Jackson (1830–1885): A Critical Bibliography of Secondary Comment." *American Literary Realism, 1870–1910*, 6 (1973), 197–241.

PROJECTS AND PROBLEMS

Compare Helen Hunt Jackson's attitude toward Mexicans with that of Davy Crockett and her attitude toward the Mexican War with that of Henry David Thoreau.

For Chief Joseph's version of the dispute with General O. O. Howard, see his account in *North American Review* for April, 1879. Consider Whittier's poem on Howard in this volume and speculate on possible explanations for the Union general's different attitudes toward blacks and Indians.

Compare *Ramona* with Harriet Beecher Stowe's romantic assault on slavery in *Uncle Tom's Cabin*. Note in particular how each author treats miscegenation.

JOEL CHANDLER HARRIS
(1848-1908)

Born and reared in a small Georgia town where his shyness led him to spend boyhood hours listening to the folk tales told in the slave quarters, Harris published his first Uncle Remus story in the *Atlanta Constitution* in 1879. Eight of the thirty volumes bearing his name as author are collections of Uncle Remus tales; the others treat various subjects from a Southern point of view. "The Wonderful Tar-Baby Story" appeared in *Uncle Remus: His Songs and His Sayings* (1881), and "Free Joe and the Rest of the World" was published in 1887 in *Free Joe and Other Georgia Sketches.*

The works of Harris are affected by the Plantation Tradition and show the contemporary influence of the doctrines of the New South and the rise of white supremacy. His contribution lies in his preservation and artistic use of the Afro-American and African lore he heard from Georgia slaves and his respect for a careful rendering of their idiom.

THE WONDERFUL TAR-BABY STORY

"Didn't the fox *never* catch the rabbit, Uncle Remus?" asked the little boy the next evening.

"He come mighty nigh it, honey, sho's you born—Brer Fox did. One day atter Brer Rabbit fool 'im wid dat calamus root, Brer Fox went ter wuk en got 'im some tar, en mix it wid some turkentime, en fix up a contrapshun wat he call a Tar-Baby, en he tuck dish yer Tar-Baby en he sot 'er in de big road, en den he lay off in de bushes fer to see wat de news wuz gwineter be. En he didn't hatter wait long, nudder, kaze bimeby here come Brer Rabbit pacin' down de road—lippity-clippity, clippity-lippity—dez ez sassy ez a jay-bird. Brer Fox, he lay low. Brer Rabbit come prancin' 'long twel he spy de Tar-Baby, en den he fotch up on his behime legs like he wuz 'stonished. De Tar-Baby, she sot dar, she did, en Brer Fox, he lay low.

" 'Mawnin'!' sez Brer Rabbit, sezee—'nice wedder dis mawnin',' sezee.

"Tar-Baby ain't sayin' nothin', en Brer Fox, he lay low.

" 'How duz yo' sym'tums seem ter segashuate?' sez Brer Rabbit, sezee.

"Brer Fox, he wink his eye slow, en lay low, en de Tar-Baby, she ain't sayin' nothin'.

" 'How you come on, den? Is you deaf?' sez Brer Rabbit, sezee. 'Kaze if you is, I kin holler louder,' sezee.

"Tar-Baby stay still, en Brer Fox, he lay low.

" 'Youer stuck up, dat's w'at you is,' says Brer Rabbit, sezee, 'en I'm gwineter kyore you, dat's w'at I'm a gwineter do,' sezee.

"Brer Fox, he sorter chuckle in his stummuck, he did, but Tar-Baby ain't sayin' nothin'.

" 'I'm gwineter larn you howter talk ter 'specttubble fokes ef hit's de las' ack,' sez Brer Rabbit, sezee. 'Ef you don't take off dat hat en tell me howdy, I'm gwineter bus' you wide open,' sezee.

"Tar-Baby stay still, en Brer Fox, he lay low.

"Brer Rabbit keep on axin' 'im, en de Tar-Baby, she keep on sayin' nothin', twel present'y Brer Rabbit draw back wid his fis', he did, en

228

blip he tuck 'er side er de head. Right dar's whar he broke his merlasses jug. His fis' stuck, en he can't pull loose. De tar hilt 'im. But Tar-Baby, she stay still, en Brer Fox, he lay low.

"'Ef you don't lemme loose, I'll knock you agin,' sez Brer Rabbit, sezee, en wid dat he fotch 'er a wipe wid de udder han', en dat stuck. Tar-Baby, she ain't sayin' nothin', en Brer Fox, he lay low.

"'Tu'n me loose, fo' I kick de natal stuffin' outen you,' sez Brer Rabbit, sezee, but de Tar-Baby, she ain't sayin' nothin'. She des hilt on, en den Brer Rabbit lose de use er his feet in de same way. Brer Fox, he lay low. Den Brer Rabbit squall out dat ef de Tar-Baby don't tu'n 'im loose he butt 'er cranksided. En den he butted, en his head got stuck. Den Brer Fox, he sa'ntered fort', lookin' des ez innercent ez one er yo' mammy's mockin'-birds.

"'Howdy, Brer Rabbit,' sez Brer Fox, sezee. 'You look sorter stuck up dis mawnin',' sezee, en den he rolled on de groun', en laughed en laughed twel he couldn't laugh no mo'. 'I speck you'll take dinner wid me dis time, Brer Rabbit. I done laid in some calamus root, en I ain't gwineter take no skuse,' sez Brer Fox, sezee."

Here Uncle Remus paused, and drew a two-pound yam out of the ashes.

"Did the fox eat the rabbit?" asked the little boy to whom the story had been told.

"Dat's all de fur de tale goes," replied the old man. "He mout, en den agin he moutent. Some say Jedge B'ar come 'long en loosed 'im —some say he didn't. I hear Miss Sally callin'. You better run 'long."

FREE JOE AND THE REST OF THE WORLD

The name of Free Joe strikes humorously upon the ear of memory. It is impossible to say why, for he was the humblest, the simplest, and the most serious of all God's living creatures, sadly lacking in all those elements that suggest the humorous. It is certain, moreover, that in 1850 the sober-minded citizens of the little Georgian village of Hillsborough were not inclined to take a humorous view of Free Joe, and neither his name nor his presence provoked a smile. He was a black atom, drifting hither and thither without an owner, blown about by all the winds of circumstance, and given over to shiftlessness.

The problems of one generation are the paradoxes of a succeeding one, particularly if war, or some such incident, intervenes to clarify the atmosphere and strengthen the understanding. Thus, in 1850, Free Joe represented not only a problem of large concern, but, in the watchful eyes of Hillsborough, he was the embodiment of that vague and mysterious danger that seemed to be forever lurking on the outskirts of slavery, ready to sound a shrill and ghostly signal in the impenetrable swamps, and steal forth under the midnight stars to murder, rapine, and pillage,—a danger always threatening, and yet never assuming shape; intangible, and yet real; impossible, and yet not improbable. Across the serene and smiling front of safety, the pale outlines of the awful shadow of insurrection sometimes fell. With this invisible panorama as a background, it was natural that the figure of Free Joe, simple and humble as it was, should assume undue proportions. Go where he would, do what he might, he could not escape the finger of observation and the kindling eye of suspicion. His lightest words were noted, his slightest actions marked.

Under all the circumstances it was natural that his peculiar condition should reflect itself in his habits and manners. The slaves laughed loudly day by day, but Free Joe rarely laughed. The slaves sang at their work and danced at their frolics, but no one ever heard Free Joe sing or saw him dance. There was something painfully plaintive and appealing in his attitude, something touching in his anxiety to please. He was of the friendliest nature, and seemed to be delighted when he could amuse the little children who had made a playground of the public square. At times he would please them by making his little dog Dan perform all sorts of curious tricks, or he would tell them quaint stories of the beasts of the field and birds of the air; and frequently he was coaxed into relating the story of his own freedom. That story was brief, but tragical.

In the year of our Lord 1840, when a negro-speculator of a sportive turn of mind reached the little village of Hillsborough on his way to the Mississippi region, with a caravan of likely negroes of both sexes, he found much to interest him. In that day and at that time there were a number of young men in the village who had not bound themselves over to repentance for the various misdeeds of the flesh. To these young men the negro-speculator (Major Frampton was his name) proceeded to address himself. He was a Virginian, he declared; and, to prove the statement, he referred all the festively inclined young men of Hillsborough to a barrel of peach-brandy in one of his covered wagons. In the minds of these young men there was less doubt in regard to the age and quality of the brandy than there was in regard to the negro-trader's birthplace. Major Frampton might or might not have been born in the Old Dominion,—that was a matter for consideration and inquiry,—but there could be no question as to the mellow pungency of the peach-brandy.

In his own estimation, Major Frampton was one of the most accomplished of men. He had summered at the Virginia Springs; he had been to Philadelphia, to Washington, to Richmond, to Lynchburg, and to Charleston, and had accumulated a great deal of experience which he found useful. Hillsborough was hid in the woods of Middle Georgia, and its general aspect of innocence impressed him. He looked on the young men who had shown their readiness to test his peach-brandy, as over-grown country boys who needed to be introduced to some of the arts and sciences he had at his command. Thereupon the major pitched his tents, figuratively speaking, and became, for the time being, a part and parcel of the innocence that characterized Hillsborough. A wiser man would doubtless have made the same mistake.

The little village possessed advantages that seemed to be providentially arranged to fit the various enterprises that Major Frampton had in view. There was the auction-block in front of the stuccoed court-house, if he desired to dispose of a few of his negroes; there was a quarter-track, laid out to his hand and in excellent order, if he chose to enjoy the pleasures of horse-racing; there were secluded pine thickets within easy reach, if he desired to indulge in the exciting pastime of cock-fighting; and various lonely and unoccupied rooms in the second story of the tavern, if he cared to challenge the chances of dice or cards.

Major Frampton tried them all with varying luck, until he began his famous game of poker with Judge Alfred Wellington, a stately gentleman with a flowing white beard and mild blue eyes that gave him the appearance of a benevolent patriarch. The history of the game in which Major Frampton and Judge Alfred Wellington took part is something more than a tradition in Hillsborough, for there are still living three or four men who sat around the table and watched its progress. It is said that at various stages of the game Major Frampton would destroy the cards with which they were playing, and send for a new pack, but the result was always the same. The mild blue eyes of Judge Wellington, with few exceptions, continued to overlook "hands" that were invincible—a habit they had acquired during a long and arduous course of training from Saratoga to New Orleans. Major Frampton lost his money, his horses, his wagons, and all his negroes but one, his body-servant. When his misfortune had reached this limit, the major adjourned the game. The sun was shining brightly, and all nature was cheerful. It is said that the major also seemed to be cheerful. However this may be, he visited the courthouse, and executed the papers that gave his body-servant his freedom. This being done, Major Frampton sauntered into a convenient pine thicket, and blew out his brains.

The negro thus freed came to be known as Free Joe. Compelled, under the law, to choose a guardian, he chose Judge Wellington, chiefly because his wife Lucinda was among the negroes won from Major Frampton. For several years Free Joe had what may be called a jovial time. His wife Lucinda was well provided for, and he found it a comparatively easy matter to provide for himself; so that, taking all the circumstances into consideration, it is not matter for astonishment that he became somewhat shiftless.

When Judge Wellington died, Free Joe's troubles began. The judge's negroes, including Lucinda, went to his half-brother, a man named Calderwood, who was a hard master and a rough customer generally,—a man of many eccentricities of mind and character. His neighbors had a habit of alluding to him as "Old Spite;" and the name seemed to fit him so completely, that he was known far and near as "Spite" Calderwood. He probably enjoyed the distinction the name gave him, at any rate, he never resented it, and it was not often that he missed an opportunity to show that he deserved it. Calderwood's place was two or three miles from the village of Hillsborough, and Free Joe visited his wife twice a week, Wednesday and Saturday nights.

One Sunday he was sitting in front of Lucinda's cabin, when Calderwood happened to pass that way.

"Howdy, marster?" said Free Joe, taking off his hat.

"Who are you?" exclaimed Calderwood abruptly, halting and staring at the negro.

"I'm name' Joe, marster. I'm Lucindy's ole man."

"Who do you belong to?"

"Marse John Evans is my gyardeen, marster."

"Big name—gyardeen. Show your pass."

Free Joe produced that document, and Calderwood read it aloud slowly, as if he found it difficult to get at the meaning:—

"To whom it may concern: This is to certify that the boy Joe Frampton has my permission to visit his wife Lucinda."

This was dated at Hillsborough, and signed *"John W. Evans."*

Calderwood read it twice, and then looked at Free Joe, elevating his eyebrows, and showing his discolored teeth.

"Some mighty big words in that there. Evans owns this place, I reckon. When's he comin' down to take hold?"

Free Joe fumbled with his hat. He was badly frightened.

"Lucindy say she speck you wouldn't min' my comin', long ez I behave, marster."

Calderwood tore the pass in pieces and flung it away.

"Don't want no free niggers 'round here," he exclaimed. "There's the big road. It'll carry you to town. Don't let me catch you here no more. Now, mind what I tell you."

Free Joe presented a shabby spectacle as he moved off with his

little dog Dan slinking at his heels. It should be said in behalf of
Dan, however, that his bristles were up, and that he looked back and
growled. It may be that the dog had the advantage of insignificance,
but it is difficult to conceive how a dog bold enough to raise his
bristles under Calderwood's very eyes could be as insignificant as
Free Joe. But both the negro and his little dog seemed to give a new
and more dismal aspect to forlornness as they turned into the road
and went toward Hillsborough.

After this incident Free Joe appeared to have clearer ideas concerning his peculiar condition. He realized the fact that though he
was free he was more helpless than any slave. Having no owner,
every man was his master. He knew that he was the object of suspicion, and therefore all his slender resources (ah! how pitifully slender they were!) were devoted to winning, not kindness and appreciation, but toleration; all his efforts were in the direction of mitigating
the circumstances that tended to make his condition so much worse
than that of the negroes around him,—negroes who had friends because they had masters.

So far as his own race was concerned, Free Joe was an exile. If the
slaves secretly envied him his freedom (which is to be doubted, considering his miserable condition), they openly despised him, and lost
no opportunity to treat him with contumely. Perhaps this was in
some measure the result of the attitude which Free Joe chose to
maintain toward them. No doubt his instinct taught him that to hold
himself aloof from the slaves would be to invite from the whites the
toleration which he coveted, and without which even his miserable
condition would be rendered more miserable still.

His greatest trouble was the fact that he was not allowed to visit
his wife; but he soon found a way out of this difficulty. After he had
been ordered away from the Calderwood place, he was in the habit
of wandering as far in that direction as prudence would permit.
Near the Calderwood place, but not on Calderwood's land, lived an
old man named Micajah Staley and his sister Becky Staley. These
people were old and very poor. Old Micajah had a palsied arm and
hand; but, in spite of this, he managed to earn a precarious living
with his turning-lathe.

When he was a slave Free Joe would have scorned these
representatives of a class known as poor white trash, but now he

found them sympathetic and helpful in various ways. From the back door of their cabin he could hear the Calderwood negroes singing at night, and he sometimes fancied he could distinguish Lucinda's shrill treble rising above the other voices. A large poplar grew in the woods some distance from the Staley cabin, and at the foot of this tree Free Joe would sit for hours with his face turned toward Calderwood's. His little dog Dan would curl up in the leaves nearby, and the two seemed to be as comfortable as possible.

One Saturday afternoon Free Joe, sitting at the foot of this friendly poplar, fell asleep. How long he slept, he could not tell; but when he awoke little Dan was licking his face, the moon was shining brightly, and Lucinda his wife stood before him laughing. The dog, seeing that Free Joe was asleep, had grown somewhat impatient, and he concluded to make an excursion to the Calderwood place on his own account. Lucinda was inclined to give the incident a twist in the direction of superstition.

"I 'uz settin' down front er de fireplace," she said, "cookin' me some meat, w'en all of a sudden I year sumpin at de do'—scratch, scratch. I tuck'n tu'n de meat over, en make out I aint year it. Bimeby it come dar 'gin—scratch, scratch. I up en open de do', I did, en, bless de Lord! dar wuz little Dan, en it look like ter me dat his ribs done grow tergeer. I gin 'im some bread, en den, w'en he start out, I tuck'n foller 'im, kaze, I say ter myse'f, maybe my nigger man mought be some'rs 'roun'. Dat ar little dog got sense, mon."

Free Joe laughed and dropped his hand lightly on Dan's head. For a long time after that he had no difficulty in seeing his wife. He had only to sit by the poplar-tree until little Dan could run and fetch her. But after a while the other negroes discovered that Lucinda was meeting Free Joe in the woods, and information of the fact soon reached Calderwood's ears. Calderwood was what is called a man of action. He said nothing; but one day he put Lucinda in his buggy, and carried her to Macon, sixty miles away. He carried her to Macon, and came back without her; and nobody in or around Hillsborough, or in that section, ever saw her again.

For many a night after that Free Joe sat in the woods and waited. Little Dan would run merrily off and be gone a long time, but he always came back without Lucinda. This happened over and over again. The "willis-whistlers" would call and call, like phantom huntsmen wandering on a far-off shore; the screech-owl would shake and shiver in the depths of the woods; the night-hawks, sweeping by on noiseless wings, would snap their beaks as though they enjoyed the huge joke of which Free Joe and little Dan were the victims; and the whip-poor-wills would cry to each other through the gloom. Each night seemed to be lonelier than the preceding, but Free Joe's patience was proof against loneliness. There came a time, however, when little Dan refused to go after Lucinda. When Free Joe motioned him in the direction of the Calderwood place, he would simply move about uneasily and whine; then he would curl up in the leaves and make himself comfortable.

One night, instead of going to the poplar-tree to wait for Lucinda, Free Joe went to the Staley cabin, and, in order to make his welcome good, as he expressed it, he carried with him an armful of fat-pine splinters. Miss Becky Staley had a great reputation in those parts as a fortune-teller, and the schoolgirls, as well as older people, often tested her powers in this direction, some in jest and some in earnest. Free Joe placed his humble offering of light-wood in the chimney-corner, and then seated himself on the steps, dropping his hat on the ground outside.

"Miss Becky," he said presently, "whar in de name er gracious you reckon Lucindy is?"

"Well, the Lord he'p the nigger!" exclaimed Miss Becky, in a tone that seemed to reproduce, by some curious agreement of sight with sound, her general aspect of peakedness. "Well, the Lord he'p the nigger! haint you been a-seein' her all this blessed time? She's over at old Spite Calderwood's if she's anywheres, I reckon."

"No'm, dat I aint, Miss Becky. I aint seen Lucindy in now gwine on mighty nigh a mont'."

"Well, it haint a-gwine to hurt you," said Miss Becky, somewhat sharply. "In my day an' time it wuz allers took to be a bad sign when niggers got to honeyin' 'roun' an' gwine on."

"Yessum," said Free Joe, cheerfully assenting to the proposition—"yessum, dat's so, but me an' my ole 'oman, we 'uz raise tergeer, en dey aint bin many days w'en we 'uz 'way fum one 'n'er like we is now."

"Maybe she's up an' took up wi' some un else," said Micajah

Staley from the corner. "You know what the sayin' is, 'New master, new nigger.'"

"Dat's so, dat's de sayin', but tain't wid my ole 'oman like 'tis wid yuther niggers. Me en her wuz des natally raise up tergeer. Dey's lots likelier niggers dan w'at I is," said Free Joe, viewing his shabbiness with a critical eye, "but I knows Lucindy mos' good ez I does little Dan dar—dat I does."

There was no reply to this, and Free Joe continued,—

"Miss Becky, I wish you please, ma'am, take en run yo' kyards en see sump'n n'er 'bout Lucindy; kaze ef she sick, I'm gwine dar. Dey ken take en take me up en gimme a stroppin', but I'm gwine dar."

Miss Becky got her cards, but first she picked up a cup, in the bottom of which were some coffee-grounds. These she whirled slowly round and round, ending finally by turning the cup upside down on the hearth and allowing it to remain in that position.

"I'll turn the cup first," said Miss Becky, "and then I'll run the cards and see what they say."

As she shuffled the cards the fire on the hearth burned low, and in its fitful light the gray-haired, thin-featured woman seemed to deserve the weird reputation which rumor and gossip had given her. She shuffled the cards for some moments, gazing intently in the dying fire; then, throwing a piece of pine on the coals, she made three divisions of the pack, disposing them about in her lap. Then she took the first pile, ran the cards slowly through her fingers, and studied them carefully. To the first she added the second pile. The study of these was evidently not satisfactory. She said nothing, but frowned heavily; and the frown deepened as she added the rest of the cards until the entire fifty-two had passed in review before her. Though she frowned, she seemed to be deeply interested. Without changing the relative position of the cards, she ran them all over again. Then she threw a larger piece of pine on the fire, shuffled the cards afresh, divided them into three piles, and subjected them to the same careful and critical examination.

"I can't tell the day when I've seed the cards run this a-way," she said after awhile. "What is an' what aint, I'll never tell you; but I know what the cards sez."

"W'at does dey say, Miss Becky?" the negro inquired, in a tone the solemnity of which was heightened by its eagerness.

"They er runnin' quare. These here that I'm a-lookin' at," said Miss Becky, "they stan' for the past. Them there, they er the present; and the t'others, they er the future. Here's a bundle,"—tapping the ace of clubs with her thumb,—"an' here's a journey as plain as the nose on a man's face. Here's Lucinda"—

"Whar she, Miss Becky?"

"Here she is—the queen of spades."

Free Joe grinned. The idea seemed to please him immensely.

"Well, well, well!" he exclaimed. "Ef dat don't beat my time! De queen er spades! W'en Lucindy year dat hit'll tickle 'er, sho'!"

Miss Becky continued to run the cards back and forth through her fingers.

"Here's a bundle an' a journey, and here's Lucinda. An' here's ole Spite Calderwood."

She held the cards toward the negro and touched the king of clubs.

"De Lord he'p my soul!" exclaimed Free Joe with a chuckle. "De faver's dar. Yesser, dat's him! W'at de matter 'long wid all un um, Miss Becky?"

The old woman added the second pile of cards to the first, and then the third, still running them through her fingers slowly and critically. By this time the piece of pine in the fireplace had wrapped itself in a mantle of flame, illuminating the cabin and throwing into strange relief the figure of Miss Becky as she sat studying the cards. She frowned ominously at the cards and mumbled a few words to herself. Then she dropped her hands in her lap and gazed once more into the fire. Her shadow danced and capered on the wall and floor behind her, as if, looking over her shoulder into the future, it could behold a rare spectacle. After a while she picked up the cup that had been turned on the hearth. The coffee-grounds, shaken around, presented what seemed to be a most intricate map.

"Here's the journey," said Miss Becky, presently; "here's the big road, here's rivers to cross, here's the bundle to tote." She paused and sighed. "They haint no names writ here, an' what it all means I'll never tell you. Cajy, I wish you'd be so good as to han' me my pipe."

"I haint no hand wi' the kyards," said Cajy, as he handed the pipe, "but I reckon I can patch out your misinformation, Becky, bekaze the other day, whiles I was a-finishin' up Mizzers Perdue's rollin'–pin, I hearn a rattlin' in the road, I looked out, an' Spite Calderwood was a-drivin' by in his buggy, an' thar sot Lucinda by him. It'd in-about drapt out er my min'."

Free Joe sat on the door-sill and fumbled at his hat, flinging it from one hand to the other.

"You aint see um gwine back, is you, Mars Cajy?" he asked after a while.

"Ef they went back by this road," said Mr. Staley, with the air of one who is accustomed to weigh well his words, "it must 'a' bin en-durin' of the time whiles I was asleep, bekaze I haint bin no furder from my shop than to yon bed."

"Well, sir!" exclaimed Free Joe in an awed tone, which Mr. Staley seemed to regard as a tribute to his extraordinary powers of state-ment.

"Ef it's my beliefs you want," continued the old man, "I'll pitch 'em at you fair and free. My beliefs is that Spite Calderwood is gone an' took Lucindy outen the county. Bless your heart and soul! when Spite Calderwood meets the Old Boy in the road they'll be a turrible scuffle. You mark what I tell you."

Free Joe, still fumbling with his hat, rose and leaned against the door-facing. He seemed to be embarrassed. Presently he said,—

"I speck I better be gittin' 'long. Nex' time I see Lucindy, I'm gwine tell 'er w'at Miss Becky say 'bout de queen er spades—dat I is. Ef dat don't tickle 'er, dey ain't no nigger 'oman never bin tickle'."

He paused a moment, as though waiting for some remark or com-ment, some confirmation of misfortune, or, at the very least, some endorsement of his suggestion that Lucinda would be greatly pleased to know that she had figured as the queen of spades; but nei-ther Miss Becky nor her brother said anything.

"One minnit ridin' in the buggy 'longside er Mars Spite, en de nex' highfalutin' 'roun' playin' de queen er spades. Mon, deze yer nigger gals gittin' up in de pictur's; dey sholy is."

With a brief "Good-night, Miss Becky, Mars Cajy," Free Joe went out into the darkness, followed by little Dan. He made his way to the poplar, where Lucinda had been in the habit of meeting him, and sat down. He sat there a long time; he sat there until little Dan, growing restless, trotted off in the direction of the Calderwood place. Dozing against the poplar, in the gray dawn of the morning, Free Joe heard Spite Calderwood's fox-hounds in full cry a mile away.

"Shoo!" he exclaimed, scratching his head, and laughing to himself, "dem ar dogs is des a-warmin' dat old fox up."

But it was Dan the hounds were after, and the little dog came back no more. Free Joe waited and waited, until he grew tired of waiting. He went back the next night and waited, and for many nights thereafter. His waiting was in vain, and yet he never regarded it as in vain. Careless and shabby as he was, Free Joe was thoughtful enough to have his theory. He was convinced that little Dan had found Lucinda, and that some night when the moon was shining brightly through the trees, the dog would rouse him from his dreams as he sat sleeping at the foot of the poplar-tree, and he would open his eyes and behold Lucinda standing over him, laughing merrily as of old; and then he thought what fun they would have about the queen of spades.

How many long nights Free Joe waited at the foot of the poplar-tree for Lucinda and little Dan, no one can ever know. He kept no account of them, and they were not recorded by Micajah Staley nor by Miss Becky. The season ran into summer and then into fall. One night he went to the Staley cabin, cut the two old people an armful of wood, and seated himself on the door-steps, where he rested. He was always thankful—and proud, as it seemed—when Miss Becky gave him a cup of coffee, which she was sometimes thoughtful enough to do. He was especially thankful on this particular night.

"You er still layin' off for to strike up wi' Lucindy out thar in the woods, I reckon," said Micajah Staley, smiling grimly. The situation was not without its humorous aspects.

"Oh, dey er comin', Mars Cajy, dey er comin', sho," Free Joe replied. "I boun' you dey'll come; en w'en dey does come, I'll des take en fetch um yer, whar you kin see um wid you own eyes, you en Miss Becky."

"No," said Mr. Staley, with a quick and emphatic gesture of disapproval. "Don't! don't fetch 'em anywheres. Stay right wi' 'em as long as may be."

Free Joe chuckled, and slipped away into the night, while the two old people sat gazing in the fire. Finally Micajah spoke.

"Look at that nigger; look at 'im. He's pine-blank as happy now as a killdee by a mill-race. You can't 'faze 'em. I'd in-about give up my t'other hand ef I could stan' flat-footed, an' grin at trouble like that there nigger."

"Niggers is niggers," said Miss Becky, smiling grimly, "an' you can't rub it out; yit I lay I've seed a heap of white people lots meaner'n Free Joe. He grins,—an' that's nigger,—but I've ketched his under jaw a-trimblin' when Lucindy's name uz brung up. An' I tell you," she went on, bridling up a little, and speaking with almost fierce emphasis, "the Old Boy's done sharpened his claws for Spite Calderwood. You'll see it."

"Me, Rebecca?" said Mr. Staley, hugging his palsied arm; "me? I hope not."

"Well, you'll know it then," said Miss Becky, laughing heartily at her brother's look of alarm.

The next morning Micajah Staley had occasion to go into the woods after a piece of timber. He saw Free Joe sitting at the foot of the poplar, and the sight vexed him somewhat.

"Git up from there," he cried, "an' go an' arn your livin'. A mighty purty pass it's come to, when great big buck niggers can lie a-snorin' in the woods all day, when t'other folks is got to be up an' a-gwine. Git up from there!"

Receiving no response, Mr. Staley went to Free Joe, and shook him by the shoulder; but the negro made no response. He was dead. His hat was off, his head was bent, and a smile was on his face. It was as if he had bowed and smiled when death stood before him, humble to the last. His clothes were ragged; his hands were rough and callous; his shoes were literally tied together with strings; he was shabby in the extreme. A passer-by, glancing at him, could have no idea that such a humble creature had been summoned as a witness before the Lord God of Hosts.

SUGGESTED ADDITIONAL READINGS

Nights with Uncle Remus
Mingo and Other Sketches in Black and White
Daddy Jake the Runaway
Balaam and His Master

SELECTED REFERENCES

Brookes, Stella Brewer. *Joel Chandler Harris, Folklorist* (1950).

Glazier, Lyle. "The Uncle Remus Stories: Two Portraits of American Negroes." *Hacettepe Bulletin of Social Sciences and Humanities,* 1 (1969), 67–74.

Ives, Sumner. "Dialect Differentiation in the Stories of Joel Chandler Harris." *American Literature,* 17 (1955), 88–96.

Light, Kathleen. "Uncle Remus and the Folklorists." *Southern Literary Journal,* 7, No. 2 (1975), 88–104.

Thurman, Wallace. "The Nephews of Uncle Remus." *Independent,* 119 (1927), 296–98.

Turner, Arlin. "Joel Chandler Harris (1848–1908)." *American Literary Realism, 1870–1910,* No. 3 (1968), 18–23.

Turner, Darwin T. "Daddy Joel Harris and His Old-Time Darkies." *Southern Literary Journal,* 1, No. 1 (1968), 20–41.

Wolfe, Bernard. "Uncle Remus and the Malevolent Rabbit." *Commentary,* 8 (1949), 31–41.

PROJECTS AND PROBLEMS

Compare Harris's Reconstruction novel, *Gabriel Tolliver,* with George W. Cable's *John March, Southerner,* or Thomas Nelson Page's *Red Rock.*

Discuss selected Uncle Remus tales as expressions of folk materials and folk values and as manifestations of the South's racial policies and attitudes before and after the Civil War.

Consider the pictures of blacks and poor whites in "Free Joe." Does the story emphasize race or class or both?

In a series of letters written for the *Atlanta Constitution* in 1882, Harris discussed racism in the North and the South. Using the letters that are reprinted in *The American Voice: Selections from the Non-fiction of Representative American Writers of Fiction, 1793–1934* (1968), ed. by Gerald Willen, compare his comments about what he saw in Cambridge, Massachusetts, with what William Dean Howells had to say about that scene in the selection from "A Pedestrian Tour" that is included in this volume.

In "Where's Duncan?" in *Balaam and His Master* there is an octoroon who does not fully conform to the stereotype. How is he exceptional? Compare the story with Charles W. Chesnutt's "The Sheriff's Children" in *The Wife of His Youth,* in which there is a similar father-son relationship. Or, considering the style and gruesome content reminiscent of Poe, compare Harris's tale with two stories about Chinese characters by Ambrose Bierce: "The Haunted Valley" and "The Night-Doings at 'Deadman's'." These are in *The Complete Short Stories of Ambrose Bierce* (1970), ed. by Ernest Jerome Hopkins.

Compare Harris's picture of race relations in Georgia with that of Will N. Harben. See Harben's *White Marie: A Story of Georgia Plantation Life* (1889) or, preferably, *Northern Georgia Sketches* (1900).

EMMA LAZARUS
(1849–1887)

The early writing of this descendant of Sephardic Jews, which won praise from Emerson and others, did not deal with minority experience. Emma Lazarus made her contribution to American letters when she became an adherent of Judaism and a spokesman for the immigrant. "The Jewish Problem," a selection from which appears below, was published in *Century Magazine* in February, 1883, a year after her *Songs of a Semite* made her the first Jewish-American poet to win wide recognition. The two sonnets here were included in *The Poems of Emma Lazarus* (1889). She wrote "The New Colossus," a classic expression of the image of America as a haven for the oppressed, to raise money for a pedestal for the Statue of Liberty.

THE JEWISH PROBLEM

The Jewish problem is as old as history, and assumes in each age a new form. The life or death of millions of human beings hangs upon its solution; its agitation revives the fiercest passions for good and for evil that inflame the human breast. From the era when the monotheistic, Semite slaves of the Pharaohs made themselves hated and feared by their polytheistic masters, till to-day when the monstrous giants Labor and Capital are arming for a supreme conflict, the Jewish question has been inextricably bound up with the deepest and gravest questions that convulse society. Religious intolerance and race-antipathy are giving place to an equally bitter and dangerous social enmity. This scattered band of Israelites, always in the minority, always in the attitude of *protestants* against the dominant creed, against society as it is, seem fated to excite the antagonism of their fellow-countrymen. Intellectually endowed...with "a high ideality and a keen sense of reality" they may be said broadly to represent Liberalism and Revolution in Germany and Russia, Conservatism and Capital in England and America. Liberty they must and will have, but when this is once obtained, their energy is transferred to the aim of fortifying and preserving it.

°   °   °   °   °

Even in America, presumably the refuge of the oppressed, public opinion has not yet reached that point where it absolves the race from the sin of the individual. Every Jew, however honorable or enlightened, has the humiliating knowledge that his security and reputation are, in a certain sense, bound up with those of the meanest rascal who belongs to his tribe, and who has it in his power to jeopardize the social status of his whole nation. It has been well said that the Jew must be of gold in order to pass for silver. Since the establishment of the American Union, Jews have here enjoyed absolute civil and political freedom and equality, and until the past few years, a large and in some places almost entire immunity from social prejudice. Their toleration, it is now asserted, has failed to produce beneficial results; on the contrary they have degenerated, rather than im-

245

246 THE MINORITY PRESENCE IN AMERICAN LITERATURE

proved, under these favorable conditions. While I admit the fact that America has no such brilliant list of Semitic names as the Europe of to-day can show, I find nothing to support the theory of the degeneracy of the race. Being subjected to the same influences as are the Christians who surround them, they simply evince the same proclivities. In this commercial country and commercial age they have been known chiefly as thriving merchants, tradesmen, and bankers who have enjoyed, as a rule, a high degree of credit and respect. If they have not surpassed, neither have they fallen behind, their competitors of other sects. They have been good citizens, furnishing, as statistics prove, proportionately fewer inmates to the prisons and fewer numbers to the proletariat than their neighbors of other descent. They have shared all national burdens and sorrows, fighting the battles of the Revolution and of the Union, grudging neither life nor money to the fortunes of the Republic. They are the prominent patrons of all musical enterprise—the only general division of art which has attained nearly as advanced a state of cultivation here as in Europe. The leader of free religious thought, and an indefatigable promoter of the better education of the poor in New York is a Jew—Felix Adler. The race is represented in every liberal profession, in the army, the navy, and the house of Congress.

And yet here, too, the everlasting prejudice is cropping out in various shapes. Within recent years, Jews have been "boycotted" at not a few places of public resort; in our schools and colleges, even in our scientific universities, Jewish scholars are frequently subjected to annoyance on account of their race. The word "Jew" is in constant use, even among so-called refined Christians, as a term of opprobrium, and is employed as a verb, to denote the meanest tricks. In other words, all the magnanimity, patience, charity, and humanity, which the Jews have manifested in return for centuries of persecution, have been thus far inadequate to eradicate the profound antipathy engendered by fanaticism and ready to break out in one or another shape at any moment of popular excitement.

THE NEW COLOSSUS

Not like the brazen giant of Greek fame,
With conquering limbs astride from land to land;
Here at our sea-washed, sunset gates shall stand
A mighty woman with a torch, whose flame
Is the imprisoned lightning, and her name
Mother of Exiles. From her beacon-hand
Glows world-wide welcome; her mild eyes command
The air-bridged harbor that twin cities frame.
"Keep, ancient lands, your storied pomp!" cries she
With silent lips. "Give me your tired, your poor,
Your huddled masses yearning to breathe free,
The wretched refuse of your teeming shore.
Send these, the homeless, tempest-tost to me:
I lift my lamp beside the golden door!"

THE NEW EZEKIEL

What, can these dead bones live, whose sap is dried
  By twenty scorching centuries of wrong?
Is this the House of Israel, whose pride
  Is as a tale that's told, an ancient song?
Are these ignoble relics all that live
  Of psalmist, priest, and prophet? Can the breath
Of very heaven bid these bones revive,
  Open the graves and clothe the ribs of death?
Yea, Prophesy, the Lord hath said. Again
  Say to the wind, Come forth and breathe afresh,
Even that they may live upon these slain,
  And bone to bone shall leap, and flesh to flesh.
The Spirit is not dead, proclaim the word,
  Where lay dead bones, a host of armed men stand!
I ope your graves, my people, saith the Lord,
  And I shall place you living in your land.

SUGGESTED ADDITIONAL READING

Emma Lazarus: Selections from Her Poetry and Prose, 3rd ed.
(1967), ed. by Morris U. Shappes.

SELECTED REFERENCES

Baym, Max I. "Emma Lazarus and Emerson." *Publications of
the American Jewish Society,* No. 38, pt. 4 (1949), 281–87.
Harap, Louis. *The Image of the Jew in American Literature*
(1974).
Merriam, Eve. *Emma Lazarus: Woman with a Torch* (1956).

PROJECTS AND PROBLEMS

Compare the attitudes of Emma Lazarus and Henry James toward
George Eliot's *Daniel Deronda,* which gave wide circulation to the
idea of a Jewish national state.

Discuss Emerson's seeming ambivalence in praising Emma Lazarus but neglecting to include her poetry in his anthology, *Parnassus,* in 1874. Compare his relationship with her with that of Edmund Clarence Stedman.

As a member of a wealthy and patrician family, Emma Lazarus was of a quite different class than the East European Jewish immigrants with whom she identified. Did she feel that middle class status meant freedom from the effects of minority identity?

See her essay on Longfellow, reprinted in Shappes's *Selections,* and compare "The Jewish Cemetery at Newport" with her poem, "In the Jewish Synagogue at Newport." Or compare her poetry with Morris Rosenfeld's *Songs from the Ghetto* (1898), translated from the Yiddish but recognized as American expression.

HENRY JAMES
(1843–1916)

Prolific author of stories, novels, plays, and criticism, James is celebrated for his attention to narrative technique and his portrayal of sophisticated, wealthy Americans and foreign aristocrats. He has enjoyed enormous influence among critics and novelists, but the very works that delight artists and intellectuals tend to be "caviare to the general." As his style became more complex and his materials more removed from the experience of American readers of his day, the expatriate author lost the popularity attained by early works like *Daisy Miller* and *Washington Square*.

The selection below is one day's diary entry in "The Impressions of a Cousin," first published in *Century Magazine* in two installments at the end of 1883 and collected in *Tales of Three Cities* the following year. James did not include it in the definitive New York edition of his works. In the story both Caliph and his non-Jewish half brother, Adrian, wish to marry Eunice, but Caliph's real object is to win control of her estate.

A DIARIST'S PREJUDICES

May 2.—Mr. Caliph is really very delightful. He made his appearance to-day and carried everything before him. When I say he carried everything, I mean he carried me; for Eunice had not my prejudices to get over. When I said to her after he had gone, "Your trustee is a very clever man," she only smiled a little, and turned away in silence. I suppose she was amused with the air of importance with which I announced this discovery. Eunice had made it several years ago, and could not be excited about it. I had an idea that some allusion would be made to the way he has neglected her— some apology at least for his long absence. But he did something better than this. He made no definite apology; he only expressed, in his manner, his look, his voice, a tenderness, a charming benevolence, which included and exceeded all apologies. He looks rather tired and preoccupied; he evidently has a great many irons of his own in the fire, and has been thinking these last weeks of larger questions than the susceptibilities of a little girl in New York who happened several years ago to have an exuberant mother. He is thoroughly genial, and is the best talker I have seen since my return. A totally different type from the young Adrian. He is not in the least handsome—is, indeed, rather ugly; but with a fine, expressive, pictorial ugliness. He is forty years old, large and stout, may even be pronounced fat; and there is something about him that I don't know how to describe except by calling it a certain richness. I have seen Italians who have it, but this is the first American. He talks with his eyes, as well as with his lips, and his features are wonderfully mobile. His smile is quick and delightful; his hands are well-shaped, but distinctly fat; he has a pale complexion and a magnificent brown beard—the beard of Haroun-al-Raschid. I suppose I must write it very small; but I have an intimate conviction that he is a Jew, or of Jewish origin. I see that in his plump, white face, of which the tone would please a painter, and which suggests fatigue but is nevertheless all alive; in his remarkable eye, which is full of old expressions— expressions which linger there from the past, even when they are not active to-day; in his profile, in his anointed beard, in the very rings on his large pointed fingers. There is not a touch of all this in his

251

step-brother; so I suppose the Jewish blood is inherited from his father. I don't think he looks like a gentleman; he is something apart from all that. If he is not a gentleman, he is not in the least a bourgeois—neither is he of the Bohemian type. In short, as I say, he is a Jew; and Jews of the upper class have a style of their own. He is very clever, and I think genuinely kind. Nothing could be more charming than his way of talking to Eunice—a certain paternal interest mingled with an air of respectful gallantry (he gives her good advice, and at the same time pays her compliments); the whole thing being not in the least overdue. I think he found her changed—"more of a person," as Mrs. Ermine says; I even think he was a little surprised. She seems slightly afraid of him, which rather surprised me—she was, from her own account, so familiar with him of old. He is decidedly florid, and was very polite to me; that was a part of the floridity. He asked if we had seen his step-brother; begged us to be kind to him and to let him come and see us often. He doesn't know many people in New York, and at that age it is everything (I quote Mr. Caliph) for a young fellow to be at his ease with one or two charming women. "Adrian takes a great deal of knowing; is horribly shy; but is most intelligent, and has one of the sweetest natures! I'm very fond of him —he's all I've got. Unfortunately the poor boy is cursed with a competence. In this country there is nothing for such a young fellow to do; he hates business, and has absolutely no talent for it. I shall send him back here the next time I see him." Eunice made no answer to this, and, in fact, had little answer to make to most of Mr. Caliph's remarks, only sitting looking at the floor with a smile. I thought it proper therefore to reply that we had found Mr. Frank very pleasant, and hoped he would soon come again. Then I mentioned that the other day I had had a long visit from him alone; we had talked for an hour, and become excellent friends. Mr. Caliph, as I said this, was leaning forward with his elbow on his knee and his hand uplifted, grasping his thick beard. The other hand, with the elbow out, rested on the other knee; his head was turned toward me, askance. He looked at me a moment with his deep bright eye—the eye of a much older man than he; he might have been posing for a water-colour. If I had painted him, it would have been in a high-peaked cap, and an amber-coloured robe, with a wide girdle of pink silk wound many times round his waist, stuck full of knives with jewelled handles. Our eyes met, and we sat there exchanging a glance. I don't know whether he's vain, but I think he must see I appreciate him; I am sure he understands everything.

"I like you when you say that," he remarked at the end of a minute.

"I am glad to hear you like me!" This sounds horrid and pert as I relate it.

"I don't like every one," said Mr. Caliph.

"Neither do Eunice and I; do we, Eunice?"

"I am afraid we only try to," she answered, smiling her most beautiful smile.

"Try to? Heaven forbid! I protest against that," I cried. I said to Mr. Caliph that Eunice was too good.

"She comes honestly by that. Your mother was an angel, my child," he said to her.

Cousin Letitia was not an angel, but I have mentioned that Mr. Caliph is florid. "You used to be very good to her," Eunice murmured, raising her eyes to him.

He had got up; he was standing there. He bent his head, smiling like an Italian. "You must be the same, my child."

"What can I do?" Eunice asked.

"You can believe in me—you can trust me."

"I do, Mr. Caliph. Try me and see!"

This was unexpectedly gushing, and I instinctively turned away. Behind my back, I don't know what he did to her—I think it possible he kissed her. When you call a girl "my child," I suppose you may kiss her; but that may be only my bold imagination. When I turned round he had taken up his hat and stick, to say nothing of buttoning a very tightly-fitting coat round a very spacious person, and was ready to offer me his hand in farewell.

"I am so glad you are with her. I am so glad she has a companion so accomplished—so capable."

"So capable of what?" I said, laughing; for the speech was absurd, as he knows nothing about my accomplishments.

There is nothing solemn about Mr. Caliph; but he gave me a look which made it appear to me that my levity was in bad taste. Yes, humiliating as it is to write it here, I found myself rebuked by a Jew with fat hands! "Capable of advising her well!" he said softly.

"Ah, don't talk about advice," Eunice exclaimed. "Advice always gives an idea of trouble, and I am very much afraid of trouble."

"You ought to get married," he said, with his smile coming back to him.

Eunice coloured and turned away, and I observed—to say something—that this was just what Mrs. Ermine said.

"Mrs. Ermine? ah, I hear she's a charming woman!" And shortly after that he went away.

That was almost the only weak thing he said—the only thing for mere form, for of course no one can really think her charming; least of all a clever man like that. I don't like Americans to resemble Italians, or Italians to resemble Americans; but putting that aside, Mr. Caliph is very prepossessing. He is wonderfully good company; he will spoil us for other people. He made no allusion to business, and no appointment with Eunice for talking over certain matters that are pending; but I thought of this only half an hour after he had gone. I said nothing to Eunice about it, for she would have noticed the omission herself, and that was enough. The only other point in Mr. Caliph that was open to criticism is his asking Eunice to believe in him—to trust him. Why shouldn't she, pray? If that speech was curious—and, strange to say, it almost appeared so—it was incredibly naïf. But this quality is insupposable of Mr. Caliph; who ever heard of a naïf Jew? After he had gone I was on the point of saying to Eunice, "By the way, why did you never mention that he is a Hebrew? That's an important detail." But an impulse that I am not able to define stopped me, and now I am glad I didn't speak. I don't believe Eunice ever made the discovery, and I don't think she would like it if she did make it. That I should have done so on the instant only proves that I am in the habit of studying the human profile!

SUGGESTED ADDITIONAL READING

The Tragic Muse

SELECTED REFERENCES

Dupee, F. W. Henry James (1965).

Harap, Louis. *The Image of the Jew in American Literature* (1974).

Levy, Leo B. "Henry James and the Jews: A Critical Study." *Commentary*, 26 (1958), 243–49.

McCarthy, Harold T. "Henry James and the American Aristocracy." *American Literary Realism: 1870–1910*, 4, No. 1 (1971), 61–71.

PROJECTS AND PROBLEMS

Is the reader encouraged to infer that the differences between Caliph and Adrian are to be explained by the fact that one of these half brothers had a Jewish father and the other did not?

James has an American character in *Roderick Hudson* object to the heroine's marriage to an Italian nobleman, saying, "If she wanted a fine bright fellow—a specimen of clean comfortable *white* humanity—I would have undertaken to find him for her without going out of my native State." In "Break of Day," a story by Brander Matthews in *Vignettes of Manhattan* (1894), the author laments the plight of a ghetto heroine whose calls for assistance reached only poor Poles, "poor-spirited . . . cowardly creatures all of them; and she could not hope for help from them as she would if they were only white men." Find instances in both earlier and later American literature of the inclination to regard only WASPs as truly "white."

Compare James's casual references to Jews in *The Awkward Age, The Spoils of Poynton,* and *What Maisie Knew* with his passing comments about other minorities in *Hawthorne, The Bostonians,* and *Washington Square.*

Such stereotypical allusions to minorities as appear in fiction by James often are expressed by characters, not by the author. Does this relieve James of responsibility for the references and clear him of racism? Examine selected works of fiction carefully to judge the author's own views. For some direct comments by James on minorities in America in 1904, see *The American Scene.*

Compare Miriam Roth of *The Tragic Muse* with an earlier half-Jewish heroine, Miriam of *The Marble Faun* by Nathaniel Hawthorne. Do these authors attach equal importance to the strain of Jewish ancestry? Are the same stereotypes evident in both novels?

Does James depict females of Jewish ancestry more favorably than their male counterparts? Would he concur with Ambrose Bierce's definition of "Hebrew" in *The Devil's Dictionary* as "a male Jew, as distinguished from a Shebrew, an altogether superior creation." Is such discrimination the rule in the treatment of minorities and aliens?

GEORGE W. CABLE
(1844–1925)

Cable's estrangement from the South he had loved and served as a Confederate soldier grew with each addition to his publications. His fiction disclosed a deepening strain of social criticism beneath the local color surface, and his essays identified him as a champion of the freedman's right to full citizenship. The early short stories collected in *Old Creole Days* (1879) and his first novel, *The Grandissimes* (1880), blend realism and romance in classic portraits of antebellum Louisiana.

The first selection that follows is from *Madame Delphine* (1881), and the second is from *The Creoles of Louisiana* (1884). Ristofalo and Mrs. Riley are characters in *Dr. Sevier*, the novel about New Orleans during and after the Civil War that Cable published in 1885. His account of the integrated school is from "The 'Haunted House' in Royal Street," one of the narratives in *Strange True Stories of Louisiana* (1889).

THE QUADROONS OF OLD NEW ORLEANS

During the first quarter of the present century, the free quadroon caste of New Orleans was in its golden age. Earlier generations—sprung, upon the one hand, from the merry gallants of a French colonial military service which had grown gross by affiliation with Spanish-American frontier life, and, upon the other hand, from comely Ethiopians culled out of the less negroidal types of African live goods, and bought at the ship's side with vestiges of quills and cowries and copper wire still in their headdresses—these earlier generations, with scars of battle or private rencontre still on the fathers, and of servitude on the manumitted mothers, afforded a mere hint of the splendor that was to result from a survival of the fairest through seventy-five years devoted to the elimination of the black pigment and the cultivation of hyperion excellence and nymphean grace and beauty. Nor, if we turn to the present, is the evidence much stronger which is offered by the *gens de couleur* whom you may see in the quadroon quarter this afternoon, with "Ichabod" legible on their murky foreheads through a vain smearing of toilet powder, dragging their chairs down to the narrow gateway of their close-fenced gardens, and staring shrinkingly at you as you pass, like a nest of yellow kittens.

But as the present century was in its second and third decades, the *quadroones* (for we must contrive a feminine spelling to define the strict limits of the caste as then established) came forth in splendor. Old travelers spare no terms to tell their praises, their faultlessness of feature, their perfection of form, their varied styles of beauty—for there were even pure Caucasian blondes among them—their fascinating manners, their sparkling vivacity, their chaste and pretty wit, their grace in the dance, their modest propriety, their taste and elegance in dress. In the gentlest and most poetic sense they were indeed the sirens of this land, where it seemed "always afternoon"—a momentary triumph of an Arcadian over a Christian civilization, so beautiful and so seductive that it became the subject of special

258

chapters by writers of the day more original than correct as social philosophers.

The balls that were got up for them by the male *sang-pur* were to that day what the carnival is to the present. Society balls given the same nights proved failures through the coincidence. The magnates of government—municipal, state, federal—those of the army, of the learned professions and of the clubs—in short, the white male aristocracy in everything save the ecclesiastical desk—were there. Tickets were high-priced to insure the exclusion of the vulgar. No distinguished stranger was allowed to miss them. They were beautiful! They were clad in silken extenuations from the throat to the feet, and wore, withal, a pathos in their charm that gave them a family likeness to innocence.

WHAT IS A CREOLE?

What is a Creole? Even in Louisiana the question would be variously answered.[1] The title did not here first belong to the descendants of Spanish, but of French settlers. But such a meaning implied a certain excellence of origin, and so came early to include any native, of French or Spanish descent by either parent, whose non-alliance with the slave race entitled him to social rank. Later, the term was adopted by—not conceded to—the natives of mixed blood, and is still so used among themselves. At length the spirit of commerce saw the money value of so honored a title, and broadened its meaning to take in any creature or thing of variety or manufacture peculiar to Louisiana that might become an object of sale: as Creole ponies, chickens, cows, shoes, eggs, wagons, baskets, cabbages, negroes, etc. Yet the Creoles proper will not share their distinction with the worthy "Acadian." He is a Creole only by courtesy, and in the second person singular. Besides French and Spanish, there are even, for convenience of speech, "colored" Creoles; but there are no Italian, or Sicilian, nor any English, Scotch, Irish, or "Yankee" Creoles, unless of parentage married into, and themselves thoroughly proselyted in, Creole society. Neither Spanish nor American domination has taken from the Creoles their French vernacular. This, also, is part of their title; and, in fine, there seems to be no more serviceable definition of the Creoles of Louisiana than this: that they are the French-speaking, native portion of the ruling class.

There is no need to distinguish between the higher and humbler grades of those from whom they sprang. A few settlers only were persons of rank and station. Many were the children of the casket-girls, and many were of such stock as society pronounces less than nothing; yet, in view of that state of society which the French revolution later overturned, any present overplus of honor may as well fall to the children of those who filled the prisons before, as of those who filled them during that bloody convulsion.

---

[1]Cable's footnote on the etymology of the word is omitted.

MR. RISTOFALO AND MRS. RILEY

Ristofalo came often. He was a man of simple words, and of few thoughts of the kind that were available in conversation; but his personal adventures had begun almost with infancy, and followed one another in close and strange succession over lands and seas ever since. He could therefore talk best about himself, though he talked modestly. "These things to hear would Desdemona seriously incline," and there came times when even a tear was not wanting to gem the poetry of the situation.

"And ye might have saved yerself from all that," was sometimes her note of sympathy. But when he asked how she silently dried her eyes.

Sometimes his experiences had been intensely ludicrous, and Mrs. Riley would laugh until in pure self-oblivion she smote her thigh with her palm, or laid her hand so smartly against his shoulder as to tip him half off his seat.

"Ye didn't!"

"Yes."

"Ah! Get out wid ye, Raphael Ristofalo,—to be telling me that for the trooth!"

At one such time she was about to give him a second push, but he took the hand in his, and quietly kept it to the end of his story.

He lingered late that evening, but at length took his hat from under his chair, rose, and extended his hand.

"Man alive!" she cried, "that's my *hand,* sur, I'd have ye to know. Begahn wid ye! Lookut heere! What's the reason ye make it so long atween yer visits, eh? Tell me that. Ah—ah—ye've no need fur to tell me, Mr. Ristofalo! Ah—now don't tell a lie!"

"Too busy. Come all time—wasn't too busy."

"Ha, ha! Yes, yes; ye're too busy. Of coorse ye're too busy. Oh, yes! ye *air* too busy—a'courtin' thim I-talian froot gerls around the Frinch Mairket. Ah! I'll bet two bits ye're a bouncer! Ah, don't tell me. I know ye, ye villain! Some o'thim's a-waitin' fur ye now, ha, ha! Go! And don't ye nivver come back heere anny more. D'ye mind?"

"Aw righ'." The Italian took her hand for the third time and held it, standing in his simple square way before her and wearing his gentle smile as he looked her in the eye. "Good-by, Kate."

Her eye quailed. Her hand pulled a little helplessly, and in a meek voice she said:—

"That's not right for you to do me that a-way, Mr. Ristofalo. I've got a handle to my name, sur."

She threw some gentle rebuke into her glance, and turned it upon him. He met it with that same amiable absence of emotion that was always in his look.

"Kate too short by itself?" he asked. "Aw righ'; make it Kate Ristofalo."

"No," said Mrs. Riley, averting and drooping her face.

"Take good care of you," said the Italian; "you and Mike. Always be kind. Good care."

Mrs. Riley turned with sudden fervor.

"Good cayre!—Mr. Ristofalo," she exclaimed, lifting her free hand and touching her bosom with the points of her fingers, "ye don't know the hairt of a woman, surr! No-o-o, surr! It's *love* we wants! 'The hairt as has trooly loved nivver furgits, but as trooly loves ahn to the close!' "

"Yes," said the Italian; "yes," nodding and ever smiling, "dass aw righ'."

But she:—

"Ah! it's no use fur you to be a-talkin' an' a-pallaverin' to Kate Riley when ye don't be lovin' her, Mr. Ristofalo, an' ye know ye don't."

A tear glistened in her eye.

"Yes, love you," said the Italian; "course, love you."

He did not move a foot or change the expression of a feature.

"H-yes!" said the widow. "H-yes!" she panted. "H-yes, a little! A little, Mr. Ristofalo! But I want"—she pressed her hand hard upon her bosom, and raised her eyes aloft—"I want to be—h—h—h—adaured above all the e'rth!"

"Aw righ'," said Ristofalo; "das aw righ'; yes—door above all you worth."

"Raphael Ristofalo," she said, "ye're a-deceivin' me! Ye came heere whin nobody axed ye,—an' that ye know is a fact, surr,—an' made yerself agree'ble to a poor, unsuspectin' widdah, an' [*tears*] rabbed me o' mie hairt, ye did; whin I nivver intinded to git married ag'in."

"Don't cry, Kate—Kate Ristofalo," quietly observed the Italian, getting an arm around her waist, and laying a hand on the farther cheek. "Kate Ristofalo."

"Shut!" she exclaimed, turning with playful fierceness, and proudly drawing back her head; "shut! Hah! It's Kate Ristofalo, is it? Ah, ye think so? Hah-h! It'll be ad least two weeks yet before the priest will be after giving you the right to call me that!"

And, in fact, an entire fortnight did pass before they were married.

THE SCHOOL IN THE
HAUNTED HOUSE

The era of political reconstruction came. The victorious national power decreed that they who had once been master and slave should enter into political partnership on terms of civil equality. The slaves grasped the boon; but the masters, trained for generations in the conviction that public safety and private purity were possible only by the subjection of the black race under the white, loathed civil equality as but another name for private companionship, and spurned, as dishonor and destruction in one, the restoration of their sovereignty at the price of political copartnership with the groveling race they had bought and sold and subjected easily to the leash and lash.

What followed took every one by surprise. The negro came at once into a larger share of power than it was ever intended he should or expected he would attain. His master, related to him long and only under the imagined necessities of plantation government, vowed the issue must and should be, not How shall the two races share public self-government in prosperous amity? but, Which race shall exclusively rule the other, race by race?

The necessities of national authority tipped the scale, and the powers of legislation and government and the spoils of office tumbled, all together, into the freedman's ragged lap. Thereupon there fell upon New Orleans, never well governed at the best, a volcanic shower of corruption and misrule.

And yet when history's calm summing-up and final judgment comes, there must this be pointed out, which was very hard to see through the dust and smoke of those days: that while plunder and fraud ran riot, yet no serious attempt was ever made by the freedman or his allies to establish any un-American principle of government, and for nothing else was he more fiercely, bloodily opposed than for measures approved by the world's best thought and in full.

264

harmony with the national scheme of order. We shall see now what these things have to do with our strange true story.

In New Orleans the American public school system, which recognizes free public instruction as a profitable investment of the public funds for the common public safety, had already long been established. The negro adopted and enlarged it. He recognized the fact that the relation of pupils in the public schools is as distinctly a public and not a private relation as that of the sidewalk, the market, the public park, or the street-car. But recognizing also the impracticabilities of place and time, he established separate schools for whites and blacks. In one instance, however, owing mainly to smallness of numbers, it seemed more feasible to allow a common enjoyment of the civil right of public instruction without separation by race than to maintain two separate schools, one at least of which would be very feeble for lack of numbers. Now, it being so decided, of all the buildings in New Orleans which one was chosen for this experiment but the "haunted house" in Royal street!

I shall never forget the day—although marked by no startling incident—when I sat in its lofty drawing-rooms and heard its classes in their annual examination. It was June, and the teachers and pupils were clad in recognition of the special occasion and in the light fabrics fitted to the season. The rooms were adorned with wreaths, garlands, and bouquets. Among the scholars many faces were beautiful, and all were fresh and young. Much Gallic blood asserted itself in complexion and feature, generally of undoubted, unadulterated "Caucasian" purity, but sometimes of visible and now and then of preponderating African tincture. Only two or three, unless I have forgotten, were of pure negro blood. There, in the rooms that had once resounded with the screams of Madame Lalaurie's little slave fleeing to her death, and with the hootings and maledictions of the enraged mob, was being tried the experiment of a common enjoyment of public benefits by the daughters of two widely divergent races, without the enforcement of private social companionship.

From such enforcement the school was as free as any school is or ought to be. The daily discipline did not require any two pupils to be social, but only every one to be civil, and civil to all. These pages are written, however, to tell a strange true story, and not to plead one cause or another. Whatever the story itself pleads, let it plead.

Outside the "haunted house," far and near, the whole community was divided into two fiercely hostile parties, often at actual war with each other, the one striving to maintain government upon a co-citizenship regardless of race in all public relations, the other sworn to make race the supreme, sufficient, inexorable condition of supremacy on the one part and subjection on the other. Yet for all this the school prospered.

Nevertheless, it suffered much internal unrest. Many a word was spoken that struck like a club, many a smile stung like a whip-lash, many a glance stabbed like a knife; even in the midst of recitations a wounded one would sometimes break into sobs or silent tears while the aggressor crimsoned and palpitated with the proud indignation of the master caste. The teachers met all such by-play with prompt, impartial repression and concentration upon the appointed duties of the hour.

Sometimes another thing restored order. Few indeed of the pupils, of whatever racial purity of preponderance, but held more or less in awe the ghostly traditions of the house; and at times it chanced to be just in the midst of one of these ebullitions of scorn, grief, and resentful tears that noiselessly and majestically the great doors of the reception-rooms, untouched by visible hands, would slowly swing open, and the hushed girls would call to mind Madame Lalaurie.

Not all who bore the tincture of the despised race suffered alike. Some were fierce and sturdy, and played a savage tit-for-tat. Some were insensible. A few bore themselves inflexibly by dint of sheer nerve; while many, generally much more white than black, quivered and winced continually under the contumely that fell, they felt, with peculiar injustice and cruelty upon them.

Odd things happened from time to time to remind one of the house's early history. One day a deep hidden well that no one had suspected the existence of was found in the basement of the main house. Another time—But we must be brief.

Matters went on thus for years. But at length there was a sudden and violent change.

VI.
EVICTIONS

The "Radical" party in Louisiana, gorged with private spoils and loathed and hated by the all but unbroken ranks of well-to-do society, though it held a *creed* as righteous and reasonable as any political party ever held, was going to pieces by the sheer weakness of its own political corruption. It was made mainly of the poor and weak elements of the people. Had it been ever so pure it could not have made headway against the strongest ranks of society concentrating against it with revolutionary intent, when deserted by the power which had called it to responsibility and—Come! this history of a house must not run into the history of a government. It is a fact in our story, however, that in the "Conservative" party there sprung up the "White League," purposing to wrest the State government from the "Radicals" by force of arms.

On the 14th of September, 1874, the White League met and defeated the Metropolitan Police in a hot and bloody engagement of infantry and artillery on the broad steamboat landing in the very middle of New Orleans. But the Federal authority interfered. The "Radical" government resumed control. But the White League survived and grew in power. In November elections were held, and the State legislature was found to be Republican by a majority of only two.

One bright, spring-like day in December, such as a northern March might give in its best mood, the school had gathered in the "haunted house" as usual, but the hour of duty had not yet struck. Two teachers sat in an upper class-room talking over the history of the house. The older of the two had lately heard of an odd new incident connected with it, and was telling of it. A distinguished foreign visitor, she said, guest at a dinner-party in the city the previous season, turned unexpectedly to his hostess, the talk being of quaint old New Orleans houses, and asked how to find "the house where that celebrated tyrant had lived who was driven from the city by a mob for maltreating her slaves." The rest of the company sat aghast, while the hostess silenced him by the severe coldness with which she replied that she "knew nothing about it." One of Madame Lalaurie's daughters was sitting there, a guest at the table.

When the teacher's story was told her companion made no comment. She had noticed a singular sound that was increasing in volume. It was out-of-doors—seemed far away; but it was drawing nearer. She started up, for she recognized it now as a clamor of human voices, and remembered that the iron gates had not yet been locked for the day. They hurried to the window, looked down, and saw the narrow street full from wall to wall for a hundred yards with men coming towards them. The front of the crowd had already reached the place and was turning towards the iron gates.

The two women went quickly to the hall, and, looking down the spiral staircase to the marble pavement of the entrance three stories below, saw the men swarming in through the wide gateway and doorway by dozens. While they still leaned over the balustrade, Marguerite, one of their pupils, a blue-eyed blonde girl of lovely complexion, with red, voluptuous lips, and beautiful hair held by a carven shell comb, came and bent over the balustrade with them. Suddenly her comb slipped from its hold, flashed downward, and striking the marble pavement flew into pieces at the feet of the men who were about to ascend. Several of them looked quickly up.

"It was my mother's comb!" said Marguerite, turned ashy pale, and sunk down in hysterics. The two teachers carried her to a remote room, the bed-chamber of the janitress, and then obeyed an order of the principal calling her associates to the second floor. A band of men were coming up the winding stair with measured, military tread towards the landing, where the principal, with her assistants gathered around her, stood to confront them.

She was young, beautiful, and of calm temper. Her skin, says one who was present, was of dazzling clearness, her abundant hair was golden auburn, and in happy hours her eyes were as "soft as velvet." But when the leader of the band of men reached the stair-landing, threw his coat open, and showed the badge of the White League, her face had blanched and hardened to marble, and her eyes darkened to black as they glowed with indignation.

"We have come," said the White Leaguer, "to remove the colored pupils. You will call your school to order." To which the principal replied:

"You will permit me first to confer with my corps of associates." He was a trifle disconcerted.

"Oh, certainly."

The teachers gathered in the principal's private room. Some were dumb, one broke into tears, another pleaded devotion to the principal, and one was just advising that the *onus* of all action be thrown upon the intruders, when the door was pushed open and the White Leaguer said:

"Ladies, we are waiting. Assemble the school; we are going to clean it out."

The pupils, many of them trembling, weeping, and terrified, were with difficulty brought to order in the assembly room. This place had once been Madame Lalaurie's dining-hall. A frieze of angels ran round its four walls, and, oddly, for some special past occasion, a legend in crimson and gold on the western side bore the words, "The Eye of God is on us."

"Gentlemen, the school is assembled," said the principal.

"Call the roll," was the reply, "and we will challenge each name."

It was done. As each name was called its young bearer rose and confronted her inquisitors. And the inquisitors began to blunder. Accusations of the fatal taint were met with denials and withdrawn with apologies. Sometimes it was truth, and sometimes pure arrogance and falsehood, that triumphed over these champions of instinctive racial antagonism. One dark girl shot up haughtily at the call of her name—

"I am of Indian blood, and can prove it!"

"You will not be disturbed."

"Coralie—," the principal next called. A thin girl of mixed blood and freckled face rose and said:

"My mother is white."

"Step aside!" commanded the White Leaguer.

"But by the law the color follows the mother, and so *I* am white."

"Step aside!" cried the man, in a fury. (In truth there was no such law.)

"Octavie—."

A pretty, Oriental-looking girl rises, silent, pale, but self-controlled.

"Are you colored?"

"Yes; I am colored." She moves aside.

"Marie O—."

A girl very fair, but with crinkling hair and other signs of negro extraction, stands up and says:

"I am the sister of the Hon.—," naming a high Democratic official, "and I shall not leave this school."

"You may remain; your case will be investigated."

"Eugénie—."

A modest girl, visibly of mixed race, rises, weeping silently.

"Step aside."

"Marcelline V—."

A bold-eyed girl of much African blood stands up and answers:

"I am not colored! We are Spanish, and *my brother will call on you and prove it.*" She is allowed to stay.

At length the roll-call is done. "Now, madam, you will dismiss these pupils that we have set aside, at once. We will go down and wait to see that they come out." The men tramped out of the room, went down-stairs, and rejoined the impatient crowd that was clamoring in the street.

Then followed a wild scene within the old house. Restraint was lost. Terror ruled. The girls who had been ordered into the street sobbed and shrieked and begged:

"Oh, save us! We cannot go out there; the mob will kill us! What shall we do?"

One girl of grand and noble air, as dark and handsome as an East Indian princess, and standing first in her class for scholarship, threw herself at her teacher's feet, crying, "Have pity on me, Miss—!"

"My poor Léontine," replied the teacher, "what can I do? There are good 'colored' schools in the city; would it not have been wiser for your father to send you to one of them?"

But the girl rose up and answered:

"Must I go to school with my own servants to escape an unmerited disdain?" And the teacher was silent, while the confusion increased.

"The shame of it will kill me!" cried gentle Eugénie L—. And thereupon, at last, a teacher, commonly one of the sternest in discipline, exclaimed:

"If Eugénie goes, Marcelline shall go, if I have to put her out myself! Spanish, indeed! And Eugénie a pearl by the side of her!"

Just then Eugénie's father came. He had forced his way through the press in the street, and now stood bidding his child have courage and return with him the way he had come.

"Tie your veil close, Eugénie," said the teacher, "and they will not know you." And so they went, the father and the daughter. But they went alone. None followed. This roused the crowd to noisy anger.

"Why don't the rest come?" it howled. But the teachers tried in vain to inspire the panic-stricken girls with courage to face the mob, and were in despair, when a school official arrived, and with calm and confident authority bade the expelled girls gather in ranks and follow him through the crowd. So they went out through the iron gates, the great leaves of which closed after them with a rasping of their key and shooting of their bolts, while a teacher said:

"Come; the reporters will soon be here. Let us go and see after Marguerite."

They found her in the room of the janitress, shut in and fast asleep.

"Do you think," one asked of the janitress, "that mere fright and the loss of that comb made this strong girl ill?"

"No. I think she must have guessed those men's errand, and her eye met the eye of some one who knew her."

"But what of that?"

"She is 'colored.' "

"Impossible!"

"I tell you, yes!"

"Why, I thought her as pure German as her name."

"No, the mixture is there; though the only trace of it is on her lips. Her mother—she is dead now—was a beautiful quadroon. A German sea-captain loved her. The law stood between them. He opened a vein in his arm, forced in some of her blood, went to court, swore he had African blood, got his license, and married her. Marguerite is engaged to be married to a white man, a gentleman who does not know this. It was like life and death, so to speak, for her not to let those men turn her out of here."

The teacher turned away, pondering.

The eviction did not, at that time, hold good. The political struggle went on, fierce and bitter. The "Radical" government was doomed, but not dead. A few weeks after the scene just described the evicted girls were reinstated. A long term of suspense followed. The new year became the old and went out. Twice this happened. In 1877 there were two governors and two governments in Louisiana. In sight from the belvedere of the "haunted house," eight squares away up Royal street, in the State House, the *de facto* government was shut up under close military siege by the *de jure* government, and the Girls' High School in Madame Lalaurie's old house, continuing faithfully their daily sessions, knew with as little certainty to which of the two they belonged as though New Orleans had been some Italian city of the fifteenth century. But to guess the White League, was not far from right, and in April the Radical government expired.

A Democratic school-board came in. June brought Commencement day, and some of the same girls who had been evicted in 1874 were graduated by the new Board in 1877. During the summer the schools and school-laws were overhauled, and in September or October the high school was removed to another place, where each pupil suspected of mixed blood was examined officially behind closed doors and only those who could prove white or *Indian* ancestry were allowed to stay. A "colored" high school was opened in Madame Lalaurie's house with a few pupils. It lasted one session, maybe two, and then perished.

In 1882 the "haunted house" had become a Conservatory of Music. Chamber concerts were frequent in Madame Lalaurie's old dining-hall. On a certain sweet evening in the spring of that year there sat among those who had gathered to hear the haunted place filled with a deluge of sweet sounds one who had been a teacher there when the house had been, as some one—Conservative or Radical, who can tell which?—said on the spot, "for the second time purged of its iniquities." The scene was "much changed," says the auditor; but the ghosts were all there, walking on the waves of harmony. And thickest and fastest they trooped in and out when a passionate song thrilled the air with the promise that

"Some day—some day
Eyes clearer grown the truth may see."

SUGGESTED ADDITIONAL READINGS

Old Creole Days
The Grandissimes
Madame Delphine
The Silent South
Bonaventure
The Negro Question
John March, Southerner

SELECTED REFERENCES

Butcher, Philip. *George W. Cable: The Northampton Years* (1959).

――――. *George W. Cable* (1962).

Rubin, Louis D., Jr. *George W. Cable: The Life and Times of a Southern Heretic* (1969).

Skaggs, Merrill Maguire. *The Folk of Southern Fiction* (1972).

Turner, Arlin. *George W. Cable, A Biography* (1956).

PROJECTS AND PROBLEMS

Compare the social status of Creole, German, Irish, and Italian characters in *Dr. Sevier*. Which group is supplied with the most "American" virtues? Why?

Discuss Cable's position on Catholicism as it is revealed in comments about Creoles in *Old Creole Days* or *The Grandissimes*. Compare this with his portrait of a backwoods Baptist minister in "Posson Jone'."

In what ways is Bras-Coupé in *The Grandissimes* a Noble Savage? Was Cable using the story of the giant African to attack the old *Code Noir* or the color line of his own day?

Compare the Cajuns of *Bonaventure* with those depicted in Kate Chopin's *Bayou Folk*. Which of these writers is more genuinely sympathetic toward this minority group?

How do the octoroons of *Old Creole Days* differ from those of Charles W. Chesnutt's *The House Behind the Cedars?*

Study the essays in *The Silent South* or *The Negro Question*, evaluate Cable's merits as an essayist, and discuss the relevance of this material to contemporary issues.

Compare Cable's treatment of miscegenation in " 'Tite Poulette" in *Old Creole Days* with that of Sherwood Bonner in "A Volcanic Interlude" in *Lippincott's,* April, 1880. Mrs. Bonner's story is reprinted in *Nineteenth Century Short Fiction,* ed. by William Holmes and Edward Mitchell in 1970. Which story is more credible? Which is more sensational? How do the stories differ in their attitude toward slavery and racism?

For an incident that closely resembles Cable's report on the paradoxes of racial identity at the school on Royal Street, see the preface to Gustav de Beaumont's *Marie* (1835), a novel about Jacksonian America by a famous visitor, companion of Alexis de Tocqueville. The English translation (1958) is by Barbara Chapman. Compare Beaumont's picture of race relations in antebellum Baltimore with Cable's treatment of postbellum New Orleans.

CHARLES W. CHESNUTT
(1858–1932)

Chesnutt's conjure stories, set in antebellum North Carolina, had pleased *Atlantic Monthly* readers, who did not know the author's ancestry included African blood, by the time he published "What Is a White Man," one of his many articles on the race problem, in the May 30, 1889, *Independent.* The conjure tales accumulated and were collected in *The Conjure Woman* in 1899. It was joined in the same year by another volume of stories, *The Wife of His Youth,* in which Chesnutt shifted his attack from slavery to caste and color prejudice. One of the earliest biographies of Frederick Douglass was the short book that Chesnutt produced, also in 1899, from which the selection below, Chapter IV, is taken.

Although he continued to be interested in the problems of the color line, Chesnutt's fiction moved from a stylized treatment of folk superstitions to assaults on lynching and a realistic rendering of an urban race riot. After the three novels he published early in the twentieth century failed to attract a wide audience, Chesnutt abandoned the effort to make a career in letters. He left a mark on the nation's literature that is finally winning appropriate attention from critics and scholars.

WHAT IS A WHITE MAN?

The fiat having gone forth from the wise men of the South that the "all-pervading, all-conquering Anglo-Saxon race" must continue forever to exercise exclusive control and direction of the government of this so-called Republic, it becomes important to every citizen who values his birthright to know who are included in this grandiloquent term. It is of course perfectly obvious that the writer or speaker who used this expression—perhaps Mr. Grady[1] of Georgia—did not say what he meant. It is not probable that he meant to exclude from full citizenship the Celts and Teutons and Gauls and Slavs who make up so large a proportion of our population; he hardly meant to exclude the Jews, for even the most ardent fire-eater would hardly venture to advocate the disfranchisement of the thrifty race whose mortgages cover so large a portion of Southern soil. What the eloquent gentleman really meant by this high-sounding phrase was simply the white race; and the substance of the argument of that school of Southern writers to which he belongs, is simply that for the good of the country the Negro should have no voice in directing the government or public policy of the Southern States or of the nation.

But it is evident that where the intermingling of the races has made such progress as it has in this country, the line which separates the races must in many instances have been practically obliterated. And there has arisen in the United States a very large class of the population who are certainly not Negroes in an ethnological sense, and whose children will be no nearer Negroes than themselves. In view, therefore, of the very positive ground taken by the white leaders of the South, where most of these people reside, it becomes in the highest degree important to them to know what race they belong to. It ought to be also a matter of serious concern to the Southern white people; for if their zeal for good government is so great that they contemplate the practical overthrow of the Constitution and laws of the United States to secure it, they ought at least to be sure that no man entitled to it by their own argument, is robbed of a

_____[1] Henry W. Grady, editor of the *Atlanta Constitution*.

276

right so precious as that of free citizenship; the "all-pervading, all-conquering Anglo-Saxon" ought to set as high a value on American citizenship as the all-conquering Roman placed upon the franchise of his State two thousand years ago. This discussion would of course be of little interest to the genuine Negro, who is entirely outside of the charmed circle, and must content himself with the acquisition of wealth, the pursuit of learning and such other privileges as his "best friends" may find it consistent with the welfare of the nation to allow him; but to every other good citizen the inquiry ought to be a momentous one. What is a white man?

In spite of the virulence and universality of race prejudice in the United States, the human intellect long ago revolted at the manifest absurdity of classifying men fifteen-sixteenths white as black men; and hence there grew up a number of laws in different states of the Union defining the limit which separated the white and colored races, which was, when these laws took their rise and is now to a large extent, the line which separated freedom and opportunity from slavery or hopeless degradation. Some of these laws are of legislative origin; others are judge-made laws, brought out by the exigencies of special cases which came before the courts for determination. Some day they will, perhaps, become mere curiosities of jurisprudence; the "black laws" will be bracketed with the "blue laws," and will be at best but landmarks by which to measure the progress of the nation. But to-day these laws are in active operation, and they are, therefore, worthy of attention; for every good citizen ought to know the law, and, if possible, to respect it; and if not worthy of respect, it should be changed by the authority which enacted it. Whether any of the laws referred to here have been in any manner changed by very recent legislation the writer cannot say, but they are certainly embodied in the latest editions of the revised statutes of the states referred to.

The colored people were divided, in most of the Southern States, into two classes, designated by law as Negroes and mulattoes respectively. The term Negro was used in its ethnological sense, and needed no definition; but the term "mulatto" was held by legislative enactment to embrace all persons of color not Negroes. The words "quadroon" and "mestizo" are employed in some of the law books, tho not defined; but the term "octoroon," as indicating a person

THE MINORITY PRESENCE IN AMERICAN LITERATURE

having one-eighth of Negro blood, is not used at all, so far as the writer has been able to observe.

The states vary slightly in regard to what constitutes a mulatto or person of color, and as to what proportion of white blood should be sufficient to remove the disability of color. As a general rule, less than one-fourth of Negro blood left the individual white—in theory; race questions being, however, regulated very differently in practice. In Missouri, by the code of 1855, still in operation, so far as not inconsistent with the Federal Constitution and laws, "any person other than a Negro, any one of whose grandmothers or grandfathers is or shall have been a Negro, tho all of his or her progenitors except those descended from the Negro may have been white persons, shall be deemed a mulatto." Thus the color-line is drawn at one-fourth of Negro blood, and persons with only one-eighth are white.

By the Mississippi code of 1880, the color-line is drawn at one-fourth of Negro blood, all persons having less being theoretically white.

Under the code noir of Louisiana, the descendant of a white and a quadroon is white, thus drawing the line at one-eighth of Negro blood. The code of 1876 abolished all distinctions of color; as to whether they have been re-enacted since the Republican Party went out of power in that state the writer is not informed.

Jumping to the extreme North, persons are white within the meaning of the Constitution of Michigan who have less than one-fourth of Negro blood.

In Ohio the rule, as established by numerous decisions of the Supreme Court, was that a preponderance of white blood constituted a person a white man in the eye of the law, and entitled him to the exercise of all the civil rights of a white man. By a retrogressive step the color-line was extended in 1861 in the case of marriage, which by statute was forbidden between a person of pure white blood and one having a visible admixture of African blood. But by act of legislature, passed in the spring of 1887, all laws establishing or permitting distinctions of color were repealed. In many parts of the state these laws were always ignored, and they would doubtless have been repealed long ago but for the sentiment of the southern counties, separated only by the width of the Ohio River from a former slaveholding state. There was a bill introduced in the legislature during the last session to re-enact the "black laws," but it was hopelessly defeated; the member who introduced it evidently mistook his latitude; he ought to be a member of the Georgia legislature.

But the state which, for several reasons, one might expect to have the strictest laws in regard to the relations of the races, has really the loosest. Two extracts from decisions of the Supreme Court of South Carolina will make clear the law of that state in regard to the color line.

"The definition of the term mulatto, as understood in this state, seems to be vague, signifying generally a person of mixed white or European and Negro parentage, in whatever proportions the blood of the two races may be mingled in the individual. But it is not invariably applicable to every admixture of African blood with the European, nor is one having all the features of a white to be ranked with the degraded class designated by the laws of this state as persons of color, because of some remote taint of the Negro race. The line of distinction, however, is not ascertained by any rule of law. . . . Juries would probably be justified in holding a person to be white in whom the admixture of African blood did not exceed the proportion of one-eighth. But it is in all cases a question for the jury, to be determined by them upon the evidence of features and complexion afforded by inspection, the evidence of reputation as to parentage, and the evidence of the rank and station in society occupied by the party. The only rule which can be laid down by the courts is that where there is a distinct and visible admixture of Negro blood, the individual is to be denominated a mulatto or person of color."

In a later case the court held:

"The question whether persons are colored or white, where color or feature are doubtful, is for the jury to decide by reputation, by reception into society, and by their exercise of the privileges of the white man, as well as by admixture of blood."

It is an interesting question why such should have been, and should still be, for that matter, the law of South Carolina, and why there should exist in that state a condition of public opinion which would accept such a law. Perhaps it may be attributed to the fact that the colored population of South Carolina always out numbered the white population, and the eagerness of the latter to recruit their ranks was sufficient to overcome in some measure their prejudice against the Negro blood. It is certainly true that the color-line is, in practice as in law, more loosely drawn in South Carolina than in any other Southern State, and that no inconsiderable element of the population of that state consists of these legal white persons, who were either born in the state, or, attracted thither by this feature of the laws, have come in from surrounding states, and, forsaking home and kindred, have taken their social position as white people. A reasonable degree of reticence in regard to one's antecedents is, however, usual in such cases.

Before the War the color-line, as fixed by law, regulated in theory the civil and political status of persons of color. What that status was, was expressed in the Dred Scott decision. But since the War, or rather since the enfranchisement of the colored people, these laws have been mainly confined—in theory, be it always remembered —to the regulation of the intercourse of the races in schools and in the marriage relation. The extension of the color-line to places of public entertainment and resort, to inns and public highways, is in most states entirely a matter of custom. A colored man can sue in the courts of any Southern State for the violation of his common-law rights, and recover damages of say fifty cents without costs. A colored minister who sued a Baltimore steamboat company a few weeks ago for refusing him first-class accommodation, he having paid first-class fare, did not even meet with that measure of success: the learned judge, a Federal judge by the way, held that the plaintiff's rights had been invaded, and that he had suffered humiliation at the hands of the defendant company, but that "the humiliation was not sufficient to entitle him to damages." And the learned judge dismissed the action without costs to either party.

Having thus ascertained what constitutes a white man, the good citizen may be curious to know what steps have been taken to preserve the purity of the white race, Nature, by some unaccountable oversight, having to some extent neglected a matter so important to the future prosperity and progress of mankind. The marriage laws referred to here are in active operation, and cases under them are by no means infrequent. Indeed, instead of being behind the age, the marriage laws in the Southern States are in advance of public opinion; for very rarely will a Southern community stop to figure on the pedigree of the contracting parties to a marriage where one is white

CHARLES W. CHESNUTT   281

and the other is known to have any strain of Negro blood.

In Virginia, under the title "Offenses against Morality," the law provides that "any white person who shall intermarry with a Negro shall be confined in jail not more than one year and fined not exceeding one hundred dollars." In a marginal note on the statute-book, attention is called to the fact that "a similar penalty is not imposed on the Negro"—a stretch of magnanimity to which the laws of other states are strangers. A person who performs the ceremony of marriage in such a case is fined two hundred dollars, one-half of which goes to the informer.

In Maryland, a minister who performs the ceremony of marriage between a Negro and a white person is liable to a fine of one hundred dollars.

In Mississippi, code of 1880, it is provided that "the marriage of a white person to a Negro or mulatto or person who shall have one-fourth or more of Negro blood, shall be unlawful"; and as this prohibition does not seem sufficiently emphatic, it is further declared to be "incestuous and void," and is punished by the same penalty prescribed for marriage within the forbidden degrees of consanguinity.

But it is Georgia, the *alma genetrix* of the chain-gang, which merits the questionable distinction of having the harshest set of color laws. By the law of Georgia the term "person of color" is defined to mean "all such as have an admixture of Negro blood, and the term 'Negro,' includes mulattoes." This definition is perhaps restricted somewhat by another provision, by which "all Negroes, mestizoes, and their descendants, having one-eighth of Negro or mulatto blood in their veins, shall be known in this State as persons of color." A colored minister is permitted to perform the ceremony of marriage between colored persons only, tho white ministers are not forbidden to join persons of color in wedlock. It is further provided that "the marriage relation between white persons and persons of African descent is forever prohibited, and such marriages shall be null and void." This is a very sweeping provision; it will be noticed that the term "persons of color," previously defined, is not employed, the expression "persons of African descent" being used instead. A court which was so inclined would find no difficulty in extending this provision of the law to the remotest strain of African blood. The marriage relation is forever prohibited. Forever is a long time.

There is a colored woman in Georgia said to be worth $300,000—an immense fortune in the poverty-stricken South. With a few hundred such women in that state, possessing a fair degree of good looks, the color-line would shrivel up like a scroll in the heat of competition for their hands in marriage. The penalty for the violation of the law against intermarriage is the same sought to be imposed by the defunct Glenn Bill for violation of its provisions; *i.e.*, a fine not to exceed one thousand dollars, and imprisonment not to exceed six months, or twelve months in the chain-gang.

Whatever the wisdom or justice of these laws, there is one objection to them which is not given sufficient prominence in the consideration of the subject, even where it is discussed at all; they make mixed blood a *prima facie* proof of illegitimacy. It is a fact that at present, in the United States, a colored man or woman whose complexion is white or nearly white is presumed, in the absence of any knowledge of his or her antecedents, to be the offspring of a union not sanctified by law. And by a curious but not uncommon process, such persons are not held in the same low estimation as white people in the same position. The sins of their fathers are not visited upon the children, in that regard at least; and their mothers' lapses from virtue are regarded either as misfortunes or as faults excusable under the circumstances. But in spite of all this, illegitimacy is not a desirable distinction, and is likely to become less so as these people of mixed blood advance in wealth and social standing. This presumption of illegitimacy was once, perhaps, true of the majority of such persons; but the times have changed. More than half of the colored people of the United States are of mixed blood; they marry and are given in marriage, and they beget children of complexions similar to their own. Whether or not, therefore, laws which stamp these children as illegitimate, and . . . establish a lower standard of morality for a large part of the population than the remaining part is judged by, are wise laws; and whether or not the purity of the white race could not be as well preserved by the exercise of virtue, and the operation of those natural laws . . . so often quoted by Southern writers as the justification of all sorts of Southern "policies"—are questions which the good citizen may at least turn over in his mind occasionally, pending the settlement of other complications which have grown out of the presence of the Negro on this continent.

FREDERICK DOUGLASS ON
THE ABOLITIONIST CIRCUIT

In 1841 Douglass entered upon that epoch of his life which brought the hitherto obscure refugee prominently before the public, and in which his services as anti-slavery orator and reformer constitute his chief claim to enduring recollection. Millions of negroes whose lives had been far less bright than Douglass's had lived and died in slavery. Thousands of fugitives under assumed names were winning a precarious livelihood in the free States and trembling in constant fear of the slave-catcher. Some of these were doing noble work in assisting others to escape from bondage. Mr. Siebert, in his *Underground Railroad,* mentions one fugitive slave, John Mason by name, who assisted thirteen hundred others to escape from Kentucky. Another picturesque fugitive was Harriet Tubman, who devoted her life to this work with a courage, skill, and success that won her a wide reputation among the friends of freedom. A number of free colored men in the North, a few of them wealthy and cultivated, lent their time and their means to this cause. But it was reserved for Douglass, by virtue of his marvellous gift of oratory, to become pre-eminently the personal representative of his people for a generation.

In 1841 the Massachusetts Anti-slavery Society, which had been for some little time weakened by faction, arranged its differences, and entered upon a campaign of unusual activity, which found expression in numerous meetings throughout the free States, mainly in New England. On August 15 of that year a meeting was held at Nantucket, Massachusetts. The meeting was conducted by John A. Collins, at that time general agent of the society, and was addressed by William Lloyd Garrison and other leading abolitionists. Douglass had taken a holiday and come from New Bedford to attend this convention, without the remotest thought of taking part except as a spectator. The proceedings were interesting, and aroused the audience to a high state of feeling. There was present in the meeting a certain abolitionist, by name William C. Coffin, who had heard Douglass speak in the little negro Sunday-school at New Bedford, and who knew of his recent escape from slavery. To him came the happy inspiration to ask Douglass to speak a few words to the convention by way of personal testimony. Collins introduced the speaker as "a graduate from slavery, with his diploma written upon his back."

Douglass himself speaks very modestly about this, his first public appearance. He seems, from his own account, to have suffered somewhat from stage fright, which was apparently his chief memory concerning it. The impressions of others, however, allowing a little for the enthusiasm of the moment, are a safer guide as to the effect of Douglass's first speech. Parker Pillsbury reported that, "though it was late in the evening when the young man closed his remarks, none seemed to know or care for the hour. . . . The crowded congregation had been wrought up almost to enchantment during the whole long evening, particularly by some of the utterances of the last speaker [Douglass], as he turned over the terrible apocalypse of his experience in slavery." Mr. Garrison bore testimony to "the extraordinary emotion it exerted on his own mind and to the powerful impression it exerted upon a crowded auditory." "Patrick Henry," he declared, "had never made a more eloquent speech than the one they had just listened to from the lips of the hunted fugitive." Upon Douglass and his speech as a text Mr. Garrison delivered one of the sublimest and most masterly efforts of his life; and then and there began the friendship between the fugitive slave and the great agitator which opened the door for Douglass to a life of noble usefulness, and secured to the anti-slavery cause one of its most brilliant and effective orators.

At Garrison's instance Collins offered Douglass employment as lecturer for the Anti-slavery Society, though the idea of thus engaging him doubtless occurred to more than one of the abolition leaders who heard his Nantucket speech. Douglass was distrustful of his own powers. Only three years out of slavery, with little learning and no experience as a public speaker, painfully aware of the prejudice which must be encountered by men of his color, fearful too of the publicity that might reveal his whereabouts to his legal owner, who might reclaim his property wherever found, he yielded only reluctantly to Mr. Collins's proposition, and agreed at first upon only a three months' term of service.

Most of the abolitionists were, or meant to be, consistent in their practice of what they preached; and so, when Douglass was enrolled as one of the little band of apostles, they treated him literally as a man and a brother. Their homes, their hearts, and their often none too well-filled purses were open to him. In this new atmosphere his mind expanded, his spirit took on high courage, and he read and studied diligently, that he might make himself worthy of his opportunity to do something for his people.

During the remainder of 1841 Douglass travelled and lectured in Eastern Massachusetts with George Foster, in the interest of the two leading abolition journals, the *Anti-slavery Standard* and the *Liberator*, and also lectured in Rhode Island against the proposed Dorr constitution, which sought to limit the right of suffrage to white male citizens only, thus disfranchising colored men who had theretofore voted. With Foster and Pillsbury and Parker and Monroe and Abby Kelly he labored to defeat the Dorr constitution and at the same time promote the abolition gospel. The proposed constitution was defeated, and colored men who could meet the Rhode Island property qualification were left in possession of the right to vote.

Douglass had plunged into this new work, after the first embarrassment wore off, with all the enthusiasm of youth and hope. But, except among the little band of Garrisonians and their sympathizers, his position did not relieve him from the disabilities attaching to his color. The feeling toward the negro in New England in 1841 was but little different from that in the State of Georgia to-day. Men of color were regarded and treated as belonging to a distinctly inferior order of creation. At hotels and places of public resort they were refused entertainment. On railroads and steamboats they were herded off by themselves in mean and uncomfortable cars. If welcomed in churches at all, they were carefully restricted to the negro pew. As in the Southern States to-day, no distinction was made among them in these respects by virtue of dress or manners or culture or means; but all were alike discriminated against because of their dark skins. Some of Douglass's abolition friends, among whom he especially mentions Wendell Phillips and two others of lesser note, won their way to his heart by at all times refusing to accept privileges that were denied to their swarthy companion. Douglass resented proscription wherever met with, and resisted it with force when the odds were not too overwhelming. More than once he was beaten and maltreated by railroad conductors and brakemen. For a time the Eastern Railroad ran its cars through Lynn, Massachusetts, without stopping, because Douglass, who resided at that time in Lynn, insisted on riding in the white people's car, and made trouble when interfered with. Often it was impossible for the abolitionists to secure a meeting-place; and in several instances Douglass paraded the streets with a bell, like a town crier, to announce that he would lecture in the open air.

Some of Douglass's friends, it must be admitted, were at times rather extreme in their language, and perhaps stirred up feelings that a more temperate vocabulary would not have aroused. None of them ever hesitated to call a spade a spade, and some of them denounced slavery and all its sympathizers with the vigor and picturesqueness of a Muggletonian or Fifth Monarchy man of Cromwell's time execrating his religious adversaries. And, while it was true enough that the Church and the State were, generally speaking, the obsequious tools of slavery, it was not easy for an abolitionist to say so in vehement language without incurring the charge of treason or blasphemy,—an old trick of bigotry and tyranny to curb freedom of thought and freedom of speech. The little personal idiosyncrasies which some of the reformers affected, such as long hair in the men and short hair in the women,—there is surely some psychological reason why reformers run to such things,— served as convenient excuses for gibes and unseemly interruptions at their public meetings. On one memorable occasion, at Syracuse, New York, in November, 1842, Douglass and his fellows narrowly escaped tar and feathers. But, although Douglass was vehemently denunciatory of slavery in all its aspects, his twenty years of training in that hard school had developed in him a vein of prudence that saved him from these verbal excesses,—perhaps there was also some element of taste involved,—and thus made his arguments more effective than if he had alienated his audiences by indiscriminate attacks on all the institutions of society. No one could justly accuse Frederick Douglass of cowardice or self-seeking; yet he was opportunist enough to sacrifice the immaterial for the essential, and to use the best means at hand to promote the ultimate object sought, although the means thus offered might not be the ideal instrument. It was doubtless this trait that led Douglass, after he separated from his abolitionist friends, to modify his views upon the subject of disunion and the constitutionality of slavery, and to support political parties whose platforms by no means expressed the full measure of his convictions.

In 1843 the New England Anti-slavery Society resolved, at its annual meeting in the spring, to stir the Northern heart and rouse the national conscience by a series of one hundred conventions in New Hampshire, Vermont, New York, Ohio, Indiana, and Pennsylvania. Douglass was assigned as one of the agents for the conduct of this undertaking. Among those associated in this work, which extended over five months, were John A. Collins, the president of the society, who mapped out the campaign; James Monroe; George Bradburn; William A. White; Charles L. Remond, a colored orator, born in Massachusetts, who rendered effective service in the abolition cause; and Sidney Howard Gay, at that time managing editor of the *National Anti-slavery Standard* and later of the New York *Tribune* and the New York *Evening Post.*

The campaign upon which this little band of missionaries set out was no inconsiderable one. They were not going forth to face enthusiastic crowds of supporters, who would meet them with brass bands and shouts of welcome. They were more likely to be greeted with hisses and cat-calls, sticks and stones, stale eggs and decayed cabbages, hoots and yells of derision, and decorations of tar and feathers.

In some towns of Vermont slanderous reports were made in advance of their arrival, their characters were assailed, and their aims and objects misrepresented. In Syracuse, afterward distinguished for its strong anti-slavery sentiment, the abolitionists were compelled to hold their meetings in the public park, from inability to procure a house in which to speak; and only after their convention was well under way were they offered the shelter of a dilapidated and abandoned church. In Rochester they met with a more hospitable reception. The indifference of Buffalo so disgusted Douglass's companions that they shook the dust of the city from their feet, and left Douglass, who was accustomed to coldness and therefore undaunted by it, to tread the wine-press alone. He spoke in an old post-office for nearly a week, to such good purpose that a church was thrown open to him; and on a certain Sunday, in the public park, he held

288 THE MINORITY PRESENCE IN AMERICAN LITERATURE

and thrilled by his eloquence an audience of five thousand people.

On leaving Buffalo, Douglass joined the other speakers, and went with them to Clinton County, Ohio, where, under a large tent, a mass meeting was held of abolitionists who had come from widely scattered points. During an excursion made about this time to Pennsylvania to attend a convention at Norristown, an attempt was made to lynch him at Manayunk; but his usual good fortune served him, and he lived to be threatened by higher powers than a pro-slavery mob.

When the party of reformers reached Indiana, where the pro-slavery spirit was always strong, the State having been settled largely by Southerners, their campaign of education became a running fight, in which Douglass, whose dark skin attracted most attention, often got more than his share. His strength and address brought him safely out of many an encounter; but in a struggle with a mob at Richmond, Indiana, he was badly beaten and left unconscious on the ground. A good Quaker took him home in his wagon, his wife bound up Douglass's wounds and nursed him tenderly,—the Quakers were ever the consistent friends of freedom, —but for the lack of proper setting he carried to the grave a stiff hand as the result of this affray. He had often been introduced to audiences as "a graduate from slavery with his diploma written upon his back": from Indiana he received the distinction of a post-graduate degree.

SUGGESTED ADDITIONAL READINGS

> The Conjure Woman
> The Wife of His Youth
> The House Behind the Cedars
> The Short Fiction of Charles W. Chesnutt (1974), ed. by Sylvia Lyons Render.

SELECTED REFERENCES

Andrews, William L. "The Significance of Charles W. Chesnutt's 'Conjure Stories.'" Southern Literary Journal, 7, No. 1 (1974), 78–99.

———. "William Dean Howells and Charles W. Chesnutt: Criticism and Race Fiction in the Age of Booker T. Washington." *American Literature*, 48 (1976), 327-29.

Chesnutt, Helen M. *Charles Waddell Chesnutt: Pioneer of the Color Line* (1952).

Hemenway, Robert. " 'Baxter's Procrustes': Irony and Protest." *CLA Journal*, 18 (1974), 172–85.

Howells, William Dean. "Mr. Charles W. Chesnutt's Stories." *Atlantic Monthly*, 75 (1900), 699–701.

———. "A Psychological Counter-Current in Recent Fiction." *North American Review*, 173 (1901), 881–83.

Keller, Dean H. "Charles Waddell Chesnutt (1858–1932)." *American Literary Realism, 1870–1910*, No. 3 (1968), 1–4.

Mason, Julian D., Jr. "Charles W. Chesnutt as Southern Author." *Mississippi Quarterly*, 20 (1967), 77–89.

Render, Sylvia Lyons. "Tar Heelia in Chesnutt." *CLA Journal*, 9 (1965), 39–50.

Teller, Walter. "Charles W. Chesnutt's Conjuring and Color-Line Stories." *American Scholar*, 42 (1972), 125–27.

Wideman, John. "Charles W. Chesnutt: *The Marrow of Tradition.*" *American Scholar*, 42 (1972), 128–34.

PROJECTS AND PROBLEMS

Compare Chesnutt's Uncle Julius, in *The Conjure Woman*, with Joel Chandler Harris's Uncle Remus and Thomas Nelson Page's Uncle Billy, in "Marse Chan."

Discuss the octoroons depicted by Chesnutt, William Wells Brown, and Frances Harper. Do the writers differ from one another, and from white authors, in their use of the "tragic octoroon" figure?

Chesnutt's subjects progressed from conjure through the color line to race conflict. Consider *The Marrow of Tradition* (1901) as an anticipation of Richard Wright and later militant black novelists. Make reference also to short stories and essays by Chesnutt that are expressions of his position on civil rights.

Compare Chesnutt's use of conjure in his fiction with George W. Cable's treatment of voodoo in *The Grandissimes*, noting in particular what these authors seem to say about how whites and blacks are affected by the folklore and superstition of their region.

Speculate on the reasons for Chesnutt's difficulty in getting "What Is a White Man?" published. Relate that essay to the work of the Open Letter Club, with which he was affiliated. See Helen M. Chesnutt's biography and Philip Butcher, *George W. Cable: The Northampton Years* (1959).

JOAQUIN MILLER
(1841?–1913)

Sometimes called "the poet of the Sierras" and "the Byron of Oregon," Joaquin Miller tried to live up to the romantic legends that circulated about his life in the West. *Songs of the Sierras* (1871), acclaimed in England, was the most successful of his many volumes of poetry. He wrote several plays, among them *The Danites in the Sierras* (1882), a drama about the Mormons. The selection below is from *My Own Story* (1890), one of several autobiographical works.

BLOOD ON THE SNOW

There was a tribe of Indians camped down on the rapid, rocky
Klamat River—a sullen, ugly set were they, too: at least so said The
Forks. Never social, hardly seeming to notice the whites, who were
now thick about them, below them, above them, on the river all
around them. Sometimes we would meet one on the narrow trail; he
would gather his skins about him, hide his bow and arrows under
their folds, and, without seeming to see any one, would move past us
still as a shadow. I do not remember that I ever saw one of these Indians laugh, not even to smile. A hard-featured, half-starved set of
savages, of whom the wise men of the camp prophesied no good.

The snow, unusually deep this winter, had driven them all down
from the mountains, and they were compelled to camp on the river.

The game, too, had been driven down along with the Indians, but
it was of but little use to them. Their bows and arrows did poor
competition with the rifles of the whites in the killing of the game.
The whites had fairly filled the cabins with deer and elk in their season, got the lion's share, and left the Indians almost destitute.

Another thing that made it rather more hard on the Indians than
anything else, was the utter failure of the annual run of salmon the
summer before, on account of the muddy water. The Klamat, which
had poured from the mountain lakes to the sea as clear as glass, was
now made muddy and turbid from the miners washing for gold on its
banks and tributaries. The trout turned on their sides and died; the
salmon from the sea came in but rarely on account of this; and what
few did come were pretty safe from the spears of the Indians, because of the colored water; so that the supply, which was more than
all others their bread and their meat, was entirely cut off. . . .

What made matters worse, there was a set of men, low men, of
the lowest type, who would hang around those lodges at night, give
the Indians whisky of the vilest sort, debauch their women, and
cheat the men out of their skins and bows and arrows.

Perhaps there was a grim sort of philosophy in the red man so disposing of his bows and arrows now that the game was gone and they
were of no further use. Sold them for bread for his starving babes,
maybe. How many tragedies are hidden here? How many tales of

devotion, self-denial, and sacrifice, as true as the white man ever lived, as pure, and brave, and beautiful as ever gave tongue to eloquence or pen to song, sleep here with the dust of these sad and silent people on the bank of the stormy river!

In this condition of things, about mid-winter, when the snow was deep and crusted stiff, and all nature seemed dead and buried in a ruffled shroud, there was a murder. The Indians had broken out! The prophesied massacre had begun!

Killed by the Indians! It swept like a telegram through the camp. Confused and incoherent, it is true, but it gathered force and form as the tale flew on from tongue to tongue, until it assumed a frightful shape.

A man had been killed by the Indians down at the rancheria. Not much of a man, it is true.

Killed, too, down in the Indian camp when he should have been in bed, or at home, or at least in company with his kind.

All this made the miners hesitate a bit as they hurriedly gathered in at The Forks, with their long Kentucky rifles, their pistols capped and primed, and bowie-knives in their belts.

But as the gathering storm that was to sweep the Indians from the earth took shape and form, these honest men stood out in little knots, leaning on their rifles in the streets, and gravely questioned whether, all things considered, the death of the "Chicken," for that was the dead man's name, was sufficient cause for interference.

To their eternal credit these men mainly decided that it was not, and two by two they turned away, went back to their cabins, hung their rifles up on the rack, and turned their thoughts to their own affairs.

But the hangers-on about the town were terribly enraged. "A man has been killed!" they proclaimed aloud. "A man has been murdered by the savages!! We shall all be massacred! butchered! burnt!!"

In one of the saloons where men were wont to meet at night, have stag-dances, and drink lightning, a short, important man, with the print of a glass-tumbler cut above his eye, arose and made a speech.

"Fellow-miners [he had never touched a pick in his life], I am ready to die for me country! [He was an Irishman sent out to Sydney at the Crown's expense.] What have I to live for? [Nothing whatever, as far as any one could tell.] Fellow-miners, a man has been kilt by the treacherous savages—kilt in cold blood! Fellow-miners, let us advance upon the inemy. Let us—let us—fellow-miners, let us take a drink and advance upon the inemy."

"Range around me. Rally to the bar and take a drink, every man of you, at me own ixpense."

The barkeeper, who was also proprietor of the place, a man not much above the type of the speaker, ventured a mild remonstrance at this wholesale generosity; but the pistol, flourished in a very suggestive way, settled the matter, and, with something of a groan, he set his decanters to the crowd, and became a bankrupt.

This was the beginning; they passed from saloon to saloon, or, rather, from door to door; the short, stout Irishman making speeches, and the mob gathering force and arms as it went, and then, wild with drink and excitement, moved down upon the Indians, some miles away on the bank of the river.

"Come," said the Prince[1] to me, as they passed out of town, "let us see this through. Here will be blood. We will see from the hill overlooking the camp. I hope the Indians are armed—hope to God they are 'heeled,' and that they will receive the wretches warmly as they deserve."

Maybe his own wretchedness had something to do with his wrath; but I think not. I should rather say that, had he been in strength and spirits, and had his pistols, which had long since been disposed of for bread, he had met this mob face to face, and sent it back to town.

We followed not far behind the crowd of fifty or sixty men armed with pistols, rifles, knives, and hatchets.

The trail led to a little point overlooking the bar on which the Indian huts were huddled.

The river made a bend about there. It ground and boiled in a crescent blocked with running ice and snow. The Indians were out in the extreme curve of a horse-shoe made by the river, and we advanced from without. They were in a net. They had only a choice of deaths; death by drowning, or death at the hands of their hereditary foe.

It was nearly night; cold and sharp the wind blew up the river, and the snow flew around like feathers. Not an Indian to be seen. The thin, blue smoke came slowly up, as if afraid to leave the wigwams, and the traditional, everwatchful and wakeful Indian dog was

[1]The author's companion, a "prince of a fellow."

not to be seen or heard. The men hurried down upon the camp, spreading out upon the horse-shoe as they advanced in a run.

"Stop here," said the Prince; and we stood from the wind behind a boulder that stood, tall as a cabin, upon the bar. The crowd advanced to within half a pistol shot, and gave a shout as they drew and leveled their arms. Old squaws came out—bang! bang! bang! shot after shot, and they were pierced and fell, or turned to run.

The whites, yelling, howling, screaming, were now among the lodges, shooting down at arm's length man, woman, or child. Some attempted the river, I should say, for I afterward saw streams of blood upon the ice, but not one escaped; nor was a hand raised in defense. It was all done in a little time. Instantly, as the shots and shouts began, we two advanced, we rushed into the camp, and, when we reached the spot, only now and then a shot was heard within a lodge, dispatching a wounded man or woman.

The few surviving children—for nearly all had been starved to death—had taken refuge under skins and under lodges overthrown, hidden away as little kittens will hide just old enough to spit and hiss, and hide when they first see the face of man. These were now dragged forth and shot. Not all these men who made this mob, bad as they were, did this—only a few; but enough to leave, as far as they could, no living thing.

The babies did not scream. Not a wail, not a sound. The murdered men and women, in the few minutes that the breath took leave, did not even groan.

As we came up a man named "Shon"—at least, that was all the name I knew for him—held up a baby by the leg, a naked, bony little thing, which he had dragged from under a lodge—held it up with one hand, and with the other blew its head to pieces with his pistol.

I must stop here to say that this man Shon soon left camp, and was afterward hung by the Vigilance Committee near Lewiston, Idaho Territory; that he whined for his life like a puppy, and he died like a coward as he was. I chronicle this fact with a feeling of delight. . . .

This man threw down the body of the child among the dead, and rushed across to where a pair of ruffians had dragged up another, a little girl, naked, bony, thin as a shadow, starved into a ghost. He caught her by the hair with a howl of delight, placed the pistol to her head, and turned around to point the muzzle out of range of his companions who stood around on the other side.

The child did not cry—she did not even flinch. Perhaps she did not know what it meant; but I should rather believe she had seen so much of death there, so much misery, the steady, silent work of the monster famine through the village day after day that she did not care. I saw her face; it did not even wince. Her lips were thin and fixed, and firm as iron.

The villain, having turned her around, now lifted his arm, cocked the pistol, and—

"Stop that! Stop that, or die! You damned assassin, let go that child, or I will pitch you neck and crop into the Klamat."

The Prince had him by the throat with one hand, and with the other he wrested the pistol from his grasp and threw it into the river. The Prince had not even so much as a knife. The man did not know this, nor did the Prince care, or he had not thrown away the weapon he wrung from his hand. The Prince pushed the child behind him, and advanced toward the short, fat Sydney convict, who had turned, pistol in hand, in his direction.

"Keep your distance, or I will send you to hell across lots in a second."

The man turned away cowed and baffled. He had looked in the Prince's face, and seen his master.

As for myself, I was not only helpless, but, as was always the case on similar occasions, stupid, awkward, speechless. I went up to the little girl, however, got a robe out of one of the lodges—for they had not yet set fire to the village—and put it around her naked little body. After that, as I moved about among the dead, or stepped aside to the river to see the streams of blood on the snow and ice, she followed close as a shadow behind me, but said nothing.

Suddenly there was a sharp yell, a volley of oaths, exclamations, a scuffle, and blows.

"Scalp him! Scalp him! the little savage! Scalp him and throw him in the river!"

From out of the piles of dead somewhere, no one could tell exactly where or when, an apparition had sprung up—a naked little Indian boy, that might have been all the way from twelve to twenty, armed with a knotted war-club, and had fallen upon his foes like a fury.

The poor little hero, starved into a shadow, stood little show there, though he had been a very Hercules in courage. He was felled almost instantly by kicks and blows; and the very number of his enemies saved his life, for they could neither shoot nor stab him with safety, as they crowded and crushed around him.

How or why he was finally spared, was always a marvel. Quite likely the example of the Prince had moved some of the men to more humanity.

When the crowd that had formed a knot about him had broken up, and I first got sight of him, he was sitting on a stone with his hands between his naked legs, and blood dripping from his long hair, which fell down in strings over his forehead. He had been stunned by a grazing shot, no doubt, and had fallen among the first. He came up to his work, though, like a man, when his senses returned, and, without counting the chances, lifted his two hands to do with all his might the thing he had been taught.

Valor, such valor as that, is not a cheap or common thing. It is rare enough to be respected even by the worst of men. It is only the coward who affects to despise such courage.

The boy sat there on the stone as the village burned, the smoke from burning skins, the wild-rye straw, willow-baskets and Indian robes, ascended, and a smell of burning bodies went up to the Indians' God and the God of us all, and no one said nay, and no one approached him; the men looked at him from under their slouched hats as they moved around, but said nothing.

I pitied him. God knows I pitied him. I was a boy myself, alone, helpless, in an army of strong and unsympathetic men. I would have gone up and put my arms about the wild and splendid little savage, bloody and desperate as he was, so lonely now, so intimate with death, so pitiful! if I had dared, dared the reproach of men-brutes.

There was a sort of nobility about him; his recklessness, his desire to die, lifting his little arms against an army of strong and reckless men, his proud and defiant courage, that made me feel at once that he was above me, stronger, somehow better, than I. Still, he was a boy, and I was a boy—the only boys in the camp, and my heart went out, strong and true, toward him.

The work of destruction was now too complete. There was not found another living thing—nothing but two or three Indians that had been shot and shot, and yet seemed determined never to die, that lay in the bloody snow down toward the rim of the river.

Naked nearly, they were, and only skeletons, with the longest and blackest hair tangled and tossed, and blown in strips and strings, or in clouds out on the white and the blood-red snow, or down their tawny backs, or over their bony breasts, about their dusky forms, fierce and unconquered, with the bloodless lips set close, and blue, and cold, and firm, like steel.

The dead lay around us, piled up in places, limbs twisted with limbs in the wrestle with death; a mother embracing her boy here; an arm thrown around a neck there; as if these wild people could love as well as die.

In the village, some of the white men claimed to have found something that had been stolen. I have no idea there is any truth in it. I wish there was; then there might be some shadow of excuse for all the murders that made up this cruel tragedy, all of which is, I believe, literally true; truer than nine-tenths of the history and official reports written, wherein these people are mentioned; and I stand ready to give names, dates, and detail to all whom it may concern.

Let me not here be misunderstood. An Indian is no better than a white man. If he sins let him suffer. But I do protest against this custom of making up a case—this custom of deciding the case against him in favor of the white man, forever, on the evidence of the white man only; even though that custom be, in the language of the law, so old "that the memory of man runneth not to the contrary."

The white man and red man are much alike, with one great difference, which you must and will set down to the advantage of the latter.

The Indian has no desire for fortune; he has no wish in his wild state to accumulate wealth; and it is in his wild state that he must be judged, for it is in this condition that he is said to sin. If "money is the root of all evil," as Solomon hath it, then the Indian has not that evil, or that root of evil, or any desire for it.

It is the white man's monopoly. If an Indian love you, trusts you, or believes in you at all, he will serve you, guide you through the country, follow you to battle, fight for you, he and all his sons and kindred, and never think of the pay or profit. He would despise it if offered, beyond some presents, some tokens of remembrance, decorations, or simplest articles of use.

Again, I do vehemently protest against taking the testimony of border Indians or any Indians with whom the white man comes in constant contact, and to whom he has taught the use of money and the art of lying.

And most particularly I do protest against taking these Indians—renegades—who affiliate, mix and strike hands with the whites, as representative Indians. Better take our own "camp followers" as respectable and representative soldiers.

When you reflect that for centuries the Indians in almost every lodge on the continent, at almost every council, have talked of the whites and their aggressions, and of these things chiefly, and always with that bitterness which characterizes people who look at and see only one side of the case, then you may come to understand, a little, their eternal hatred of their hereditary enemy—how deeply seated this is, how it has become a part of their nature, and, above all, how low, fallen, and how unlike a true Indian one must be who leaves his retreating tribe and lingers in a drunken and debauched fellowship with the whites, losing all his virtues, and taking on all the vices of his enemy.

The true Indian retires before the white man's face to the forest and to the mountain tops. It is very true he leaves a surf, a sort of kelp and driftwood, and trash, the scum, the idlers, and the cowards and prostitutes of his tribe, as the sea leaves weeds and drift and kelp. But the true Indian is to be found only in his fastnesses or on the heights, gun in hand.

SUGGESTED ADDITIONAL READINGS

"The Song of Creation"
"Kit Carson's Ride"
"The Sioux Chief's Daughter"
"The Tale of Tall Alcide"
"El Vaquero"
Shadows of Shasta

SELECTED REFERENCES

Frost, O. W. *Joaquin Miller* (1967).
Keiser, Albert. *The Indian in American Literature* (1931).
Peterson, Martin S. *Joaquin Miller* (1937).

PROJECTS AND PROBLEMS -

Compare Miller's portrayal of Indian character with that of Helen Hunt Jackson or of Lydia Maria Child in *Hobomok.*

Weigh the contrasting elements in Miller's writing and decide whether he was essentially realistic or romantic. How much was he affected by the local color tradition and by writers like Bret Harte?

JACOB A. RIIS
(1849–1914)

Born in Denmark, Riis emigrated to the United States in
1870 and by 1877 had become a police reporter on New
York newspapers. In the tenement sections of the city he
recorded with camera and pen the poverty of the ghetto
dwellers. His exposure of conditions in the slums
contributed to the establishment of revised housing and
health codes. The first selection presented here is from
Chapter 20 of *How the Other Half Lives* (1890) and the
second is extracted from "Merry Christmas in the
Tenements," a story in *Out of Mulberry Street* (1898).

ITALIANS AND OTHERS IN THE TENEMENTS OF NEW YORK

Where Mulberry Street crooks like an elbow within hail of the old depravity of the Five Points, is "the Bend," foul core of New York's slums. Long years also, the cows coming home from the pasture trod a path over this hill. Echoes of tinkling bells linger there still, but they do not call up memories of green meadows and summer fields; they proclaim the homecoming of the ragpicker's cart. In the memory of man the old cowpath has never been other than a vast human pigsty. There is but one Bend in the world, and it is enough. The city authorities, moved by the angry protests of ten years of sanitary reform effort, have decided that it is too much and must come down. Another Paradise Park will take its place and let in sunlight and air to work such transformation as at the Five Points, around the corner of the next block. Never was change more urgently needed. Around the Bend cluster the bulk of the tenements that are stamped as altogether bad, even by the optimists of the Health Department. Incessant raids cannot keep down the crowds that make them their home. In the scores of back alleys, of stable lanes, and hidden byways, of which the rent collector alone can keep track, they share such shelter as the ramshackle structures afford with every kind of abomination rifled from the dumps and ash barrels of the city. Here, too, shunning the light, skulks the unclean beast of dishonest idleness. The Bend is the home of the tramp as well as the ragpicker.

It is not much more than twenty years since a census of the Bend district returned only twenty-four of the six hundred and nine tenements as in decent condition. Three-fourths of the population of the "Bloody Sixth" Ward were then Irish. The army of tramps that grew up after the disbandment of the armies in the field, and has kept up its muster roll, together with the inrush of the Italian tide, have ever since opposed a stubborn barrier to all efforts at permanent improvement. The more that has been done, the less it has seemed to accomplish in the way of real relief, until it has at last become clear

302

that nothing short of entire demolition will ever prove of radical benefit. Corruption could not have chosen ground for its stand with better promise of success. The whole district is a maze of narrow, often unsuspected passageways—necessarily, for there is scarce a lot that has not two, three, or four tenements upon it, swarming with unwholesome crowds. What a bird's eye view of the Bend would be like is a matter of bewildering conjecture. Its everyday appearance, as seen from the corner of Bayard Street on a sunny day, is one of the sights of New York.

Bayard Street is the high road to Jewtown across the Bowery, picketed from end to end with the outposts of Israel. Hebrew faces, Hebrew signs, and incessant chatter in the queer lingo that passes for Hebrew on the East Side attend the curious wanderer to the very corner of Mulberry Street. But the moment he turns the corner the scene changes abruptly. Before him lies spread out what might better be the market place in some town in Southern Italy than a street in New York—all but the houses; they are still the same old tenements of the unromantic type. But for once they do not make the foreground in a slum picture from the American metropolis. The interest centers not in them, but in the crowd they shelter only when the street is not preferable, and that with the Italian is only when it rains or he is sick. When the sun shines, the entire population seeks the street, carrying on its household work, its bargaining, its love-making on street or sidewalk, or idling there when it has nothing better to do, with the reverse of the impulse that makes the Polish Jew coop himself up in his den with the thermometer at stewing heat. Along the curb women sit in rows, young and old alike, with the odd head covering, pad or turban, that is their badge of servitude—hers to bear the burden as long as she lives—haggling over baskets of frowsy weeds, some sort of salad probably, stale tomatoes, and oranges not above suspicion. Ash barrels serve them as counters, and not infrequently does the arrival of the official cart enroute for the dump cause a temporary suspension of trade until the barrels have been emptied and restored. Hucksters' and peddlers' carts make two rows of booths in the street itself, and along the houses is still another—a perpetual market doing a very lively trade in its own queer staples, found nowhere on American ground save in the Bend. Two old hags, camping on the pavement, are dispensing stale bread, baked not in loaves, but in the shape of big wreaths like exaggerated crullers, out of bags of dirty bedtick. There is no use disguising the fact: they look like and they probably are old mattresses mustered into service under the pressure of a rush of trade. Stale bread was the one article the health officers, after a raid on the market, once reported as "not unwholesome." It was only disgusting. Here is a brawny butcher, sleeves rolled up above the elbows and clay pipe in mouth, skinning a kid that hangs from his hook. They will tell you with a laugh at the Elizabeth Street police station that only a few days ago when a dead goat had been reported lying in Pell Street it was mysteriously missing by the time the offal-cart came to take it away. It turned out that an Italian had carried it off in his sack to a wake or feast of some sort in one of the back alleys.

On either side of the narrow entrance to Bandits' Roost, one of the most notorious of these, is a shop that is a fair sample of the sort of invention necessity is the mother of in the Bend. It is not enough that trucks and ash barrels have provided four distinct lines of shops that are not down on the insurance maps, to accommodate the crowds. Here have the very hallways been made into shops. Three feet wide by four deep, they have just room for one, the shopkeeper, who, himself within, does his business outside, his wares displayed on a board hung across what was once the hall door. Back of the rear wall of this unique shop a hole has been punched from the hall into the alley and the tenants go that way. One of the shops is a "tobacco bureau," presided over by an unknown saint, done in yellow and red —there is not a shop, a stand, or an ash barrel doing duty for a counter, that has not its patron saint—the other is a fishstand full of slimy, odd-looking creatures, fish that never swam in American waters, or if they did, were never seen on an American fishstand, and snails. Big, awkward sausages, anything but appetizing, hang in the grocer's doorway, knocking against the customer's head as if to remind him that they are there waiting to be bought. What they are, I never had the courage to ask. Down the street comes a file of women carrying enormous bundles of firewood on their heads, loads of decaying vegetables from the market wagons in their aprons, and each a baby at the breast supported by a sort of sling that prevents it from tumbling down. The women do all the carrying, all the work one sees going on in the Bend. The men sit or stand in the streets, on trucks, or in the open doors of the saloons smoking black clay pipes, talking and gesticulating as if forever on the point of coming to blows. Near a particularly boisterous group, a really pretty girl with a string of amber beads twisted artlessly in the knot of her raven hair has been bargaining long and earnestly with an old granny, who presides over a wheelbarrow load of secondhand stockings and faded cotton yarn, industriously darning the biggest holes while she extols the virtues of her stock. One of the rude swains, with patched overalls tucked into his boots, to whom the girl's eyes have strayed more than once, steps up and gallantly offers to pick her out the handsomest pair, whereat she laughs and pushes him away with a gesture which he interprets as an invitation to stay; and he does, evidently to the satisfaction of the beldame, who forthwith raises her prices fifty per cent without being detected by the girl.

Red bandannas and yellow kerchiefs are everywhere; so is the Italian tongue, infinitely sweeter than the harsh gutturals of the Russian Jew around the corner. So are the *ristorantes* of innumerable Pasquales; half of the people in the Bend are christened Pasquale, or get the name in some other way. When the police do not know the name of an escaped murderer, they guess at Pasquale and send the name out on alarm; in nine cases out of ten it fits. So are the "banks" that hang out their shingle as tempting bait on every hand. There are half a dozen in the single block, steamship agencies, employment offices, and savings banks, all in one. So are the toddling youngsters, bowlegged half of them, and so are no end of mothers, present and prospective, some of them scarce yet in their teens. . . .

A JEWISH WEDDING IN LIBERTY HALL

In Liberty Hall a Jewish wedding is in progress. Liberty! Strange
how the word echoes through these sweaters' tenements, where starvation is at home half the time. It is as an all-consuming passion
with these people, whose spirit a thousand years of bondage have
not availed to daunt. It breaks out in strikes, when to strike is to
hunger and die. Not until I stood by a striking cloakmaker whose
last cent was gone, with not a crust in the house to feed seven
hungry mouths, yet who had voted vehemently in the meeting that
day to keep up the strike to the bitter end,—bitter indeed, nor far
distant,—and heard him at sunset recite the prayer of his fathers:
"Blessed art thou, O Lord our God, King of the world, that thou hast
redeemed us as thou didst redeem our fathers, hast delivered us from
bondage to liberty, and from servile dependence to redemption!"—
not until then did I know what of sacrifice the word might mean,
and how utterly we of another day had forgotten. But for once shop
and tenement are left behind. Whatever other days may have in
store, this is their day of play, when all may rejoice.

The bridegroom, a cloak-presser in a hired dress-suit, sits alone
and ill at ease at one end of the hall, sipping whisky with a fine air of
indifference, but glancing apprehensively toward the crowd of
women in the opposite corner that surrounds the bride, a pale little
shop-girl with a pleading, winsome face. From somewhere unexpectedly appears a big man in an ill-fitting coat and skull cap,
flanked on either side by a fiddler, who scrapes away and away, ac-
companying the improvisator in a plaintive minor key as he halts
before the bride and intones his lay. With many a shrug of stooping
shoulders and queer excited gesture, he drones, in the harsh, guttural
Yiddish of Hester street, his story of life's joys and sorrows, its
struggles and victories in the land of promise. The women listen,
nodding and swaying their bodies sympathetically. He works himself
into a frenzy, in which the fiddlers vainly try to keep up with him.
He turns and digs the laggard angrily in the side without losing the
meter. The climax comes. The bride bursts into hysterical sobs,

while the women wipe their eyes. A plate, heretofore concealed under his coat, is whisked out. He has conquered; the inevitable collection is taken up.

The tuneful procession moves upon the bridegroom. An Essex-street girl in the crowd, watching them go, says disdainfully: "None of this humbug when I get married." It is the straining of young America at the fetters of tradition. Ten minutes later, when, between double files of women holding candles, the couple pass to the canopy where the rabbi waits, she has already forgotten; and when the crunching of a glass under the bridegroom's heel announces that they are one, and that until the broken pieces be reunited he is hers and hers alone, she joins with all the company in the exulting shout of "Mozzel tov!" ("Good luck!"). Then the *dupka*, men and women joining in, forgetting all but the moment, hands on hips, stepping in time, forward, backward, and across. And then the feast.

They sit at the long tables by squads and tribes. Those who belong together sit together. There is no attempt at pairing off for conversation or mutual entertainment, at speech-making or toasting. The business in hand is to eat, and it is attended to. The bridegroom, at the head of the table, with his shiny silk hat on, sets the example; and the guests emulate it with zeal, the men smoking big, strong cigars between mouthfuls. "Gosh! ain't it fine?" is the grateful comment of one curly-headed youngster, bravely attacking his third plate of chicken-stew. "Fine as silk," nods his neighbor in knickerbockers. Christmas, for once, means something to them that they can understand. The crowd of hurrying waiters make room for one bearing aloft a small turkey adorned with much tinsel and many paper flowers. It is for the bride, the one thing not to be touched until the next day—one day off from the drudgery of housekeeping; she, too, can keep Christmas.

A group of bearded, dark-browed men sit apart, the rabbi among them. They are the orthodox, who cannot break bread with the rest, for fear, though the food be kosher, the plates have been defiled. They brought their own to the feast, and sit at their own table, stern and justified. Did they but know what depravity is harbored in the impish mind of the girl yonder, who plans to hang her stocking overnight by the window! There is no fireplace in the tenement. Queer things happen over here, in the strife between the old and the new.

The girls of the College Settlement, last summer, felt compelled to explain that the holiday in the country which they offered some of these children was to be spent in an Episcopal clergyman's house, where they had prayers every morning. "Oh," was the indulgent answer, "they know it isn't true, so it won't hurt them."

SUGGESTED ADDITIONAL READING

The Children of the Poor

SELECTED REFERENCES

Meyer, Edith Patterson. *"Not Charity but Justice": The Story of Jacob A. Riis* (1974).
Ware, Louise. *Jacob A. Riis* (1938).

PROJECTS AND PROBLEMS

Does Riis challenge or support the notion that a great many Italians were named Pasquale and operated restaurants?

Compare the ghetto stories of *Vignettes of Manhattan* (1894), by Brander Matthews, with those of *Out of Mulberry Street*. Which writer seems to demonstrate greater authority? Which shows more compassion?

Does Riis seem to indicate that the "melting pot" is working? Does he suggest that the Americanization process involves the alteration or abandonment of the immigrant's cultural heritage? Is his portrait clearly that of one who was himself an immigrant?

Does the picture Riis gives of the progression of immigrant groups in a given city area resemble the report on a suburban neighborhood in transition that William Dean Howells offered in *Suburban Sketches* in 1871?

STEPHEN CRANE
(1871–1900)

A pioneer naturalist, Stephen Crane presented so grim a portrait of the experiences of an Irish family in a New York ghetto that he had to publish *Maggie: A Girl of the Streets* (1893) at his own expense. A revised version was issued under commercial auspices after the success of his great novel of the Civil War, *The Red Badge of Courage* (1895). Though he produced important poetry and stories during the remaining years of his short life, much of his time was spent as journalist and war correspondent.

Chapter 9 of the first version of *Maggie* appears below. It is followed by portions of "The Monster" from *The Monster and Other Stories* (1899). The third selection is a fragment from "The Knife," first published in *Harper's Magazine*, March, 1900.

THE JOHNSONS OF RUM ALLEY

A group of urchins were intent upon the side door of a saloon. Expectancy gleamed from their eyes. They were twisting their fingers in excitement.

"Here she comes," yelled one of them suddenly.

The group of urchins burst instantly asunder and its individual fragments were spread in a wide, respectable half circle about the point of interest. The saloon door opened with a crash, and the figure of a woman appeared upon the threshold. Her gray hair fell in knotted masses about her shoulders. Her face was crimsoned and wet with perspiration. Her eyes had a rolling glare.

"Not a damn cent more of me money will yehs ever get, not a damn cent. I spent me money here fer t'ree years an' now yehs tells me yeh'll sell me no more stuff! T'hell wid yeh, Johnnie Murckre! 'Disturbance?' Disturbance be damned! T'hell wid yeh, Johnnie—"

The door received a kick of exasperation from within and the woman lurched heavily out on the sidewalk.

The gamins in the half-circle became violently agitated. They began to dance about and hoot and yell and jeer. Wide dirty grins spread over each face.

The woman made a furious dash at a particularly outrageous cluster of little boys. They laughed delightedly and scampered off a short distance, calling out over their shoulders to her. She stood tottering on the curbstone and thundered at them.

"Yeh devil's kids," she howled, shaking red fists. The little boys whooped in glee. As she started up the street they fell in behind and marched uproariously. Occasionally she wheeled about and made charges on them. They ran nimbly out of reach and taunted her.

In the frame of a gruesome doorway she stood for a moment cursing them. Her hair straggled, giving her crimson features a look of insanity. Her great fists quivered as she shook them madly in the air.

The urchins made terrific noises until she turned and disappeared. Then they filed quietly in the way they had come.

The woman floundered about in the lower hall of the tenement house and finally stumbled up the stairs. On an upper hall a door was opened and a collection of heads peered curiously out, watching her. With a wrathful snort the woman confronted the door, but it was slammed hastily in her face and the key was turned.

She stood for a few minutes, delivering a frenzied challenge at the panels.

"Come out in deh hall, Mary Murphy, damn yeh, if yehs want a row. Come ahn, yeh overgrown terrier, come ahn."

She began to kick the door with her great feet. She shrilly defied the universe to appear and do battle. Her cursing trebles brought heads from all doors save the one she threatened. Her eyes glared in every direction. The air was full of her tossing fists.

"Come ahn, deh hull damn gang of yehs, come ahn," she roared at the spectators. An oath or two, cat-calls, jeers and bits of facetious advice were given in reply. Missles clattered about her feet.

"What deh hell's deh matter wid yeh?" said a voice in the gathered gloom, and Jimmie came forward. He carried a tin dinner-pail in his hand and under his arm a brown truckman's apron done in a bundle. "What deh hell's wrong?" he demanded.

"Come out, all of yehs, come out," his mother was howling. "Come ahn an' I'll stamp yer damn brains under me feet."

"Shet yer face, an' come home, yer damned old fool," roared Jimmie at her. She strided up to him and twirled her fingers in his face. Her eyes were darting flames of unreasoning rage and her frame trembled with eagerness for a fight.

"T'hell wid yehs! An' who deh hell are yehs? I ain't givin' a snap of me fingers fer yehs," she bawled at him. She turned her huge back in tremendous disdain and climbed the stairs to the next floor.

Jimmie followed, cursing blackly. At the top of the flight he seized his mother's arm and started to drag her toward the door of their room.

"Come home, damn yeh," he gritted between his teeth.

"Take yer hands off me! Take yer hands off me," shrieked his mother.

She raised her arm and whirled her great fist at her son's face. Jimmie dodged his head and the blow struck him in the back of the neck. "Damn yeh," gritted he again. He threw out his left hand and writhed his fingers about her middle arm. The mother and the son began to sway and struggle like gladiators.

"Whoop!" said the Rum Alley tenement house. The hall filled with interested spectators.

"Hi, ol' lady, dat was a dandy!"

"T'ree to one on deh red!"

"Ah, stop yer dam scrappin'!"

The door of the Johnson home opened and Maggie looked out. Jimmie made a supreme cursing effort and hurled his mother into the room. He quickly followed and closed the door. The Rum Alley tenement swore disappointedly and retired.

The mother slowly gathered herself up from the floor. Her eyes glittered menacingly upon her children.

"Here, now," said Jimmie, "we've had enough of dis. Sit down, an' don' make no trouble."

He grasped her arm, and twisting it, forced her into a creaking chair.

"Keep yer hands off me," roared his mother again.

"Damn yer ol' hide," yelled Jimmie, madly. Maggie shrieked and ran into the other room. To her there came the sound of a storm of crashes and curses. There was a great final thump and Jimmie's voice cried: "Dere damn yeh, stay still." Maggie opened the door now, and went warily out. "Oh, Jimmie."

He was leaning against the wall and swearing. Blood stood upon bruises on his knotty fore-arms where they had scraped against the floor or the walls in the scuffle. The mother lay screeching on the floor, the tears running down her furrowed face.

Maggie, standing in the middle of the room, gazed about her. The usual upheaval of the tables and chairs had taken place. Crockery was strewn broadcast in fragments. The stove had been disturbed on its legs, and now leaned idiotically to one side. A pail had been upset and water spread in all directions.

The door opened and Pete appeared. He shrugged his shoulders. "Oh, Gawd," he observed.

He walked over to Maggie and whispered in her ear. "Ah, what deh hell, Mag? Come ahn and we'll have a hell of a time."

The mother in the corner upreared her head and shook her tangled locks.

"Teh hell wid him and you," she said, glowering at her daughter in the gloom. Her eyes seemed to burn balefully. "Yeh've gone teh deh devil, Mag Johnson, yehs knows yehs have gone teh deh devil. Yer a disgrace teh yer people, damn yeh. An' now, git out an' go ahn wid dat doe-faced jude of yours. Go teh hell wid him, damn yeh, an' a good riddance. Go teh hell an' see how yeh likes it."

Maggie gazed long at her mother.

"Go teh hell now, an' see how yeh likes it. Git out. I won't have sech as yehs in me house! Get out, d'yeh hear! Damn yeh, git out!"

The girl began to tremble.

At this instant Pete came forward. "Oh, what deh hell, Mag, see," whispered he softly in her ear. "Dis all blows over. See? Deh ol' woman 'ill be all right in deh mornin'. Come ahn out wid me! We'll have a hell of a time."

The woman on the floor cursed. Jimmie was intent upon his bruised fore-arms. The girl cast a glance about the room filled with a chaotic mass of debris, and at the red, writhing body of her mother.

"Go teh hell an' good riddance."

She went.

A HERO IN LAVENDER TROUSERS

II.

It was apparent from Jimmie's manner that he felt some kind of desire to efface himself. He went down to the stable. Henry Johnson, the negro who cared for the doctor's horses, was sponging the buggy. He grinned fraternally when he saw Jimmie coming. These two were pals. In regard to almost everything in life they seemed to have minds precisely alike. Of course there were points of emphatic divergence. For instance, it was plain from Henry's talk that he was a very handsome negro, and he was known to be a light, a weight, and an eminence in the suburb of the town, where lived the larger number of the negroes, and obviously this glory was over Jimmie's horizon; but he vaguely appreciated it and paid deference to Henry for it mainly because Henry appreciated it and deferred to himself. However, on all points of conduct as related to the doctor, who was the moon, they were in complete but unexpressed understanding. Whenever Jimmie became the victim of an eclipse he went to the stable to solace himself with Henry's crimes. Henry, with the elasticity of his race, could usually provide a sin to place himself on a footing with the disgraced one. Perhaps he would remember that he had forgotten to put the hitching-strap in the back of the buggy on some recent occasion, and had been reprimanded by the doctor. Then these two would commune subtly and without words concerning their moon, holding themselves sympathetically as people who had committed similar treasons. On the other hand, Henry would sometimes choose to absolutely repudiate this idea, and when Jimmie appeared in his shame would bully him most virtuously, preaching with assurance the precepts of the doctor's creed, and pointing out to Jimmie all his abominations. Jimmie did not discover that this was odious in his comrade. He accepted it and lived in its shadow with humility, merely trying to conciliate the saintly Henry with acts of deference. Won by this attitude, Henry would sometimes allow the child to enjoy the felicity of squeezing the sponge over a buggy-wheel, even when Jimmy was still gory from unspeakable deeds.

Whenever Henry dwelt for a time in sackcloth, Jimmie did not

314

patronize him at all. This was a justice of his age, his condition. He did not know. Besides, Henry could drive a horse, and Jimmie had a full sense of this sublimity. Henry personally conducted the moon during the splendid journeys through the country roads, where farms spread on all sides, with sheep, cows, and other marvels abounding.

"Hello, Jim!" said Henry, poising his sponge. Water was dripping from the buggy. Sometimes the horses in the stalls stamped thunderingly on the pine floor. There was an atmosphere of hay and of harness.

For a minute Jimmie refused to take an interest in anything. He was very downcast. He could not even feel the wonders of wagon washing. Henry, while at his work, narrowly observed him.

"Your pop done wallop yer, didn't he?" he said at last.

"No," said Jimmie, defensively; "he didn't."

After this casual remark Henry continued his labor, with a scowl of occupation. Presently he said: "I done tol' yer many's th' time not to go a-foolin' an' a-projjeckin' with them flowers. Yer pop don' like it nohow." As a matter of fact, Henry had never mentioned flowers to the boy.

Jimmie preserved a gloomy silence, so Henry began to use seductive wiles in this affair of washing a wagon. It was not until he began to spin a wheel on the tree, and the sprinkling water flew everywhere, that the boy was visibly moved. He had been seated on the sill of the carriage-house door, but at the beginning of this ceremony he arose and circled toward the buggy, with an interest that slowly consumed the remembrance of a late disgrace.

Johnson could then display all the dignity of a man whose duty it was to protect Jimmie from a splashing. "Look out, boy! look out! You done gwi' spile yer pants. I raikon your mommer don't 'low this foolishness, she know it. I ain't gwi' have you round yere spilin' yer pants, an' have Mis' Trescott light on me pressen'ly. 'Deed I ain't."

He spoke with an air of great irritation, but he was not annoyed at all. This tone was merely a part of his importance. In reality he was always delighted to have the child there to witness the business of the stable. For one thing, Jimmie was invariably overcome with reverence when he was told how beautifully a harness was polished or a horse groomed. Henry explained each detail of this kind with unction, procuring great joy from the child's admiration.

III.

After Johnson had taken his supper in the kitchen, he went to his loft in the carriage-house and dressed himself with much care. No belle of a court circle could bestow more mind on a toilet than did Johnson. On second thought, he was more like a priest arraying himself for some parade of the church. As he emerged from his room and sauntered down the carriage-drive, no one would have suspected him of ever having washed a buggy.

It was not altogether a matter of the lavender trousers, nor yet the straw hat with its bright silk band. The change was somewhere far in the interior of Henry. But there was no cake-walk hyperbole in it. He was simply a quiet, well-bred gentleman of position, wealth, and other necessary achievements out for an evening stroll, and he had never washed a wagon in his life.

In the morning, when in his working-clothes, he had met a friend —"Hello, Pete!" "Hello, Henry!" Now, in his effulgence, he encountered this same friend. His bow was not at all naughty. If it expressed anything, it expressed consummate generosity—"Good-evenin', Misteh Washington." Pete, who was very dirty, being at work in a potato-patch, responded in a mixture of abasement and appreciation—"Good-evenin', Misteh Johnsing."

The shimmering blue of the electric arc-lamps was strong in the main street of the town. At numerous points it was conquered by the orange glare of the outnumbering gaslights in the windows of shops. Through this radiant lane moved a crowd, which culminated in a throng before the post-office, awaiting the distribution of the evening mails. Occasionally there came into it a shrill electric street-car, the motor singing like a cageful of grasshoppers, and possessing a great gong that clanged forth both warnings and simple noise. At the little theatre, which was a varnish and red-plush miniature of one of the famous New York theatres, a company of strollers was to play "East Lynne." The young men of the town were mainly gathered at the corners, in distinctive groups, which expressed various shades and lines of chumship, and had little to do with any social gradations. There they discussed everything with critical insight, passing the whole town in review as it swarmed in the street. When the gongs of the electric cars ceased for a moment to harry the ears, there could be heard the sound of the feet of the leisurely crowd on the bluestone pavement, and it was like the peaceful evening lashing at the shore of a lake. At the foot of the hill, where two lines of maples sentinelled the way, an electric lamp glowed high among the embowering branches, and made most wonderful shadow-etchings on the road below it.

When Johnson appeared amid the throng, a member of one of the profane groups at a corner instantly telegraphed news of this extraordinary arrival to his companions. They hailed him. "Hello, Henry! Going to walk for a cake to-night?"

"Ain't he smooth?"

"Why you've got that cake right in your pocket, Henry!"

"Throw out your chest a little more."

Henry was not ruffled in any way by these quiet admonitions and compliments. In reply he laughed a supremely good-natured, chuckling laugh, which nevertheless expressed an underground complacency of superior metal.

Young Griscom, the lawyer, was just emerging from Reifsnyder's barber shop, rubbing his chin contentedly. On the steps he dropped his hand and looked with wide eyes into the crowd. Suddenly he bolted back into the shop. "Wow!" he cried to the parliament; "you ought to see the coon that's coming!"

Reifsnyder and his assistant instantly poised their razors high and turned towards the window. Two belathered heads reared from the chairs. The electric shine in the street caused an effect like water to them who looked through the glass from the yellow glamour of Reifsnyder's shop. In fact, the people without resembled the inhabitants of a great aquarium that here had a square pane in it. Presently into this frame swam the graceful form of Henry Johnson.

"Chee!" said Reifsnyder. He and his assistant with one accord threw their obligations to the winds, and leaving their lathered victims helpless, advanced to the window. "Ain't he a taisy?" said Reifsnyder, marvelling.

But the man in the first chair, with a grievance in his mind, had found a weapon. "Why, that's only Henry Johnson, you blamed idiots! Come on now, Reif, and shave me. What do you think I am—a mummy?"

Reifsnyder turned, in a great excitement. "I bait you any money that vas not Henry Johnson! Henry Johnson! Rats!" The scorn put into this last word made it an explosion. "That man was a Pullman-car porter or someding. How could that be Henry Johnson?" he demanded, turbulently. "You vas crazy."

The man in the first chair faced the barber in a storm of indignation. "Didn't I give him those lavender trousers?" he roared.

And young Griscom, who had remained attentively at the window, said: "Yes, I guess that was Henry. It looked like him."

"Oh, vell," said Reifsnyder, returning to his business, "if you think so! Oh, vell!" He implied that he was submitting for the sake of amiability.

Finally the man in the second chair, mumbling from a mouth made timid by adjacent lather, said: "That was Henry Johnson all right. Why, he always dresses like that when he wants to make a front! He's the biggest dude in town—anybody knows that."

"Chinger!" said Reifsnyder.

Henry was not at all oblivious of the wake of wondering ejaculation that streamed out behind him. On other occasions he had reaped this same joy, and he always had an eye for the demonstration. With a face beaming with happiness he turned away from the scene of his victories into a narrow side street, where the electric light still hung high, but only to exhibit a row of tumble-down houses leaning together like paralytics.

The saffron Miss Bella Farragut, in a calico frock, had been crouched on the front stoop, gossiping at long range, but she espied her approaching caller at a distance. She dashed around the corner of the house, galloping like a horse. Henry saw it all, but he preserved the polite demeanor of a guest when a waiter spills claret down his cuff. In this awkward situation he was simply perfect.

The duty of receiving Mr. Johnson fell upon Mrs. Farragut, because Bella, in another room, was scrambling wildly into her best gown. The fat old woman met him with a great ivory smile, sweeping back with the door, and bowing low. "Walk in, Misteh Johnson, walk in. How is you dis ebenin', Misteh Johnson—how is you?"

Henry's face showed like a reflector as he bowed and bowed, bending almost from his head to his ankles. "Good-evenin', Mis' Fa'gut; good-evenin'. How is you dis evenin'? Is all you' folks well, Mis' Fa'gut?"

After a great deal of kowtow, they were planted in two chairs opposite each other in the living-room. Here they exchanged the most tremendous civilities, until Miss Bella swept into the room, when there was more kowtow on all sides, and a smiling show of teeth that was like an illumination.

The cooking-stove was of course in this drawing-room, and on the fire was some kind of long-winded stew. Mrs. Farragut was obliged to arise and attend to it from time to time. Also young Sim came in and went to bed on his pallet in the corner. But to all these domesticities the three maintained an absolute dumbness. They bowed and smiled and ignored and imitated until a late hour, and if they had been the occupants of the most gorgeous salon in the world they could not have been more like three monkeys.

After Henry had gone, Bella, who encouraged herself in the appropriation of phrases, said, "Oh, Ma, isn't he divine?"

THE JACKSONS OF WHILOMVILLE

. . . The scattered colony of negroes which hovered near Whilom-ville was of interesting origin, being the result of some contrabands who had drifted as far north as Whilomville during the great civil war. The descendants of these adventurers were mainly conspicuous for their bewildering number, and the facility which they possessed for adding even to this number. Speaking, for example, of the Jack-sons—one couldn't hurl a stone into the hills about Whilomville without having it land on the roof of a hut full of Jacksons. The town reaped little in labor from these curious suburbs. There were a few men who came in regularly to work in gardens, to drive teams, to care for horses, and there were a few women who came in to cook or to wash. These latter had usually drunken husbands. In the main the colony loafed in high spirits, and the industrious minority gained no direct honor from their fellows, unless they spent their earnings on raiment, in which case they were naturally treated with distinction. On the whole, the hardships of these people were the wind, the rain, the snow, and any other physical difficulties which they could cultivate. About twice a year the lady philanthropists of Whilomville went up against them, and came away poorer in goods but rich in complacence. After one of these attacks the colony would preserve a comic air of rectitude for two days, and then re-lapse again to the genial irresponsibility of a crew of monkeys.

SELECTED REFERENCES

Cady, Edwin H. *Stephen Crane* (1962).

Cunliffe, Marcus. "Stephen Crane and the American Background of *Maggie.*" *American Quarterly,* 7 (1955), 31–44.

Ellison, Ralph. "Stephen Crane and the Mainstream of American Fiction." *Shadow and Act* (1967).

Fine, L. H., ed. "Two Unpublished Plays by Stephen Crane." *Resources for American Literary Study,* 1 (1971), 200–16.

Gibson, Donald B. *The Fiction of Stephen Crane* (1968).

Nye, Russel B. "Stephen Crane as Social Critic." *Modern Quarterly,* 11 (1940), 48–54.

Westbrook, Max. "Stephen Crane's Social Ethic." *American Quarterly,* 14 (1962), 587–96.

PROJECTS AND PROBLEMS

Maggie and *George's Mother* are accounts of life in New York's Bowery, but this polyglot slum resembles ghettos in other places and other times. Compare Crane's treatment of race relations in his ghetto with that of Michael Gold in *Jews Without Money* (1930), or Richard Wright in *Native Son* (1940), or Samuel Ornitz in *Bride of the Sabbath* (1951).

How is it that Nellie, the woman "of brilliance and audacity" in *Maggie,* escapes the fate that befalls Maggie Johnson? To what minority, if any, does Nellie belong?

Evidently it was Crane's intention in exposing man's inhumanity to man in a small town in "The Monster" to appeal for racial brotherhood, and he has been praised for showing a black man performing a truly heroic act, rare in American fiction at the time. But Cora Crane said "Henry Johnson was a hero only as he was a horror," and it may be argued that Crane's story is seriously marred by his reliance on the minstrel stereotype. Discuss the portrayal of all the black characters in Crane's stories about Whilomville.

Compare *Maggie* with Edwin O'Connor's modern novel about Irish life in the slums of Boston, *The Edge of Sadness* (1962), or with Ann Petry's *The Street* (1946), a novel about a black woman's plight in Harlem.

For a study of Crane and his contemporaries, compare his treatment of minority characters with that of Frank Norris in *McTeague*, or discuss the relationship between *Maggie* and Theodore Dreiser's "Sanctuary" (in *Chains—Lesser Novels and Stories*), or compare his tenement tales with selected works by Abraham Cahan.

Compare Crane's portrayal of Indian peons and Mexicans with his treatment of ghetto dwellers in New York. See Volume VIII of *The Works of Stephen Crane* (1973), ed. by Fredson Bowers; *Stephen Crane in the West and Mexico* (1971), ed. by Joseph Katz; and *The New York City Sketches of Stephen Crane* (1966), ed. by Robert W. Stallman and Edward R. Hagemann.

Study carefully Crane's rendering of Negro dialect. Is there any significance to be found in the inconsistencies in the speech of Henry Johnson in "The Monster," who says "Your pop" to young Jimmie Trescott at one moment and "Yer pop" the next?

Speculate on Crane's reasons for changing certain details of his newspaper report, "Stephen Crane's Own Story," in writing "The Open Boat." Consult *The Stephen Crane Reader* (1972), ed. by R. W. Stallman, or *The Portable Stephen Crane* (1969), ed. by Joseph Katz.

Compare *Maggie* with J. W. Sullivan's "Minnie Kelsey's Wedding," reprinted from *Tenement Tales of New York* in *A Gathering of Ghetto Writers: Irish, Italian, Jewish, Black, and Puerto Rican* (1972), ed. by Wayne Miller. Why would Sullivan's story have been more acceptable to the general reading public of the time than was Crane's novel?

THOMAS NELSON PAGE
(1853–1922)

Page's sentimental fiction about old Virginia brought the defeated Confederacy a measure of victory. A whole school of writers followed his lead in creating an aristocratic society of gentle white masters and loyal happy bondsmen, a skillful revival of the Plantation Tradition that J. P. Kennedy had introduced more than half a century earlier. A celebrated example of Page's work is "Marse Chan" in his first book, *In Ole Virginia* (1887). His idealization of the antebellum order, in stories, novels, poems, and nonfiction, was intended to denigrate Reconstruction and justify the racial policies of the New South. Here is one of the narratives collected in *Pastime Stories* (1894).

UNCLE JACK'S VIEWS OF GEOGRAPHY

When the war ended and the negroes were free there was a great enthusiasm for educating them. One of the first schools started was built on the edge of his place by Colonel Trigg, who got a little "school-marm," as they were termed, to come down and teach it. It was soon filled by the colored population, the pupils ranging from five to seventy-five years, all studying "a-b ab, e-b, eb." Even "Uncle Jack Scott," the colonel's head man, one of the "old-timers," went in, and was transferred from the stable to the school-room. The colonel fumed about it; but it was laid to the door of Uncle Jack's new wife, "Mrs. Scott," who was a "citified" lady, and had many airs. Uncle Jack was an acquisition to the school, and was given a prominent position by the stove, the little school-mistress paying him especial attention, putting him through his "a-b ab's and e-b eb's" with much pride, and holding him up to her younger scholars as a shining example. A few days later Uncle Jack appeared, armed with a long hickory switch, which he presented to the teacher with a remark about "lazy niggers needin' hick'ry's much's bread," and loud enough to be heard by the whole school. Miss Barr (called "Bear" by Mrs. Scott) took the hickory with visible emotion, made a speech to the school upon Uncle Jack's wisdom and appreciation of educational advantages, and Uncle Jack, with much grandeur, went to his task. The lesson that day was "b-a ba, b-e be." Unhappily, Uncle Jack had learned "a-b ab, e-b eb" too well, and b and a were never anything but ab, and b and e never anything but eb, no matter in what order they came. Miss Barr was at her wits' end. She had established her rules, and she stood by them. Had she believed it her duty, she would have gone to perdition without a tremor. One of her most invariable rules was to thrash for missing lessons. When Uncle Jack missed his lesson two days hand-running, she was in despair; but discipline was to be preserved, and after hours of painful suspense, when he still failed, she ordered him to stand up. He obeyed. She glanced around, seeking some alternative; fifty pairs of eyes were fastened upon her. She reached under her desk, and slowly drew out a hickory, the very one Uncle Jack had brought her. Fifty pairs of eyes showed their whites.

"Take off your coat."

There was a gasp throughout the room.

Uncle Jack paused a moment as if stupefied, then laid down his book and took off his coat.

"Take off your waistcoat."

He obeyed.

"You ain't gwine meck me teck off my shirt, is you?" he asked tremulously.

"No. Clasp your hands."

He did so, and she raised the hickory and brought it down "swauo" across his back. Again there was a gasp throughout the room, which came every time a lick was given. Uncle Jack was the only one who uttered no sound. He stood like a statue. When she finished, he put on his coat and sat down. School was dismissed.

Next day Uncle Jack was at his old place at the stable.

"Why, I thought you were at school?" said his master, who had heard something of the trouble.

"Nor, suh; I got 'nough edication," he said. He stuck his curry-comb into his brush. There was a pause; then: "I tell you de fac', Marse Conn. I is too ole to be whupt by a ooman, an' a po' white ooman at dat."

It was several years after this that Uncle Jack was working one day at a water-gate in a field, when the children came down the road from school. They stopped and peeped stolidly through the fence. Among them was "Jawnie," Mrs. Scott's hopeful, who had proved an apter scholar than his father. His bag was on his arm. He climbed over the fence, and from the bank gazed down apathetically at his father in the water below. Presently he said:

"Or, poppa, de teacher say you mus' git me a geography."

Uncle Jack's jaw set. He dug on as if he had not heard. Then he repeated to himself: "Geog'aphy—geog'aphy. Marse Conn, whut is dat? Whut is a geog'aphy?" he asked, looking up at his employer, who happened to be by.

"A geography?" said the Colonel. "Why, a geography is a—is a book—a book that tells about places, and where they are, and so on." He gave a comprehensive sweep with his arm around the horizon.

"Yas, suh; now I onderstands," said Jack, going back to digging.

Presently he stopped, and looked up at "Jawnie." "I say, boy, you tell de teacher *I* say you better stick to you' a-b ab's an' you' e-b eb's, an' let geog'aphy alone. You knows de way now to de spring an' de wood-pile an' de mill, an' when you gits a little bigger I's gwine to show you de way to de hoe-handle an' de cawn-furrer, an' dat's all de geog'aphy a nigger's got to know."

He dug on.

SUGGESTED ADDITIONAL READINGS

In Ole Virginia
Befo' de War (with A. C. Gordon)
Elsket and Other Stories
The Old South
The Burial of the Guns
Social Life in Old Virginia
Red Rock

SELECTED REFERENCES

Gross, Theodore. "The Negro in the Literature of Reconstruction." *Phylon*, 22 (1961), 5–14.
———. *Thomas Nelson Page* (1967).
Wilson, Edmund. *Patriotic Gore* (1962).

PROJECTS AND PROBLEMS

Compare *Red Rock* with a Reconstruction novel by George W. Cable, Joel Chandler Harris, Albion Tourgée, John W. DeForest, or Thomas Dixon. Discuss in detail the treatment of the character of the freedmen and the rise of white supremacy.

Appraise the literary merit of such colleagues of Page as James Lane Allen, Harry Stillwell Edwards, F. Hopkinson Smith, Ruth

McEnery Stuart, Octave Thanet (Alice French), Grace King, and Constance Fenimore Woolson. See *A Bibliographical Guide to the Study of Southern Literature* (1969), ed. by Louis D. Rubin, Jr.

On the basis of a careful reading of Page's "Marse Chan," J. C. Harris's "Free Joe," and Mark Twain's "A True Story," compare the attitudes of the three authors toward slavery, racial differences, and civil rights. Are the three men equally romantic (or realistic)? Do they use dialect in the same way?

Are there consequential differences between the idyllic old Virginia of Page and the idealized old Kentucky presented in the fiction of James Lane Allen? Use specific works for a comparison.

KATE CHOPIN
(1851–1904)

Five years after the death of her Creole husband, Mrs. Chopin returned to her native St. Louis and began to write about the people and the life-styles she had come to know during her residence in Louisiana. Her tales of blacks, Cajuns, and Creoles were collected in *Bayou Folk* (1894), from which "Old Aunt Peggy" and "La Belle Zoraïde" are taken, and *A Night in Acadie* (1897). From these stories, showing the influence of both local color and regionalism, she moved to the psychological realism of *The Awakening* (1899), a novel that shocked readers by its portrait of a respectable woman's discovery of sensual needs that lead to adultery. The book is now much admired by literary critics and supporters of women's liberation.

OLD AUNT PEGGY

When the war was over, old Aunt Peggy went to Monsieur, and said:—

"Massa, I ain't never gwine to quit yer. I'm gittin' ole an' feeble, an' my days is few in dis heah lan' o' sorrow an' sin. All I axes is a li'le co'ner whar I kin set down an' wait peaceful fu de en'."

Monsieur and Madame were very much touched at this mark of affection and fidelity from Aunt Peggy. So, in the general reconstruction of the plantation which immediately followed the surrender, a nice cabin, pleasantly appointed, was set apart for the old woman. Madame did not even forget the very comfortable rocking-chair in which Aunt Peggy might "set down," as she herself feelingly expressed it, "an' wait fu de en'."

She has been rocking ever since.

At intervals of about two years Aunt Peggy hobbles up to the house, and delivers the stereotyped address which has become more than familiar:—

· "Mist'ess, I's come to take a las' look at you all. Le' me look at you good. Le' me look at de chillun,—de big chillun an' de li'le chillun. Le' me look at de picters an' de photygraphts an' de pianny, an' eve'ything 'fo' it's too late. One eye is done gone, an' de udder's a-gwine fas'. Any mo'nin' yo' po' ole Aunt Peggy gwine wake up an' fin' herse'f stone-bline."

After such a visit Aunt Peggy invariably returns to her cabin with a generously filled apron.

The scruple which Monsieur one time felt in supporting a woman for so many years in idleness has entirely disappeared. Of late his attitude towards Aunt Peggy is simply one of profound astonishment, —wonder at the surprising age which an old black woman may attain when she sets her mind to it, for Aunt Peggy is a hundred and twenty-five, so she says.

It may not be true, however. Possibly she is older.

LA BELLE ZORAÏDE

The summer night was hot and still; not a ripple of air swept over the *marais*. Yonder, across Bayou St. John, lights twinkled here and there in the darkness, and in the dark sky above a few stars were blinking. A lugger that had come out of the lake was moving with slow, lazy motion down the bayou. A man in the boat was singing a song.

The notes of the song came faintly to the ears of old Manna-Loulou, herself as black as the night, who had gone out upon the gallery to open the shutters wide.

Something in the refrain reminded the woman of an old, half-forgotten Creole romance, and she began to sing it low to herself while she threw the shutters open:—

> "Lisett' to kité la plaine,
> Mo perdi bonhair à moué;
> Ziés à moué semblé fontaine,
> Dépi mo pa miré toué."

And then this old song, a lover's lament for the loss of his mistress, floating into her memory, brought with it the story she would tell to Madame, who lay in her sumptuous mahogany bed, waiting to be fanned and put to sleep to the sound of one of Manna-Loulou's stories. The old negress had already bathed her mistress's pretty white feet and kissed them lovingly, one, then the other. She had brushed her mistress's beautiful hair, that was as soft and shining as satin, and was the color of Madame's wedding-ring. Now, when she reëntered the room, she moved softly toward the bed, and seating herself there began gently to fan Madame Delisle.

Manna-Loulou was not always ready with her story, for Madame would hear none but those which were true. But to-night the story was all there in Manna-Loulou's head—the story of la belle Zoraïde—and she told it to her mistress in the soft Creole patois, whose music and charm no English words can convey.

"La belle Zoraïde had eyes that were so dusky, so beautiful, that any man who gazed too long into their depths was sure to lose his head, and even his heart sometimes. Her soft, smooth skin was the color of *café-au-lait.* As for her elegant manners, her *svelte* and graceful figure, they were the envy of half the ladies who visited her mistress, Madame Delarivière.

"No wonder Zoraïde was as charming and as dainty as the finest lady of la rue Royale: from a toddling thing she had been brought up at her mistress's side; her fingers had never done rougher work than sewing a fine muslin seam; and she even had her own little black servant to wait upon her. Madame, who was her godmother as well as her mistress, would often say to her:—

" 'Remember, Zoraïde, when you are ready to marry, it must be in a way to do honor to your bringing up. It will be at the Cathedral. Your wedding gown, your *corbeille,* all will be of the best; I shall see to that myself. You know, M'sieur Ambroise is ready whenever you say the word; and his master is willing to do as much for him as I shall do for you. It is a union that will please me in every way.'

"M'sieur Ambroise was then the body servant of Doctor Langlé. La belle Zoraïde detested the little mulatto, with his shining whiskers like a white man's, and his small eyes, that were cruel and false as a snake's. She would cast down her own mischievous eyes, and say:—

" 'Ah, nénaine, I am so happy, so contented here at your side just as I am. I don't want to marry now; next year, perhaps, or the next.' And Madame would smile indulgently and remind Zoraïde that a woman's charms are not everlasting.

"But the truth of the matter was, Zoraïde had seen le beau Mézor dance the Bamboula in Congo Square. That was a sight to hold one rooted to the ground. Mézor was as straight as a cypress-tree and as proud looking as a king. His body, bare to the waist, was like a column of ebony and it glistened like oil.

"Poor Zoraïde's heart grew sick in her bosom with love for le beau Mézor from the moment she saw the fierce gleam of his eye, lighted by the inspiring strains of the Bamboula, and beheld the stately movements of his splendid body swaying and quivering through the figures of the dance.

"But when she knew him later, and he came near her to speak with her, all the fierceness was gone out of his eyes, and she saw only kindness in them and heard only gentleness in his voice; for love had taken possession of him also, and Zoraïde was more distracted than ever. When Mézor was not dancing Bamboula in Congo Square, he was hoeing sugar-cane, barefooted and half naked, in his master's field outside of the city. Doctor Langlé was his master as well as M'sieur Ambroise's.

"One day, when Zoraïde kneeled before her mistress, drawing on Madame's silken stockings, that were of the finest, she said:

" 'Nénaine, you have spoken to me often of marrying. Now, at last, I have chosen a husband, but it is not M'sieur Ambroise; it is le beau Mézor that I want and no other.' And Zoraïde hid her face in her hands when she had said that, for she guessed, rightly enough, that her mistress would be very angry. And, indeed, Madame Delarivière was at first speechless with rage. When she finally spoke it was only to gasp out, exasperated:—

" 'That negro! that negro! Bon Dieu Seigneur, but this is too much!'

" 'Am I white, nénaine?' pleaded Zoraïde.

" 'You white! *Malheureuse!* You deserve to have the lash laid upon you like any other slave; you have proven yourself no better than the worst.'

" 'I am not white,' persisted Zoraïde, respectfully and gently. 'Doctor Langlé gives me his slave to marry, but he would not give me his son. Then, since I am not white, let me have from out of my own race the one whom my heart has chosen.'

"However, you may well believe that Madame would not hear to that. Zoraïde was forbidden to speak to Mézor, and Mézor was cautioned against seeing Zoraïde again. But you know how the negroes are, Ma'zélle Titite," added Manna-Loulou, smiling a little sadly. "There is no mistress, no master, no king nor priest who can hinder them from loving when they will. And these two found ways and means.

"When months had passed by, Zoraïde, who had grown unlike herself,—sober and preoccupied,—said again to her mistress:—

" 'Nénaine, you would not let me have Mézor for my husband; but I have disobeyed you, I have sinned. Kill me if you wish, nénaine: forgive me if you will; but when I heard le beau Mézor say to me, "Zoraïde, mo l'aime toi," I could have died, but I could not have helped loving him.'

"This time Madame Delarivière was so actually pained, so wounded at hearing Zoraïde's confession, that there was no place left in her heart for anger. She could utter only confused reproaches. But she was a woman of action rather than of words, and she acted promptly. Her first step was to induce Doctor Langlé to sell Mézor. Doctor Langlé, who was a widower, had long wanted to marry Madame Delarivière, and he would willingly have walked on all fours at noon through the Place d'Armes if she wanted him to. Naturally he lost no time in disposing of le beau Mézor, who was sold away into Georgia, or the Carolinas, or one of those distant countries far away, where he would no longer hear his Creole tongue spoken, nor dance Calinda, nor hold la belle Zoraïde in his arms.

"The poor thing was heartbroken when Mézor was sent away from her, but she took comfort and hope in the thought of her baby that she would soon be able to clasp to her breast.

"La belle Zoraïde's sorrows had now begun in earnest. Not only sorrows but sufferings, and with the anguish of maternity came the shadow of death. But there is no agony that a mother will not forget when she holds her first-born to her heart, and presses her lips upon the baby flesh that is her own, yet far more precious than her own.

"So, instinctively, when Zoraïde came out of the awful shadow she gazed questioningly about her and felt with her trembling hands upon either side of her. 'Où li, mo piti a moin? (Where is my little one?)' she asked imploringly. Madame who was there and the nurse who was there both told her in turn, 'To piti à toi, li mouri' ('Your little one is dead'), which was a wicked falsehood that must have caused the angels in heaven to weep. For the baby was living and well and strong. It had at once been removed from its mother's side, to be sent away to Madame's plantation, far up the coast. Zoraïde could only moan in reply, 'Li mouri, li mouri,' and she turned her face to the wall.

"Madame had hoped, in thus depriving Zoraïde of her child, to have her young waiting-maid again at her side free, happy, and beautiful as of old. But there was a more powerful will than Madame's at work—the will of the good God, who had already designed that Zoraïde should grieve with a sorrow that was never more to be lifted in this world. La belle Zoraïde was no more. In her stead was a sad-eyed woman who mourned night and day for her baby. 'Li mouri, li mouri,' she would sigh over and over again to those about her, and to herself when others grew weary of her complaint.

"Yet, in spite of all, M'sieur Ambroise was still in the notion to marry her. A sad wife or a merry one was all the same to him so long as that wife was Zoraïde. And she seemed to consent, or rather submit, to the approaching marriage as though nothing mattered any longer in this world.

"One day, a black servant entered a little noisily the room in which Zoraïde sat sewing. With a look of strange and vacuous happiness upon her face, Zoraïde arose hastily. 'Hush, hush,' she whispered, lifting a warning finger, 'my little one is asleep; you must not awaken her.'

"Upon the bed was a senseless bundle of rags shaped like an infant in swaddling clothes. Over this dummy the woman had drawn the mosquito bar, and she was sitting contentedly beside it. In short, from that day Zoraïde was demented. Night nor day did she lose sight of the doll that lay in her bed or in her arms.

"And now was Madame stung with sorrow and remorse at seeing this terrible affliction that had befallen her dear Zoraïde. Consulting with Doctor Langlé, they decided to bring back to the mother the real baby of flesh and blood that was now toddling about, and kicking its heels in the dust yonder upon the plantation.

"It was Madame herself who led the pretty, tiny little "griffe" girl to her mother. Zoraïde was sitting upon a stone bench in the courtyard, listening to the soft splashing of the fountain, and watching the fitful shadows of the palm leaves upon the broad, white flagging.

" 'Here,' said Madame, approaching, 'here, my poor dear Zoraïde, is your own little child. Keep her; she is yours. No one will ever take her from you again.'

"Zoraïde looked with sullen suspicion upon her mistress and the child before her. Reaching out a hand she thrust the little one mistrustfully away from her. With the other hand she clasped the rag bundle fiercely to her breast; for she suspected a plot to deprive her of it.

"Nor could she ever be induced to let her own child approach her; and finally the little one was sent back to the plantation, where she was never to know the love of mother or father.

"And now this is the end of Zoraïde's story. She was never known again as la belle Zoraïde, but ever after as Zoraïde la folle, who no one ever wanted to marry—not even M'sieur Ambroise. She lived to be an old woman, whom some people pitied and others laughed at—always clasping her bundle of rags—her 'piti.'

"Are you asleep, Ma'zélle Titite?"

"No, I am not asleep; I was thinking. Ah, the poor little one, Man Loulou, the poor little one! better had she died!"

But this is the way Madame Delisle and Manna-Loulou really talked to each other:—

"Vou pré droumi, Ma'zélle Titite?"

"Non, pa pré droumi; mo yapré zongler. Ah, la pauv' piti, Man Loulou. La pauv' piti! Mieux li mouri!"

SUGGESTED ADDITIONAL READINGS

At Fault
A Night in Acadie
The Awakening

SELECTED REFERENCES

Arner, Robert D. "Pride and Prejudice: Kate Chopin's 'Désirée's Baby.' " Mississippi Quarterly, 25 (1972), 131–40.

Butcher, Philip. "Two Early Southern Realists in Revival." CLA Journal, 14 (1970), 91–95.

Eble, Kenneth. "A Forgotten Novel: Kate Chopin's The Awakening." Western Humanities Review, 10 (1956), 261–69.

Fletcher, Marie. "The Southern Woman in the Fiction of Kate Chopin." Louisiana Historical Quarterly, 7 (1966), 117–32.

Leary, Lewis. "Kate Chopin's Other Novel." Southern Literary Journal, 1, No. 1 (1968), 60–74.

Seyersted, Per. Kate Chopin: A Critical Biography (1969).

PROJECTS AND PROBLEMS

Compare the Cajuns of Bayou Folk and A Night in Acadie with those of George W. Cable's Bonaventure, or compare the Creoles of

Chopin's stories with those of Grace King's *Monsieur Motte* or *Balcony Stories*.

Is Kate Chopin best described, on the basis of her minority characters, as local colorist, realist, regionalist, or romanticist?

For a modern treatment of the materials of Kate Chopin's fiction see Shirley Ann Grau's "Joshua," in *The Black Prince and Other Stories*. Are the two writers in essentially the same tradition?

Discuss Kate Chopin as a pioneer feminist whose female protagonists are heralds of the movement for women's liberation. Consider Syersted's contention that "La Belle Zoraïde" "is more a plea for woman's right to choose her husband than a direct condemnation of slavery."

BOOKER T. WASHINGTON
(1856–1915)

Washington's *Up from Slavery*, which began its serial run in *Outlook* in 1900, is another in the long list of autobiographies recounting the struggles and triumphs of a self-made American. As founder and principal of Tuskegee Institute in Alabama, Washington was the most influential black leader of his time. His strategy of accommodation and emphasis on industrial training for the freedmen brought opposition from advocates of full civil rights and academic education. His controversial address at the Atlanta Exposition of 1895, which serves as Chapter 24 of *Up from Slavery*, is the most famous of his many speeches.

THE ATLANTA EXPOSITION
ADDRESS

Mr. President and Gentleman of the Board of Directors and Citizens:

One third of the population of the South is of the Negro race. No enterprise seeking the material, civil, or moral welfare of this section can disregard this element of our population and reach the highest success. I but convey to you, Mr. President and Directors, the sentiment of the masses of my race when I say that in no way have the value and manhood of the American Negro been more fittingly and generously recognized than by the managers of this magnificent Exposition at every stage of its progress. It is a recognition that will do more to cement the friendship of the two races than any occurrence since the dawn of our freedom.

Not only this, but the opportunity here afforded will awaken among us a new era of industrial progress. Ignorant and inexperienced, it is not strange that in the first years of our new life we began at the top instead of at the bottom; that a seat in Congress or the State Legislature was more sought than real estate or industrial skill; that the political convention of stump speaking had more attractions than starting a dairy farm or truck garden.

A ship lost at sea for many days suddenly sighted a friendly vessel. From the mast of the unfortunate vessel was seen a signal, "Water, water; we die of thirst!" The answer from the friendly vessel at once came back, "Cast down your bucket where you are." A second time the signal, "Water, water; send us water!" ran up from the distressed vessel, and was answered, "Cast down your bucket where you are." And a third and fourth signal for water was answered, "Cast down your bucket where you are." The captain of the distressed vessel, at last heeding the injunction, cast down his bucket, and it came up full of fresh, sparkling water from the mouth of the Amazon River. To those of my race who depend on bettering their condition in a foreign land or who underestimate the importance of cultivating friendly relations with the Southern white man, who is their next door neighbor, I would say: "Cast down your bucket where you are"

338

—cast it down in making friends in every manly way of the people of all races by whom we are surrounded.

Cast it down in agriculture, mechanics, in commerce, in domestic service, and in the professions. And in this connection it is well to bear in mind that whatever other sins the South may be called to bear, when it comes to business, pure and simple, it is in the South that the Negro is given a man's chance in the commercial world, and in nothing is this Exposition more eloquent than in emphasizing this chance. Our greatest danger is that in the great leap from slavery to freedom we may overlook the fact that the masses of us are to live by the productions of our hands, and fail to keep in mind that we shall prosper in proportion as we learn to dignify and glorify common labor and put brains and skill into the common occupations of life; shall prosper in proportion as we learn to draw the line between the superficial and the substantial, the ornamental gew-gaws of life and the useful. No race can prosper till it learns that there is as much dignity in tilling a field as in writing a poem. It is at the bottom of life we must begin, and not at the top. Nor should we permit our grievances to overshadow our opportunities.

To those of the white race who look to the incoming of those of foreign birth and strange tongue and habits for the prosperity of the South, were I permitted I would repeat what I say to my own race, "Cast down your bucket where you are." Cast it down among the eight millions of Negroes whose habits you know, whose fidelity and love you have tested in days when to have proved treacherous meant the ruin of your firesides. Cast down your bucket among these people who have, without strikes and labor wars, tilled your fields, cleared your forests, builded your railroads and cities, and brought forth treasures from the bowels of the earth, and helped make possible this magnificent representation of the progress of the South. Casting down your bucket among my people, helping and encouraging them as you are doing on these grounds, and to education of head, hand, and heart, you will find that they will buy your surplus land, make blossom the waste places in your fields, and run your factories. While doing this, you can be sure in the future, as in the past, that you and your families will be surrounded by the most patient, faithful, law-abiding, and unresentful people that the world has seen. As we have proved our loyalty to you in the past, in nursing your children, watching by the sickbed of your mothers and fathers, and often following them with tear-dimmed eyes to their graves, so in the future, in our humble way, we shall stand by you with a devotion that no foreigner can approach, ready to lay down our lives, if need be, in defense of yours, interlacing our industrial, commercial, civil, and religious life with yours in a way that shall make the interests of both races one. In all things that are purely social we can be as separate as the fingers, yet one as the hand in all things essential to mutual progress.

There is no defense or security for any of us except in the highest intelligence and development of all. If anywhere there are efforts tending to curtail the fullest growth of the Negro, let these efforts be turned into stimulating, encouraging, and making him the most useful and intelligent citizen. Effort or means so invested will pay a thousand per cent interest. These efforts will be twice blessed— "blessing him that gives and him that takes."

There is no escape through law of man or God from the inevitable:

> The laws of changeless justice bind
> Oppressor with oppressed;
> And close as sin and suffering joined
> We march to fate abreast.

Nearly sixteen millions of hands will aid you in pulling the load upward, or they will pull against you the load downward. We shall constitute one-third and more of the ignorance and crime of the South, or one-third its intelligence and progress; we shall contribute one-third to the business and industrial prosperity of the South, or we shall prove a veritable body of death, stagnating, depressing, retarding every effort to advance the body politic.

Gentlemen of the Exposition, as we present to you our humble effort at an exhibition of our progress, you must not expect overmuch. Starting thirty years ago with ownership here and there in a few quilts and pumpkins and chickens (gathered from miscellaneous sources), remember the path that has led from these to the inventions and production of agricultural implements, buggies, steam engines, newspapers, books, statuary, carving, paintings, the management of drugstores and banks, has not been trodden without contact with thorns and thistles. While we take pride in what we exhibit as a result of our independent efforts, we do not for a moment forget that our part in this exhibition would fall far short of your expectations but for the constant help that has come to our educational life, not only from the Southern states, but especially from Northern philanthropists, who have made their gifts a constant stream of blessing and encouragement.

The wisest among my race understand that the agitation of questions of social equality is the extremest folly, and that progress in the enjoyment of all the privileges that will come to us must be the result of severe and constant struggle rather than of artificial forcing. No race that has anything to contribute to the markets of the world is long in any degree ostracized. It is important and right that all privileges of the law be ours, but it is vastly more important that we be prepared for the exercises of these privileges. The opportunity to earn a dollar in a factory just now is worth infinitely more than the opportunity to spend a dollar in an opera house.

In conclusion, may I repeat that nothing in thirty years has given us more hope and encouragement, and drawn us so near to you of the white race, as this opportunity offered by the Exposition; and here bending, as it were, over the altar that represents the results of the struggles of your race and mine, both starting practically empty-handed three decades ago, I pledge that in your effort to work out the great and intricate problem which God has laid at the doors of the South, you shall have at all times the patient, sympathetic help of my race; only let this be constantly in mind, that, while from representations in these buildings of the product of field, of forest, of mine, of factory, letters, and art, much good will come, yet far above and beyond material benefits will be that higher good, that, let us pray God, will come, in a blotting out of sectional differences and racial animosities and suspicions, in a determination to administer absolute justice, in a willing obedience among all classes to the mandates of law. This, this, coupled with our material prosperity, will bring into our beloved South a new heaven and a new earth.

SUGGESTED ADDITIONAL READING

The Future of the American Negro

The Story of My Life and Work
Selected Speeches of Booker T. Washington, (1932) ed. by T. Davidson Washington.

SELECTED REFERENCES

Butcher, Philip. "George W. Cable and Booker T. Washington." *Journal of Negro Education,* 17 (1948), 462–68.

Harlan, Louis R. *Booker T. Washington: The Making of a Black Leader, 1865–1901* (1972).

Hawkins, Hugh, ed. *Booker T. Washington and His Critics: The Problem of Negro Leadership* (1962).

PROJECTS AND PROBLEMS

Did Washington regard "those of foreign birth and strange tongue and habits" as fellow victims of racism or as hostile aliens who posed a threat to the interests of the black minority? At what point in his Atlanta speech did he resort to the minstrel tradition in the interest of comic relief?

Compare *Up from Slavery* with *The Autobiography of Benjamin Franklin* or with *The Making of an American,* the autobiography of Jacob A. Riis that was published in 1901. Discuss the extent to which each man's achievement was affected by the status of the group to which he belonged.

Examine the relationship of Washington and William Monroe Trotter, the militant black editor of the Boston *Guardian,* or W. E. B. Du Bois, who published *The Souls of Black Folk* in 1903.

PAUL LAURENCE DUNBAR
(1872–1906)

The poems below were all written by 1896 when
Dunbar's third book, *Lyrics of Lowly Life*, was
published with an introduction in which William Dean
Howells praised the poet as "the only man of pure
African blood and of American civilization to feel the
negro life aesthetically and express it lyrically." The
young man from Dayton, Ohio, was on his way to
become the first black poet to win a national audience.

Writing stories and poems about antebellum days he
knew only from hearsay, Dunbar both exploited and was
shackled by the vogue for dialect literature and the hold
of the imagined past on the minds of his readers. In his
efforts to escape the stereotypes he wrote three novels
devoted mainly to white characters, but in *The Sport of
the Gods* (1902) he turned with more success to a
pioneer treatment of life in the growing black
community in New York. "Negro Life in Washington,"
which appeared in *Harper's Weekly*, January 13, 1900,
shows his interest in the urban scene and the
contemporary race problem.

343

LITTLE BROWN BABY

Little brown baby wif spa'klin' eyes,
   Come to yo' pappy an' set on his knee.
What you been doin', suh—makin' san' pies?
   Look at dat bib—you's ez du'ty ez me.
Look at dat mouf—dat's merlasses, I bet;
   Come hyeah, Maria, an' wipe off his han's.
Bees gwine to ketch you an' eat you up yit,
   Bein' so sticky an' sweet—goodness lan's!

Little brown baby wif spa'klin' eyes,
   Who's pappy's darlin' an' who's pappy's chile?
Who is it all de day nevah once tries
   Fu' to be cross, er once loses dat smile?
Whah did you git dem teef? My, you's a scamp!
   Whah did dat dimple come f'om in yo' chin?
Pappy do' know you—I b'lieves you's a tramp;
   Mammy, dis hyeah's some ol' straggler got in!

Let's th'ow him outen de do' in de san',
   We do' want stragglers a-layin' 'roun' hyeah;
Let's gin him 'way to de big buggah-man;
   I know he's hidin' erroun' hyeah right neah.
Buggah-man, buggah-man, come in de do',
   Hyeah's a bad boy you kin have fu' to eat.
Mammy an' pappy do' want him no mo',
   Swaller him down f'om his haid to his feet!

Dah, now, I t'ought dat you'd hug me up close.
   Go back, ol' buggah, you sha'n't have dis boy.
He ain't no tramp, ner no straggler, of co'se;
   He's pappy's pa'dner an' playmate an' joy.
Come to you' pallet now—go to yo' res';
   Wisht you could allus know ease an' cleah skies;
Wisht you could stay jes' a chile on my breas'—
   Little brown baby wif spa'klin' eyes!

WE WEAR THE MASK

We wear the mask that grins and lies,
It hides our cheeks and shades our eyes,—
This debt we pay to human guile;
With torn and bleeding hearts we smile,
And mouth with myriad subtleties.

Why should the world be overwise,
In counting all our tears and sighs?
Nay, let them only see us, while
    We wear the mask.

We smile, but, O great Christ, our cries
To Thee from tortured souls arise.
We sing, but oh, the clay is vile
Beneath our feet, and long the mile;
But let the world dream otherwise,
    We wear the mask!

AN ANTE–BELLUM SERMON

We is gathahed hyeah, my brothahs,
    In dis howlin' wildaness,
Fu' to speak some words of comfo't
    To each othah in distress.
An' we chooses fu' ouah subjic'
    Dis—we'll 'splain it by an' by;
"An' de Lawd said, 'Moses, Moses,'
    An' de man said, 'Hyeah am I.' "

Now ole Pher'oh, down in Egypt,
    Was de wuss man evah bo'n,
An' he had de Hebrew chillun
    Down dah wukin' in his co'n;
'T well de Lawd got tiahed o' his foolin',
    An' sez he: "I'll let him know—
Look hyeah, Moses, go tell Pher'oh
    Fu' to let dem chillun go."

"An' ef he refuse to do it,
    I will make him rue de houah,
Fu' I'll empty down on Egypt
    All de vials of my powah."
Yes, he did—an' Pher'oh's ahmy
    Wasn't wuth a ha'f a dime;
Fu' de Lawd will he'p his chillun,
    You kin trust him evah time.

An' yo' enemies may 'sail you
    In de back an' in de front;
But de Lawd is all aroun' you,
    Fu' to ba' de battle's brunt.
Dey kin fo'ge yo' chains an' shackles
    F'om de mountains to de sea;
But de Lawd will sen' some Moses
    Fu' to set his chillun free.

An' de lan' shall hyeah his thundah,
    Lak a blas' f'om Gab'el's ho'n,
Fu' de Lawd of hosts is mighty
    When he girds his ahmor on.
But fu' feah some one mistakes me,
    I will pause right hyeah to say,
Dat I'm still a-preachin' ancient,
    I ain't talkin' 'bout to-day.

But I tell you, fellah christuns,
    Things'll happen mighty strange;
Now, de Lawd done dis fu' Isrul,
    An' his ways don't nevah change,
An' de love he showed to Isrul
    Wasn't all on Isrul spent;
Now don't run an' tell yo' mastahs
    Dat I's preachin' discontent.

'Cause I isn't; I'se a-judgin'
    Bible people by deir ac's;
I'se a-givin' you de Scriptuah,
    I'se a-handin' you de fac's.
Cose ole Pher'oh b'lieved in slav'ry,
    But de Lawd he let him see,
Dat de people he put bref in,—
    Evah mothah's son was free.

An' dahs othahs thinks lak Pher'oh,
    But dey calls de Scriptuah liar,
Fu' de Bible says "a servant
    Is a-worthy of his hire."
An' you cain't get roun' nor thoo dat,
    An' you cain't git ovah it,
Fu' whatevah place you git in,
    Dis hyeah Bible too 'll fit.

So you see de Lawd's intention,
    Evah sence de worl' began,

Was dat His almighty freedom
    Should belong to evah man,
But I think it would be bettah,
    Ef I'd pause agin to say,
Dat I'm talkin' 'bout ouah freedom
    In a Bibleistic way.

But de Moses is a-comin',
    An' he's comin', suah and fas'
We kin hyeah his feet a-trompin',
    We kin hyeah his trumpit blas'.
But I want to wa'n you people,
    Don't you git too brigity;
An' don't you git to braggin'
    'Bout dese things, you wait an' see.

But when Moses wif his powah
    Comes an' sets us chillun free,
We will praise de gracious Mastah
    Dat has gin us liberty;
An' we'll shout ouah halleluyahs,
    On dat mighty reck'nin' day,
When we'se reco'nised ez citiz'—
    Huh uh! Chillun, let us pray!

NEGRO LIFE IN WASHINGTON

Washington is the city where the big men of little towns come to be disillusioned. Whether black or white, the little great soon seek their level here. It matters not whether it is Ezekiel Corncray of Podunk Center, Vermont, or Isaac Johnson of the Alabama black belt —in Washington he is apt to come to a realization of his true worth to the world.

In a city of such diverse characteristics it is natural that the life of any portion of its people should be interesting. But when it is considered that here the experiment of sudden freedom has been tried most earnestly, and, I may say, most successfully, upon a large percentage of the population, it is to the lives of these people that one instinctively turns for color, picturesqueness, and striking contrast.

It is the delicately blended or boldly differentiated light and shade effects of Washington negro life that are the despair of him who tries truthfully to picture it.

It is the middle-class negro who has imbibed enough of white civilization to make him work to be prosperous. But he has not partaken of civilization so deeply that he has become drunk and has forgotten his own identity. The church to him is still the centre of his social life, and his preacher a great man. He has not—and I am not wholly sorry that he has not—learned the repression of his emotions, which is the mark of a high and dry civilization. He is impulsive, intense, fervid, and—himself. He has retained some of his primitive ingenuousness. When he goes to a party he goes to enjoy himself and not to pose. If there be onlookers outside his own circle, and he be tempted to pose, he does it with such childlike innocence and good-humor that no one is for a moment anything but amused, and he is forgiven his little deception.

Possibly in even the lower walks of life a warmer racial color is discoverable. For instance, no other race can quite show the counterpart of the old gentleman who passes me on Sunday on his way to church. An ancient silk hat adorns a head which I know instinctively is bald and black and shiny on top; but the edges are fringed with a growth of crisp white hair, like a frame around the mild old face.

349

The broadcloth coat which is buttoned tightly around the spare form is threadbare, and has faded from black to gray-green; but although bent a little with the weight of his years, his glance is alert, and he moves briskly along, like a character suddenly dropped out of one of Page's stories. He waves his hand in salute, and I have a vision of Virginia of fifty years ago.

A real bit of the old South, though, as one sees it in Washington, is the old black mammy who trundles to and fro a little baby-carriage with its load of laundry-work, but who tells you, with manifest pride, "Yes, suh, I has nussed, off'n on, mo'n a dozen chillun of de X fambly, an' some of de men dat's ginuls now er in Cong'ess was jes nachully raised up off'n me." But she, like so many others, came to Washington when it was indeed the Mecca for colored people, where lay all their hopes of protection, of freedom, and of advancement. Perhaps in the old days, when labor brought better rewards, she saved something and laid it by in the ill-fated Freedman's Savings Bank. But the story of that is known; so the old woman walks the streets to-day, penniless, trundling her baby-carriage, a historic but pathetic figure.

Some such relic of the past, but more prosperous withal, is the old lady who leans over the counter of a tiny and dingy restaurant on Capitol Hill and dispenses coffee and rolls and fried pork to her colored customers. She wears upon her head the inevitable turban or handkerchief in which artists delight to paint the old mammies of the South. She keeps unwavering the deep religious instinct of her race, and is mighty in her activities on behalf of one or the other of the colored churches. Under her little counter she always has a contribution-book, and not a customer, white or black, high or low, who is not levied upon to "he'p de chu'ch outen hits 'stress." But one who has sat and listened to her, as, leaning chin on hand, she recounted one of her weird superstitious stories of the night-doctors and their doings, or the "awful jedgement on a sinnah man," is not unwilling to be put at some expense for his pleasure.

The old lady and her stories are of a different cast from that part of the Washington life which is the pride of her proudest people. It is a far cry from the smoky little restaurant on the Hill, with its genial and loquacious old owner, to the great business block on Fourteenth Street and its wealthy, shrewd, and cultivated proprietor.

Colored men have made money here, and some of them have known how to keep it. There are several of them on the Board of Trade—five, I think—and they are regarded by their fellows as solid, responsible, and capable business men. The present assessment law was drafted by a colored member of the board, and approved by them before it was submitted to Congress.

As for the professions, there are so many engaged in them that it would keep one busy counting or attempting to count the dark-skinned lawyers and doctors one meets in a day.

The cause of this is not far to seek. Young men come here to work in the departments. Their evenings are to a certain extent free. It is the most natural thing in the world that they should improve their time by useful study. But why such a preponderance in favor of the professions, you say. Are there not other useful pursuits—arts and handicrafts? To be sure there are. But then your new people dearly love a title, and Lawyer Jones sounds well, Dr. Brown has an infinitely more dignified ring, and as for Professor—well, that is the acme of titular excellence, and there are more dark professors in Washington than one could find in a day's walk through a European college town.

However, it is well that these department clerks should carry something away with them when they leave Washington, for their condition is seldom financially improved by their sojourn here. This, though, is perhaps apart from the aim of the present article, for it is no more true of the negro clerks than of their white confrères. Both generally live up to the limit of their salaries.

The clerk has much leisure, and is in consequence a society man. He must dress well and smoke as good a cigar as an Eastern Congressman. It all costs money, and it is not unnatural that at the end of the year he is a little long on unreceipted bills and short on gold. The tendency of the school-teachers, now, seems to be entirely different. There are a great many of them here, and on the average they receive less than the government employés. But perhaps the discipline which they are compelled to impart to their pupils has its salutary effect upon their own minds and impulses. However that may be, it is true that the banks and building associations receive each month a part of the salaries of a large proportion of these instructors.

The colored people themselves have a flourishing building association and a well-conducted bank, which do part—I am sorry I cannot say the major part—of their race's business.

The influence which the success of a few men will have upon a
whole community is indicated in the spirit of venture which actu-
ates the rising generation of this city. A few years ago, if a man secured a political position, he was never willing or fit to do anything
else afterward. But now the younger men, with the example of some
of their successful elders before them, are beginning to see that an
easy berth in one of the departments is not the best thing in life, and
they are getting brave enough to do other things. Some of these ven-
tures have proven failures, even disasters, but it has not daunted the
few, nor crushed the spirit of effort in them.

It has been said, and not without some foundation in fact, that a
colored man who came to Washington never left the place. Indeed,
the city has great powers of attracting and holding its colored population; for, belong to whatever class or condition they may, they are
always sure to find enough of that same class or condition to make
their residence pleasant and congenial. But this very spirit of enterprise of which I have spoken is destroying the force of this dictum,
and men of color are even going so far as to resign government posi-
tions to go away and strike out for themselves. I have in mind now
two young men who are Washingtonians of the Washingtonians,
and who have been in office here for years. But the fever has taken
them, and they have voluntarily given up their places to go and try
their fortunes in the newer and less crowded West.

Such things as these are small in themselves, but they point to a
condition of affairs in which the men who have received the training
and polish which only Washington can give to a colored man can go
forth among their fellows and act as leaveners to the crudity of their
race far and wide.

That the pleasure and importance of negro life in Washington are
overrated by the colored people themselves is as true as that it is
underrated and misunderstood by the whites. To the former the social aspect of this life is a very dignified and serious drama. To the
latter it is nothing but a most amusing and inconsequential farce.
But both are wrong: it is neither the one thing nor the other. It is a
comedy of the period played out by earnest actors, who have

learned their parts well, but who on that very account are disposed to mouth and strut a little and watch the gallery.

Upon both races the truth and significance of the commercial life among the negroes have taken a firmer hold, because the sight of their banks, their offices, and places of business are evidences which cannot be overlooked or ignored.

As for the intellectual life, a university set on a hill cannot be hid, and the fact that about this university and about this excellent high-school clusters a community in which people, unlike many of the educational fakirs which abound, have taken their degrees from Cambridge, Oxford, Edinburgh, Harvard, Yale, Cornell, Wellesley, and a score of minor colleges, demands the recognition of a higher standard of culture among people of color than obtains in any other city.

But, taking it all in all and after all, negro life in Washington is a promise rather than a fulfillment. But it is worthy of note for the really excellent things which are promised.

SUGGESTED ADDITIONAL READINGS

Folks from Dixie
The Strength of Gideon and Other Stories
The Complete Poems of Paul Laurence Dunbar
The Paul Laurence Dunbar Reader (1975), ed. by Jay Martin
    and Gossie H. Hudson.

SELECTED REFERENCES

Brawley, Benjamin. *Paul Laurence Dunbar: Poet of His People* (1936).

Burch, Charles E. "The Plantation Negro in Dunbar's Poetry." *Southern Workman,* 50 (1921), 227–29.

Butcher, Philip. "Mutual Appreciation: Dunbar and Cable." *CLA Journal,* 1 (1958), 101–02.

Cunningham, Virginia. *Paul Laurence Dunbar and His Song* (1947).

354 THE MINORITY PRESENCE IN AMERICAN LITERATURE

Howells, William Dean. "Paul Laurence Dunbar." *North American Review*, 23 (1906), 185–86.

Lawson, Victor. *Dunbar Critically Examined* (1941).

Martin, Jay, ed. *A Singer in the Dawn: Reinterpretations of Paul Laurence Dunbar* (1975).

Redding, J. Saunders. *To Make a Poet Black* (1939).

Stronks, James B. "Paul Laurence Dunbar and William Dean Howells." *Ohio Historical Quarterly*, 68 (1957), 95–108.

Turner, Darwin T. "Paul Laurence Dunbar: The Poet and the Myths." *CLA Journal*, 18 (1974), 155–71.

————. "Paul Laurence Dunbar: The Rejected Symbol." *Journal of Negro History*, 52 (1967), 1–13.

PROJECTS AND PROBLEMS

Discuss the relative merit of Dunbar's poems in dialect and those in standard English. Include in this comparison "When Dey 'Listed Colored Soldiers" and "The Colored Soldiers."

Do Dunbar's poems and stories conform entirely with the stereotypes of the Plantation Tradition? Are they full expressions of his opinions about racial characteristics and the race problem?

Compare some of Dunbar's poems in Hoosier dialect with those of James Whitcomb Riley and discuss the relationship of these two writers.

Study Dunbar's articles on black society in Washington, D.C., one reprinted in this volume and the other in *Saturday Evening Post*, December 14, 1901, and see Chapter 14 of *The Fanatics* (1901). Does Dunbar's picture of the black upper class agree with that presented in Charles W. Chesnutt's *The Wife of His Youth?*

The incident at the bar in Chapter 9 of *The Sport of the Gods* resembles early bar scenes in Stephen Crane's *George's Mother*. Both writers had careers marked by tragedy, and both died young. Compare the ambivalent attitudes toward religion that may be found in their works.

Speculate on Dunbar's reasons for writing "Circumstances Alter Cases," published in 1905, in Irish brogue. Compare the Irish characters of the poem with the German immigrants in Chapter 23 of *The Fanatics*.

"The Haunted Oak" (1903) is about lynching. Was Dunbar more realistic and bitter in treating the racial problems of his own day than he was in handling the antebellum past? Take into account his fugitive nonfiction.

Compare Dunbar's "The Party" with Irwin Russell's "Christmas-Night in the Quarters," first published in *Scribner's Magazine*, January, 1878, and highly praised by Joel Chandler Harris in his introduction to Russell's *Poems* (1888). Do the two poets differ in their treatment of black character and the antebellum plantation?

HAROLD FREDERIC
(1856–1898)

This selection is from Chapter V of *The Damnation of Theron Ware* (1896), the work for which Harold Frederic is best known. The realistic novel traces the fall of a simple Methodist preacher in a New York town as he discovers his ignorance, examines his prejudices, and recognizes the shortcomings of his faith and his followers. Frederic's other fiction includes stories about the Civil War and a novel about a Northern farmer's reaction to abolitionism.

THE IRISH RECONSIDERED

Though the parsonage was only three blocks away, the young minister had time to think about a good many things before he reached home.

First of all, he had to revise in part the arrangement of his notions about the Irish. Save for an occasional isolated and taciturn figure among the nomadic portion of the hired help in the farm country, Theron had scarcely ever spoken to a person of this curiously alien race before. He remembered now that there had been some dozen or more Irish families in Tyre, quartered in the outskirts among the brickyards, but he had never come in contact with any of them, or given to their existence even a passing thought. So far as personal acquaintance went, the Irish had been to him only a name.

But what a sinister and repellent name! His views on this general subject were merely those common to his communion and his environment. He took it for granted, for example, that in the large cities most of the poverty and all the drunkenness, crime, and political corruption were due to the perverse qualities of this foreign people, —qualities accentuated and emphasized in every evil direction by the baleful influence of a false and idolatrous religion. It is hardly too much to say that he had never encountered a dissenting opinion on this point. His boyhood had been spent in those bitter days when social, political, and blood prejudices were fused at white heat in the public crucible together. When he went to the Church Seminary, it was a matter of course that every member of the faculty was a Republican, and that every one of his classmates had come from a Republican household. When, later on, he entered the ministry, the rule was still incredulous of exceptions. One might as well have looked in the Nedahma Conference for a divergence of opinion on the Trinity as for a difference in political conviction. Indeed, even among the laity, Theron could not feel sure that he had ever known a Democrat; that is, at all closely. He understood very little about politics, it is true. If he had been driven into a corner, and forced to attempt an explanation of this tremendous partisan unanimity in which he had a share, he would probably have first mentioned the

War,—the last shots of which were fired while he was still in pet-
ticoats. Certainly his second reason, however, would have been that
the Irish were on the other side.

He had never before had occasion to formulate, even in his own
thoughts, this tacit race and religious aversion in which he had been
bred. It rose now suddenly in front of him, as he sauntered from
patch to patch of sunlight under the elms, like some huge, shadowy,
and symbolical monument. He looked at it with wondering curiosity, as at something he had heard of all his life, but never seen before,—an abhorrent spectacle, truly! The foundations upon which its
dark bulk reared itself were ignorance, squalor, brutality, and vice.
Pigs wallowed in the mire before its base, and burrowing into this
base were a myriad of narrow doors, each bearing the hateful sign of
a saloon, and giving forth from its recesses of night the sounds of
screams and curses. Above were sculptured rows of lowering, ape-
like faces from Nast's and Keppler's cartoons, and out of these
sprang into the vague upper gloom, on the one side, lamp-posts
from which negroes hung by the neck, and on the other gibbets for
dynamiters and Molly Maguires; and between the two glowed a
spectral picture of some black-robed, tonsured men, with leering sa-
tanic masks, making a bonfire of the Bible in the public schools.

Theron stared this phantasm hard in the face, and recognized it
for a very tolerable embodiment of what he had heretofore supposed he thought about the Irish. For an instant, the sight of it made
him shiver, as if the sunny May had of a sudden lapsed into bleak
December. Then he smiled, and the bad vision went off into space.
He saw instead Father Forbes, in the white and purple vestments,
standing by poor MacEvoy's bedside, with his pale, chiselled, lumi-
nous, uplifted face, and he heard only the proud, confident clanging
of the girl's recital,—*beatum Michaelem Archangelum, beatum Jo-
annem Baptistam, Petrum et Paulum*—em! am! um!—like strokes on
a great resonant alarm-bell, attuned for the hearing of heaven. He
caught himself on the very verge of feeling that heaven must have
heard.

Then he smiled again, and laid the matter aside, with a parting admission that it had been undoubtedly picturesque and impressive,
and that it had been a valuable experience to him to see it. At least
the Irish, with all their faults, must have a poetic strain, or they

would not have clung so tenaciously to those curious and ancient forms. He recalled having heard somewhere, or read, it might be, that they were a people much given to songs and music. And the young lady, that very handsome and friendly Miss Madden, had told him that she was a musician! He had a new pleasure in turning this over in his mind. Of all the closed doors which his choice of a career had left along his pathway, no other had for him such a magical fascination as that on which was graven the lute of Orpheus. He knew not even the alphabet of music, and his conceptions of its possibilities ran but little beyond the best of the hymn-singing he had heard at Conferences, yet none the less the longing for it raised on occasion such mutiny in his soul that more than once he had specifically prayed against it as a temptation.

Dangerous though some of its tendencies might be, there was no gainsaying the fact that a love for music was in the main an uplifting influence,—an attribute of cultivation. The world was the sweeter and more gentle for it. And this brought him to musing upon the odd chance that the two people of Octavius who had given him the first notion of polish and intellectual culture in the town should be Irish. The Romish priest must have been vastly surprised at his intrusion, yet had been at the greatest pains to act as if it were quite the usual thing to have Methodist ministers assist at Extreme Unction. And the young woman,—how gracefully, with what delicacy, had she comprehended his position and robbed it of all its possible embarrassments! It occurred to him that they must have passed, there in front of her home, the very tree from which the luckless wheelwright had fallen some hours before; and the fact that she had forborne to point it out to him took form in his mind as an added proof of her refinement of nature.

The midday dinner was a little more than ready when Theron reached home, and let himself in by the front door. On Mondays, owing to the moisture and "clutter" of the weekly washing in the kitchen, the table was laid in the sitting-room, and as he entered from the hall the partner of his joys bustled in by the other door, bearing the steaming platter of corned beef, dumplings, cabbages, and carrots, with arms bared to the elbows, and a red face. It gave him great comfort, however, to note that there were no signs of the morning's displeasure remaining on this face; and he immediately remembered again those interrupted projects of his about the piano and the hired girl.

"Well! I'd just about begun to reckon that I was a widow," said Alice, putting down her fragrant burden. There was such an obvious suggestion of propitiation in her tone that Theron went around and kissed her. He thought of saying something about keeping out of the way because it was "Blue Monday," but held it back lest it should sound like a reproach.

"Well, what kind of a washerwoman does *this* one turn out to be? " he asked, after they were seated, and he had invoked a blessing and was cutting vigorously into the meat.

"Oh, so-so," replied Alice; "she seems to be particular, but she's mortal slow. If I hadn't stood right over her, we shouldn't have had the clothes out till goodness knows when. And of course she's Irish!"

"Well, what of *that?*" asked the minister, with a fine unconcern.

Alice looked up from her plate, with knife and fork suspended in air. "Why, you know we were talking only the other day of what a pity it was that none of our own people went out washing," she said. "That Welsh woman we heard of couldn't come, after all; and they say, too, that she presumes dreadfully upon the acquaintance, being a church member, you know. So we simply *had* to fall back on the Irish. And even if they do go and tell their priest everything they see and hear, why, there's one comfort, they can tell about *us* and welcome. Of course I see to it she doesn't snoop around in here."

Theron smiled. "That's all nonsense about their telling such things to their priests," he said with easy confidence.

"Why, you told me so yourself," replied Alice, briskly. "And I've always understood so, too; they're bound to tell *everything* in confession. That's what gives the Catholic Church such a tremendous hold. You've spoken of it often."

"It must have been by way of a figure of speech," remarked Theron, not with entire directness. "Women are great hands to separate one's observations from their context, and so give them meanings quite unintended. They are also great hands," he added genially, "or at least one of them is, at making the most delicious dumplings in the world. I believe these are the best even you ever made."

Alice was not unmindful of the compliment, but her thoughts were on other things. "I shouldn't like that woman's priest, for example," she said, "to know that we had no piano."

"But if he comes and stands outside our house every night and listens,—as of course he will," said Theron, with mock gravity, "it is
only a question of time when he must reach that conclusion for himself. Our only chance, however, is that there are some sixteen hundred other houses for him to watch, so that he may not get around to
us for quite a spell. Why, seriously, Alice, what on earth do you suppose Father Forbes knows or cares about our poor little affairs, or
those of any other Protestant household in this whole village? He
has his work to do, just as I have mine,—only his is ten times as ex-
acting in everything except sermons,—and you may be sure he is
only too glad when it is over each day, without bothering about
things that are none of his business."

"All the same, I'm afraid of them," said Alice, as if argument were
exhausted.

SUGGESTED ADDITIONAL READINGS

> *In the Valley*
> *The Return of the O'Mahony*
> *Marsena, and Other Stories of the Wartime*
> *Gloria Mundi*
> *The Market-Place*

SELECTED REFERENCES

Milne, W. Gordon. "Frederic's 'Free' Woman." *American Literary Realism, 1870–1910*, 6 (1973), 258–60.

O'Donnell, Thomas F. and Hoyt C. Franchere. *Harold Frederic*
(1961).

———. "Theron Ware, the Irish Picnic, and *Comus*." *American
Literature*, 46, (1975), 528–37.

Walcutt, Charles C. "Harold Frederic and American Naturalism." *American Literature*, 10 (1939), 11–22.

Ziff, Larzer. *The American 1890's: Life and Times of a Lost
Generation* (1966).

PROJECTS AND PROBLEMS

Compare Frederic's *Marsena, and Other Stories of the Wartime* with Thomas Nelson Page's *The Burial of the Guns,* published in the same year. Consider also Frederic's *The Copperhead.*

What counterparts of the Irish Molly Maguires, mentioned in the selection by Frederic in this volume, might be found among other minority groups in the 1970s? Discuss similarities and differences. In the selection, Alice Ware's notions about Irish character conform to the established stereotype. In what details do the Irish stereotype and those applied to other minorities agree?

Frederic may be regarded as an early champion of the liberated woman. Observe the changes that may be seen in Celia, the heroine of *The Damnation of Theron Ware,* when she reappears in his last novel, *The Market-Place.* Compare her with Edna Pontellier, the heroine of Kate Chopin's *The Awakening.*

Compare Frederic's portrait of the Dutch of New York State in his historical romance, *In the Valley,* with the representation of the Dutch in selected works by Cooper or Irving.

Sarah Orne Jewett depicts Irish and other newcomers to New England in *Strangers and Wayfarers* (1890) and *The Queen's Twin and Other Stories* (1899). Discuss the difference between her characters and attitudes and those of Frederic.

Compare Frederic's treatment of Jews in *Gloria Mundi* or *The Market-Place* with that in selected works by Henry James.

THEODORE DREISER
(1871–1945)

Dreiser's great importance to American literature rests mainly on two novels, *Sister Carrie* (1900) and *An American Tragedy* (1925). Although his impact was felt after the period covered in this book, his inclusion here is justified by the relevance of many of his works and by the narratives involving minority characters that he wrote around 1899. The selection below is the closing section of one of these stories, "Nigger Jeff," which Dreiser published in *Ainslee's* about a year after he wrote it and collected in *Free and Other Stories* in 1918. It is based on an incident he observed as a reporter in St. Louis.

THE DECEASED'S
SURVIVORS

It was sundown again before he remembered that he had not discovered whether the body had been removed. Nor had he heard why
the negro came back, nor exactly how he was caught. A nine o'clock
evening train to the city giving him a little more time for investiga-
tion, he decided to avail himself of it. The negro's cabin was two
miles out along a pine-shaded road, but so pleasant was the evening
that he decided to walk. En route, the last rays of the sinking sun
stretched long shadows of budding trees across his path. It was not
long before he came upon the cabin, a one-story affair set well back
from the road and surrounded with a few scattered trees. By now it
was quite dark. The ground between the cabin and the road was
open, and strewn with the chips of a woodpile. The roof was sagged,
and the windows patched in places, but for all that it had the glow
of a home. Through the front door, which stood open, the blaze of a
wood-fire might be seen, its yellow light filling the interior with a
golden glow.

Hesitating before the door, Davies finally knocked. Receiving no
answer he looked in on the battered cane chairs and aged furniture
with considerable interest. It was a typical negro cabin, poor beyond
the need of description. After a time a door in the rear of the room
opened and a little negro girl entered carrying a battered tin lamp
without any chimney. She had not heard his knock and started per-
ceptibly at the sight of his figure in the doorway. Then she raised her
smoking lamp above her head in order to see better, and approached.

There was something ridiculous about her unformed figure and
loose gingham dress, as he noted. Her feet and hands were so large.
Her black head was strongly emphasized by little pigtails of hair
done up in white twine, which stood out all over her head. Her dark
skin was made apparently more so by contrast with her white teeth
and the white of her eyes.

Davies looked at her for a moment but little moved now by the
oddity which ordinarily would have amused him, and asked, "Is this
where Ingalls lived?"

The girl nodded her head. She was exceedingly subdued, and looked as if she might have been crying.

"Has the body been brought here?"

"Yes, suh," she answered, with a soft negro accent.

"When did they bring it?"

"Dis moanin'."

"Are you his sister?"

"Yes, suh."

"Well, can you tell me how they caught him? When did he come back, and what for?" He was feeling slightly ashamed to intrude thus.

"In de afternoon, about two."

"And what for?" repeated Davies.

"To see us," answered the girl. "To see my motha'."

"Well, did he want anything? He didn't come just to see her, did he?"

"Yes, suh," said the girl, "he came to say good-by. We doan know when dey caught him." Her voice wavered.

"Well, didn't he know he might get caught?" asked Davies sympathetically, seeing that the girl was so moved.

"Yes, suh, I think he did."

She still stood very quietly holding the poor battered lamp up, and looking down.

"Well, what did he have to say?" asked Davies.

"He didn' have nothin' much to say, suh. He said he wanted to see motha'. He was a-goin' away."

The girl seemed to regard Davies as an official of some sort, and he knew it.

"Can I have a look at the body?" he asked.

"The girl did not answer, but started as if to lead the way.

"When is the funeral?" he asked.

"Tomorra'."

The girl then led him through several bare sheds of rooms strung in a row to the furthermost one of the line. This last seemed a sort of storage shed for odds and ends. It had several windows, but they were quite bare of glass and open to the moonlight save for a few wooden boards nailed across from the outside. Davies had been wondering all the while where the body was and at the lonely and forsaken air of the place. No one but this little pig-tailed girl seemed about. If they had any colored neighbors they were probably afraid to be seen here.

Now, as he stepped into this cool, dark, exposed outer room, the desolation seemed quite complete. It was very bare, a mere shed or wash-room. There was the body in the middle of the room, stretched upon an ironing board which rested on a box and a chair, and covered with a white sheet. All the corners of the room were quite dark. Only its middle was brightened by splotches of silvery light.

Davies came forward, the while the girl left him, still carrying her lamp. Evidently she thought the moon lighted up the room sufficiently, and she did not feel equal to remaining. He lifted the sheet quite boldly, for he could see well enough, and looked at the still, black form. The face was extremely distorted, even in death, and he could see where the rope had tightened. A bar of cool moonlight lay just across the face and breast. He was still looking, thinking soon to restore the covering, when a sound, half sigh, half groan, reached his ears.

At it he started as if a ghost had made it. It was so eerie and unexpected in this dark place. His muscles tightened. Instantly his heart went hammering like mad. His first impression was that it must have come from the dead.

"Oo-o-ohh!" came the sound again, this time whimpering, as if someone were crying.

Instantly he turned, for now it seemed to come from a corner of the room, the extreme corner to his right, back of him. Greatly disturbed, he approached, and then as his eyes strained he seemed to catch the shadow of something, the figure of a woman, perhaps, crouching against the walls, huddled up, dark, almost indistinguishable.

"Oh, oh, oh!" the sound now repeated itself, even more plaintively than before.

Davies began to understand. He approached slowly, then more swiftly desired to withdraw, for he was in the presence of an old black mammy, doubled up and weeping, She was in the very niche of the two walls, her head sunk on her knees, her body quite still. "Oh, oh, oh!" she repeated, as he stood there near her.

Davies drew silently back. Before such grief his intrusion seemed cold and unwarranted. The guiltlessness of the mother—her love—how could one balance that against the other? The sensation of tears came to his eyes. He instantly covered the dead and withdrew.

Out in the moonlight he struck a brisk pace, but soon stopped and looked back. The whole dreary cabin, with its one golden eye, the door, seemed such a pitiful thing. The weeping mammy, alone in her corner—and he had come back to say "Good-by!" Davies swelled with feeling. The night, the tragedy, the grief, he saw it all. But also with the cruel instinct of the budding artist that he already was, he was beginning to meditate on the character of story it would make—the color, the pathos. The knowledge now that it was not always exact justice that was meted out to all and that it was not so much the business of the writer to indict as to interpret was borne in on him with distinctness by the cruel sorrow of the mother, whose blame, if any, was infinitesimal.

"I'll get it all in!" he exclaimed feelingly, if triumphantly at last. "I'll get it all in!"

SELECTED REFERENCES

Gerber, Philip L. *Theodore Dreiser* (1964).

McAleer, John J. *Theodore Dreiser: An Introduction and Interpretation* (1968).

Pizer, Donald. "Theodore Dreiser's 'Nigger Jeff': The Development of an Aesthetic." *American Literature*, 41 (1969), 331–41.

Trilling, Lionel. "Dreiser and the Liberal Mind." *Nation*, 162 (1946), 466, 468–72.

PROJECTS AND PROBLEMS

Consider the references to Jews in *Sister Carrie, An American Tragedy, Dawn,* and elsewhere in connection with the question of anti-Semitism in Dreiser's career.

"Nigger Jeff," an early attack on lynching, differs considerably from earlier romantic fiction assailing slavery or espousing civil rights. Compare Dreiser's story with the two selections in this volume by Mark Twain which emphasize the family attachment of blacks.

In Chapter 28 of The "Genius" Dreiser has the Irish overseer of a force of Italian day laborers say that these "guineas" are "naat white. Any man kin tell that be lookin' at thim." Discuss physical appearance as a factor in the relationship of the Irish and Italian figures in this scene. Does Dreiser sometimes use physical appearance to demean minority characters?

Discuss Dreiser's portrait of the conflict of cultures and the Americanization of a German immigrant's daughter in "Old Rogaum and His Theresa" in Free and Other Stories. Does the story condemn the commercialized vice of the ghetto? Compare Theresa with Stephen Crane's Maggie Johnson.

What is the significance of the use of An American Tragedy, Dreiser's classic account of lower class frustration with a cast of characters drawn from the majority, as a model for works depicting minority experience? Consider carefully Richard Wright's Native Son (1940) or Willard Motley's Knock on Any Door (1947).

FRANK NORRIS
(1870–1902)

Norris planned an epic of the West and completed two impressive volumes, *The Octopus* and *The Pit,* before his death. Admired as a pioneer of American naturalism, he produced in *McTeague* (1899) a novel heavily affected by his feeling for melodrama. The story recounts the tragedy of a San Francisco dentist, the victim of inordinate greed, whose fate it is to die of thirst in Death Valley. That the subplot also features greed—and melodrama—may be seen in this selection from Chapter 3. Maria and Zerkow are important characters. The use of Germans and other ethnic groups in the action of the novel is limited but provocative.

MISMATED SCHEMERS

When Maria entered his shop, Zerkow had just come in from his daily rounds. His decrepit wagon stood in front of his door like a stranded wreck; the miserable horse, with its lamentable swollen joints, fed greedily upon an armful of spoiled hay in a shed at the back.

The interior of the junk shop was dark and damp, and foul with all manner of choking odors. On the walls, on the floor, and hanging from the rafters was a world of debris, dust-blackened, rust-corroded. Everything was there, every trade was represented, every class of society; things of iron and cloth and wood; all the detritus that a great city sloughs off in its daily life. Zerkow's junk shop was the last abiding-place, the almshouse, of such articles as had out-lived their usefulness.

Maria found Zerkow himself in the back room, cooking some sort of a meal over an alcohol stove. Zerkow was a Polish Jew—curiously enough his hair was fiery red. He was a dry, shrivelled old man of sixty-odd. He had the thin, eager, cat-like lips of the covetous; eyes that had grown keen as those of a lynx from long searching amidst muck and debris; and claw-like, prehensile fingers—the fingers of a man who accumulates, but never disburses. It was impossible to look at Zerkow and not know instantly that greed—inordinate, insatiable greed—was the dominant passion of the man. He was the Man with the Rake, groping hourly in the muck-heap of the city for gold, for gold, for gold. It was his dream, his passion; at every instant he seemed to feel the generous solid weight of the crude fat metal in his palms. The glint of it was constantly in his eyes; the jangle of it sang forever in his ears as the jangling of cymbals.

"Who is it? Who is it?" exclaimed Zerkow, as he heard Maria's footsteps in the outer room. His voice was faint, husky, reduced almost to a whisper by his prolonged habit of street crying.

"Oh, it's you again, is it?" he added, peering through the gloom of the shop. "Let's see; you've been here before, ain't you? You're the Mexican woman from Polk Street. Macapa's your name, hey?"

Maria nodded. "Had a flying squirrel an' let him go," she muttered, absently. Zerkow was puzzled; he looked at her sharply for a

370

moment, then dismissed the matter with a movement of his head.

"Well, what you got for me?" he said. He left his supper to grow cold, absorbed at once in the affair.

Then a long wrangle began. Every bit of junk in Maria's pillow-case was discussed and weighed and disputed. They clamored into each other's faces over Old Grannis's cracked pitcher, over Miss Baker's silk gaiters, over Marcus Schouler's whiskey flasks, reaching the climax of disagreement when it came to McTeague's instruments.

"Ah, no, no!" shouted Maria. "Fifteen cents for the lot! I might as well make you a Christmas present! Besides, I got some gold fillings off him; look at um."

Zerkow drew a quick breath as the three pellets suddenly flashed in Maria's palm. There it was, the virgin metal, the pure, unalloyed ore, his dream, his consuming desire. His fingers twitched and hooked themselves into his palms, his thin lips drew tight across his teeth.

"Ah, you got some gold," he muttered, reaching for it.

Maria shut her fist over the pellets. "The gold goes with the others," she declared. "You'll gi' me a fair price for the lot, or I'll take um back."

In the end a bargain was struck that satisfied Maria. Zerkow was not one who would let gold go out of his house. He counted out to her the price of all her junk, grudging each piece of money as if it had been the blood of his veins. The affair was concluded.

But Zerkow still had something to say. As Maria folded up the pillow-case and rose to go, the old Jew said:

"Well, see here a minute, we'll—you'll have a drink before you go, won't you? Just to show that it's all right between us." Maria sat down again.

'Yes, I guess I'll have a drink," she answered.

Zerkow took down a whiskey bottle and a red glass tumbler with a broken base from a cupboard on the wall. The two drank together, Zerkow from the bottle, Maria from the broken tumbler. They wiped their lips slowly, drawing breath again. There was a moment's silence.

"Say," said Zerkow at last, "how about those gold dishes you told me about the last time you were here?"

"What gold dishes?" inquired Maria, puzzled.

"Ah, you know," returned the other. "The plate your father owned in Central America a long time ago. Don't you know, it rang like so many bells? Red gold, you know, like oranges?"

"Ah," said Maria, putting her chin in the air as if she knew a long story about that if she had a mind to tell it. "Ah, yes, that gold service."

"Tell us about it again," said Zerkow, his bloodless lower lip moving against the upper, his claw-like fingers feeling about his mouth and chin. "Tell us about it; go on."

He was breathing short, his limbs trembled a little. It was as if some hungry beast of prey had scented a quarry. Maria still refused, putting up her head, insisting that she had to be going.

"Let's have it," insisted the Jew. "Take another drink." Maria took another swallow of the whiskey. "Now, go on," repeated Zerkow; "let's have the story." Maria squared her elbows on the deal table, looking straight in front of her with eyes that saw nothing.

"Well, it was this way," she began. "It was when I was little. My folks must have been rich, oh, rich into the millions—coffee, I guess —and there was a large house, but I can only remember the plate. Oh, that service of plate! It was wonderful. There were more than a hundred pieces, and every one of them gold. You should have seen the sight when the leather trunk was opened. It fair dazzled your eyes. It was a yellow blaze like a fire, like a sunset; such a glory, all piled up together, one piece over the other. Why, if the room was dark you'd think you could see just the same with all that glitter there. There wa'n't a piece that was so much as scratched; every one was like a mirror, smooth and bright, just like a little pool when the sun shines into it. There was dinner dishes and soup tureens and pitchers; and great, big platters as long as that and wide too; and cream-jugs and bowls with carved handles, all vines and things; and drinking mugs, every one a different shape; and dishes for gravy and sauces; and then a great, big punch-bowl with a ladle, and the bowl was all carved out with figures and bunches of grapes. Why, just only that punch-bowl was worth a fortune, I guess. When all that plate was set out on a table, it was a sight for a king to look at. Such a service as that was! Each piece was heavy, oh, so heavy! and thick, you know; thick, fat gold, nothing but gold—red, shining, pure gold, orange red—and when you struck it with your knuckle, ah, you should have heard! No church bell ever rang sweeter or clearer. It was soft gold, too; you could bite into it, and leave the dent of your teeth. Oh, that gold plate! I can see it just as plain—solid, solid, heavy, rich, pure gold; nothing but gold, gold, heaps and heaps of it. What a service that was!"

Maria paused, shaking her head, thinking over the vanished splendor. Illiterate enough, unimaginative enough on all other subjects, her distorted wits called up this picture with marvellous distinctness. It was plain she saw the plate clearly. Her description was accurate, was almost eloquent.

Did that wonderful service of gold plate ever exist outside of her diseased imagination? Was Maria actually remembering some reality of a childhood of barbaric luxury? Were her parents at one time possessed of an incalculable fortune derived from some Central American coffee plantation, a fortune long since confiscated by armies of insurrectionists, or squandered in the support of revolutionary governments?

It was not impossible. Of Maria Macapa's past prior to the time of her appearance at the "flat" absolutely nothing could be learned. She suddenly appeared from the unknown, a strange woman of a mixed race, sane on all subjects but that of the famous service of gold plate; but unusual, complex, mysterious, even at her best.

But what misery Zerkow endured as he listened to her tale! For he chose to believe it, forced himself to believe it, lashed and harassed by a pitiless greed that checked at no tale of treasure, however preposterous. The story ravished him with delight. He was near someone who had possessed this wealth. He saw someone who had seen this pile of gold. He seemed near it; it was there, somewhere close by, under his eyes, under his fingers; it was red, gleaming, ponderous. He gazed about him wildly; nothing, nothing but the sordid junk shop and the rust-corroded tins. What exasperation, what positive misery, to be so near to it and yet to know that it was irrevocably, irretrievably lost! A spasm of anguish passed through him. He gnawed at his bloodless lips, at the hopelessness of it, the rage, the fury of it.

"Go on, go on," he whispered; "let's have it all over again. Polished like a mirror, hey, and heavy? Yes, I know, I know. A punch-bowl worth a fortune. Ah! and you saw it, you had it all!"

Maria rose to go. Zerkow accompanied her to the door, urging another drink upon her.

"Come again, come again," he croaked. "Don't wait till you've got junk; come any time you feel like it, and tell me more about the plate."

He followed her a step down the alley.

"How much do you think it was worth?" he inquired, anxiously.

"Oh, a million dollars," answered Maria, vaguely.

When Maria had gone, Zerkow returned to the back room of the shop, and stood in front of the alcohol stove, looking down into his cold dinner, preoccupied, thoughtful.

"A million dollars," he muttered in his rasping, guttural whisper, his finger-tips wandering over his thin, cat-like lips. "A golden service worth a million dollars; a punch-bowl worth a fortune; red gold plates, heaps and piles. God!"

SUGGESTED ADDITIONAL READINGS

> Moran of the Lady Letty
> Vandover and the Brute
> Frank Norris of "The Wave" (1931), ed. by Oscar Lewis.

SELECTED REFERENCES

> Berthoff, Warner. *The Ferment of Realism: American Literature, 1884–1919* (1965).
> Crisler, Jesse S. and Joseph R. McElrath, Jr. *Frank Norris: A Reference Guide* (1974).
> French, Warren. *Frank Norris* (1962).

PROJECTS AND PROBLEMS

Norris and Stephen Crane are often linked because of their roles in advancing naturalism and other similarities in their careers. Crane's *Maggie* and Norris's *Vandover and the Brute* invite comparison. Is Crane's prostitute, Maggie, significantly different from Norris's Flossie?

The notions about Anglo-Saxon superiority that Norris revealed in *McTeague* may be seen also in *Moran of the Lady Letty* and in his contributions to *The Wave*. See "A Case for Lombroso" and "The Wife of Chino" for instances of minority stereotyping. Was Norris influenced by class and regional prejudice as well as racism? Consider in particular his Chinese characters in *Moran of the Lady Letty*.

ABRAHAM CAHAN
(1860–1951)

Born in Lithuania, Cahan migrated to the United States in 1882, entered journalism, and became editor of an influential Jewish daily paper. In the 1890s he began to write realistic stories about East Side life in New York. William Dean Howells helped find a publisher for his first novel, *Yekl* (1896), the earliest immigrant novel in English. The story below appeared in *Century Magazine*, November, 1899. Cahan's major work, *The Rise of David Levinsky* (1917) preserves in fiction an important part of our national heritage.

THE APOSTATE OF CHEGOCHEGG

I

"So this is America, and I am a Jewess no longer!" brooded Michalina, as she looked at the stretch of vegetable gardens across the road from the threshold where she sat. "They say farm-hands work shorter hours on Saturdays, yet God knows when Wincas will get home." Her slow, black eyes returned to the stocking and the big darning-needle in her hands.

She was yearning for her Gentile husband and their common birthplace, and she was yearning for her father's house and her Jewish past. Wincas kept buzzing in her ear that she was a Catholic, but he did not understand her. She was a *meshumedeste*—a convert Jewess, an apostate, a renegade, a traitoress, something beyond the vituperative resources of Gentile speech. The bonfires of the Inquisition had burned into her people a point of view to which Wincas was a stranger. Years of religious persecution and enforced clannishness had taught them to look upon the Jew who deserts his faith for that of his oppressors with a horror and a loathing which the Gentile brain could not conceive. Michalina's father had sat seven days shoeless on the ground, as for the dead, but death was what he naturally invoked upon the "defiled head," as the lesser of the two evils. Atheism would have been a malady; *shmad* (conversion to a Gentile creed) was far worse than death. Michalina felt herself buried alive. She was a meshumedeste. She shuddered to think what the word meant.

At first she seemed anxious to realize the change she had undergone. "You are a Jewess no longer—you are a Gentile woman," she would say to herself. But the words were as painful as they were futile, and she turned herself adrift on the feeling that she was the same girl as of old, except that something terrible had befallen her. "God knows where it will all end," she would whisper. She had a foreboding that something far more terrible, a great crushing blow that was to smite her, was gathering force somewhere.

Hatred would rise in her heart at such moments—hatred for her "sorceress of a stepmother," whose cruel treatment of Michalina had driven her into the arms of the Gentile lad and to America. It was owing to her that Rivka (Rebecca) had become a Michalina, a meshumedeste.

The Long Island village (one of a dozen within half an hour's walk from one another) was surrounded by farms which yielded the Polish peasants their livelihood. Their pay was about a dollar a day, but potatoes were the principal part of their food, and this they got from their American employers free. Nearly every peasant owned a fiddle or a banjo. A local politican had humorously dubbed the settlement Chego-Chegg (this was his phonetic summary of the Polish Language), and the name clung.

Wincas and Michalina had been only a few days in the place, and although they spoke Polish as well as Lithuanian, they were shy of the other peasants and felt lonely. Michalina had not seen any of her former coreligionists since she and her husband had left the immigrant station, and she longed for them as one for the first time in mid-ocean longs for a sight of land. She had heard that there were two Jewish settlements near by. Often she would stand gazing at the horizon, wondering where they might be; whereupon her vague image of them at once allured and terrified her.

The sun shone dreamily, like an old man smiling at his own drowsiness. It was a little world of blue, green, gray, and gold, heavy with sleep. A spot of white and a spot of red came gleaming down the road. Rabbi Nehemiah was on his way home from Greyton, where he had dined with the "finest householder" and "said some law" to the little congregation at the afternoon service. For it was Sabbath, and that was why his unstarched shirt-collar was so fresh and his red bandana was tied around the waist of his long-skirted coat. Carrying things on the seventh day being prohibited, Rabbi Nehemiah *wore* his handkerchief.

The door of the general store (it was also the inn), overlooking the cross-roads from a raised platform, was wide open. A Polish peasant in American trousers and undershirt, but with a Warsaw pipe dangling from his mouth, sat on a porch, smoking quietly. A barefooted boy was fast asleep in the grass across the road, a soldier's cap by his side, like a corpse on the battle-field.

As Michalina glanced up the gray road to see if Wincas was not coming, her eye fell upon Rabbi Nehemiah. A thrill ran through her. She could tell by his figure, his huge white collar, and the handkerchief around his waist that he was a pious, learned Jew. As he drew near she saw that his face was overgrown with wisps of silken beard of a yellowish shade, and that he was a man of about twenty-seven.

As he walked along he gesticulated and murmured to himself. It was one of his bickerings with Satan.

"It's labor lost, Mr. Satan!" he said, with a withering smile. "You won't catch me again, if you burst. Go try your tricks on somebody else. If you hope to get me among your regular customers you are a very poor businessman, I tell you that. Nehemiah is as clever as you, depend upon it. Go, mister, go!"

All this he said quite audibly, in his velvety, purring bass, which set one wondering where his voice came from.

As he came abreast of Michalina he stopped short in consternation.

"Woe is me, on the holy Sabbath!" he exclaimed in Yiddish, dropping his hands to his sides.

The color rushed to Michalina's face. She stole a glance at the Pole down the road. He seemed to be half asleep. She lowered her eyes and went on with her work.

"Will you not stop this, my daughter? Come, go indoors and dress in honor of the Sabbath," he purred on, with a troubled, appealing look.

"I don't understand what you say, sir," she answered, in Lithuanian, without raising her eyes.

The devout man started. "I thought she was a child of Israel!" he exclaimed, in his native tongue, as he hastily resumed his way. "Fie upon her! But what a pretty Gentile maiden!—just like a Jewess—" Suddenly he interrupted himself. "You are at it again, aren't you?" he burst out upon Satan. "Leave me alone, will you?"

Michalina's face was on fire. She was following the pious man with her glance. He was apparently going to one of those two Jewish villages. Every step he took gave her a pang, as if he were tied to her heart. As he disappeared on a side road behind some trees she hastily took her darning indoors and set out after him.

II.

About three quarters of an hour had passed when, following the pious little man, she came in sight of a new town that looked as if it had sprung up overnight. It was Burkdale, the newest offshoot of an old hamlet, and it owed its existence to the "Land Improvement Company," to the president of which, Madison Burke, it owed its name. Some tailoring contractors had moved their "sweatshops" here, after a prolonged strike in New York, and there were, besides, some fifty or sixty peddlers who spent the week scouring the island for custom and who came here for the two Sabbath days—their own and that of their Christian patrons. The improvised little town was lively with the whir of sewing-machines and the many-colored display of shop windows.

As the man with the red girdle made his appearance, a large, stout woman in a black wig greeted him from across the street.

"Good Sabbath, Rabbi Nehemiah!" she called out to him, with a faint smile.

"A good Sabbath and a good year!" he returned.

. Michalina was thrilled once more. She was now following close behind the pious man. She ran the risk of attracting his attention, but she no longer cared. Seeing a boy break some twigs, Rabbi Nehemiah made a dash at him, as though to rescue him from death, and seizing him by the arms, he shook the sticks out of his hands. Then, stroking the urchin's swarthy cheeks, he said fondly:

"It is prohibited, my son. God will give one a lashing for desecrating the Sabbath. Oh, what a lashing!"

A sob rose to Michalina's throat.

A short distance farther on Rabbi Nehemiah paused to remonstrate with a group of young men who stood smoking cigarettes and chatting by a merchandise wagon.

"Woe! Woe! Woe!" he exclaimed. "Do throw it away, pray! Are you not children of Israel? Do drop your cigarettes."

"Rabbi Nehemiah is right," said a big fellow, with a wink, concealing his cigarette behind him. The others followed his example, and Rabbi Nehemiah, flushed with his easy victory, went on pleading for a life of piety and divine study. He spoke from the bottom of his heart, and his face shone, but this did not prevent his plea from being flavored with a certain humor, for the most part at his own expense.

"The world to come is the tree, while this world is only the shadow it casts," he said in his soft, thick voice. "Smoking on the Sabbath, staying away from the synagogue, backbiting, cheating in business, dancing with maidens, or ogling somebody else's wife—all this is a great pleasure, is it not? Well, the sages of this world, the dudes, the educated, and even a high-priced adornment like myself, think it is. We hunt for these delights. Behold, we have caught them. Close your fist tight! Hold the precious find with might and main, Rabbi Nehemiah! Presently, hark! the Angel of Death is coming. 'Please, open your hand, Rabbi Nehemiah. Let us see what you have got.' Alas! it's empty, empty, empty—*Ai-ai!*'' he suddenly shrieked in a frightened, piteous voice. While he was speaking the big fellow had stolen up behind him and clapped his enormous high hat over his eyes. The next moment another young man slipped up to Rabbi Nehemiah's side, snatched off his bandana, and set it on fire.

"Woe is me! Woe is me! On the holy Sabbath!" cried the devout man, in despair.

Michalina, who had been looking on at a distance, every minute making ready to go home, rushed up to Rabbi Nehemiah's side.

"Don't—pray don't!" she begged his tormentors, in Yiddish. "You know he did not touch you; why should you hurt him?"

A crowd gathered. The learned man was looking about him with a perplexed air, when along came Sorah-Elka, the bewigged tall woman who had saluted him a short while ago. The young men made way for her.

"What's the matter? Got a licking again?" she inquired, between a frown and a smile, and speaking in phlegmatic, articulate accents. Her smile was like her voice—pleasingly cold. She was the cleverest, the most pious, and the most ill-natured woman in the place. "Serves you right, Rabbi Nehemiah. You look for trouble and you get it. What more do you want? What did they do to him, the scamps?"

"Nothing. They only knocked his hat over his eyes. They were fooling," answered a little boy.

Sorah-Elka's humor and her calm, authoritative manner won

Michalina's heart. Oh, if she were one of this Jewish crowd! She wished she could speak to them. Well, who knew her here? As to Rabbi Nehemiah, he did not seem to recognize her, so she ventured to say, ingratiatingly:

"He didn't do them anything. He only talked to them and they hit him on the head."

Many eyes were leveled at the stranger. The young fellow who had burned Rabbi Nehemiah's handkerchief was scanning her face.

Suddenly he exclaimed:

"I sha'n't live till next week if she is not the meshumedeste of Chego-Chegg! I peddle over there."

The terrible untranslatable word, the most loathsome to the Yiddish ear, struck Michalina cold. She wondered whether this was the great calamity which her heart had been predicting. Was it the beginning of her end? Rabbi Nehemiah recognized her. With a shriek of horror, and drawing his skirts about him, as if for fear of contamination, he proceeded to describe his meeting with Michalina at the Polish village.

"What! this plague the meshumedeste who has a peasant for a husband!" said Sorah-Elka, as she swept the young woman with contemptuous curiosity. "May all the woes that are to befall me, you, or any good Jew—may they all strike the head of this horrid thing—fie upon her!" And the big woman spat with the same imperturbable smile with which she had drawled out her malediction.

Michalina went off toward Chego-Chegg. When the crowd was a few yards behind her somebody shouted:

"Meshumedeste! Meshumedeste!"

The children and some full-grown rowdies took up the cry:

"Meshumedeste! Meshumedeste! Meshumedeste!" they sang in chorus, running after her and pelting her with stones.

Michalina was frightened to death. And yet her pursuers and the whole Jewish town became dearer to her heart than ever.

"Where have you been?" Wincas asked, shaking her furiously.

"Don't! Don't! People are looking!" she protested, in her quietly strenuous way.

The village was astir. Children were running about; women sat on the porches, gossiping; two fiddles were squeaking themselves hoarse in the tavern. A young negro, lank, tattered, and grinning, was twanging a banjo to a crowd of simpering Poles. He it was who got the peasants to forsake their accordions, or even fiddles, for banjos. He was the civilizing and Americanizing genius of the place, although he had learned to jabber Polish long before any of his pupils picked up a dozen English words.

"Tell me where you have been," raged Wincas.

"Suppose I don't? Am I afraid of you? I felt lonesome—so lonesome! I thought I would die of loneliness, so I went for a walk and lost my way. Are you satisfied?"

They went indoors, where their landlady had prepared for them a meal of herring, potatoes, and beef-stew.

Half an hour later they were seated on the lawn, conversing in whispers amid the compact blackness of the night. The two tavern windows gleamed like suspended sheets of gold. Diving out of these into the sea of darkness was a frisky host of banjo notes.

"How dark it is!" whispered Michalina.

"Are you afraid of devils?"

"No—why?"

"I thought you might be," he said.

After a pause he suddenly pointed at his heart.

"Does it hurt you?" he asked.

"What do you mean, darling?" she demanded, interlacing her fingers over his shoulder and peering into his beardless face.

"Something has got into me. It's right here. It's pulling me to pieces, Michalinka!"

"That's nothing," she said. "It's only homesickness. It will wear off."

Wincas complained of his employer, the queer ways of American farming, the tastelessness of American food.

"God has cursed this place and taken the life out of everything," he said. "I suppose it's all because the people here are so wicked. Everything looks as it should, but you just try to put it into your mouth, and you find out the swindle. Look here, Michalinka, maybe it is the Jewish god getting even on me?"

She was bent upon her own thoughts and made no reply. Presently she began to caress him as she would a sick baby.

"Don't worry, my love," she comforted him. "America is a good country. Everybody says so. Wait till we get used to it. Then you won't go, even if you are driven with sticks from here."

They sat mutely clinging to each other, their eyes on the bright tavern windows, when a fresh, fragrant breeze came blowing upon them. Wincas fell to inhaling it thirstily. The breeze brought his native village to his nostrils.

"Mi-Michalinka darling!" he suddenly sobbed out, clasping her to his heart.

III.

When Michalina, pale, weak, and beautiful, lay in bed, and the midwife bade her look at her daughter, the young mother opened her flashing black eyes and forthwith shut them again. The handful of flesh and her own splitting headache seemed one and the same thing. After a little, as her agonizing sleep was broken and her torpid gaze found the baby by the wall, she was overcome with terror and disgust. It was a *shikse* (Gentile girl), a heap of defilement. What was it doing by her side?

She had not nursed the baby a week before she grew attached to it. By the time little Marysia was a month old, she was dearer than her own life to her.

The little railroad-station about midway between the two settlements became Michalina's favorite resort. Her neighbors she shunned. She had been brought up to look down upon their people as "a race like unto an ass." At home she could afford to like them. Now that she was one of them, they were repugnant to her. They, in their turn, often mocked her and called her "Jew woman." And so she would often go to spend an hour or two in the waiting-room of the station or on the platform outside. Some of the passengers were Jews, and these would eye her curiously, as if they had heard of her. She blushed under their glances, yet she awaited them impatiently each time a train was due.

One morning a peddler, bending under his pack, stopped to look at her. When he had dropped his burden his face seemed familiar to Michalina. He was an insignificant little man, clean-shaven, with close-clipped yellowish hair, and he wore a derby hat and a sack-coat.

All at once his face broke into a broad, affectionate smile.

"How do you do?" he burst out in a deep, mellow voice which she recognized instantly. "I once spoke to you in Chego-Chegg, do you remember? I see you are amazed to see me in a short coat and without beard and sidelocks."

"You look ten years younger," she said in a daze of embarrassment.

"I am Rabbi Nehemiah no longer," he explained bashfully. "They call me Nehemiah the Atheist now."

"Another sinner!" Michalina thought, with a little thrill of pleasure.

Nehemiah continued, with a shamefaced smile:

"When my coat and my side-locks were long my sight was short, while now—why, now I am so saturated with wisdom that pious Jews keep away from me for fear of getting wet, don't you know? Well, joking aside, I had ears, but could not hear because of my ear-locks; I had eyes, and could not see because they were closed in prayer. Now I am cured of my idiocy. And how are you? How are you getting along in America?"

His face beamed. Michalina's wore a pained look. She was bemoaning the fall of an idol.

"I am all right, thank you. Don't the Burkdale people trouble you?" she asked, reddening violently.

"Men will be men and rogues will be rogues. Do you remember that Saturday? It was not the only beating I got, either. They regaled me quite often—the oxen! However, I bear them no ill will. Who knows but it was their cuffs and buffets that woke me up? The one thing that gives me pain is this: the same fellows who used to break my bones for preaching religion now beat me because I expose its idiocies. I am like the great rabbi who had once been a chief of high-waymen. 'What of it?' he used to say. 'I was a leader then, and a leader I am now.' I was whipped when I was Rabbi Nehemiah, and now that I am Nehemiah the Atheist I am whipped again. By the way, do you remember how they hooted you? There's nothing to blush about, missus. Religion is all humbug. There are no Jews and no Gentiles, missus. This is America. All are noblemen here, and all are brothers—children of one mother—Nature, dear little missus." The word was apparently a titbit to his tongue. He uttered it with relish, peering admiringly into Michalina's face. "Go forth, dear little missus! Go forth, O thou daughter of Zion, and proclaim to all those who are groveling in the mire of Judaism—"

"S-s-s-sh!" she interrupted imploringly.

"Why should you speak like that? Don't—oh, don't!"

He began a long and heated argument. She could not follow him.

Marysia was asleep in her arms, munching her little lips and smiling. As Michalina stole a glance at her, she could not help smiling, too. She gazed at the child again and again, pretending to listen. For the twentieth time she noticed that in the upper part of her face Marysia bore a striking resemblance to Wincas.

Michalina and Nehemiah often met. All she understood of his talk was that it was in Yiddish, and this was enough. Though he preached atheism, to her ear his words were echoes from the world of synagogues, rabbis, purified meat, blessed Sabbath lights. Another thing she gathered from his monologues was that he was a fellow-outcast. Of herself she never spoke. Being a mystery to him made her a still deeper mystery to herself, and their secret interviews had an irresistible charm for her.

One day Michalina found him clean-shaven and in a new necktie.

"Good morning!" he said, with unusual solemnity. And drawing a big red apple from his pocket, he shamefacedly placed it in her hand.

"What was it you wanted to tell me?" she inquired, blushing.

"Oh, nothing. I meant it for fun. It's only a story I read. It's about a great man who was in love with a beautiful woman all his life. She was married to another man and true to him, yet the stranger loved her. His soul was bewitched. He sang of her, he dreamed of her. The man's name was Petrarca and the woman's was Laura."

"I don't know what you mean by your story," she said, with an embarrassed shrug of her shoulders.

"How do you know it is only a story?" he rejoined, his eye on the glistening rail. "Maybe it is only a parable? Maybe you are Laura? Laura mine!" he whispered.

"Stop that!" she cried, with a pained gesture.

At that moment he was repulsive.

"Hush, don't eat your heart, little kitten. I was only joking."

IV.

Michalina ventured to visit Burkdale once again. This time she was not bothered. Only here and there someone would whisper, "Here comes the apostate of Chego-Chegg." Little by little she got to making most of her purchases in the Jewish town. Wincas at first stormed, and asked whether it was true that the Jew had bedeviled his wife's heart; but before long she persuaded him to go with her on some of her shopping expeditions. Michalina even decided that her husband should learn to press coats, which was far more profitable than working on a farm; but after trying it for a few days, he stubbornly gave it up. The soil called him back, he said, and if he did not obey it, it might get square on him when he was dead and buried in it.

By this time they had moved into a shanty on the outskirts of the village, within a short distance from Burkdale.

At first Michalina forbade Wincas to write to his father, but he mailed a letter secretly. The answer inclosed a note from Michalina's father, in Yiddish, which Wincas, having in his ecstasy let out his secret, handed her.

> Your dear father-in-law [the old man wrote] goes about mocking me about you and his precious son. "Will you send her your love?" he asked. "Very well, I will," said I. And here it is, Rivka. May eighty toothaches disturb your peace even as you have disturbed the peace of your mother in her grave. God grant that your impure limbs be hurled from one end of the world to the other, as your damned soul will be when you are dead like a vile cur. Your dear father-in-law (woe to you, Rivka!) asks me what I am writing. "A blessing," say I. May similar blessings strew your path, accursed meshumedeste. That's all.

"What does he write?" asked Wincas.

"Nothing. He is angry," she muttered. In her heart she asked herself: "Who is this Gentile? What is he doing here?" At this moment she felt sure that her end was near.

Nehemiah and Michalina had taken root in the little town as the representatives of two inevitable institutions. Burkdale without an atheist and a convert seemed as impossible as it would have been without a marriage-broker, a synagogue, or a bath-house "for all daughters of Israel."

Nehemiah continued his frenzied agitation. Neglecting his business, half-starved, and the fair game of every jester, but plumed with some success, the zealot went on scouting religious ceremonies, denouncing rabbis, and preaching assimilation with the enlightened Gentiles. Nehemiah was an incurably religious man, and when he had lost his belief disbelief became his religion.

And so the two were known as the *appikoros* (atheist) and the meshumedeste. Between the two there was, however, a wide difference. Disclaim Judaism as Nehemiah would, he could not get the Jews to disclaim him; while Michalina was more alien to the Mosaic community than any of its Christian neighbors. With her child in her arms she moved about among the people of the place like a lone shadow. Nehemiah was a Jew who "sinned and led others to sin"; she was not a Jewess who had transgressed, but a living stigma, all the more accursed because she had once been a Jewess.

Some of the Jewish women were friendly to her. Zelda the Busybody exchanged little favors with her, but even she stopped at cooking-utensils, for Michalina's food was *treife*[1] and all her dishes were contaminated. One day, when the dumpy little woman called at the lonely hovel, the convert offered her a wedge of her first lemon-pie. It was Zelda who had taught her to make it, and in her exultation and shamefacedness Michalina forgot the chasm that separated her from her caller.

"Taste it and tell me what is wrong about it," she said, blushing.

Zelda became confused.

"No, thank you. I've just had dinner, as true as I'm living," she stammered.

The light in Michalina's eyes went out. For a moment she stood with the saucer containing the piece of pie in her hand. When the Burkdale woman was gone she threw the pie away.

She bought a special set of dishes which she kept *kosher*, according to the faith of the people of Burkdale. Sometimes she would buy her meat of a Jewish butcher, and, on coming home, she would salt

[1]Not prepared according to Mosaic law, proscribed; the opposite of *kosher*. [Cahan's note.]

and purify it. Not that she expected this to be set to her credit in the
world to come, for there was no hope for her soul, but she could not
help, at least, playing the Jewess. It both soothed and harrowed her
to prepare food or to bless Sabbath light as they did over in Burkdale. But her Sabbath candles burned so stern, so cold, so unhal-
lowed. As she embraced the space about them and with a scooping
movement brought her hands together over her shut eyes and fell to
whispering the benediction, her heart beat fast. She felt like a thief.

"Praised be Thou, O Lord, King of the world, who hast sanctified
us by Thy commandments and commanded us to kindle the light of
Sabbath."

When she attempted to recite this she could not speak after the
third word.

Michalina received another letter from her father. The old man's
heart was wrung with compunction and yearning. He was panting to
write to her, but, alas! who ever wrote a meshumedeste except to
curse her?

> It is to gladden your treacherous heart that I am writing
> again [ran the letter]. Rejoice, accursed apostate, rejoice! We
> cannot raise our heads for shame, and our eyes are darkened
> with disgrace. God give that your eyes become so dark that
> they behold neither your cur of a husband nor your vile pup.
> May you be stained in the blood of your own heart even as
> you have stained the name of our family.
>
> Written by me, who curse the moment when I became
> your father.

Michalina was in a rage. "We cannot raise our heads"? Who are
"we"? He and his sorceress of a wife? First she makes him drive his
own daughter to "the impurity" of the Gentile faith, and then she
gets him to curse this unhappy child of his for the disgrace she
brought on her head! What are they worrying about? Is it that they
are afraid it will be hard for Michalina's stepsister to get a husband
because there is a meshumedeste in the family? Ah, she is writhing
and twitching with pain, the sorceress, isn't she? Writhe away, mur-
deress! Let her taste some of the misery she has heaped on her step-
daughter. "Rejoice, apostate, rejoice!" Michalina did rejoice. She
was almost glad to be a meshumedeste.

"But why should it have come out like this?" Michalina thought.
"Suppose I had never become a meshumedeste, and Nehemiah, or
some handsomer Jew, had married me at home.... Would not the
sorceress and her daughter burst with envy! Or suppose I became a
Jewess again, and married a pious, learned, and wealthy Jew who
fainted with love for me, and my stepmother heard of it, and I sent
my little brother lots of money—wouldn't she burst, the sorceress!
... And I should live in Burkdale, and Sorah-Elka and the other
Jews and Jewesses would call at my house, and eat, and drink. On
Saturdays I should go to the synagogue with a big prayer-book, and
on meeting me on the road people would say, 'Good Sabbath!' and I
should answer, 'A good Sabbath and a good year!' "
Michalina began to cry.

v.

Spring was coming. The air was mild, pensive, yearning.
Michalina was full of tears.

"Don't rail at the rabbis—don't!" she said, with unusual irritation,
to Nehemiah at her house. "Do you think I can bear to hear it?"

She cried. Nehemiah's eyes also filled with tears.

"Don't, little kitten," he said, "I didn't mean to hurt you. Are you
sorry you became a Christian?" he added, in an embarrassed whisper.

For the first time she recounted her story to him. When she had
finished the atheist was walking up and down.

"Ai-ai-ai! Ai-ai!" All at once he stopped. "So it was out of revenge for your stepmother that you married Wincas!" he exclaimed.
Then he dropped his voice to a shamefaced undertone. "I thought
you had fallen in love with him."

"What's that got to do with him?" she flamed out.

His face changed. She went on:

"Anyhow, he is my husband, and I am his wife and a Gentile
woman, an accursed soul, doomed to have no rest either in this
world or in the other. May the sorceress have as much darkness on
her heart as I have on mine!"

"Why should you speak like that, little kitten? Of course I am an atheist, and religion is humbug, but you are grieving for nothing. According to the Jewish law, you are neither his wife nor a Gentile woman. You are a Jewess. Mind, I don't believe in the Talmud; but, according to the Talmud, your marriage does not count. Yes, you are unmarried!" he repeated, noting her interest. "You are a maiden, free as the birds in the sky, my kitten. You can marry a Jew 'according to the laws of Moses and Israel,' and be happy."

His voice died away.

"Lau-au-ra!" he wailed, as he seized her hand and began to kiss its fingers.

"Stop—oh, stop! What has come to you!" she shrieked. Her face was crimson. After an awkward silence, she sobbed out: "Nobody will give me anything but misery—nobody, nobody, nobody! What shall I do? Oh, what shall I do?"

Under the pretense of consulting a celebrated physician, Michalina had obtained Wincas's permission to go to New York. In a secluded room, full of dust and old books, on the third floor of an Orchard street tenement-house, she found a gray-bearded man with a withered face. Before him were an open folio and a glass half filled with tea. His rusty skullcap was pushed back on his head.

The blood rushed to her face as she stepped to the table. She could not speak. "A question of law?" asked the rabbi. "Come, my daughter, what is the trouble?"

Being addressed by the venerable man as a Jewess melted her embarrassment and her fear into tears.

"I have married a Gentile," she murmured, with bowed head.

"A Gentile! Woe is me!" exclaimed the rabbi, with a look of dismay and pity.

"And I have been baptized, too."

Here an old bonnetless woman came in with a chicken. The rabbi was annoyed. After hastily inspecting the fowl, he cried:

"Kosher! Kosher! You may eat it in good health."

When the old woman was gone he leaped up from his seat and bolted the door.

"Well, do you want to do penance?" he demanded, adjusting his skullcap.

She nodded ruefully.

"Well, where is the hindrance? Go ahead, my daughter; and if you do it from a pure heart, the Most High will help you."

"But how am I to become a Jewess again? Rabbi, a man told me I never ceased to be one. Is it true?"

"Foolish young woman! What, then, are you? A Frenchwoman? The God of Israel is not in the habit of refunding one's money. Oh, no! 'Once a Jew, forever a Jew'—that's the way he does business."

"But I am married to a Gentile," she urged, with new light in her black eyes.

"Married? Not in the eye of our faith, my child. You were born a Jewess, and a Jewess cannot marry a Gentile. Now, if your marriage is no marriage—what, then, is it? A sin! Leave the Gentile, if you want to return to God. Cease sinning, and live like a daughter of Israel. Of course—of course the laws of the land—of America—do you understand?—they look upon you as a married woman, and they must be obeyed. But the laws of our faith say you are not married, and were a Jew to put the ring of dedication on your finger, you would be his wife. Do you understand, my child?"

"And how about the baby, rabbi? Suppose I wanted to make a proselyte of her?"

"A proselyte! Your learning does not seem to go very far," laughed the old man. "Why, your little girl is even a better Jewess than you have been, for she has not sinned, while you have."

"But her father—"

"Her father! What of him? Did *he* go through the throes of child-birth when the girl was born to you? Don't be uneasy, my daughter. According to our faith, children follow their mother. You are a Jewess, and so is she. She is a pure child of Israel. What is her name? Marysia? Well, call her some Jewish name—say Mindele or Shayndele. What does it amount to?"

As Michalina was making her way down the dingy staircase, she hugged the child and kissed her convulsively.

"Sheindele! Sheindele! Pure child of Israel," she said between sobs, for the first time addressing her in Yiddish. "A Jewish girlie! A Jewish girlie!"

VI.

The charitable souls who had joined to buy the steamship tickets were up with the larks. At seven o'clock Sorah-Elka's apartments on the second floor of a spick-and-span frame-house were full of pious women come to behold their "good deed" in the flesh. It was the greatest event in the eventful history of Burkdale. Michalina, restored to her Hebrew name, was, of course, the center of attention. Sorah-Elka and Zelda addressed her in the affectionate diminutive; the other women, in the most dignified form of the name; and so "Rievele dear" and "Rieva, if you please" flew thick and fast.

Nehemiah kept assuring everybody that he was an atheist, and that it was only to humor Rebecca that he was going to marry her according to the laws of Moses and Israel. But then nobody paid any heed to him. The pious souls were all taken up with the young woman they were "rescuing from the impurity."

Rebecca was polite, grateful, smiling, and nervous. Sorah-Elka was hovering about, flushed and morose.

"You have kissed her enough," she snarled at Zelda. "Kisses won't take her to the ship. You had better see about the lemons. As long as the ship is in harbor I won't be sure of the job. For one thing, too many people are in the secret. I wish we were in New York, at least."

The preparations were delayed by hitch after hitch. Besides, a prosperous rescuer bethought herself at the eleventh hour that she had a muff, as good as new, which might be of service to Rebecca; and then another rescuer, as prosperous and as pious, remembered that her jar of preserved cherries would be a godsend to Rebecca on shipboard. Still, the train was due fully an hour later; the English steamer would not sail before two o'clock, so there was plenty of time.

As to Wincas, he had gone to work at five in the morning and would not be back before seven in the evening.

Zelda was frisking about with the little girl, whom she exultantly addressed as Shayndele; and so curious was it to call a former Gentile child by a Yiddish name that the next minute everybody in the room was shouting: "Shayndele, come to me!" "Shayndele, look!" "Shayndele going to London to be a pious Jewess!" or "Shayndele, a health to your head, arms, and feet!"

"Never fear, Nehemiah will be a good father to her, won't you, Nehemiah?" said one matron.

Suddenly a woman who stood by the window gave a start.

"Her husband!" she gasped.

There was a panic. Sorah-Elka was excitedly signing to the others to be cool. Rebecca, pale and wild-eyed, burst into the bedroom, whence she presently emerged on tiptoe, flushed and biting her lip.

"What can he be doing here at this hour? I told him I was going to the New York professor," she said under her breath. Concealing herself behind the window-frame, she peeped down into the street.

"Get away from there!" whizzed Sorah-Elka, gnashing her teeth and waving her arms violently.

Rebecca lingered. She saw the stalwart figure of her husband, his long blond hair curling at the end, and his pale, oval face. He was trudging along aimlessly, gaping about him in a perplexed, forlorn way.

"He is wandering about like a cow in search of her calf," Michalina remarked, awkwardly.

"Let him go whistle!" snapped Sorah-Elka. "We shall have to tuck you away somewhere. When the coast is clear again, I'll take you to the other railroad station. Depend upon it, we'll get you over to New York and on board the ship before his pumpkin-head knows what world he is in. But I said that too many people were in the secret."

Sorah-Elka was a fighter. She was mistaken, however, as to the cause of Wincas's sudden appearance. Even the few Poles who worked in the Burkdale sweat-shops knew nothing of the great conspiracy. Water and oil won't swap secrets even when in the same bottle. It was Michalina's manner during the last few days, especially on parting with him this morning, which had kindled suspicion in the peasant's breast. What had made her weep so bitterly, clinging to him and kissing him as he was leaving? As the details of it came back to him, anxiety and an overpowering sense of loneliness had gripped his heart. He could not go on with his work.

There was a cowardly stillness in Sorah-Elka's parlor. Nehemiah was rubbing his hands and gazing at Rebecca like a prisoner mutely praying for his life. Her eye was on the window.

"What can he be doing here at such an early hour?" she muttered, sheepishly. "Maybe he has lost his job."

"And what if he did? Is it any business of yours? Let him hang and drown himself!" declared Sorah-Elka.

"Why should you curse him like that? Where is his fault?" Rebecca protested feebly.

"Look at her—look at her! She *is* dead stuck on the lump of uncleanliness, isn't she? Well, hurry up, Rievela darling. Zelda will see to the express. Come, Rievela, come!"

Rebecca tarried.

"What has got into you? Why don't you get a move on you? You know one minute may cost us the whole game."

There was a minute of suspense. All at once Rebecca burst out sobbing:

"I cannot! I cannot!" she said, with her fists at her temples. "Curse me; I deserve it. I know I am doomed to have no rest either in this world or in the other, but I cannot leave him—I cannot. Forgive me, Nehemiah, but I cannot. What shall I do? Oh, what shall I do?"

The gathering was dumfounded. Sorah-Elka dropped her immense arms. For several moments she stood bewildered. Then she said:

"A pain on my head! The good women have spent so much on the tickets!"

"I'll pay it all back—every cent—every single cent of it," pleaded Michalina. Again her own Yiddish sounded like a foreign tongue to her.

"You pay back! From the treasures of your beggarly peasant husband, perhaps? May you spend on doctor's bills a thousand dollars for every cent you have cost us, plaguy meshumedeste that you are!"

A bedlam of curses let itself loose. Michalina fled.

"Let her go to all the eighty dark, bitter, and swampy years!" Sorah-Elka concluded, as the door closed upon the apostate. "A meshumedeste will be a meshumedeste."

SUGGESTED ADDITIONAL READINGS

The Imported Bridegroom and Other Stories of the New York Ghetto

Yekl: A Tale of the New York Ghetto
"The Daughter of Reb Avrom Leib"
"Dumitru and Sigrid"
"A Marriage by Proxy: A Story of the City"
"Rabbi Eliezer's Christmas"
"The Russian Jew in America"

SELECTED REFERENCES

Fine, David M. "Immigrant Ghetto Fiction, 1885–1918: An Annotated Bibliography." *American Literary Realism, 1870–1910,* 6 (1973), 169–95.

Higham, John. Introduction to *The Rise of David Levinsky,* by Abraham Cahan (1960).

Kirk, Rudolph and Clara M. "Abraham Cahan and William Dean Howells: The Story of a Friendship." *American Jewish Historical Quarterly,* 52 (1962), 25–57.

Marovitz, Sanford E. and Lewis Fried. "Abraham Cahan: An Annotated Bibliography." *American Literary Realism, 1870–1910,* 3 (1970), 197–243.

Marovitz, Sanford E. "The Lonely New Americans of Abraham Cahan." *American Quarterly,* 20 (1968), 196–210.

PROJECTS AND PROBLEMS

Is Michalina, the heroine of the story included in this volume, a classic minority figure in the sense that her allegiance is divided between two cultures? Is she another Pocahontas figure? Discuss.

Search Cahan's uncollected stories for Swedes, other non-Jewish immigrants, and blacks and comment on his treatment of these minority characters. Does he employ the prevailing stereotypes? Does he emphasize the common problems of these ethnic groups or their differences?

The Rise of David Levinsky (1917), the novel that is Cahan's major achievement, invites comparison with James Weldon Johnson's *The Autobiography of an Ex-Coloured Man* (1912), since both depict the sacrifice of a rich cultural heritage in return for acceptance and success in the American mainstream. Discuss. Consider the possible relationship of these novels to William Dean Howells's *The Rise of Silas Lapham* (1885).

Compare *The Imported Bridegroom* with *Out of Mulberry Street* (1898), by Jacob A. Riis.

FINLEY PETER DUNNE
(1867–1936)

A Chicago journalist who became editor of national magazines, Dunne is remembered mainly as the creator of Martin Dooley, a sharp-witted Irish saloonkeeper whose wry comments on current affairs bring to mind the early Yankee cracker-box philosopher. Dunne's newspaper humor was very popular, for his characters offered sharp social criticism without losing the reader's respect and affection. The first two selections are from *Mr. Dooley in Peace and in War* (1898), while "The Negro Problem" is from *Mr. Dooley's Philosophy* (1900).

ON THE ANGLO-SAXON

"Well," said Mr. Dooley, "I see be th' pa-apers that th' snow-white pigeon iv peace have tied up th' dogs iv war. It's all over now. All we've got to do is to arrest th' pathrites an' make th' reconcen-thradios pay th' stamp tax, an' be r-ready f'r to take a punch at Germany or France or Rooshia or anny counthry on th' face iv th' globe.

"An' I'm glad iv it. This war, Hinnissy, has been a gr-reat sthrain on me. To think iv th' suffrin' I've endured! F'r weeks I lay awake at nights fearin' that th' Spanish ar-rmadillo'd lave the Cape Verde Islands, where it wasn't, an' take th' train out here, an' hur-rl death an' desthruction into my little store. Day be day th' pitiless exthries come out an' beat down on me. Ye hear iv Teddy Rosenfelt plungin' into ambus-cades an' Sicrety iv Wars: but d'ye hear iv Martin Dooley, th' man behind th' guns, four thousan' miles behind thim, an' willin' to be further? They ar-re no bokays f'r me. I'm what Hogan calls wan iv th' mute, ingloryous heroes iv th' war; an' not so dam mute, ayther. Some day, Hinnissy, justice'll be done me, an' th' likes iv me; an', whin th' story iv a gr-reat battle is written, they'll print th' kilt, th' wounded, th' missin', an' th' seryously disturbed. An' thim that have bore thimsilves well an' bravely an' paid th' taxes an' faced th' deadly newspa-apers without flinchin' 'll be advanced six pints an' given a chanst to tur-rn jack f'r th' game.

"But me wurruk ain't over jus' because Mack has inded th' war an' Teddy Rosenfelt is comin' home to bite th' Sicrety iv War. You an' me, Hinnissy, has got to bring on this here Anglo-Saxon 'lieance. An Anglo-Saxon, Hinnissy, is a German that's forgot who was his parents. They're a lot iv thim in this counthry. There must be as manny as two in Boston: they'se wan up in Maine, an' another lives at Bogg's Ferry in New York State, an' dhrives a milk wagon. Mack is an Anglo-Saxon. His folks come fr'm th' County Armagh, an' their naytional Anglo-Saxon hymn is 'O'Donnell Aboo.' Teddy Rosenfelt is another Anglo-Saxon. An' I'm an Anglo-Saxon. I'm wan iv th' hottest Anglo-Saxons that iver come out iv Anglo-Saxony. Th' name iv Dooley has been th' proudest Anglo-Saxon name in th' County Roscommon f'r many years.

"Schwartzmeister is an Anglo-Saxon, but he doesn't know it, an' won't till some wan tells him. Pether Bowbeen down be th' Frinch church is formin' th' Circle Francaize Anglo-Saxon club, an' me ol' frind Dominigo that used to boss th' Ar-rchey R-road wagon whin Callaghan had th' sthreet conthract will march at th' head iv th' Dago Anglo-Saxons whin th' time comes. There ar-re twenty thou-san' Rooshian Jews at a quarther a vote in th' Sivinth Ward; an', ar-rmed with rag hooks, they'd be a tur-rble thing f'r anny inimy iv th' Anglo-Saxon 'lieance to face. Th' Bohemians an' Pole Anglo-Saxons may be a little slow in wakin' up to what th' pa-apers calls our com-mon hurtage, but ye may be sure they'll be all r-right whin they're called on. We've got together an Anglo-Saxon 'lieance in this wa-ard, an' we're goin' to ilict Sarsfield O'Brien prisidint, Hugh O'Neill Darsey vice-prisidint. Robert Immitt Clancy sicrety, an' Wolfe Tone Malone three-as-urer. O'Brien'll be a good wan to have. He was in the Fenian r-raid, an' his father carrid a pike in forty-eight. An' he's in th' Clan. Besides, he has a sthrong pull with th' Ancient Ordher iv Anglo-Saxon Hibernyans.

"I tell ye, whin th' Clan an' th' Sons iv Sweden an' th' Banana Club an' th' Circle Francaize an' th' Pollacky Benivolent Society an' th' Rooshian Sons of Dinnymite an' th' Benny Brith an' th' Coffee Clutch that Schwartzmeister r-runs an' th' Tur-rnd' ye-mind an' th' Holland society an' th' Afro-Americans an' th' other Anglo-Saxons begin f'r to raise their Anglo-Saxon battle-cry, it'll be all day with th' eight or nine people in th' wurruld that has th' misfortune iv not bein' brought up Anglo-Saxons."

"They'se goin' to be a debate on th' 'lieance at th' ninety-eight picnic at Ogden's gr-rove," said Mr. Hennessy.

"P'r'aps," said Mr. Dooley, sweetly, "ye might like to borry th' loan iv an ice-pick."

ON THE INDIAN WAR

"Gin'ral Sherman was wan iv th' smartest men we iver had," said Mr. Dooley. "He said so manny bright things. 'Twas him said, 'War is hell'; an' that's wan iv th' finest sayin's I know annything about. 'War is hell': 'tis a thrue wurrud an' a fine sintiment. An' Gin'ral Sherman says, 'Th' on'y good Indyun is a dead Indyun. An' that's a good sayin', too. So, be th' powers, we've started in again to improve th' race; an', if we can get in Gatlin' guns enough befure th' winter's snows, we'll tur-rn thim Chippeways into a cimitry branch iv th' Young Men's Christyan Association. We will so.

"Ye see, Hinnissy, th' Indyun is bound f'r to give way to th' onward march iv white civilization. You an' me, Hinnissy, is th' white civilization. I come along, an' I find ol' Snakes-in-his-Gaiters livin' quite an' dacint in a new frame house. Thinks I, 'Tis a shame f'r to lave this savage man in possession iv this fine abode, an' him not able f'r to vote an' without a frind on th' polis foorce.' So says I: 'Snakes,' I says, 'get along,' says I. 'I want ye'er house, an' ye best move out west iv th' thracks, an' dig a hole f'r ye'ersilf,' I says. 'Divvle th' fut I will step out iv this house,' says Snakes. 'I built it, an' I have th' law on me side,' he says. 'F'r why should I take Mary Ann, an' Terence, an' Honoria, an' Robert Immitt Snakes, an' all me little Snakeses, an' rustle out west iv th' thracks,' he says, 'far fr'm th' bones iv me ancestors,' he says, 'an beyond th' water-pipe extinsion,' he says. 'Because,' says I, 'I am th' walkin' dilygate iv white civilization,' I says. 'I'm jus' as civilized as you,' says Snakes. 'I wear pants,' he says, 'an' a plug hat,' he says. 'Ye might wear tin pair,' says I, 'an' all at wanst,' I says, 'an' ye'd still be a savage,' says I; 'an' I'd be civilized,' I says, 'if I hadn't on so much as a bangle bracelet,' I says. 'So get out,' says I. 'So get out,' says I, 'f'r th' pianny movers is outside, r-ready to go to wurruk,' I says.

"Well, Snakes he fires a stove lid at me; an' I go down to th' polis station, an' says I, 'Loot,' I says, 'they'se a dhrunken Indyun not votin' up near th' mills, an he's carryin' on outrageous, an' he won't let me hang me pitchers on his wall,' says I. 'Vile savage,' says th' loot, 'I'll tache him to rayspict th' rules iv civilization,' he says. An' he takes out a wagon load, an' goes afther Snakes. Well, me frind

Snakes gives him battle, an', knowin' th' premises well, he's able to put up a gr-reat fight; but afther a while they rip him away, an' have him in th' pathrol wagon, with a man settin' on his head. An' thin he's put undher bonds to keep the peace, an' they sind him out west iv th' thracks; an' I move into th' house, an' tear out th' front an' start a faro bank. Some day, whin I get tired or th' Swedes dhrive me out or Schwartzmeister makes his lunch too sthrong f'r competition, I'll go afther Snakes again.

"Th' on'y hope f'r th Indyun is to put his house on rollers, an' keep a team hitched to it, an', whin he sees a white man, to start f'r th' settin' sun. He's rooned whin he has a cellar. He ought to put all th' plugged dollars that he gets from th' agent an' be pickin' blue berries into rowlin' stock. If he knew annything about balloons, he'd have a chanst; but we white men, Hinnissy, has all th' balloons. But, annyhow, he's doomed, as Hogan says. Th' onward march iv th' white civilization, with morgedges an' other modhern improvements, is slowly but surely, as Hogan says, chasin' him out; an' th' last iv him'll be livin' in a divin'-bell somewhere out in th' Pac-ific Ocean."

"Well," said Mr. Hennessy, the stout philanthropist, "I think so, an' thin again I dinnaw. I don't think we threat thim r-right. If I was th' gover'mint, I'd take what they got, but I'd say, 'Here, take this tin-dollar bill an' go out an' dhrink ye'ersilf to death,' I'd say. They ought to have some show."

"Well," said Mr. Dooley, "if ye feel that way, ye ought to go an' inlist as an Indyun."

THE NEGRO PROBLEM

"What's goin' to happen to th' naygur?" asked Mr. Hennessy.

"Well," said Mr. Dooley, "he'll ayther have to go to th' north an' be a subjick race, or stay in th' south an' be an objick lesson. 'Tis a har-rd time he'll have, annyhow. I'm not sure that I'd not as lave be gently lynched in Mississippi as baten to death in New York. If I was a black man, I'd choose th' cotton belt in prifrince to th' belt on th' neck fr'm th' polisman's club. I wud so.

"I'm not so much throubled about th' naygur whin he lives among his opprissors as I am whin he falls into th' hands iv his liberators. Whin he's in th' south he can make up his mind to be lynched soon or late an' give his attintion to his other pleasures iv composin' rag-time music on a banjo, an' wurrukin' f'r th' man that used to own him an' now on'y owes him his wages. But 'tis th' divvle's own hardship f'r a coon to step out iv th' rooms iv th' S'ciety f'r th' Brother-hood iv Ma-an where he's been r-readin' a pome on th' 'Future of th' Moke' an' be pursooed by a mob iv abolitionists till he's dhriven to seek polis protection, which, Hinnissy, is th' polite name f'r fracture iv th' skull.

"I was f'r sthrikin' off th' shackles iv th' slave, me la-ad. 'Twas thrue I didn't vote f'r it, bein' that I heerd Stephen A. Douglas say 'twas onconstitootional, an' in thim days I wud go to th' flure with anny man f'r th' constitootion. I'm still with it, but not sthrong. It's movin' too fast f'r me. But no matther. Annyhow I was f'r makin' th' black man free, an' though I shtud be th' south as a spoortin' prop-osition I was kind iv glad in me heart whin Gin'ral Ulyss S. Grant bate Gin'ral Lee an' th' rest iv th' Union officers captured Jeff Davis. I says to mesilf, 'Now,' I says, 'th' coon 'll have a chanst f'r his life,' says I, 'an' in due time we may injye him,' I says.

"An' sure enough it looked good f'r awhile, an' th' time come whin th' occas'nal dollar bill that wint acrost this bar on pay night wasn't good money onless it had th' name iv th' naygur on it. In thim days they was a young la-ad—a frind iv wan iv th' Donohue boys—that wint to th' public school up beyant, an' he was as bright a la-ad as ye'd want to see in a day's walk. Th' larnin' iv him wud sind Father Kelly back to his grammar. He cud spell to make a hare iv th' hedge schoolmasther, he was as quick at figures as th' iddycated pig they showed in th' tint las' week in Haley's vacant lot, and in jogger-phy, asthronomy, algybbera, jommethry, chimisthry, physiojnomy, bassoophly an' fractions, I was often har-rd put mesilf to puzzle him. I heerd him gradyooate an' his composition was so fine very few cud make out what he meant.

"I met him on th' sthreet wan day afther he got out iv school. 'What ar-re ye goin' to do f'r ye'ersilf, Snowball,' says I—his name was Andhrew Jackson George Wash'n'ton Americus Caslateras Be-resford Vanilla Hicks, but I called him 'Snowball,' him bein' as black as coal, d'ye see—I says to him: 'What ar-re ye goin' to do f'r ye'ersilf?' I says. 'I'm goin' to enther th' profission iv law,' he says, 'where be me acooman an' industhry I hope,' he says, 'f'r to rise to be a judge,' he says, 'a congrissman,' he says, 'a sinator,' he says, 'an' p'rhaps,' he says, 'a prisidint iv th' United States,' he says. 'They'se nawthin' to prevint,' he says. 'Divvle a thing,' says I. 'Whin we made ye free,' says I, 'we opened up all these opporchunities to ye', says I. 'Go on,' says I, 'an' enjye th' wealth an' position conferred on ye be th' constitootion,' I says. 'Om'y,' 'I says, 'don't be too free,' I says. 'Th' freedom iv th' likes iv ye is a good thing an' a little iv it goes a long way,' I says, 'an' if I ever hear iv ye bein' prisidint iv th' United States,' I says, 'I'll take me whitewashin' away fr'm ye'er father, ye excelsior hair, poached-egg eyed, projiny iv tar,' I says, f'r me Anglo-Saxon feelin' was sthrong in thim days.

"Well, I used to hear iv him afther that defindin' coons in th' polis coort, an' now an' thin bein' mintioned among th' scatthrin' in ray-publican county con-vintions, an' thin he dhropped out iv sight. 'Twas years befure I see him again. Wan day I was walkin' up th' levee smokin' a good tin cint seegar whin a coon wearin' a suit iv clothes that looked like a stained glass window in th' house iv a Dutch brewer an' a pop bottle in th' fr-ront iv his shirt, steps up to me an' he says: 'How d'ye do, Mistah Dooley,' says he. 'Don't ye know me—Mistah Hicks?' he says. 'Snowball,' says I. 'Step inside this dureway,' says I, 'less Clancy, th' polisman on th' corner, takes me f'r an octoroon,' I says. 'What ar-re ye do-in'?' says I. 'How did ye enjye th' presidincy?' says I. He laughed an' told me th' story iv his life. He wint to practisin' law an' found his on'y clients was coons, an' they had no assets but their vote at th' prim'ry. Besides a warrant f'r a moke was the same as a letther iv inthroduction to th' warden iv th' pinitinchry. Th' on'y thing left f'r th' lawyer to do was to move f'r a new thrile an' afther he'd got two or three he thought ol' things was th' best an' ye do well to lave bad enough alone. He got so sick iv chicken he cudden't live on his fees an' he quit th' law an' wint into journalism. He r-run 'Th' Colored Supplimint,' but it was a failure, th' taste iv th' public lanin' more to quadhroon publications, an' no man that owned a resthrant or theaytre or dhrygoods store'd put in an adver-tisemint f'r fear th' subscribers'd see it an' come ar-round. Thin he attimpted to go into pollytics, an' th' best he cud get was carryin' a bucket iv wather f'r a Lincoln Club. He thried to larn a thrade an' found th' on'y place a naygur can larn a thrade is in prison an' he can't wurruk at that without committin' burglary. He started to take up subscriptions f'r a sthrugglin' church an' found th' profis-sion was overcrowded. 'Fin'ly,' says he, ''twas up to me to be a por-ther in a saloon or go into th' on'y business,' he says, 'in which me race has a chanst,' he says. 'What's that?' says I. 'Craps,' says he. 'I've opened a palachal imporyium,' he says, 'where,' he says, ''twud please me very much,' he says, 'me ol' abolitionist frind,' he says, 'if ye'd dhrop in some day,' he says, 'an' I'll roll th' sweet, white bones f'r ye,' he says. ''Tis th' hope iv me people,' he says. 'We have an even chanst at ivry other pursoot,' he says, 'but 'tis on'y in craps we have a shade th' best iv it,' he says.

"So there ye ar-re, Hinnissy. An' what's it goin' to come to, says ye? Faith, I don't know an' th' naygurs don't know, an' be hivins, I think if th' lady that wrote th' piece we used to see at th' Halsted Sthreet Opry House come back to earth, she wudden't know. I used to be all broke up about Uncle Tom, but cud I give him a job tindin' bar in this here liquor store? I freed th' slave, Hinnissy, but, faith, I think 'twas like tur-rnin' him out iv a panthry into a cellar."

"Well, they got to take their chances," said Mr. Hennessy. "Ye can't do annything more f'r thim than make thim free."

"Ye can't," said Mr. Dooley; "on'y whin ye tell thim they're free they know we're on'y sthringin' thim."

SUGGESTED ADDITIONAL READING

Finley Peter Dunne: *Mr. Dooley at His Best* (1938), ed. by Elmer Ellis.

Mr. Dooley on Iverything and Ivrybody (1963), ed. by Robert Hutchinson.

SELECTED REFERENCES

Blair, Walter. *Horse Sense in American Humor* (1942).
Ellis, Elmer. *Mr. Dooley's America: A Life of Finley Peter Dunne* (1941).

PROJECTS AND PROBLEMS

Compare Mr. Dooley, the persona employed by Dunne in his columns to express his criticisms of society and his sympathy for the underdog, with Jesse B. Semple, spokesman for Langston Hughes.

Do Dunne's use of an Irish bartender as his principal character and his reliance on brogue indicate a decline in the force of the Irish stereotype and an advance in status for this minority? Explain your reasoning.

Dissertations by Mr. Dooley (1906) includes both "The Race Question" and "The Irish Question." Blacks and Irish are shown in these sketches as victims of majority prejudice. Are the problems the same for both groups, according to Mr. Dooley?

Discussing the Spanish-American War, Mr. Dooley, in "Mr. Dooley on the Philippines," says, "Th' inhabitants is mostly naygurs and Chinnymen, peaceful, industhrus, and law-abidin', but savage and bloodthirsty in their methods." He decides to leave the question of the annexation of the Philippines to President McKinley and Admiral Dewey. Compare his references to the islanders with those of George W. Peck, his fellow humorist, in *Peck's Uncle Ike and the Red-headed Boy* (1901).

Discuss the significance of these lines from "Mr. Dooley on Immigration" to the study of the minority presence in American literature: "As a pilgrim father that missed th' first boats, I must raise me claryon voice again' th' invasion iv this fair land be th' paupers an' arnychists iv effete Europe. Ye bet I must—because I'm here first."

SELECTED BIBLIOGRAPHY

I. Reference Books

Brown, Sterling A. *The Negro in American Fiction*. Washington D.C.: Associates in Negro Folk Education, 1937.

_____.*Negro Poetry and Drama*. Washington, D.C.: Associates in Negro Folk Education, 1937.

Butcher, Margaret Just. *The Negro in American Culture*. New York: Knopf, 1956.

Chapman, Abraham, ed. *Literature of the American Indians: Views and Interpretations*. New York: New American Library, 1975.

Friedman, Lawrence J. *The White Savage: Racial Fantasies in the Post-Bellum South*. Englewood Cliffs, N.J.: Prentice-Hall, 1970.

Gloster, Hugh Morris. *Negro Voices in American Fiction*. Chapel Hill: Univ. of North Carolina Press, 1948.

Gross, Seymour L., and John Edward Hardy, eds. *Images of the Negro in American Literature*. Chicago: Univ. of Chicago Press, 1966.

Keiser, Albert. *The Indian in American Literature*. New York: Oxford Univ. Press, 1933.

Liptzin, Sol. *The Jew in American Literature*. New York: Bloch Publishing Co., 1966.

Robinson, Cecil. *With the Ears of Strangers: The Mexican in American Literature*. Tucson: Univ. of Arizona Press, 1963.

Skaggs, Merrill Maguire. *The Folk of Southern Fiction*. Athens: Univ. of Georgia Press, 1972.

Starke, Catherine Juanita. *Black Portraiture in American Fiction*. New York: Basic Books, 1971.

Turner, Darwin T., comp. *Afro-American Writers*. A Bibliography. New York: Appleton-Century-Crofts, 1970.

Turner, Lorenzo Dow. *Anti-Slavery Sentiment in American Literature Prior to 1865*. Port Washington, N. Y.: Kennikat Press, 1966.

Yellin, Jean Fagan. *The Intricate Knot: Black Figures in American Literature, 1776–1863.* New York: New York Univ. Press, 1972.

II. Anthologies

Anderson, David D., and Robert L. Wright, eds. *The Dark and Tangled Path: Race in America.* Boston: Houghton Mifflin, 1971.

Armstrong, Virginia Irving, comp. *I Have Spoken: American History Through the Voices of the Indians.* Chicago: The Swallow Press, 1971.

Barksdale, Richard, and Keneth Kinnamon, eds. *Black Writers in America.* New York: The Macmillan Company, 1972.

Brown, Sterling A., Arthur P. Davis, and Ulysses Lee, eds. *Negro Caravan.* New York: Dryden Press, 1941.

Curti, Merle, Willard Thorp, and Carlos Baker, eds. *American Issues: The Social Record.* Fourth ed. Philadelphia: J.B. Lippincott Co., 1960.

Davis, Arthur P., and Saunders Redding, eds. *Cavalcade: Negro American Writing from 1760 to the Present.* Boston: Houghton Mifflin, 1971.

Freimarck, Vincent, and Bernard Rosenthal, eds. *Race and the American Romantics.* New York: Schocken Books, 1971.

Kearns, Francis E., ed. *The Black Experience: An Anthology of American Literature for the 1970s.* New York: Viking Press, 1970.

Lerner, Gerda, ed. *Black Women in White America: A Documentary History.* New York: Vantage Books, 1973.

Moquin, Wayne, ed. *Great Documents in American Indian History.* New York: Praeger Publishers, 1973.

VanDerBeets, Richard, ed. *Held Captive by Indians: Selected Narratives, 1642–1836.* Knoxville: Univ. of Tennessee Press, 1973.

Washburn, Wilcomb E., ed. *The Indian and the White Man.* Garden City, N.Y.: Doubleday, 1964.

III. Background

Allport, Gordon W. *The Nature of Prejudice.* Garden City, N.Y.: Doubleday, 1958.

Bissell, Benjamin. *The American Indian in English Literature of the Eighteenth Century.* New Haven: Yale Univ. Press, 1925.

Brandon, William. *The American Heritage Book of Indians.* New York: American Heritage Publishing Co., 1961.

Brown, Dee. *Bury My Heart at Wounded Knee: An Indian History of the American West.* New York: Holt, Rinehart & Winston, 1970.

Brown, Francis J., and Joseph S. Roucek, eds. *One America: The History, Contributions and Present Problems of Our Racial and National Minorities.* Third ed. Englewood Cliffs, N.J.: Prentice-Hall, 1952.

Burrows, Edwin G. *Hawaiian Americans: An Account of the Mingling of Japanese, Chinese, Polynesian, and American Cultures.* New Haven: Yale Univ. Press, 1947.

Coffin, Tristram P., and Hennig Cohen, eds. *Folklore in America.* Garden City, N.Y.: Doubleday, 1970.

Dorson, Richard M. *American Folklore.* Chicago: Univ. of Chicago Press, 1959.

Dykes, Eva Beatrice. *The Negro in English Romantic Thought.* Washington, D.C.: Associated Publishers, 1942.

Fiedler, Leslie A. *The Return of the Vanishing American.* New York: Stein & Day, 1968.

Franklin, John Hope. *From Slavery to Freedom.* Rev. ed. New York: Knopf, 1968.

Gossett, Thomas F. *Race: The History of an Idea in America.* Dallas: Southern Methodist Univ. Press, 1963.

Halliburton, Warren J., and William Loren Katz. *American Majorities and Minorities: A Syllabus of United States History for Secondary Schools.* New York: Arno, 1970.

Handlin, Oscar. *Adventure in Freedom: Three Hundred Years of Jewish Life in America.* New York: McGraw-Hill, 1954.

Hosokawa, Bill. *Nisei: The Quiet Americans.* New York: William Morrow, 1969.

Huthmacher, J. Joseph. *A Nation of Newcomers: Ethnic Minority Groups in American History.* New York: Dell, 1967.

Jordan, Winthrop D. *Historical Origins of Racism in the United States.* New York: Oxford Univ. Press, 1974.

——————. *White Over Black: American Attitudes Toward the Negro, 1550–1812.* Baltimore: Penguin Books, 1969.

Kennedy, John F. *A Nation of Immigrants.* New York: Harper & Row, 1964.

Lader, Lawrence. *The Bold Brahmins: New England's War Against Slavery: 1831–1863.* New York: E.P. Dutton, 1961.

Litwack, Leon F. *North of Slavery: The Negro in the Free States, 1790–1860.* Chicago: Phoenix Books, 1965.

Logan, Rayford W., and Irving S. Cohen. *The American Negro: Old World Background and New World Experience.* Boston: Houghton Mifflin, 1970.

McIlwaine, Shields. *The Southern Poor-White from Lubberland to Tobacco Road.* Norman: Univ. of Oklahoma Press, 1939.

McPherson, James M., *et al. Blacks in America: Bibliographical Essays.* Garden City, N.Y.: Doubleday, 1971.

Marden, Charles F., and Gladys Meyer. *Minorities in American Society.* Fourth ed. New York: D. Van Nostrand Co., 1973.

Marriott, Alice, and Carol K. Rachlin. *American Epic: The Story of the American Indian.* New York: New American Library, 1969.

Melendy, H. Brett. *The Oriental Americans.* New York: Twayne Publishers, 1972.

Mellon, Matthew T. *Early American Views on Negro Slavery.* New York: New American Library, 1969.

Miller, John C. *The First Frontier: Life in Colonial America.* New York: Dell, 1966.

Nash, Gary B. *Red, White, and Black: The Peoples of Early America.* Englewood-Cliffs, N.J.: Prentice-Hall, 1974.

Nye, Russel. *The Unembarrassed Muse: The Popular Arts in America.* New York: Dial Press, 1970.

Quarles, Benjamin. *The Negro in the Making of America.* New York: Collier Books, 1964.

Ruchames, Louis. *Racial Thought in America: From the Puritans to Abraham Lincoln.* New York: Grosset & Dunlap, 1970.

Williamson, Juanita V., and Virginia M. Burke, eds. *A Various Language: Perspectives on American Dialects.* New York: Holt, Rinehart and Winston, 1971.

Wittke, Carl. *We Who Built America: the Saga of the Immigrant.* Cleveland: Western Reserve Univ. Press, 1964.

Wright, Louis B. *The Cultural Life of the American Colonies.* New York: Harper & Row, 1962.

IV. Articles in Periodicals

Appel, John J. "American Negro and Immigrant Experience: Similarities and Differences." *American Quarterly,* 18 (1966), 95–103.

Brown, Sterling A. "The American Race Problem as Reflected in American Literature." *Journal of Negro Education*, 7 (1939), 275–90.

————. "A Century of Negro Portraiture in American Literature." *Massachusetts Review*, 7 (1966), 73–96.

————. "Negro Character as Seen by White Authors." *Journal of Negro Education*, 2 (1933), 179–203.

Cantor, Milton. "The Image of the Negro in Colonial Literature." *New England Quarterly*, 36 (1963), 452–77.

Fine, David M. "Immigrant Ghetto Fiction, 1885–1918: An Annotated Bibliography." *American Literary Realism*, 1870–1910, 6 (1973), 169–95.

Gross, Theodore L. "The Negro in the Literature of Reconstruction." *Phylon*, 22 (1961), 5–14.

Jordan, Winthrop D. "American Chiaroscuro: The Status and Definition of Mulattoes in the British Colonies." *William and Mary Quarterly*, 19 (1962), 183–200.

Kaiser, Ernest. "American Indians and Mexican Americans: A Selected Bibliography." *Freedomways*, 9 (1969), 298–327.

Kent, George E. "Ethnic Impact in American Literature: Reflections on a Course." *CLA Journal*, 11 (1967), 1–17.

Lamplugh, G.R. "The Image of the Negro in Popular Magazine Fiction, 1875–1900." *Journal of Negro History*, 57 (1972), 177–89.

Levy, David W. "Racial Stereotypes in Anti-Slavery Fiction." *Phylon*, 31 (1970), 265–79.

MacDonald, J. Frederick. "'The Foreigner' in Juvenile Series Fiction, 1900–1945." *Journal of Popular Culture*, 8 (1974), 534–48.

Mead, Margaret. "Racial Differences and Cultural Attitudes." *Columbia University Forum*, 10 (1967), 35–36.

Mintz, Sidney W. "Creating Culture in the Americas." *Columbia Forum*, 13 (1970), 4–11.

Moore, Jack B. "Images of the Negro in Early American Short Fiction." *Mississippi Quarterly*, 22 (1969), 47–57.

Musgrave, Marian E. "Patterns of Violence and Non-Violence in Pro-Slavery and Anti-Slavery Fiction." *CLA Journal*, 16 (1973), 426–37.

Nichols, Charles H., Jr. "Slave Narratives and the Plantation Legend." *Phylon*, 10 (1949), 201–10.

Patterson, Orlando. "Ethnicity and the Pluralist Fallacy." *Change*, March, 1975, pp. 10–11.

Read, Allen Walker. "The Speech of Negroes in Colonial America." *Journal of Negro History*, 24 (1939), 247–58.

Rollins, H.E. "The Negro in the Southern Short Story." *Sewanee Review*, 24 (1916), 42–60.

Simms, H.H. "A Critical Analysis of Abolition Literature, 1830–1840." *Journal of Southern History,* 6 (1940), 368–82.

Soderbergh, Peter A. "Bibliographical Essay: The Negro in Juvenile Series Books, 1899–1930." *Journal of Negro History,* 58 (1973), 179–86.

Tandy, Jeanette. "Pro-Slavery Propaganda in American Fiction of the Fifties." *South Atlantic Quarterly,* 21 (1922), 41–50, 170–78.

Thompson, Lawrence S. "The Negro in Kentucky Fiction." *Midwest Journal,* 5 (1953), 75–81.

Towner, Lawrence W. " 'A Fondness for Freedom': Servant Protest in Puritan Society." *William and Mary Quarterly,* 19 (1962), 201–19.

Turner, Darwin T. "The Teaching of Afro-American Literature." *College English,* 31 (1970), 666–70.

Twombly, Robert C., and Richard H. Moore. "Black Puritan: The Negro in Seventeenth Century Massachusetts." *William and Mary Quarterly,* 24 (1967), 224–42.

VanDerBeets, Richard. "The Indian Captivity Narrative as Ritual." *American Literature,* 43 (1972), 548–62.

Zanger, Jules. "The 'Tragic Octoroon' in Pre-Civil War Fiction." *American Quarterly,* 18 (1966), 63–70.

INDEX

"Where's Duncan," 242
Whitman, Walt (1819–1892), 15, 26–40, 98
White Anglo-Saxon Protestants, 5–6, 16, 18, 255, 375, 399–400
White Marie, 243
White Servitude in Pennsylvania, 72
Whitney, Eli, 12
Whittier, John Greenleaf (1807–1892), 11, 15, 87–93, 226

"The Wife of Chino," 375
The Wife of His Youth, 243, 275, 354
Willen, Gerald, 242
Williams, James, 93
Woolson, Constance Fenimore, 327
Wounded Knee massacre, 17
Wright, Richard, 289, 321, 368

Yekl, 376